INJUSTICE

GODS AMONG US: YEAR FIVE

VOLUME 2

INJU

GODS AMON

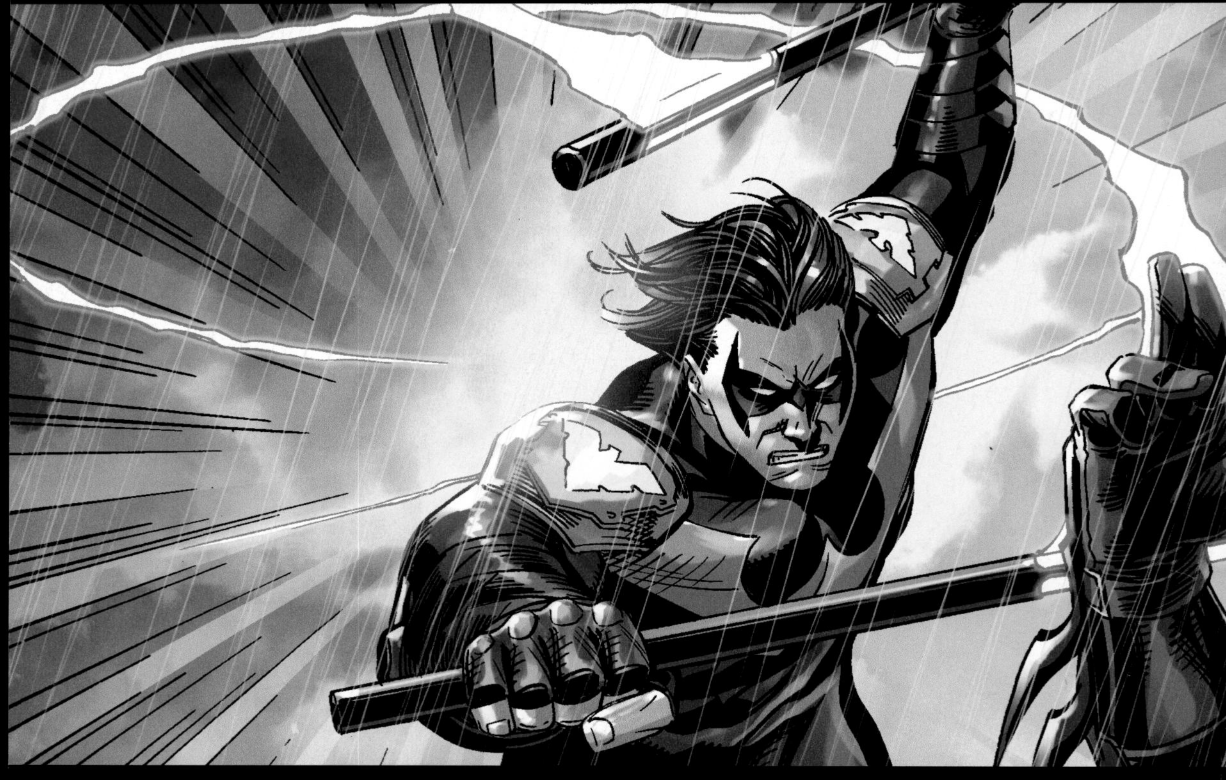

STICE
G US: YEAR FIVE
VOLUME 2

SUPERMAN created by JERRY SIEGEL and JOE SHUSTER.
By special Arrangement with the Jerry Siegel Family.

DOOMSDAY created by Brett Breeding, Dan Jurgens, Jerry Ordway,
Louise Simonson and Roger Stern.

BASED ON THE VIDEO GAME *INJUSTICE: GODS AMONG US.*

JIM CHADWICK Editor – Original Series
DAVID PIÑA Assistant Editor – Original Series
JEB WOODARD Group Editor – Collected Editions
PAUL SANTOS Editor – Collected Edition
STEVE COOK Design Director – Books
AMIE BROCKWAY-METCALF Publication Design

BOB HARRAS Senior VP – Editor-in-Chief, DC Comics

DIANE NELSON President
DAN DiDIO Publisher
JIM LEE Publisher
GEOFF JOHNS President & Chief Creative Officer
AMIT DESAI Executive VP – Business & Marketing Strategy,
    Direct to Consumer & Global Franchise Management
SAM ADES Senior VP – Direct to Consumer
BOBBIE CHASE VP – Talent Development
MARK CHIARELLO Senior VP – Art, Design & Collected Editions
JOHN CUNNINGHAM Senior VP – Sales & Trade Marketing
ANNE DEPiES Senior VP – Business Strategy, Finance & Administration
DON FALLETTI VP – Manufacturing Operations
LAWRENCE GANEM VP – Editorial Administration & Talent Relations
ALISON GILL Senior VP – Manufacturing & Operations
HANK KANALZ Senior VP – Editorial Strategy & Administration
JAY KOGAN VP – Legal Affairs
THOMAS LOFTUS VP – Business Affairs
JACK MAHAN VP – Business Affairs
NICK J. NAPOLITANO VP – Manufacturing Administration
EDDIE SCANNELL VP – Consumer Marketing
COURTNEY SIMMONS Senior VP – Publicity & Communications
JIM (SKI) SOKOLOWSKI VP – Comic Book Specialty Sales & Trade Marketing
NANCY SPEARS VP – Mass, Book, Digital Sales & Trade Marketing

INJUSTICE: GODS AMONG US – YEAR FIVE VOLUME 2

Published by DC Comics. Compilation and all new material
Copyright © 2017 DC Comics. All Rights Reserved. Originally
published in single magazine form in INJUSTICE: GODS
AMONG US – YEAR FIVE 8-14. Copyright © 2016 DC Comics.
All Rights Reserved. All characters, their distinctive likenesses
and related elements featured in this publication are
trademarks of DC Comics. The stories, characters and incidents
featured in this publication are entirely fictional. DC Comics
does not read or accept unsolicited submissions of ideas,
stories or artwork.

DC Comics, 2900 West Alameda Ave., Burbank, CA 91505
Printed by LSC Communications, Salem, VA, USA. 1/20/17.
First Printing.
ISBN: 978-1-4012-6884-8

Library of Congress Cataloging-in-Publication Data is available.

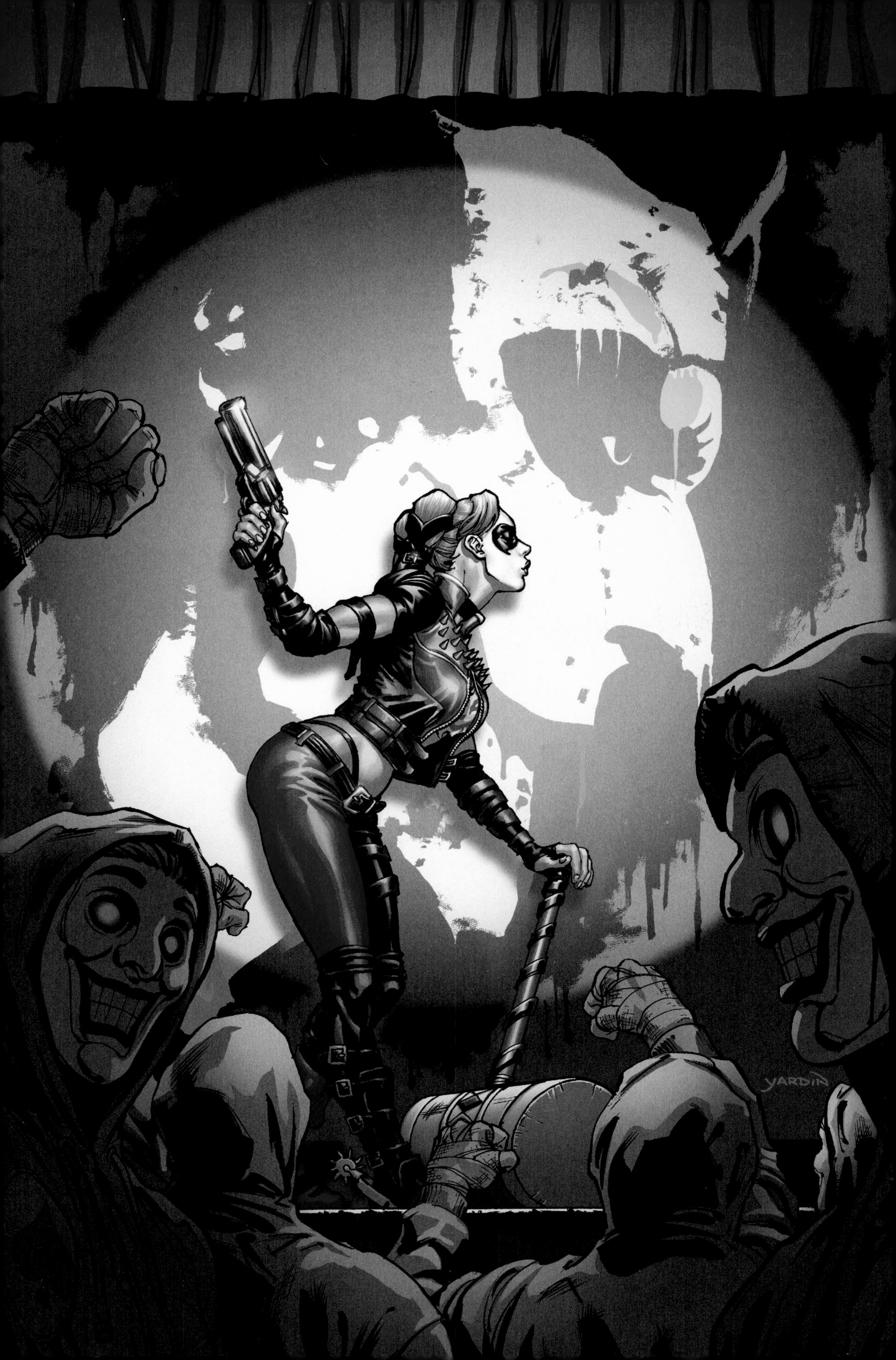
YARDIN

"Revolutionary" **Bruno Redondo** Penciller **Juan Albarrán** Inker **Rex Lokus** Colorist

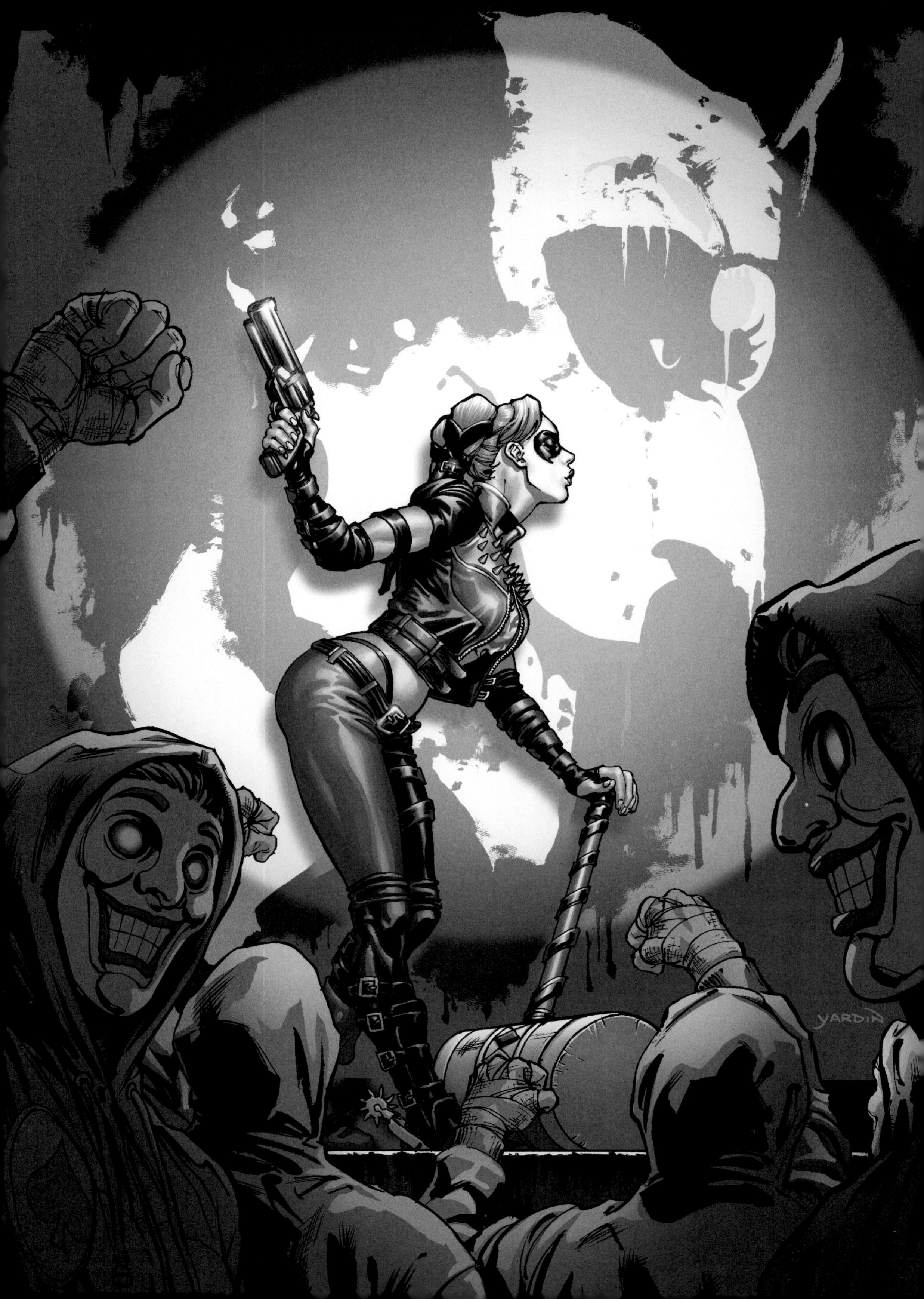
YARDIN

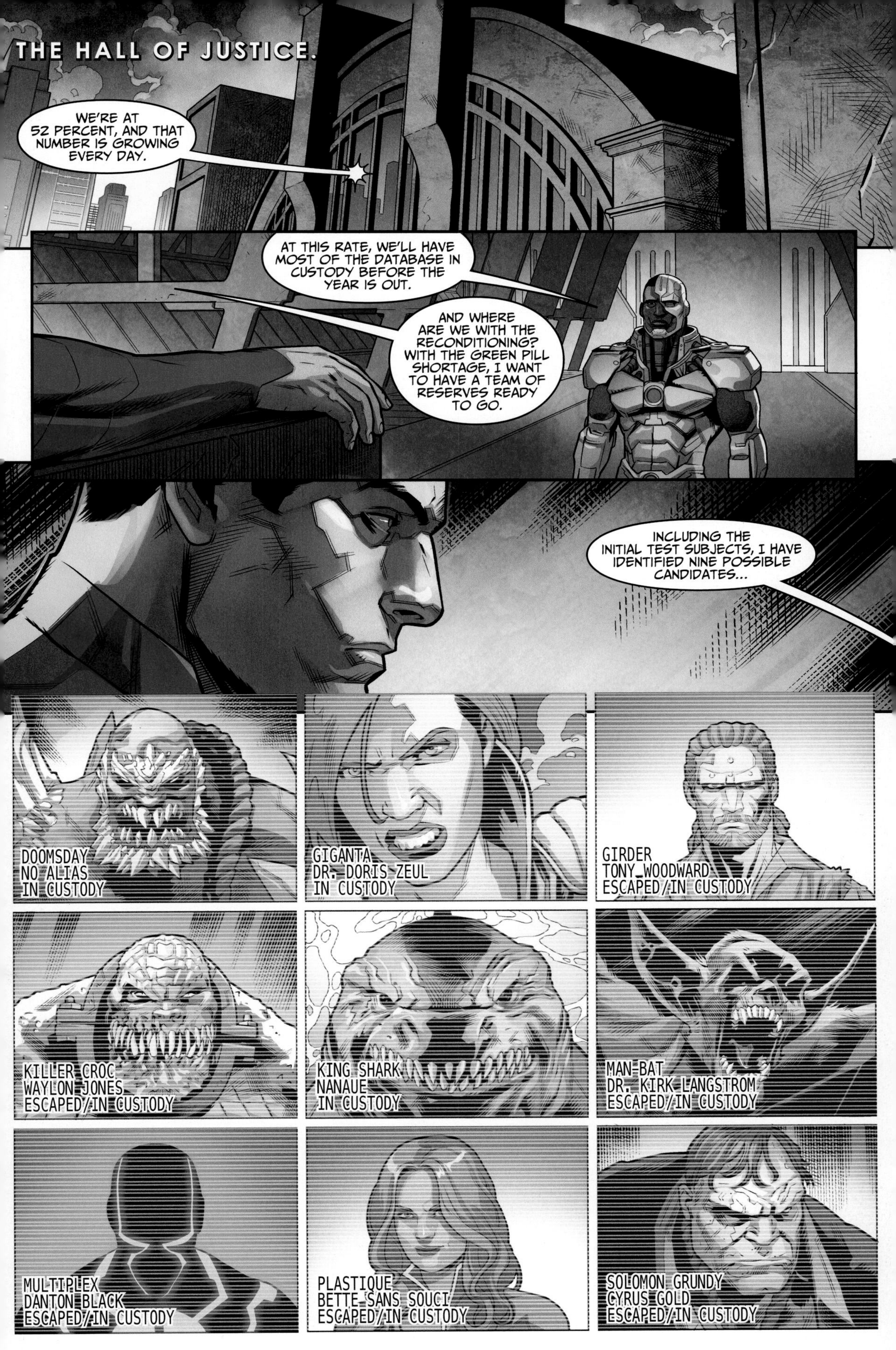
THE HALL OF JUSTICE.
WE'RE AT 52 PERCENT, AND THAT NUMBER IS GROWING EVERY DAY.
AT THIS RATE, WE'LL HAVE MOST OF THE DATABASE IN CUSTODY BEFORE THE YEAR IS OUT.
AND WHERE ARE WE WITH THE RECONDITIONING? WITH THE GREEN PILL SHORTAGE, I WANT TO HAVE A TEAM OF RESERVES READY TO GO.
INCLUDING THE INITIAL TEST SUBJECTS, I HAVE IDENTIFIED NINE POSSIBLE CANDIDATES...
DOOMSDAY
NO ALIAS
IN CUSTODY
GIGANTA
DR. DORIS ZEUL
IN CUSTODY
GIRDER
TONY WOODWARD
ESCAPED/IN CUSTODY
KILLER CROC
WAYLON JONES
ESCAPED/IN CUSTODY
KING SHARK
NANAUE
IN CUSTODY
MAN-BAT
DR. KIRK LANGSTROM
ESCAPED/IN CUSTODY
MULTIPLEX
DANTON BLACK
ESCAPED/IN CUSTODY
PLASTIQUE
BETTE SANS SOUCI
ESCAPED/IN CUSTODY
SOLOMON GRUNDY
CYRUS GOLD
ESCAPED/IN CUSTODY

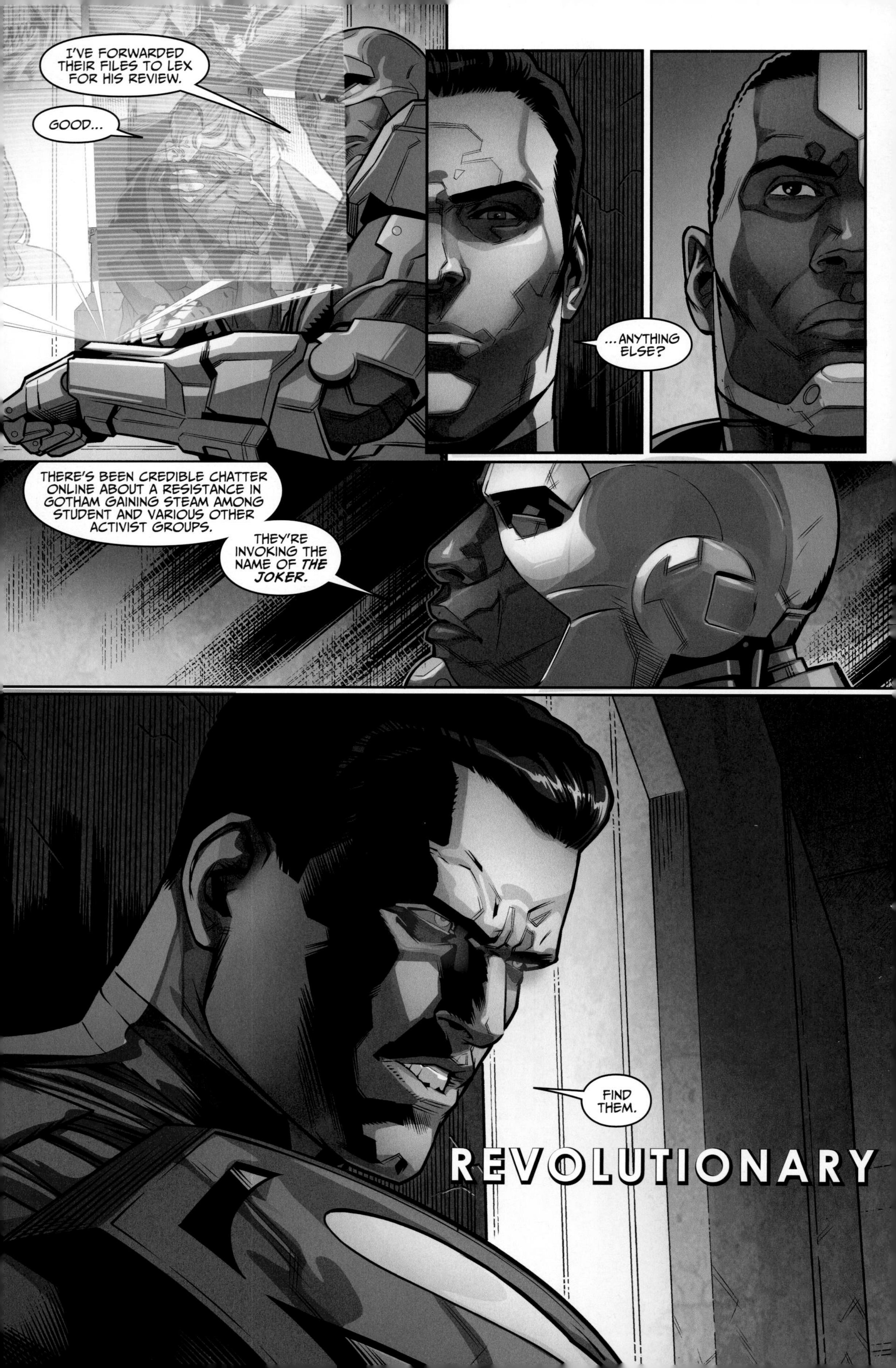
I'VE FORWARDED THEIR FILES TO LEX FOR HIS REVIEW.
GOOD...
...ANYTHING ELSE?
THERE'S BEEN CREDIBLE CHATTER ONLINE ABOUT A RESISTANCE IN GOTHAM GAINING STEAM AMONG STUDENT AND VARIOUS OTHER ACTIVIST GROUPS.
THEY'RE INVOKING THE NAME OF *THE JOKER.*
FIND THEM.
REVOLUTIONARY

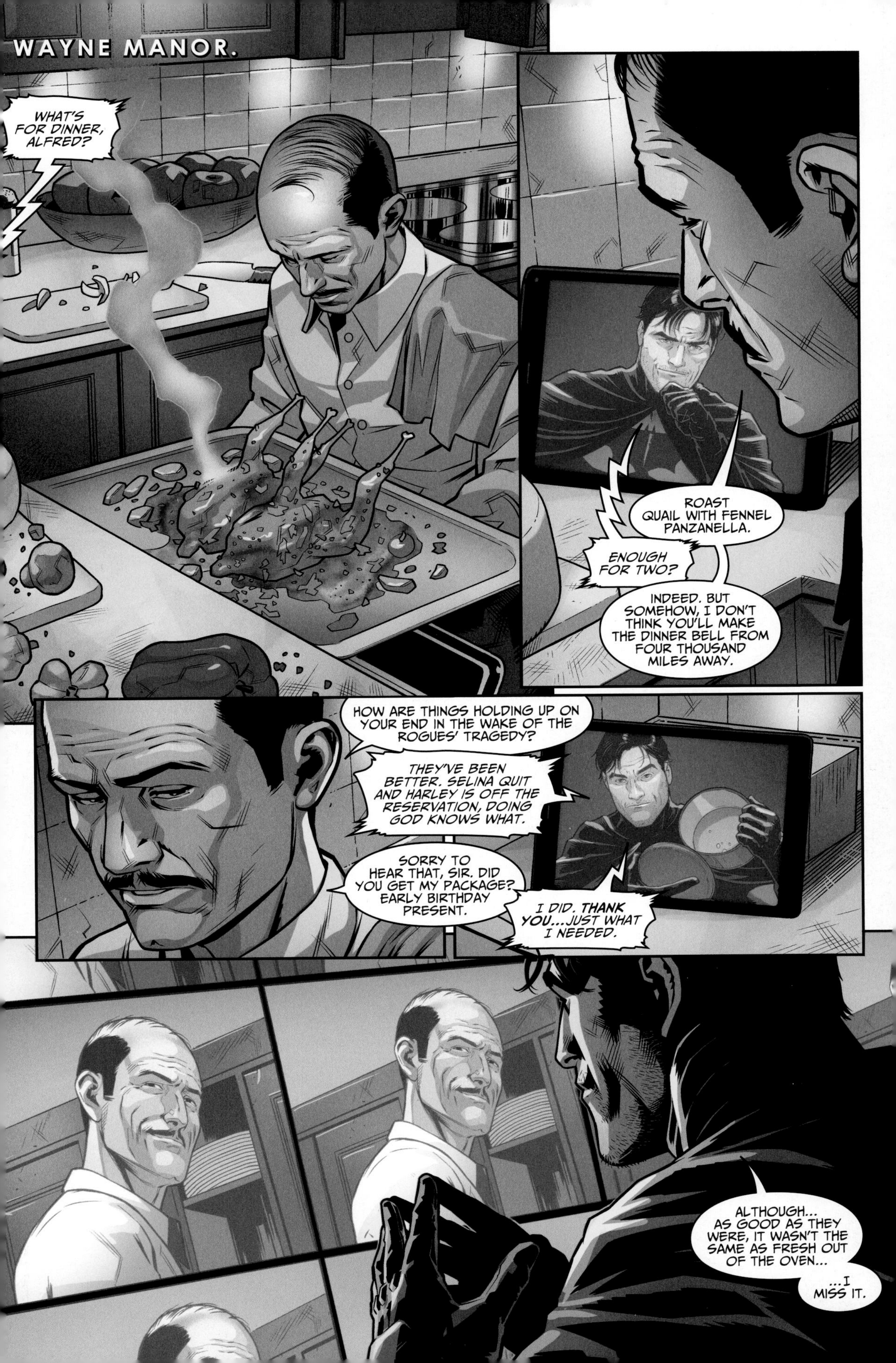
WAYNE MANOR.
WHAT'S FOR DINNER, ALFRED?
ROAST QUAIL WITH FENNEL PANZANELLA.
ENOUGH FOR TWO?
INDEED. BUT SOMEHOW, I DON'T THINK YOU'LL MAKE THE DINNER BELL FROM FOUR THOUSAND MILES AWAY.
HOW ARE THINGS HOLDING UP ON YOUR END IN THE WAKE OF THE ROGUES' TRAGEDY?
THEY'VE BEEN BETTER. SELINA QUIT AND HARLEY IS OFF THE RESERVATION, DOING GOD KNOWS WHAT.
SORRY TO HEAR THAT, SIR. DID YOU GET MY PACKAGE? EARLY BIRTHDAY PRESENT.
I DID. THANK YOU...JUST WHAT I NEEDED.
ALTHOUGH... AS GOOD AS THEY WERE, IT WASN'T THE SAME AS FRESH OUT OF THE OVEN...
...I MISS IT.

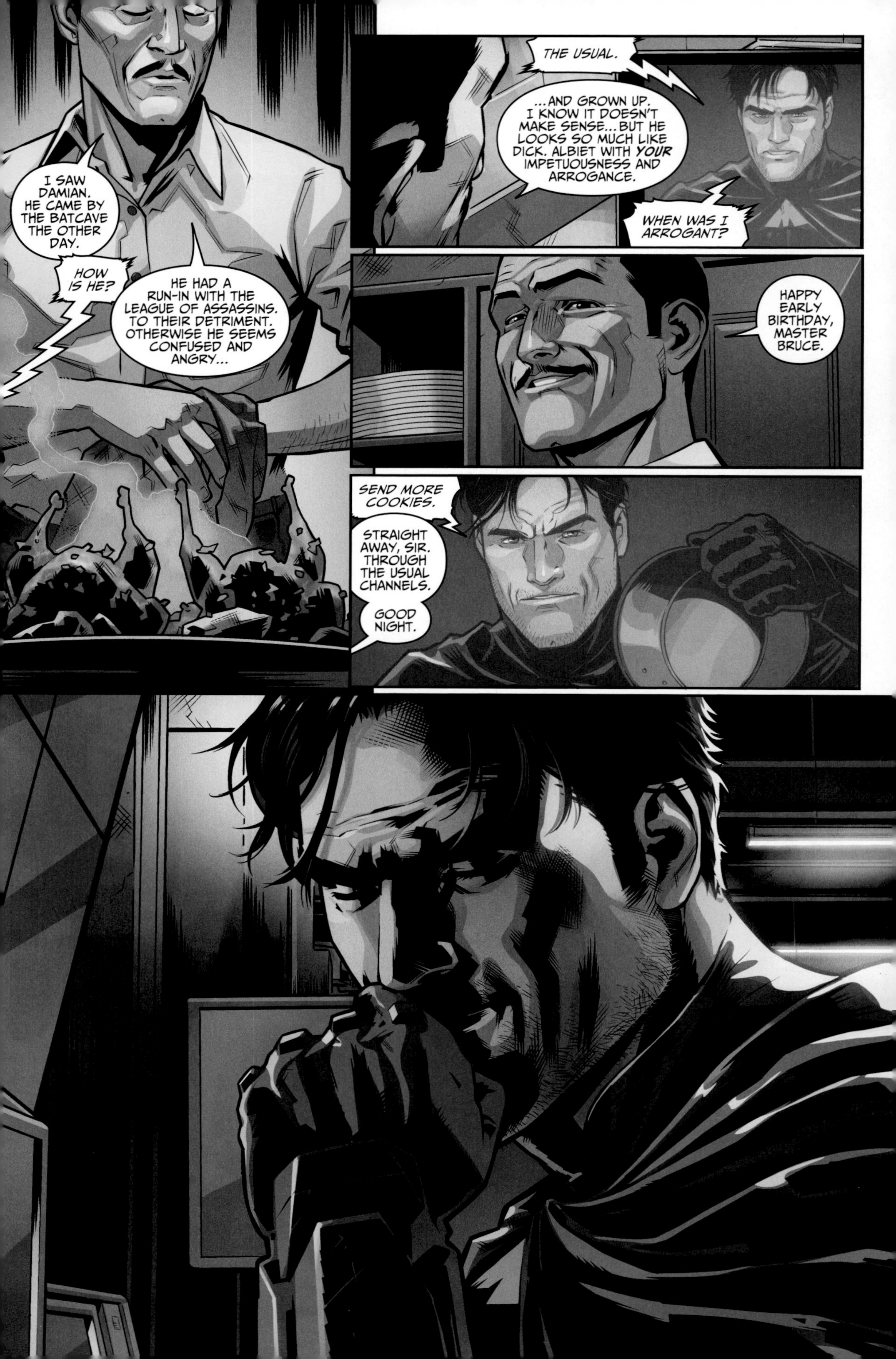
I SAW DAMIAN. HE CAME BY THE BATCAVE THE OTHER DAY.
HOW IS HE?
HE HAD A RUN-IN WITH THE LEAGUE OF ASSASSINS. TO THEIR DETRIMENT. OTHERWISE HE SEEMS CONFUSED AND ANGRY...
THE USUAL.
...AND GROWN UP. I KNOW IT DOESN'T MAKE SENSE...BUT HE LOOKS SO MUCH LIKE DICK. ALBIET WITH YOUR IMPETUOUSNESS AND ARROGANCE.
WHEN WAS I ARROGANT?
HAPPY EARLY BIRTHDAY, MASTER BRUCE.
SEND MORE COOKIES.
STRAIGHT AWAY, SIR. THROUGH THE USUAL CHANNELS.
GOOD NIGHT.

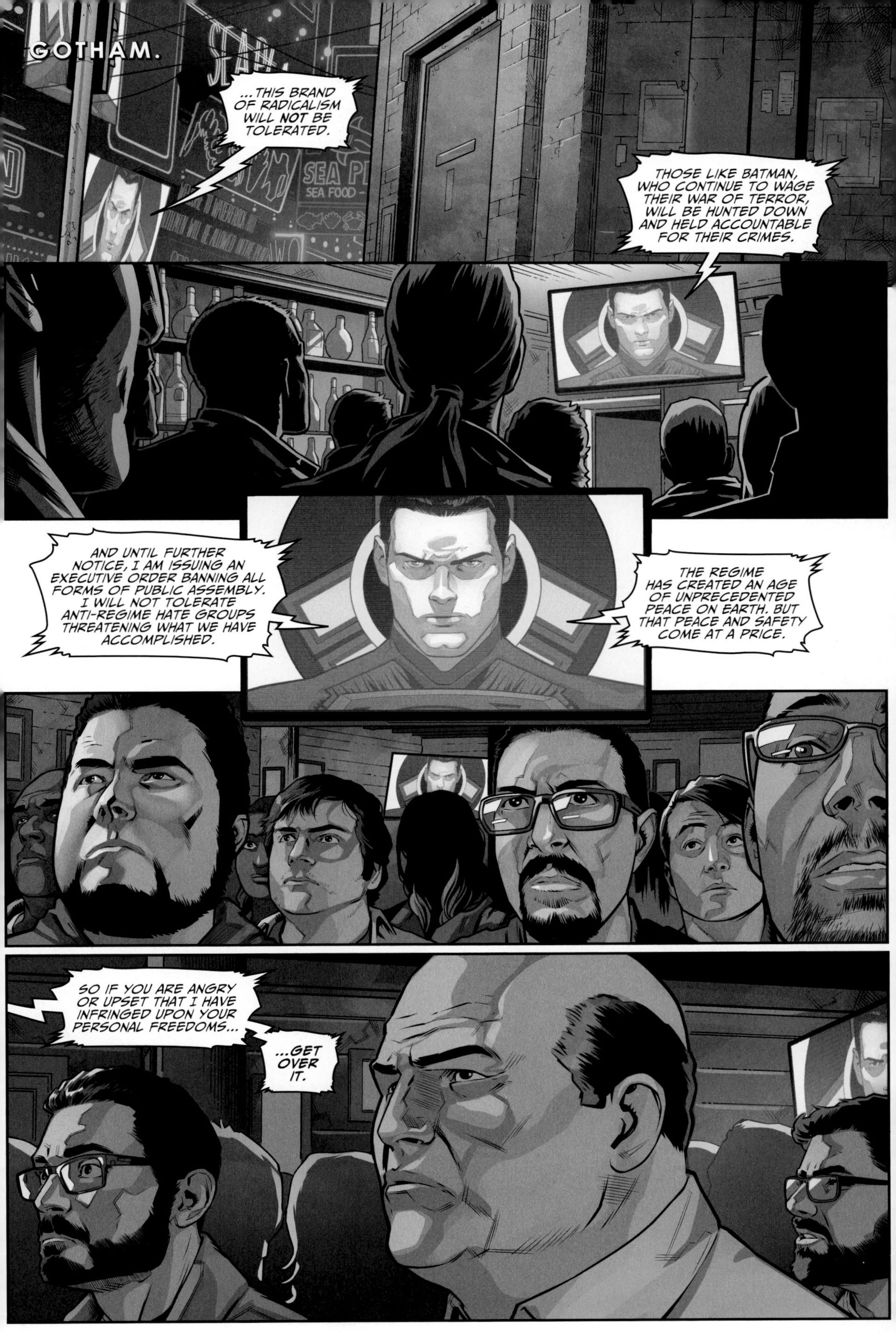
GOTHAM.
...THIS BRAND OF RADICALISM WILL NOT BE TOLERATED.
THOSE LIKE BATMAN, WHO CONTINUE TO WAGE THEIR WAR OF TERROR, WILL BE HUNTED DOWN AND HELD ACCOUNTABLE FOR THEIR CRIMES.
AND UNTIL FURTHER NOTICE, I AM ISSUING AN EXECUTIVE ORDER BANNING ALL FORMS OF PUBLIC ASSEMBLY. I WILL NOT TOLERATE ANTI-REGIME HATE GROUPS THREATENING WHAT WE HAVE ACCOMPLISHED.
THE REGIME HAS CREATED AN AGE OF UNPRECEDENTED PEACE ON EARTH. BUT THAT PEACE AND SAFETY COME AT A PRICE.
SO IF YOU ARE ANGRY OR UPSET THAT I HAVE INFRINGED UPON YOUR PERSONAL FREEDOMS...
...GET OVER IT.

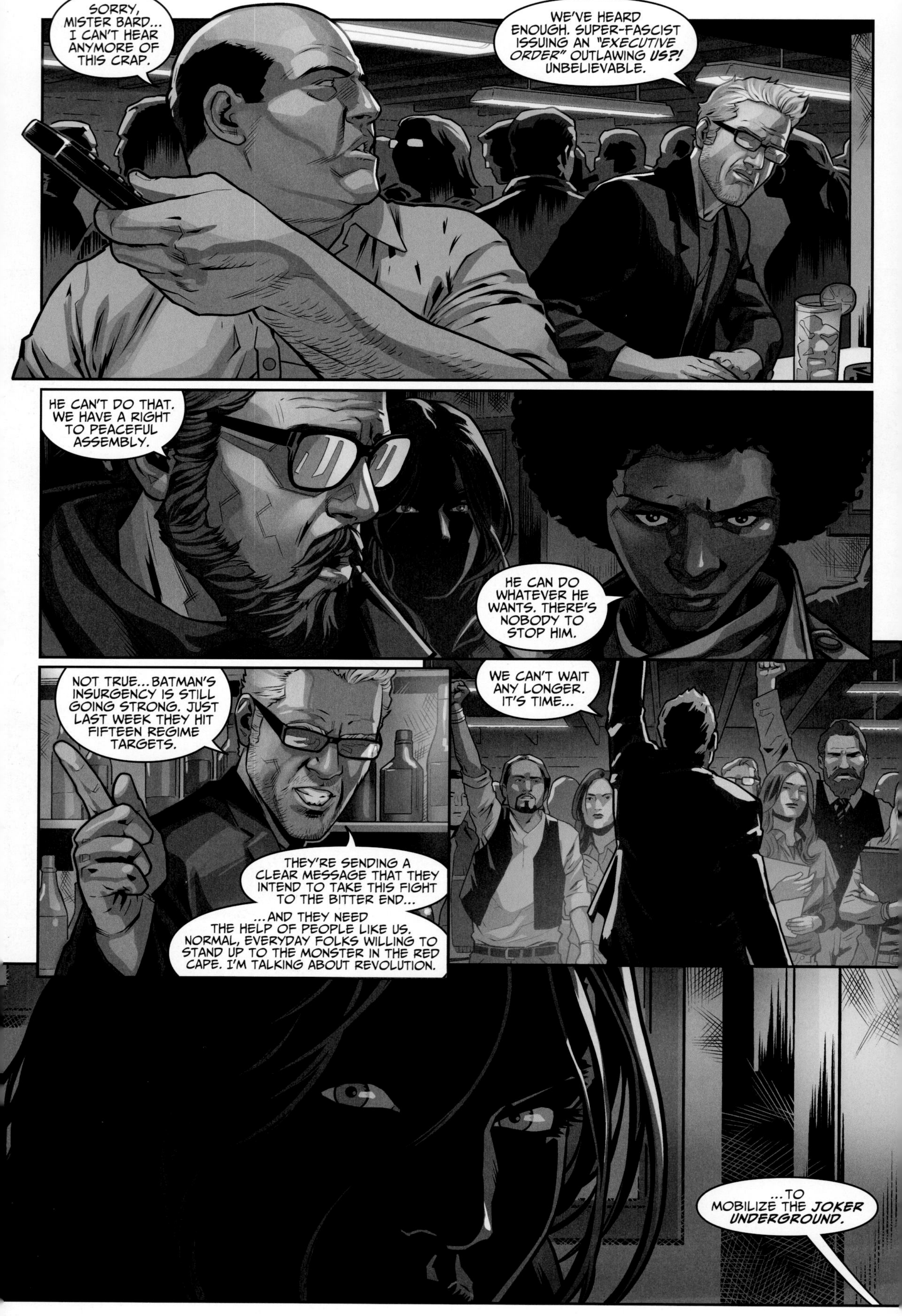
SORRY, MISTER BARD... I CAN'T HEAR ANYMORE OF THIS CRAP.
WE'VE HEARD ENOUGH. SUPER-FASCIST ISSUING AN "EXECUTIVE ORDER" OUTLAWING US?! UNBELIEVABLE.
HE CAN'T DO THAT. WE HAVE A RIGHT TO PEACEFUL ASSEMBLY.
HE CAN DO WHATEVER HE WANTS. THERE'S NOBODY TO STOP HIM.
NOT TRUE...BATMAN'S INSURGENCY IS STILL GOING STRONG. JUST LAST WEEK THEY HIT FIFTEEN REGIME TARGETS.
THEY'RE SENDING A CLEAR MESSAGE THAT THEY INTEND TO TAKE THIS FIGHT TO THE BITTER END...
...AND THEY NEED THE HELP OF PEOPLE LIKE US. NORMAL, EVERYDAY FOLKS WILLING TO STAND UP TO THE MONSTER IN THE RED CAPE. I'M TALKING ABOUT REVOLUTION.
WE CAN'T WAIT ANY LONGER. IT'S TIME...
...TO MOBILIZE THE JOKER UNDERGROUND.

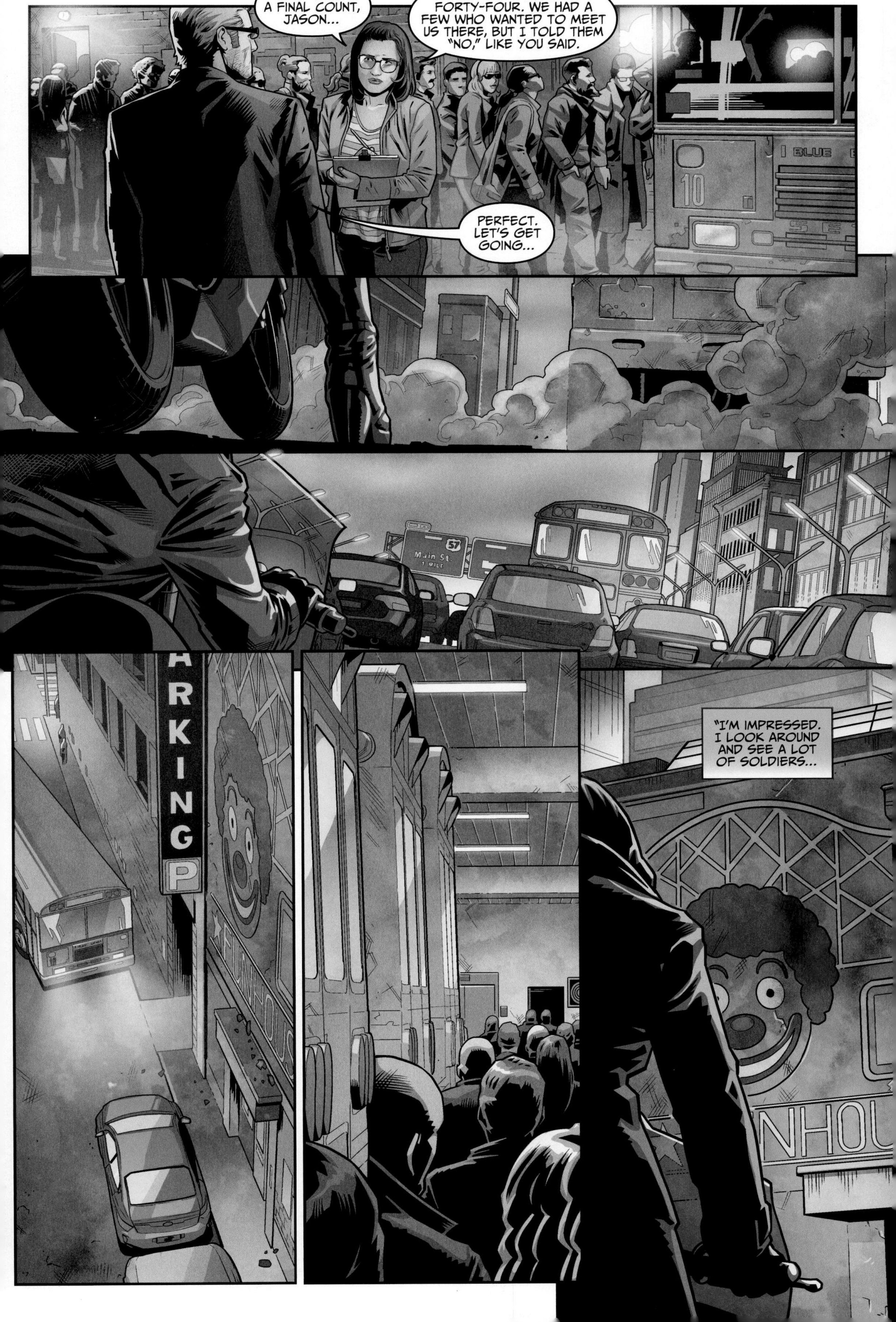
I'VE GOT A FINAL COUNT, JASON...
...THAT MAKES FORTY-FOUR. WE HAD A FEW WHO WANTED TO MEET US THERE, BUT I TOLD THEM "NO," LIKE YOU SAID.
PERFECT. LET'S GET GOING...
Main St.
1 MILE
57
ARKING
P
FUNHOUS
"I'M IMPRESSED. I LOOK AROUND AND SEE A LOT OF SOLDIERS...
NHOU

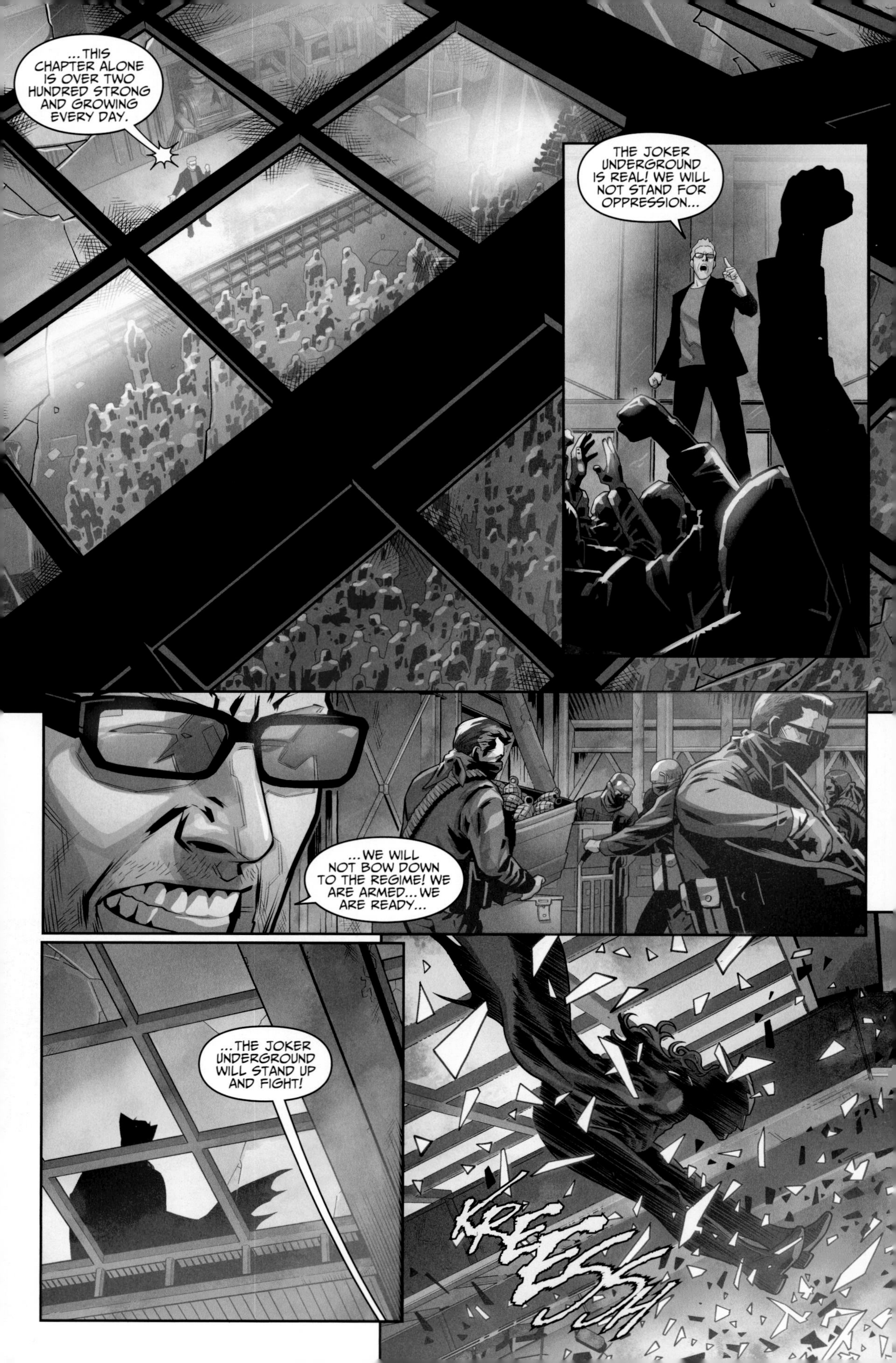
...THIS CHAPTER ALONE IS OVER TWO HUNDRED STRONG AND GROWING EVERY DAY.
THE JOKER UNDERGROUND IS REAL! WE WILL NOT STAND FOR OPPRESSION...
...WE WILL NOT BOW DOWN TO THE REGIME! WE ARE ARMED...WE ARE READY...
...THE JOKER UNDERGROUND WILL STAND UP AND FIGHT!
KREESSH

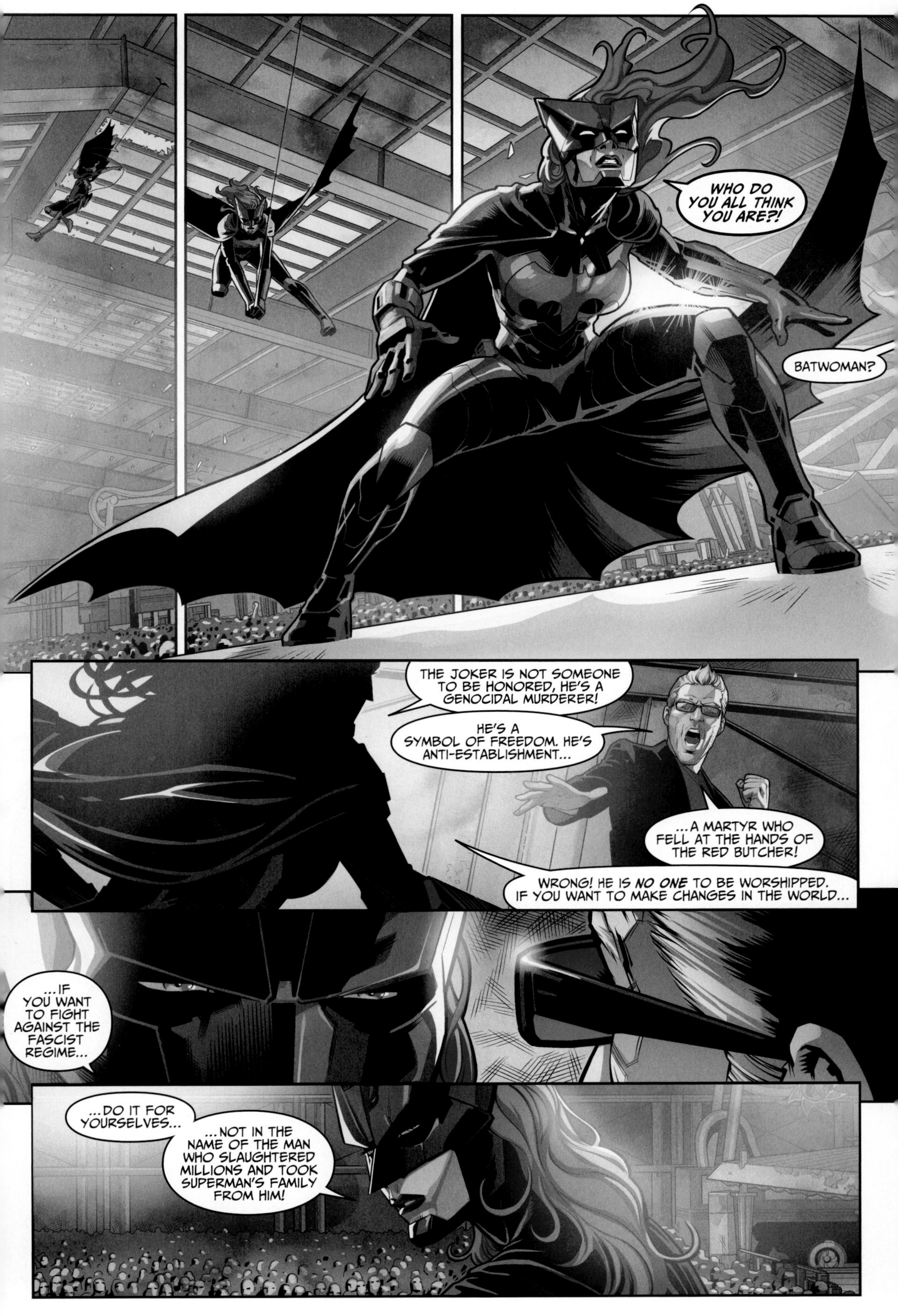
WHO DO YOU ALL THINK YOU ARE?!
BATWOMAN?
THE JOKER IS NOT SOMEONE TO BE HONORED, HE'S A GENOCIDAL MURDERER!
HE'S A SYMBOL OF FREEDOM. HE'S ANTI-ESTABLISHMENT...
...A MARTYR WHO FELL AT THE HANDS OF THE RED BUTCHER!
WRONG! HE IS NO ONE TO BE WORSHIPPED. IF YOU WANT TO MAKE CHANGES IN THE WORLD...
...IF YOU WANT TO FIGHT AGAINST THE FASCIST REGIME...
...DO IT FOR YOURSELVES...
...NOT IN THE NAME OF THE MAN WHO SLAUGHTERED MILLIONS AND TOOK SUPERMAN'S FAMILY FROM HIM!

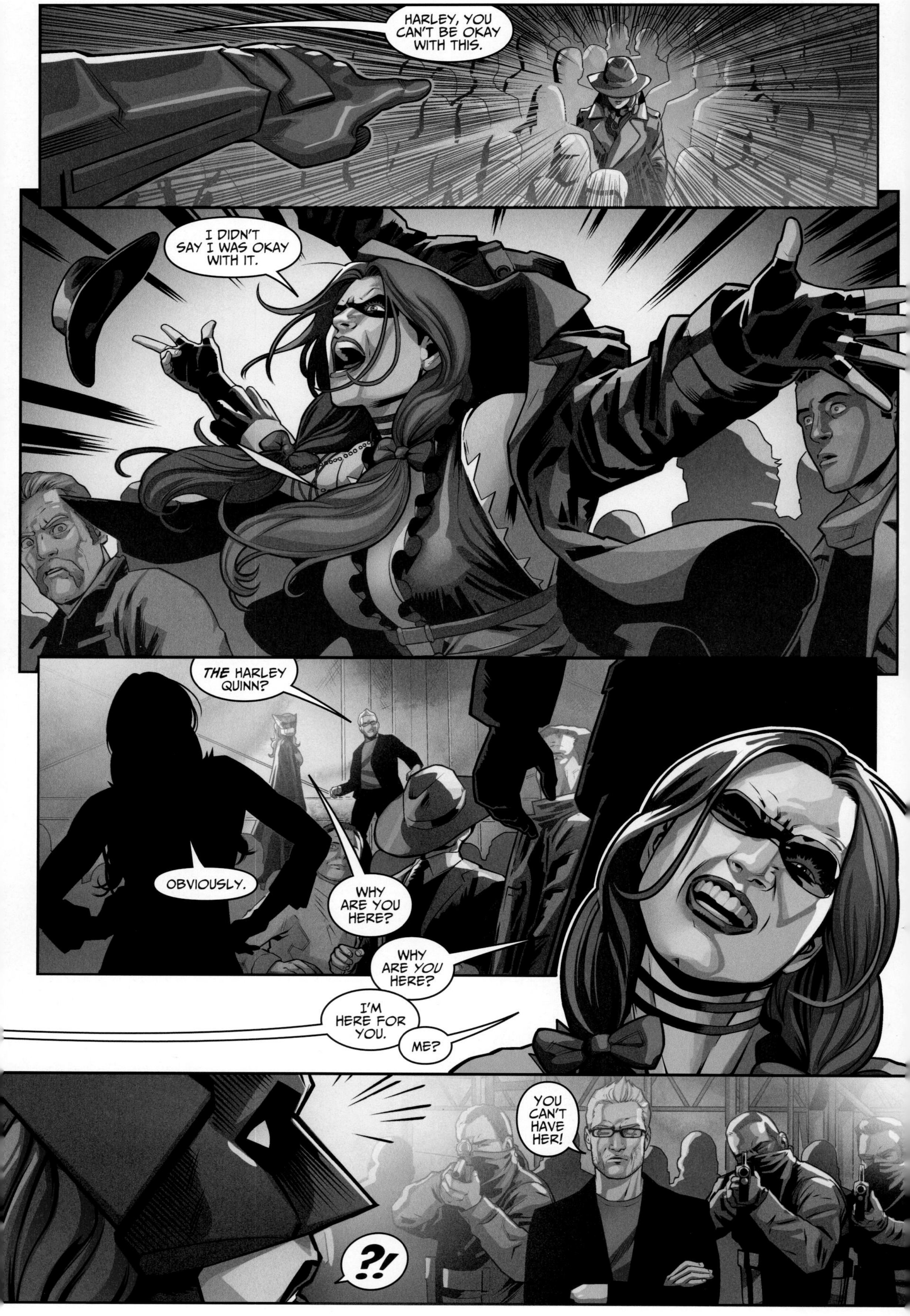
HARLEY, YOU CAN'T BE OKAY WITH THIS.
I DIDN'T SAY I WAS OKAY WITH IT.
THE HARLEY QUINN?
OBVIOUSLY.
WHY ARE YOU HERE?
WHY ARE YOU HERE?
I'M HERE FOR YOU.
ME?
YOU CAN'T HAVE HER!
?!

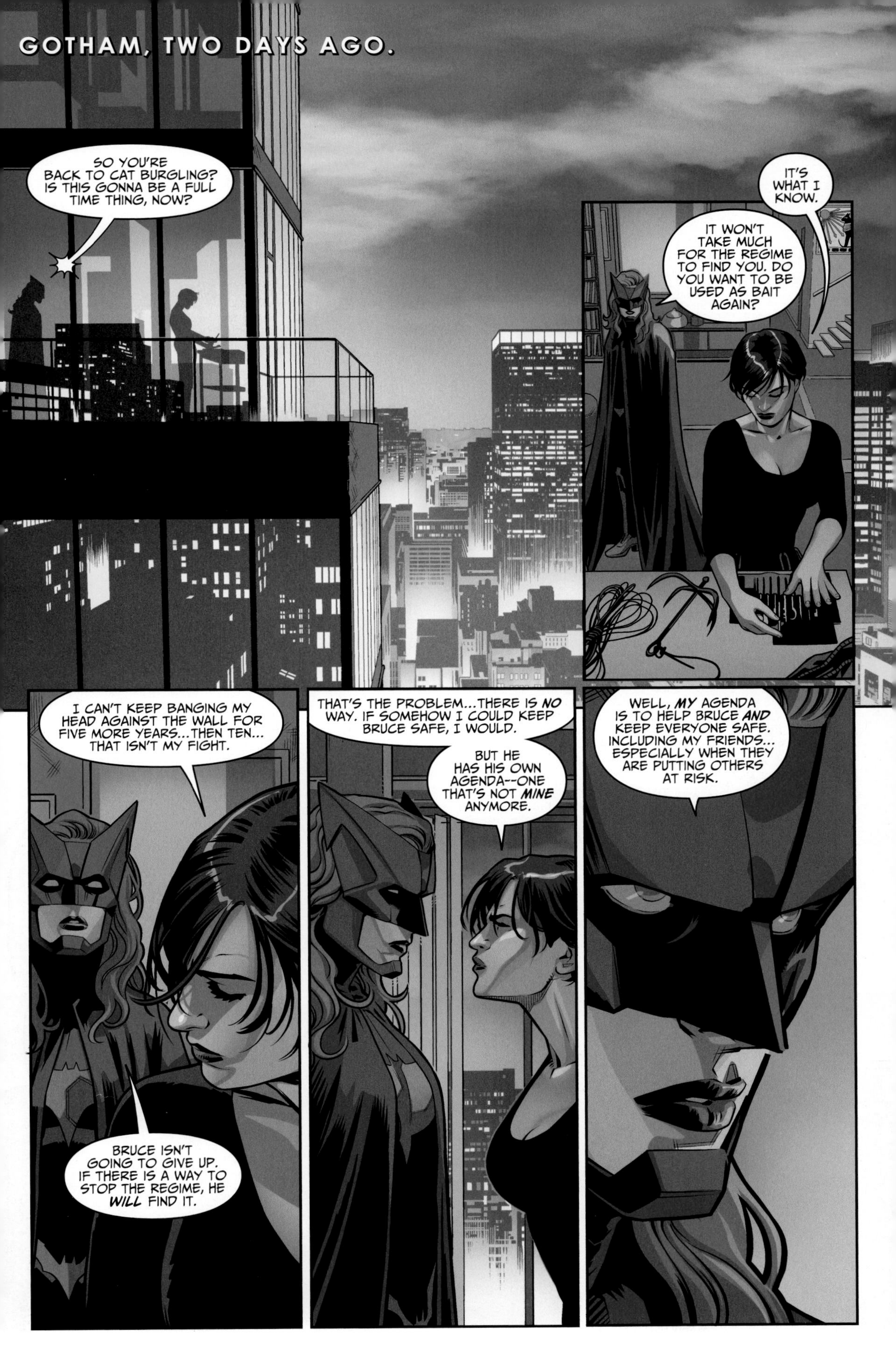
GOTHAM, TWO DAYS AGO.
SO YOU'RE BACK TO CAT BURGLING? IS THIS GONNA BE A FULL TIME THING, NOW?
IT'S WHAT I KNOW.
IT WON'T TAKE MUCH FOR THE REGIME TO FIND YOU. DO YOU WANT TO BE USED AS BAIT AGAIN?
I CAN'T KEEP BANGING MY HEAD AGAINST THE WALL FOR FIVE MORE YEARS...THEN TEN... THAT ISN'T MY FIGHT.
BRUCE ISN'T GOING TO GIVE UP. IF THERE IS A WAY TO STOP THE REGIME, HE *WILL* FIND IT.
THAT'S THE PROBLEM...THERE IS *NO* WAY. IF SOMEHOW I COULD KEEP BRUCE SAFE, I WOULD.
BUT HE HAS HIS OWN AGENDA--ONE THAT'S NOT *MINE* ANYMORE.
WELL, *MY* AGENDA IS TO HELP BRUCE *AND* KEEP EVERYONE SAFE. INCLUDING MY FRIENDS... ESPECIALLY WHEN THEY ARE PUTTING OTHERS AT RISK.

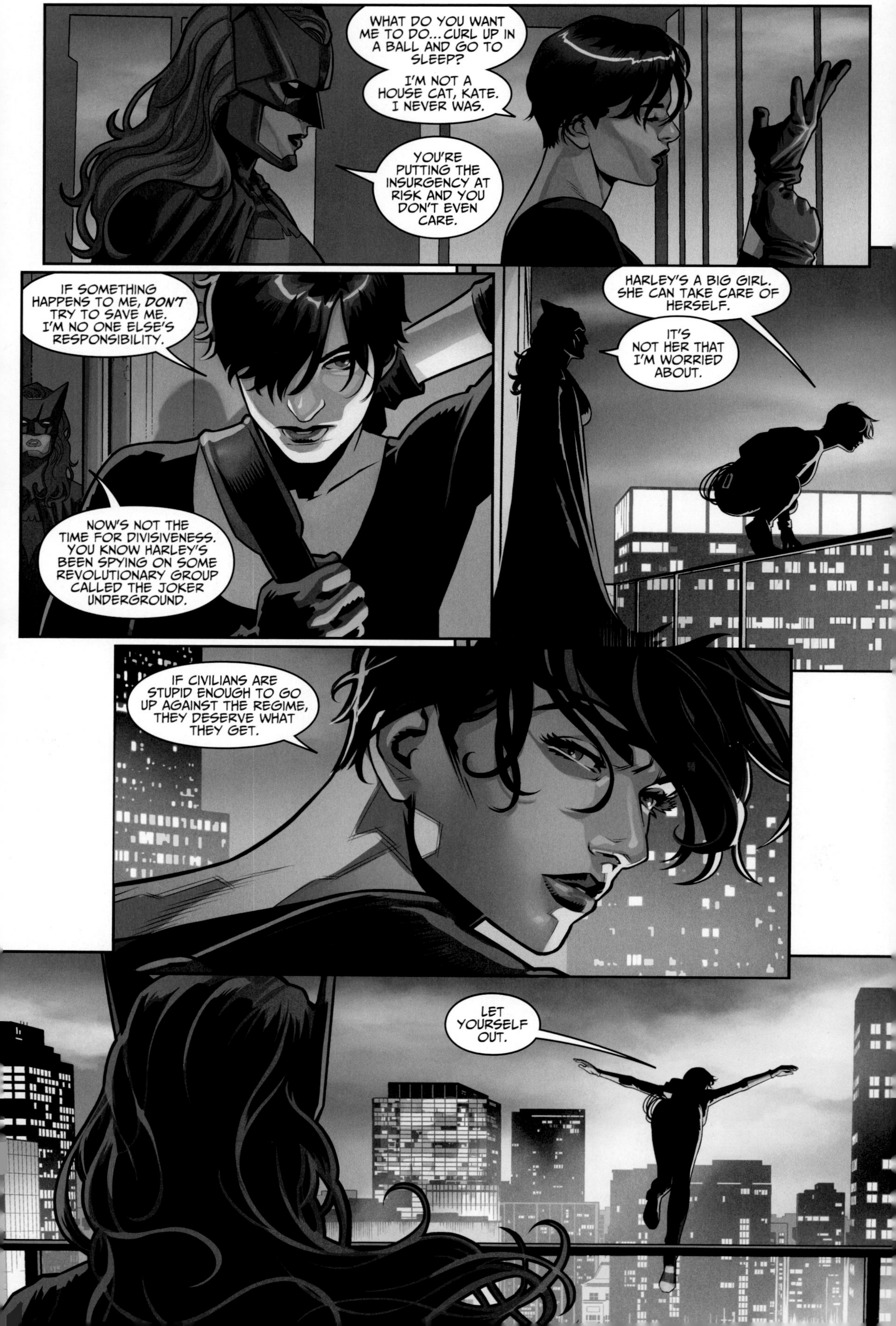
WHAT DO YOU WANT ME TO DO...CURL UP IN A BALL AND GO TO SLEEP?
I'M NOT A HOUSE CAT, KATE. I NEVER WAS.
YOU'RE PUTTING THE INSURGENCY AT RISK AND YOU DON'T EVEN CARE.
IF SOMETHING HAPPENS TO ME, *DON'T* TRY TO SAVE ME. I'M NO ONE ELSE'S RESPONSIBILITY.
NOW'S NOT THE TIME FOR DIVISIVENESS. YOU KNOW HARLEY'S BEEN SPYING ON SOME REVOLUTIONARY GROUP CALLED THE JOKER UNDERGROUND.
HARLEY'S A BIG GIRL. SHE CAN TAKE CARE OF HERSELF.
IT'S NOT HER THAT I'M WORRIED ABOUT.
IF CIVILIANS ARE STUPID ENOUGH TO GO UP AGAINST THE REGIME, THEY DESERVE WHAT THEY GET.
LET YOURSELF OUT.

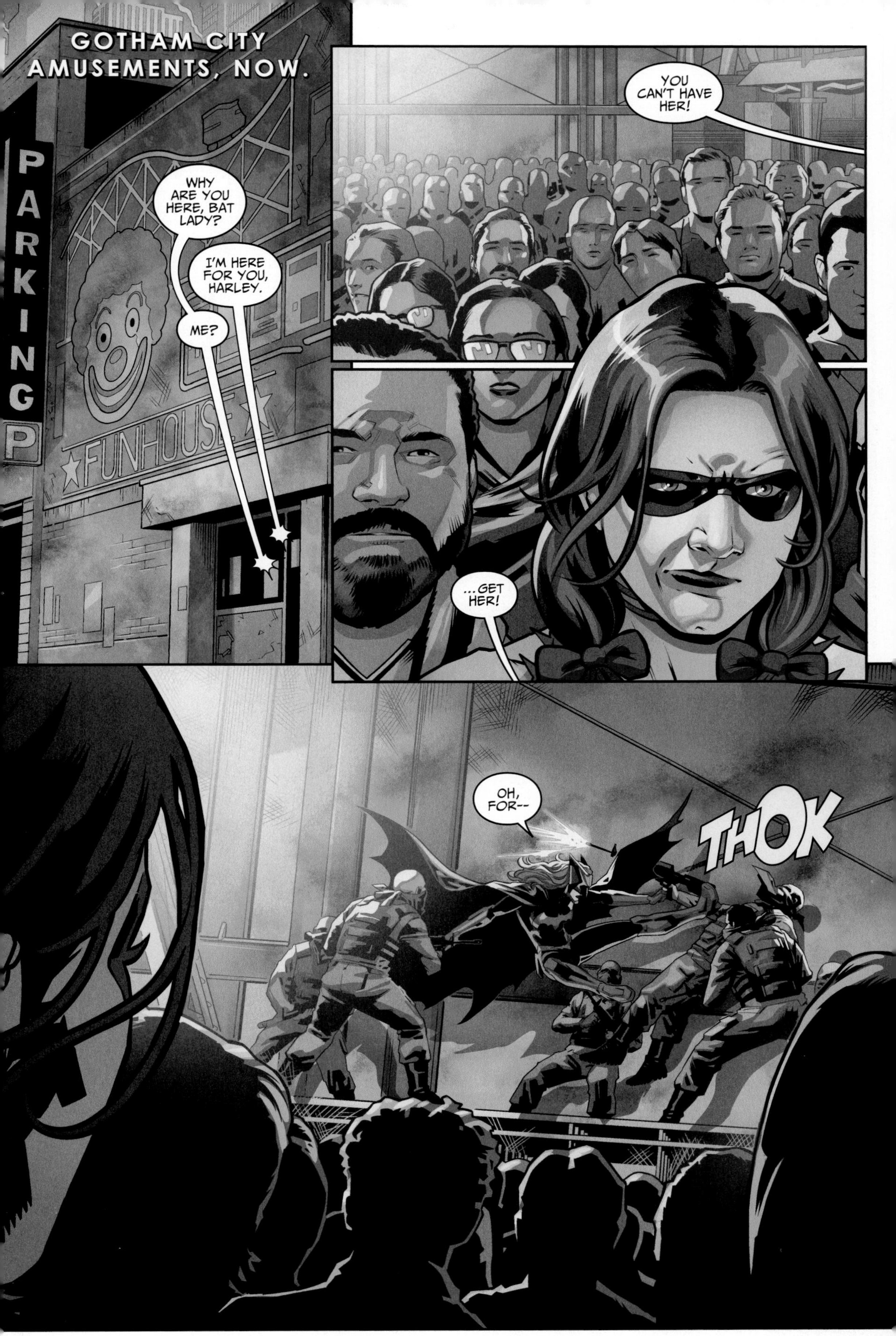
GOTHAM CITY AMUSEMENTS, NOW.
PARKING
P
FUNHOUSE
WHY ARE YOU HERE, BAT LADY?
I'M HERE FOR YOU, HARLEY.
ME?
YOU CAN'T HAVE HER!
...GET HER!
OH, FOR--
THOK

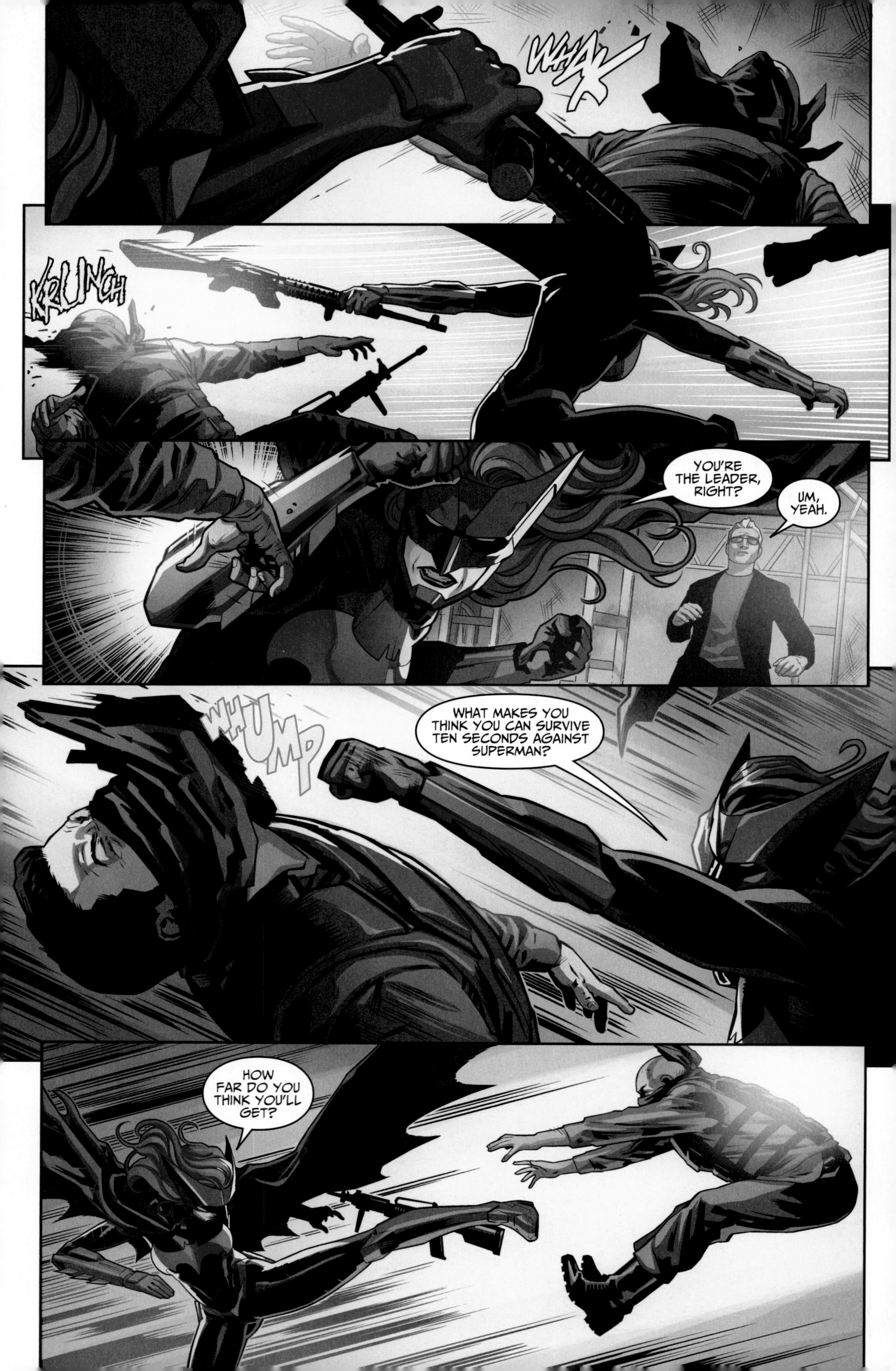
WHAK
KRUNCH
YOU'RE THE LEADER, RIGHT?
UM, YEAH.
WHUMP
WHAT MAKES YOU THINK YOU CAN SURVIVE TEN SECONDS AGAINST SUPERMAN?
HOW FAR DO YOU THINK YOU'LL GET?

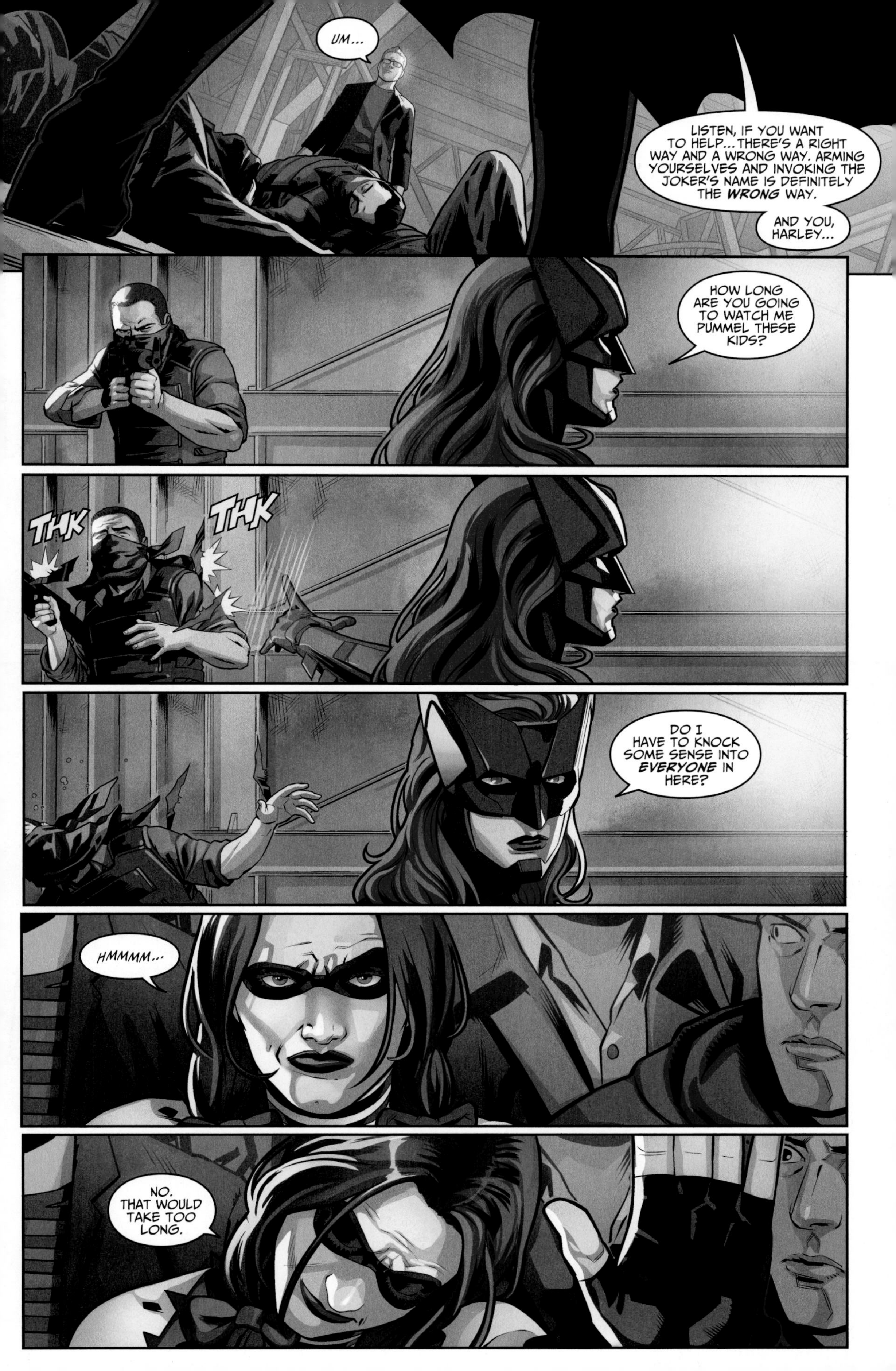
UM...
LISTEN, IF YOU WANT TO HELP... THERE'S A RIGHT WAY AND A WRONG WAY. ARMING YOURSELVES AND INVOKING THE JOKER'S NAME IS DEFINITELY THE **WRONG** WAY.
AND YOU, HARLEY...
HOW LONG ARE YOU GOING TO WATCH ME PUMMEL THESE KIDS?
THK
THK
DO I HAVE TO KNOCK SOME SENSE INTO **EVERYONE** IN HERE?
HMMMM...
NO. THAT WOULD TAKE TOO LONG.

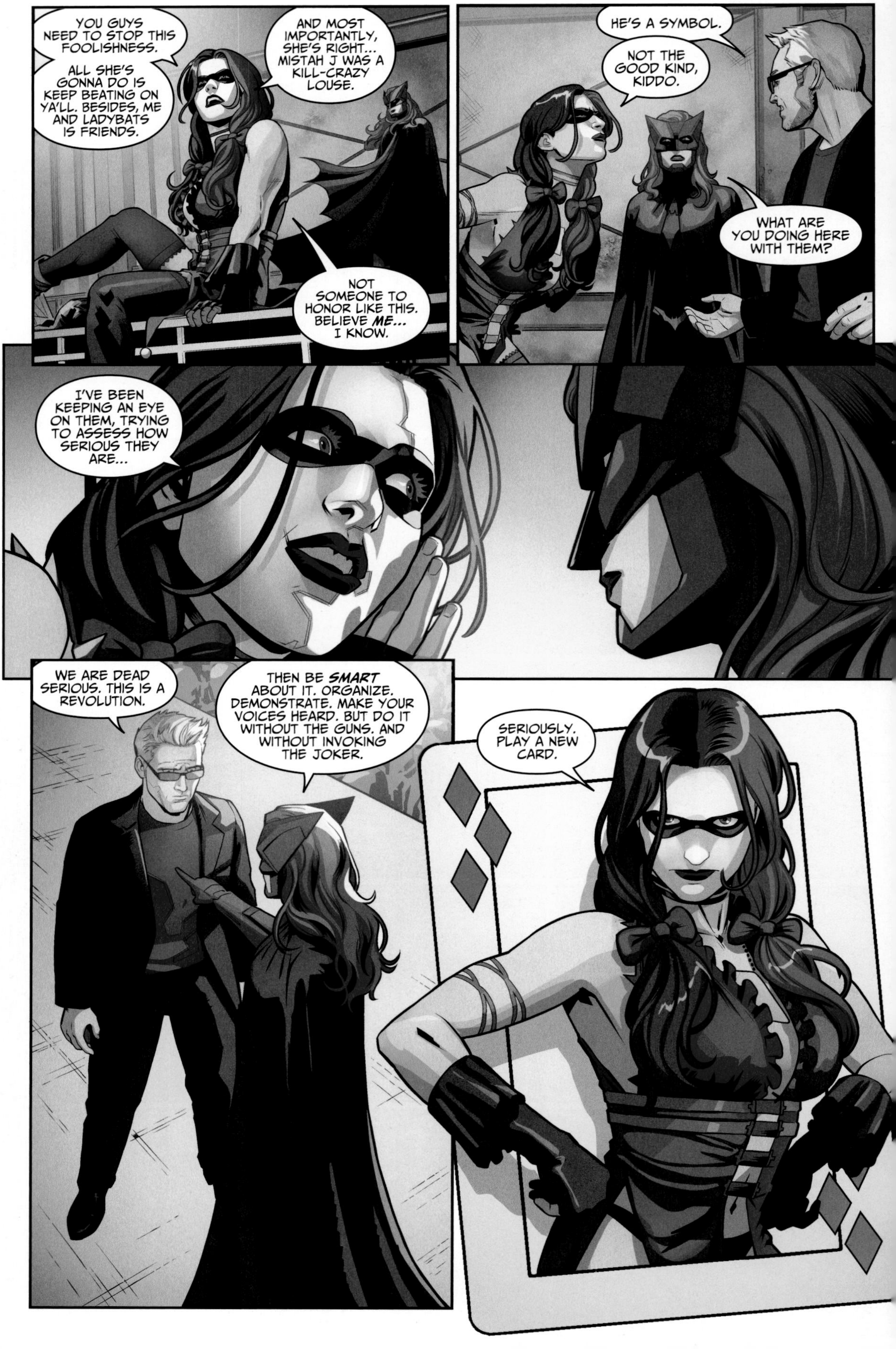
YOU GUYS NEED TO STOP THIS FOOLISHNESS.
ALL SHE'S GONNA DO IS KEEP BEATING ON YA'LL. BESIDES, ME AND LADYBATS IS FRIENDS.
AND MOST IMPORTANTLY, SHE'S RIGHT... MISTAH J WAS A KILL-CRAZY LOUSE.
NOT SOMEONE TO HONOR LIKE THIS. BELIEVE ME... I KNOW.
HE'S A SYMBOL.
NOT THE GOOD KIND, KIDDO.
WHAT ARE YOU DOING HERE WITH THEM?
I'VE BEEN KEEPING AN EYE ON THEM, TRYING TO ASSESS HOW SERIOUS THEY ARE...
WE ARE DEAD SERIOUS. THIS IS A REVOLUTION.
THEN BE SMART ABOUT IT. ORGANIZE. DEMONSTRATE. MAKE YOUR VOICES HEARD. BUT DO IT WITHOUT THE GUNS. AND WITHOUT INVOKING THE JOKER.
SERIOUSLY. PLAY A NEW CARD.

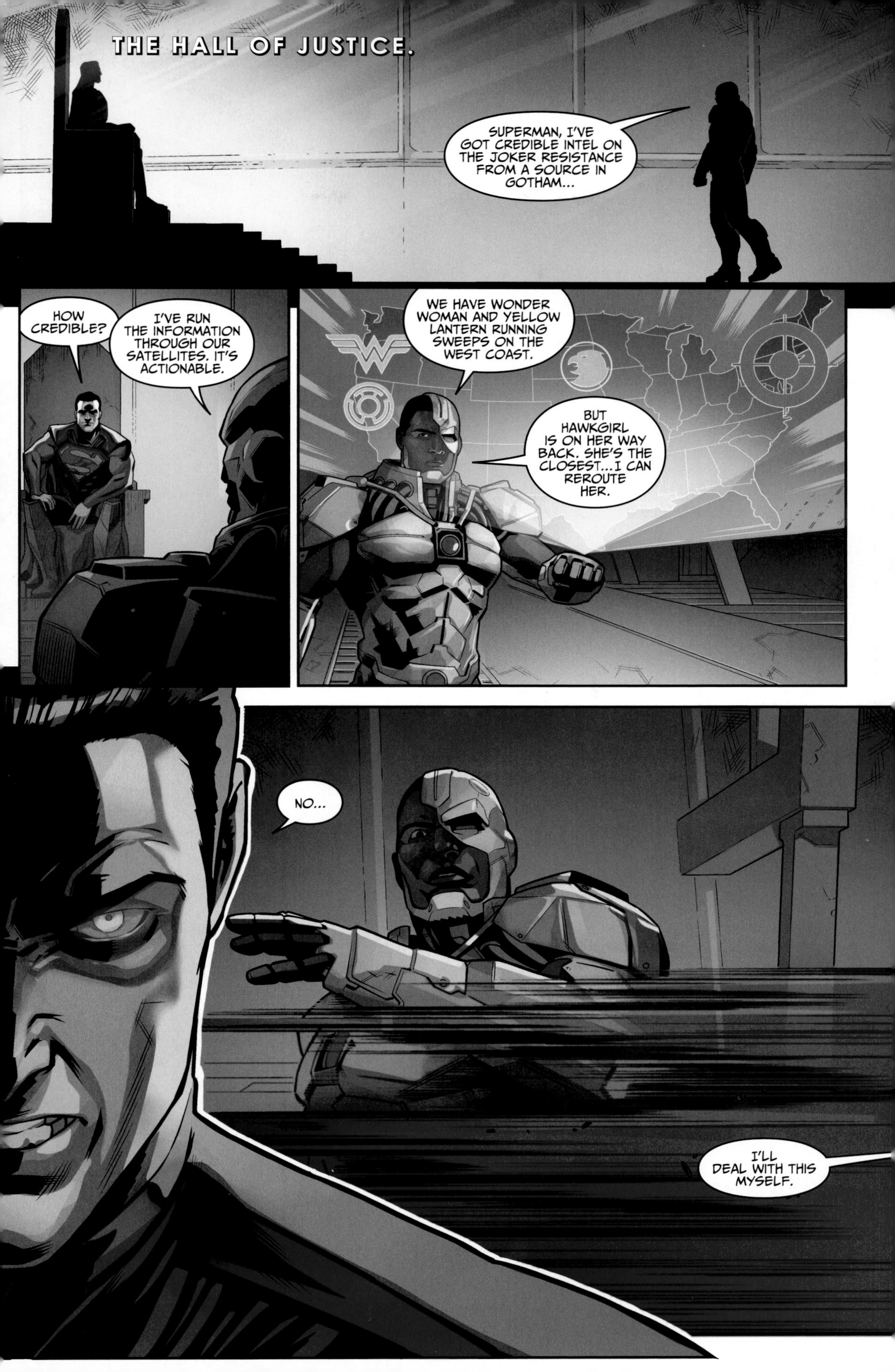
THE HALL OF JUSTICE.
SUPERMAN, I'VE GOT CREDIBLE INTEL ON THE JOKER RESISTANCE FROM A SOURCE IN GOTHAM...
HOW CREDIBLE?
I'VE RUN THE INFORMATION THROUGH OUR SATELLITES. IT'S ACTIONABLE.
WE HAVE WONDER WOMAN AND YELLOW LANTERN RUNNING SWEEPS ON THE WEST COAST.
BUT HAWKGIRL IS ON HER WAY BACK. SHE'S THE CLOSEST...I CAN REROUTE HER.
NO...
I'LL DEAL WITH THIS MYSELF.

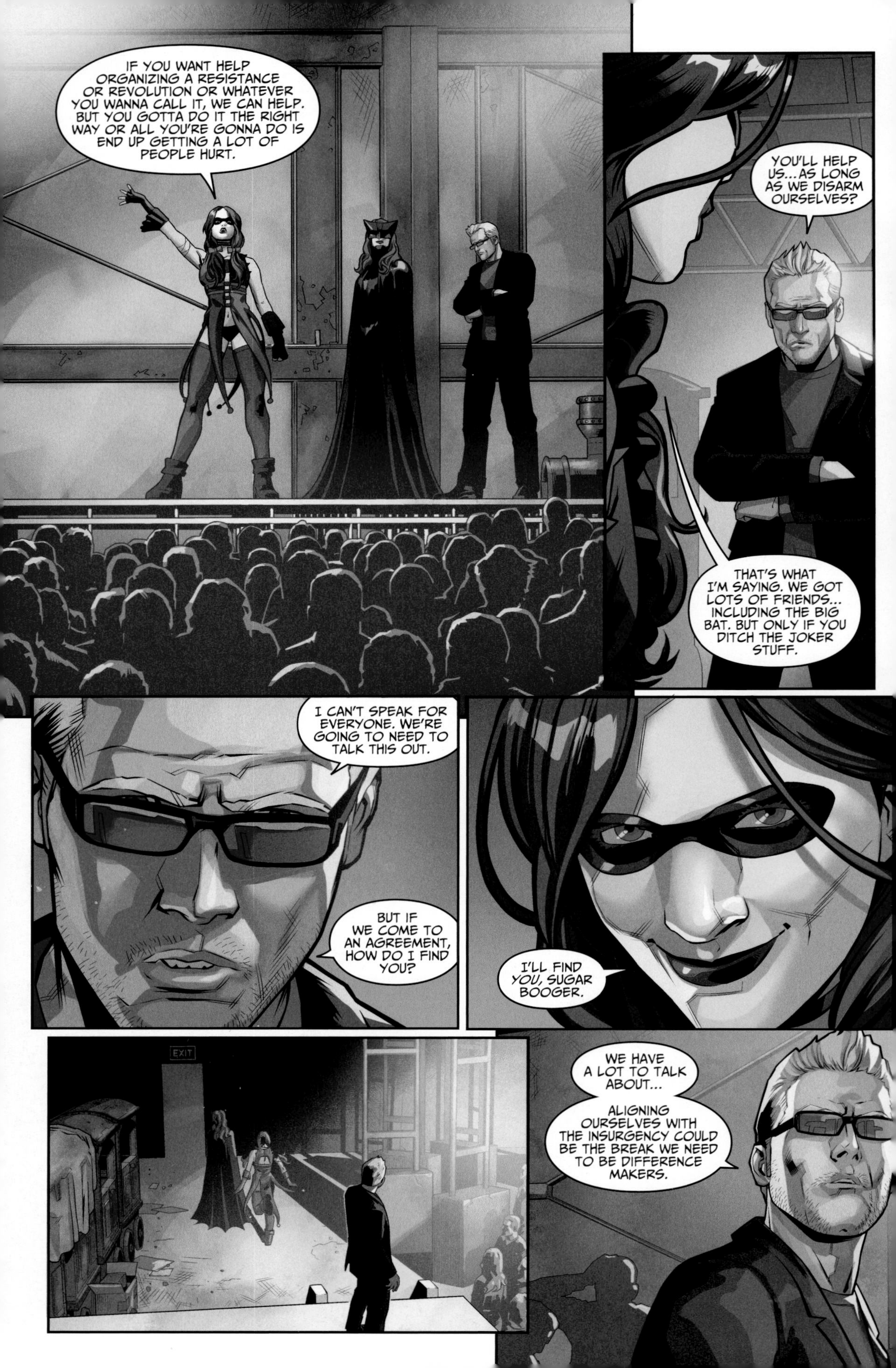
IF YOU WANT HELP ORGANIZING A RESISTANCE OR REVOLUTION OR WHATEVER YOU WANNA CALL IT, WE CAN HELP. BUT YOU GOTTA DO IT THE RIGHT WAY OR ALL YOU'RE GONNA DO IS END UP GETTING A LOT OF PEOPLE HURT.
YOU'LL HELP US...AS LONG AS WE DISARM OURSELVES?
THAT'S WHAT I'M SAYING. WE GOT LOTS OF FRIENDS... INCLUDING THE BIG BAT. BUT ONLY IF YOU DITCH THE JOKER STUFF.
I CAN'T SPEAK FOR EVERYONE. WE'RE GOING TO NEED TO TALK THIS OUT.
BUT IF WE COME TO AN AGREEMENT, HOW DO I FIND YOU?
I'LL FIND YOU, SUGAR BOOGER.
EXIT
WE HAVE A LOT TO TALK ABOUT...
ALIGNING OURSELVES WITH THE INSURGENCY COULD BE THE BREAK WE NEED TO BE DIFFERENCE MAKERS.

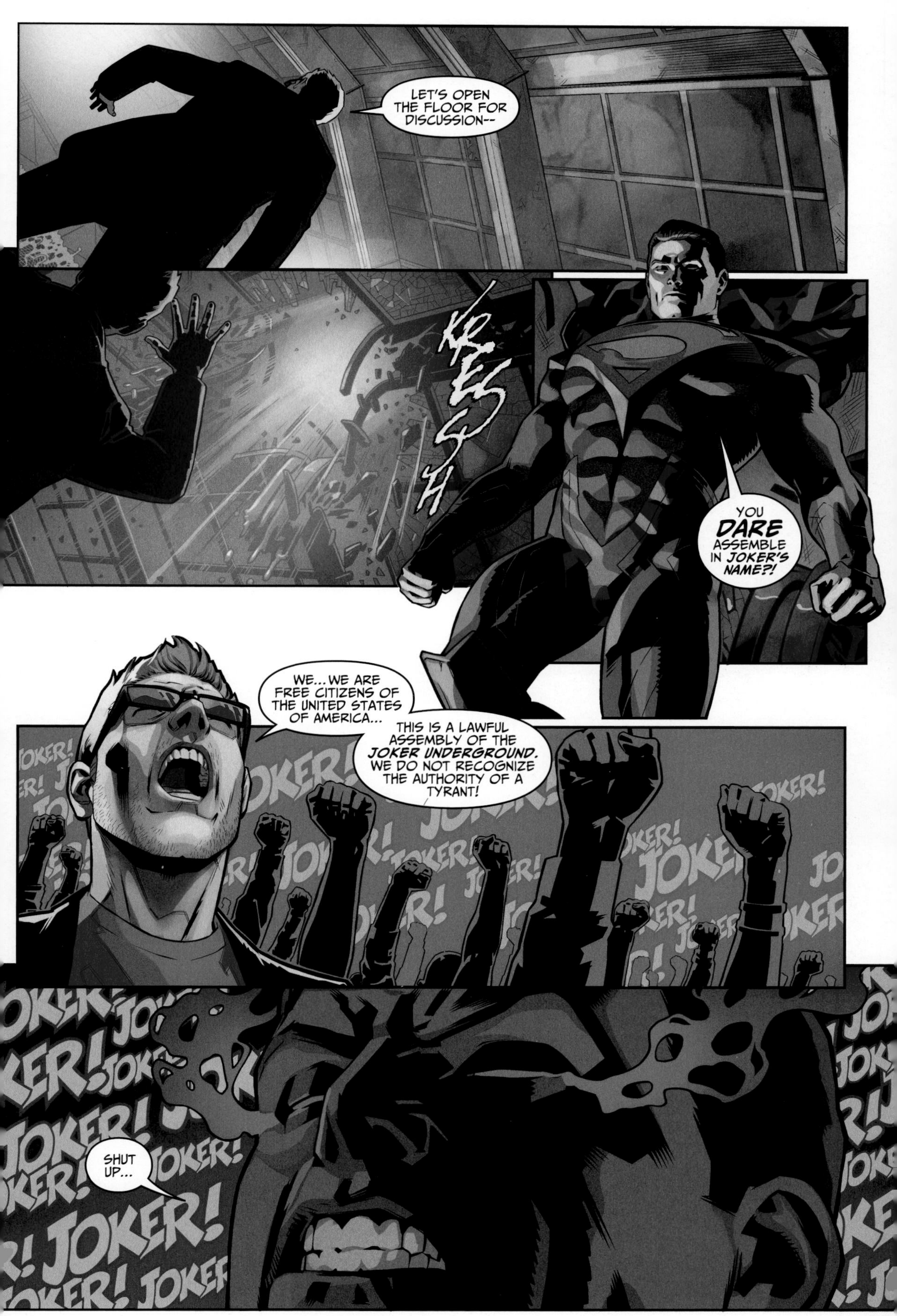
LET'S OPEN THE FLOOR FOR DISCUSSION--
KRESSHH
YOU DARE ASSEMBLE IN JOKER'S NAME?!
WE...WE ARE FREE CITIZENS OF THE UNITED STATES OF AMERICA...
THIS IS A LAWFUL ASSEMBLY OF THE JOKER UNDERGROUND. WE DO NOT RECOGNIZE THE AUTHORITY OF A TYRANT!
JOKER! JOKER! JOKER! JOKER!
SHUT UP...
JOKER! JOKER! JOKER!

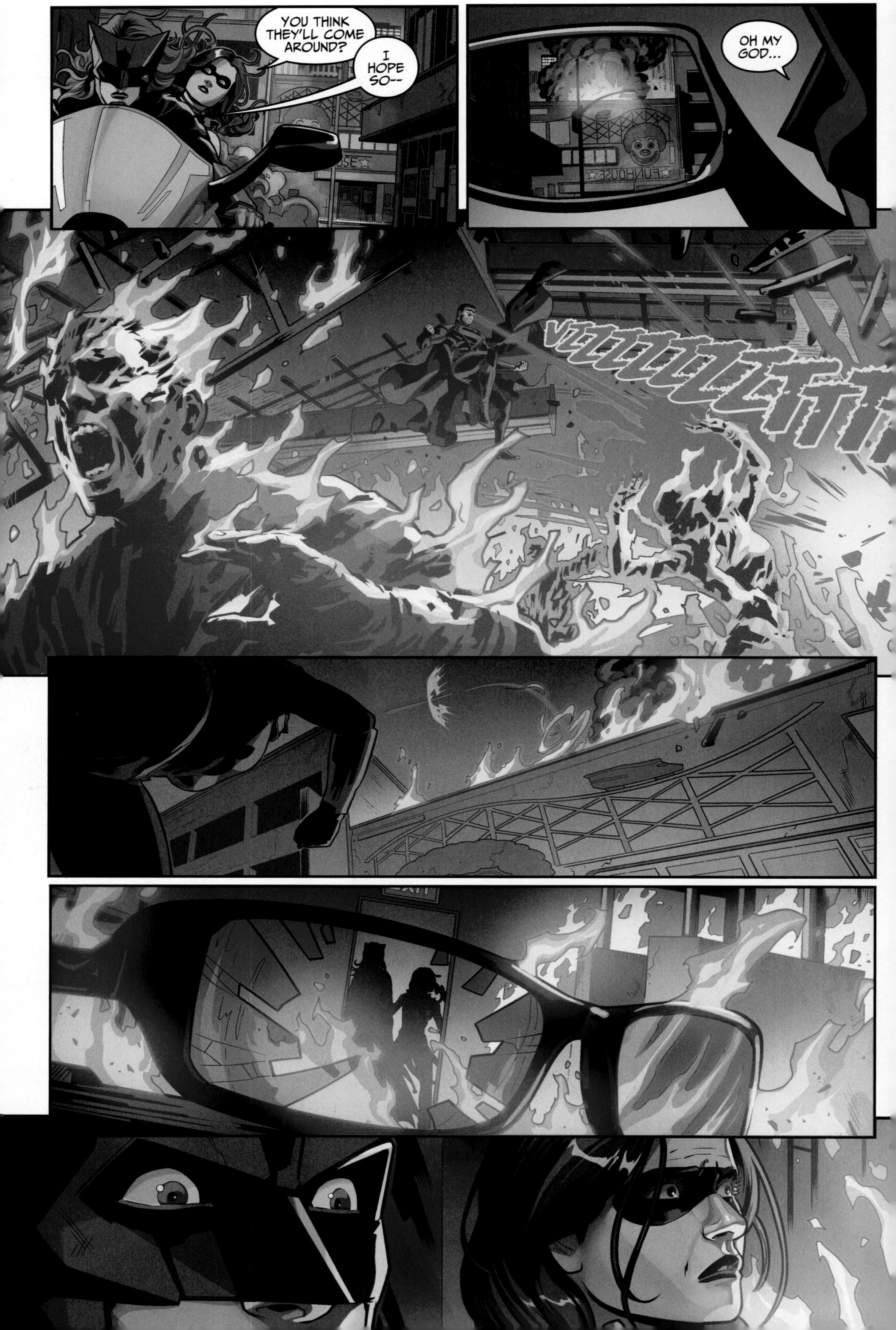
YOU THINK THEY'LL COME AROUND?
I HOPE SO--
OH MY GOD...
VZZZZZZZZTTTT

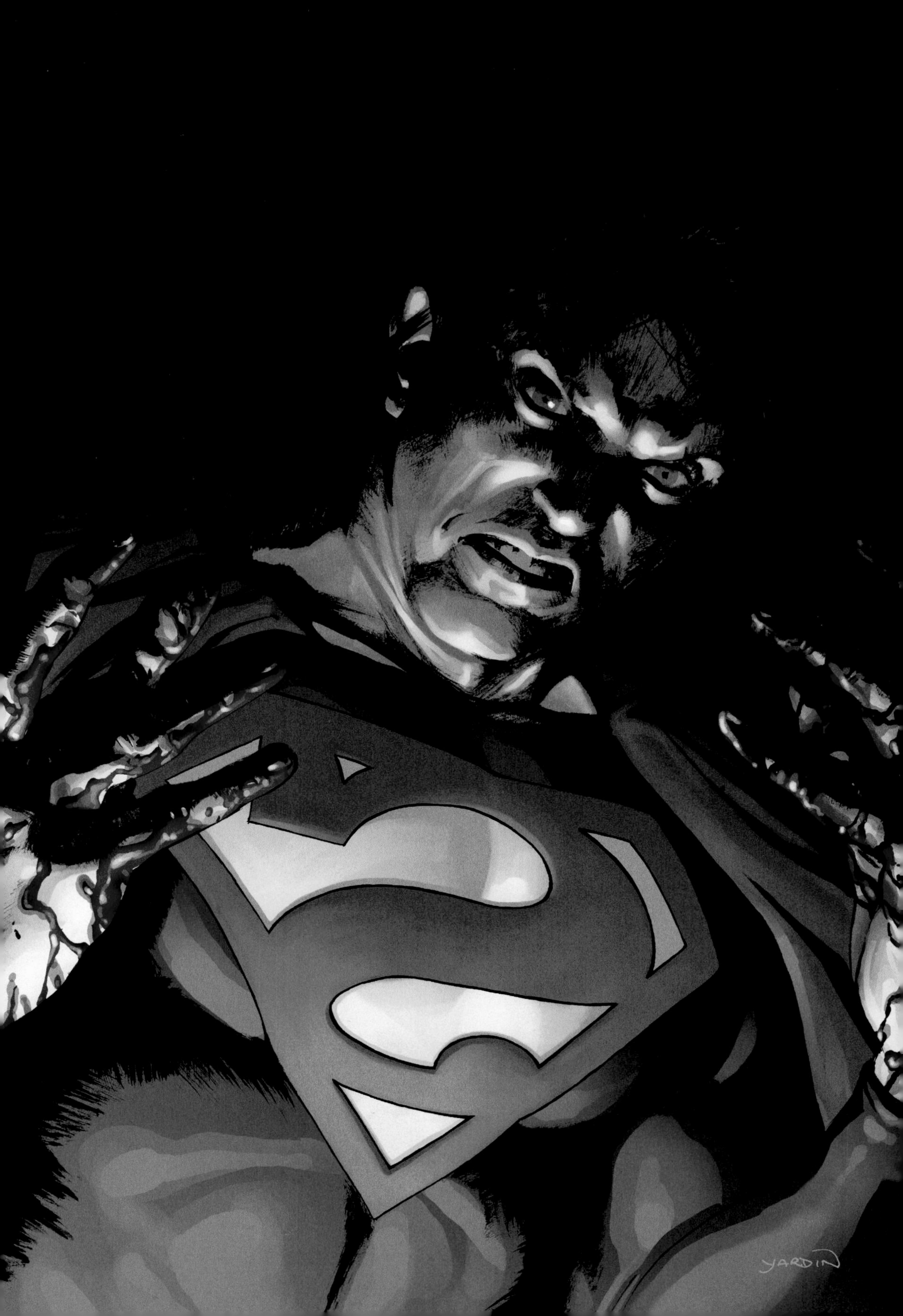
YARDIN

Of Might and Men   Tom Derenick Artist   Rex Lokus Colorist

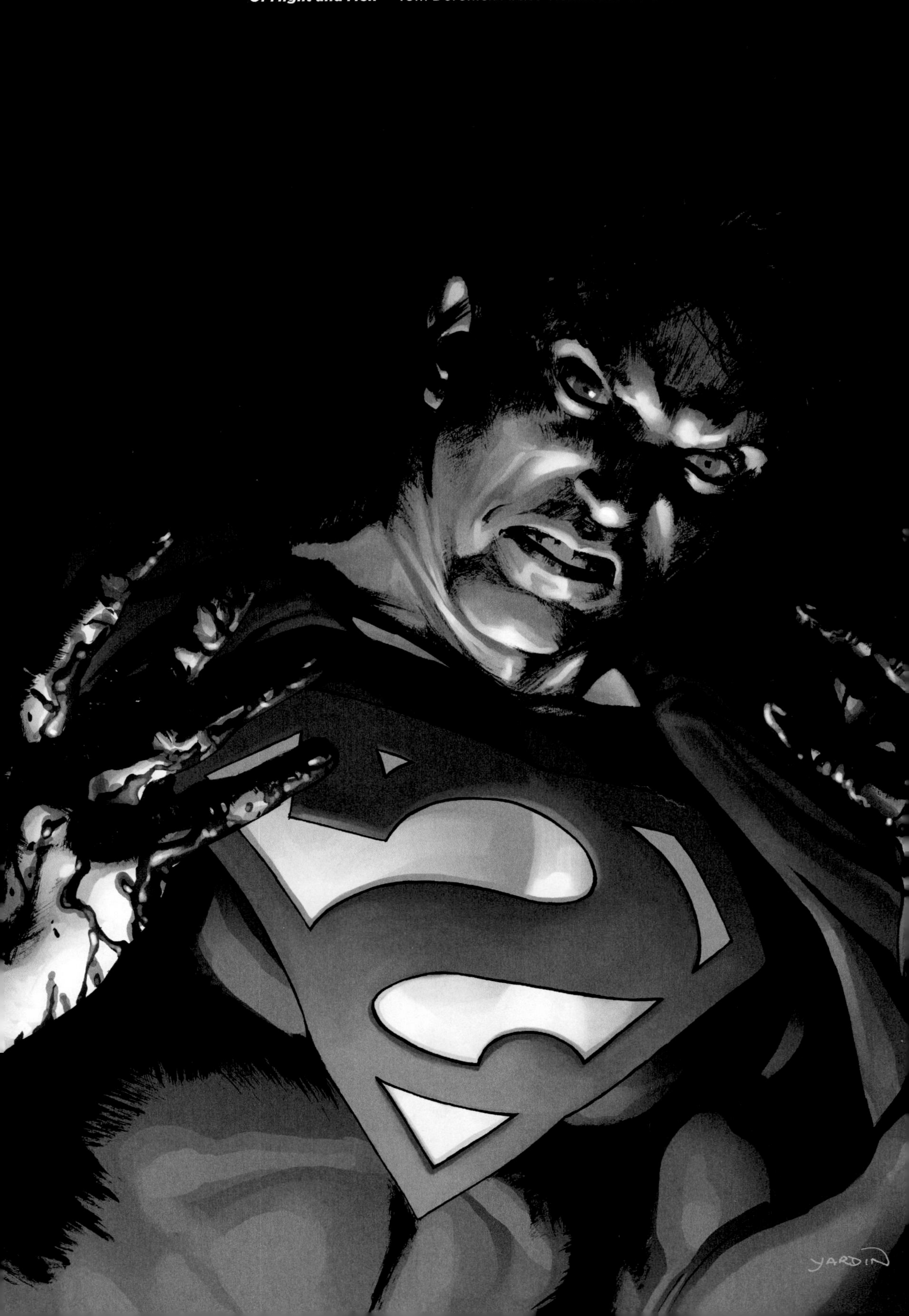
YARDIN

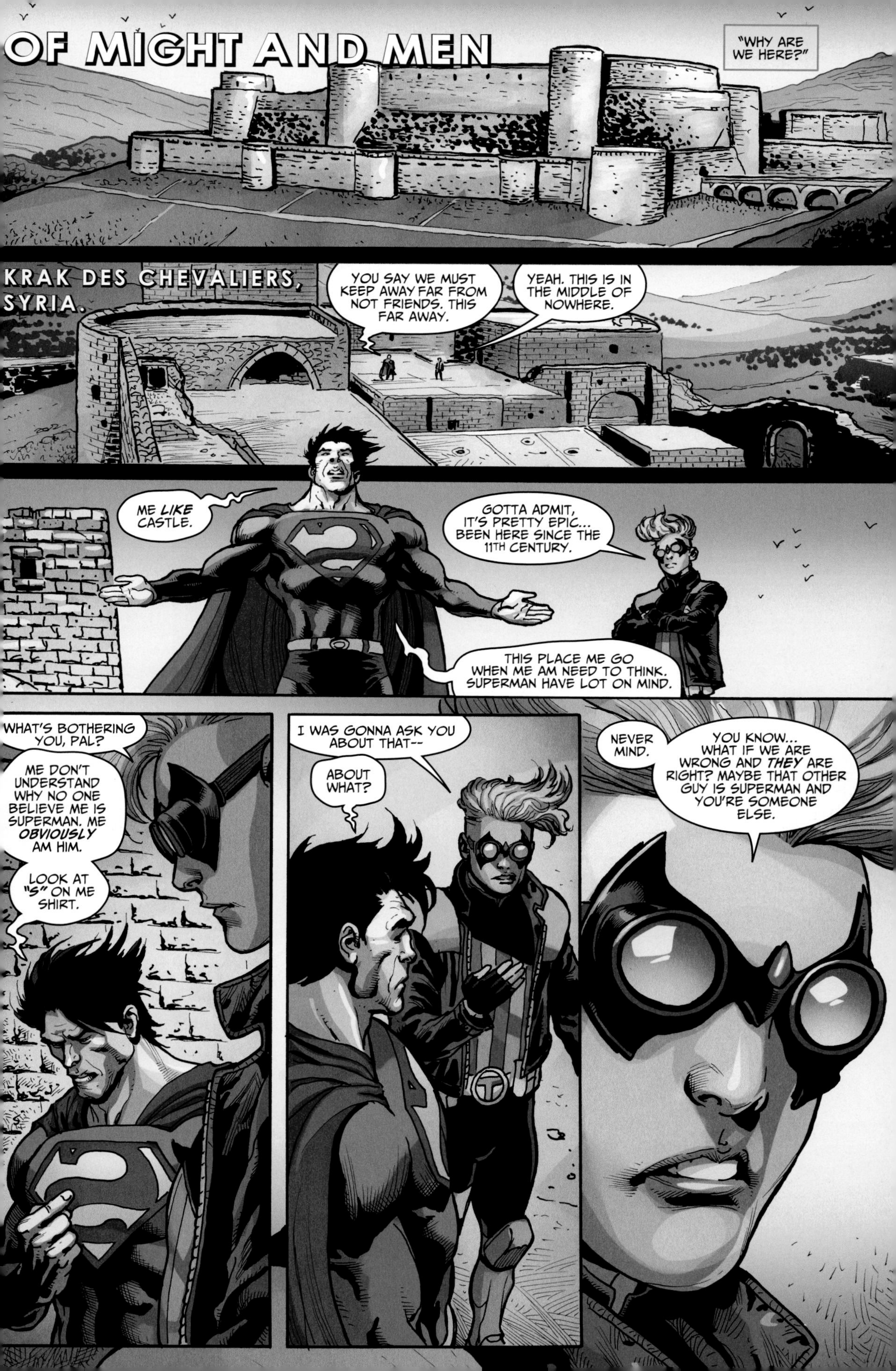
OF MIGHT AND MEN
"WHY ARE WE HERE?"
KRAK DES CHEVALIERS, SYRIA.
YOU SAY WE MUST KEEP AWAY FAR FROM NOT FRIENDS. THIS FAR AWAY.
YEAH. THIS IS IN THE MIDDLE OF NOWHERE.
ME LIKE CASTLE.
GOTTA ADMIT, IT'S PRETTY EPIC... BEEN HERE SINCE THE 11TH CENTURY.
THIS PLACE ME GO WHEN ME AM NEED TO THINK. SUPERMAN HAVE LOT ON MIND.
WHAT'S BOTHERING YOU, PAL?
ME DON'T UNDERSTAND WHY NO ONE BELIEVE ME IS SUPERMAN. ME OBVIOUSLY AM HIM.
LOOK AT "S" ON ME SHIRT.
I WAS GONNA ASK YOU ABOUT THAT--
ABOUT WHAT?
NEVER MIND.
YOU KNOW... WHAT IF WE ARE WRONG AND THEY ARE RIGHT? MAYBE THAT OTHER GUY IS SUPERMAN AND YOU'RE SOMEONE ELSE.

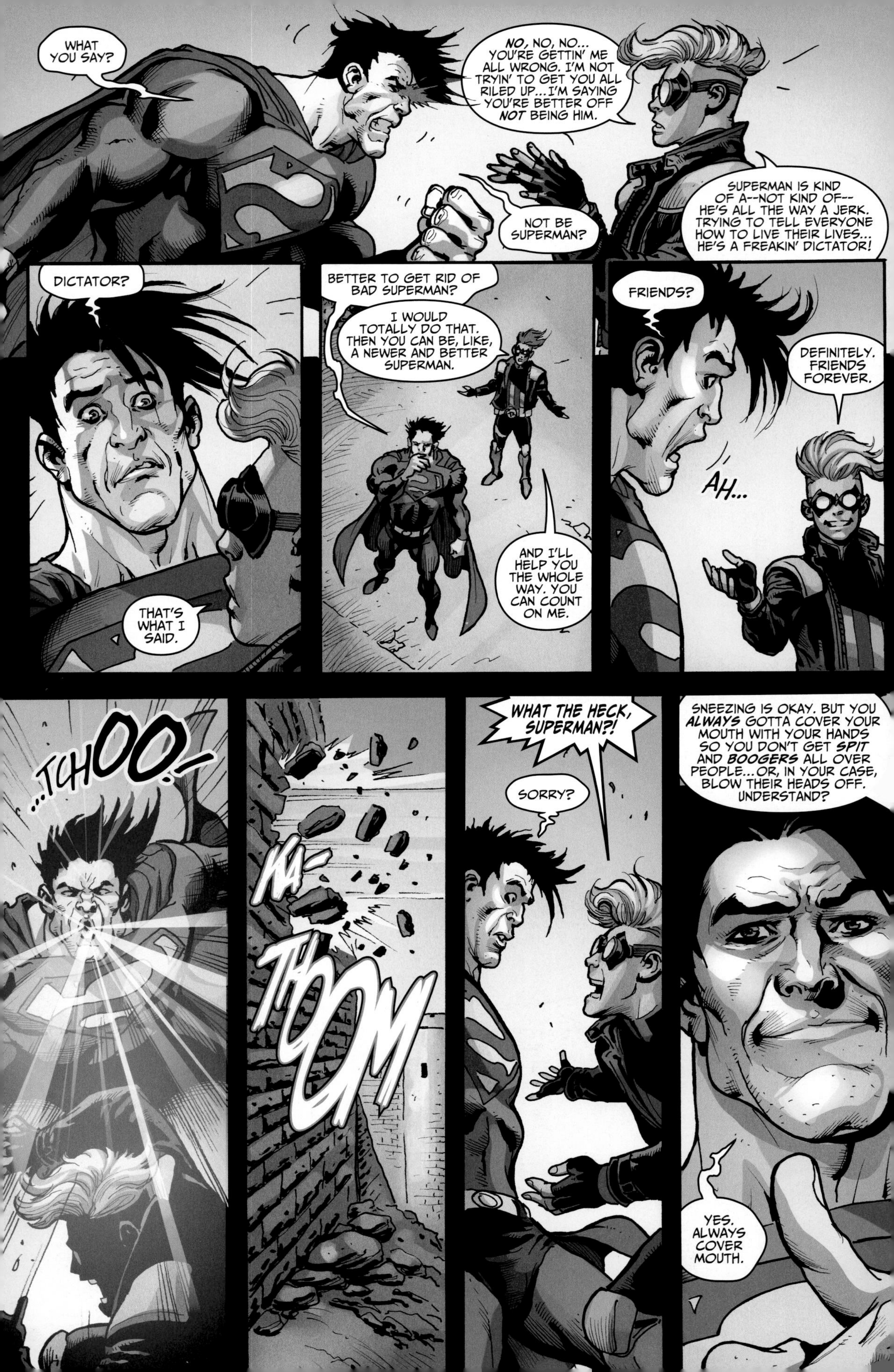
WHAT YOU SAY?
NO, NO, NO... YOU'RE GETTIN' ME ALL WRONG. I'M NOT TRYIN' TO GET YOU ALL RILED UP...I'M SAYING YOU'RE BETTER OFF NOT BEING HIM.
NOT BE SUPERMAN?
SUPERMAN IS KIND OF A--NOT KIND OF--HE'S ALL THE WAY A JERK. TRYING TO TELL EVERYONE HOW TO LIVE THEIR LIVES... HE'S A FREAKIN' DICTATOR!
DICTATOR?
THAT'S WHAT I SAID.
BETTER TO GET RID OF BAD SUPERMAN?
I WOULD TOTALLY DO THAT. THEN YOU CAN BE, LIKE, A NEWER AND BETTER SUPERMAN.
AND I'LL HELP YOU THE WHOLE WAY. YOU CAN COUNT ON ME.
FRIENDS?
DEFINITELY. FRIENDS FOREVER.
AH...
...TCHOO--
KA-THOOM
WHAT THE HECK, SUPERMAN?!
SORRY?
SNEEZING IS OKAY. BUT YOU ALWAYS GOTTA COVER YOUR MOUTH WITH YOUR HANDS SO YOU DON'T GET SPIT AND BOOGERS ALL OVER PEOPLE...OR, IN YOUR CASE, BLOW THEIR HEADS OFF. UNDERSTAND?
YES. ALWAYS COVER MOUTH.

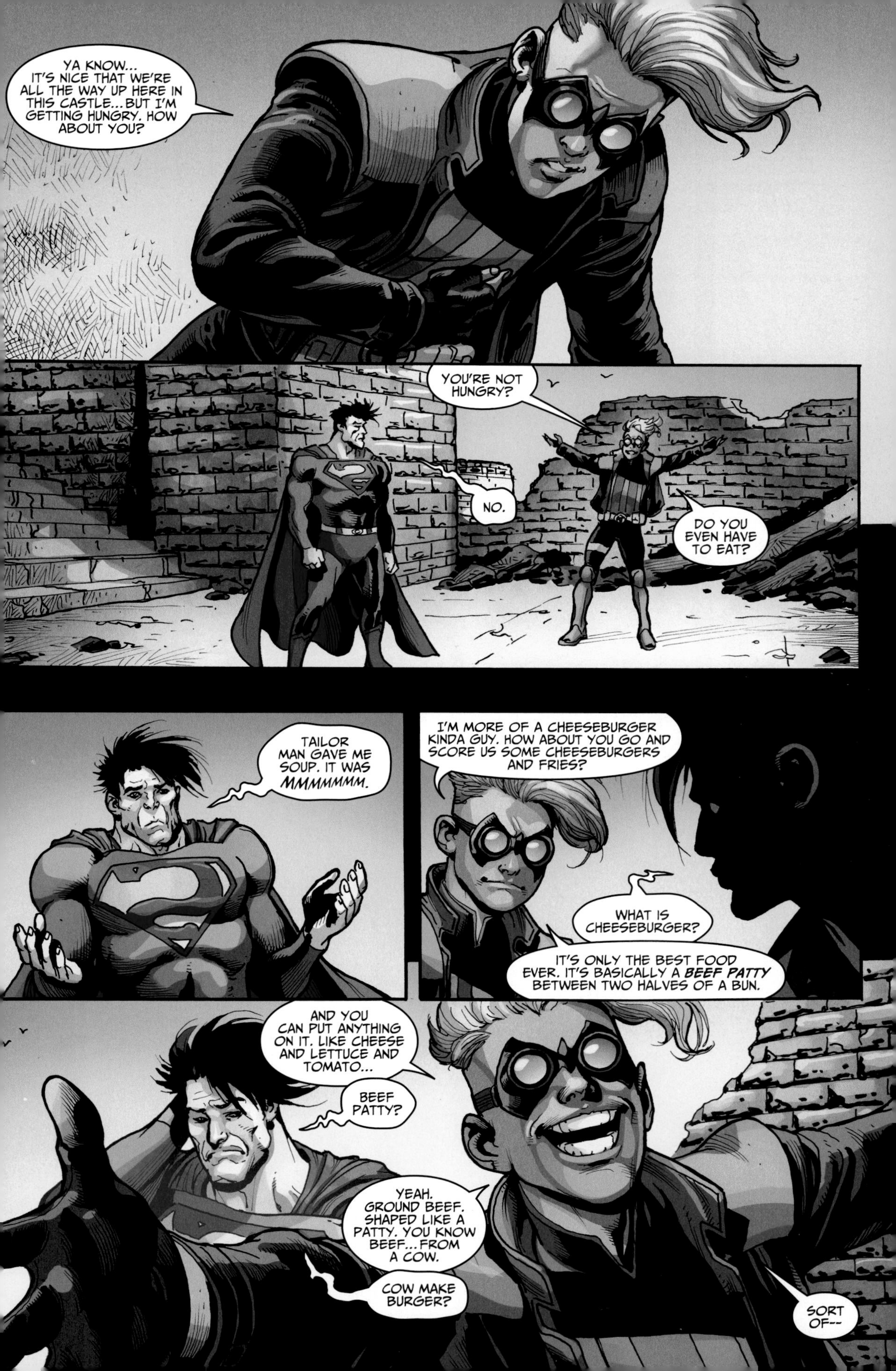
YA KNOW... IT'S NICE THAT WE'RE ALL THE WAY UP HERE IN THIS CASTLE...BUT I'M GETTING HUNGRY. HOW ABOUT YOU?
YOU'RE NOT HUNGRY?
NO.
DO YOU EVEN HAVE TO EAT?
TAILOR MAN GAVE ME SOUP. IT WAS MMMMMMM.
I'M MORE OF A CHEESEBURGER KINDA GUY. HOW ABOUT YOU GO AND SCORE US SOME CHEESEBURGERS AND FRIES?
WHAT IS CHEESEBURGER?
IT'S ONLY THE BEST FOOD EVER. IT'S BASICALLY A BEEF PATTY BETWEEN TWO HALVES OF A BUN.
AND YOU CAN PUT ANYTHING ON IT. LIKE CHEESE AND LETTUCE AND TOMATO...
BEEF PATTY?
YEAH. GROUND BEEF. SHAPED LIKE A PATTY. YOU KNOW BEEF...FROM A COW.
COW MAKE BURGER?
SORT OF--

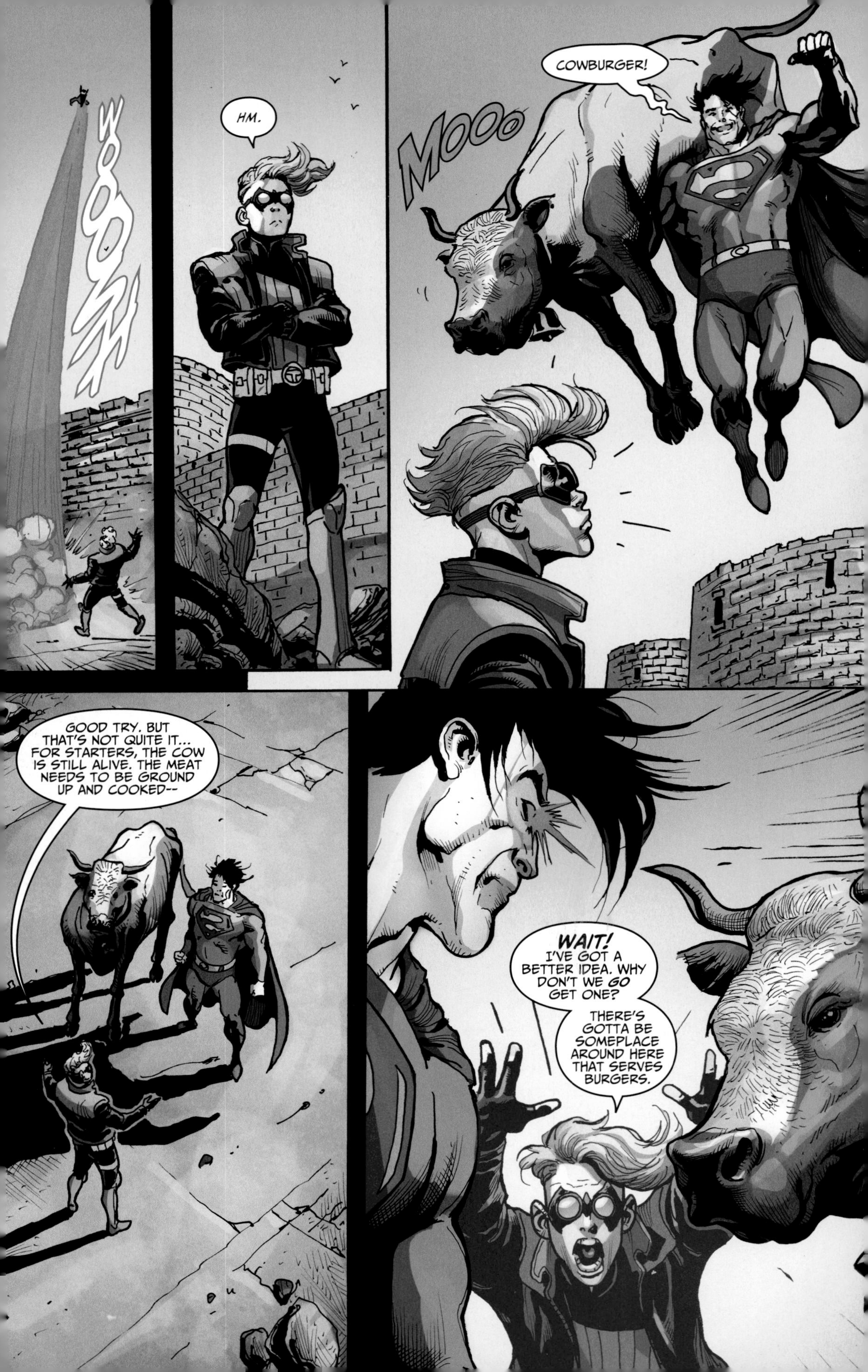
WOOOSH
HM.
COWBURGER!
MOOOO
GOOD TRY. BUT THAT'S NOT QUITE IT... FOR STARTERS, THE COW IS STILL ALIVE. THE MEAT NEEDS TO BE GROUND UP AND COOKED--
WAIT! I'VE GOT A BETTER IDEA. WHY DON'T WE GO GET ONE?
THERE'S GOTTA BE SOMEPLACE AROUND HERE THAT SERVES BURGERS.

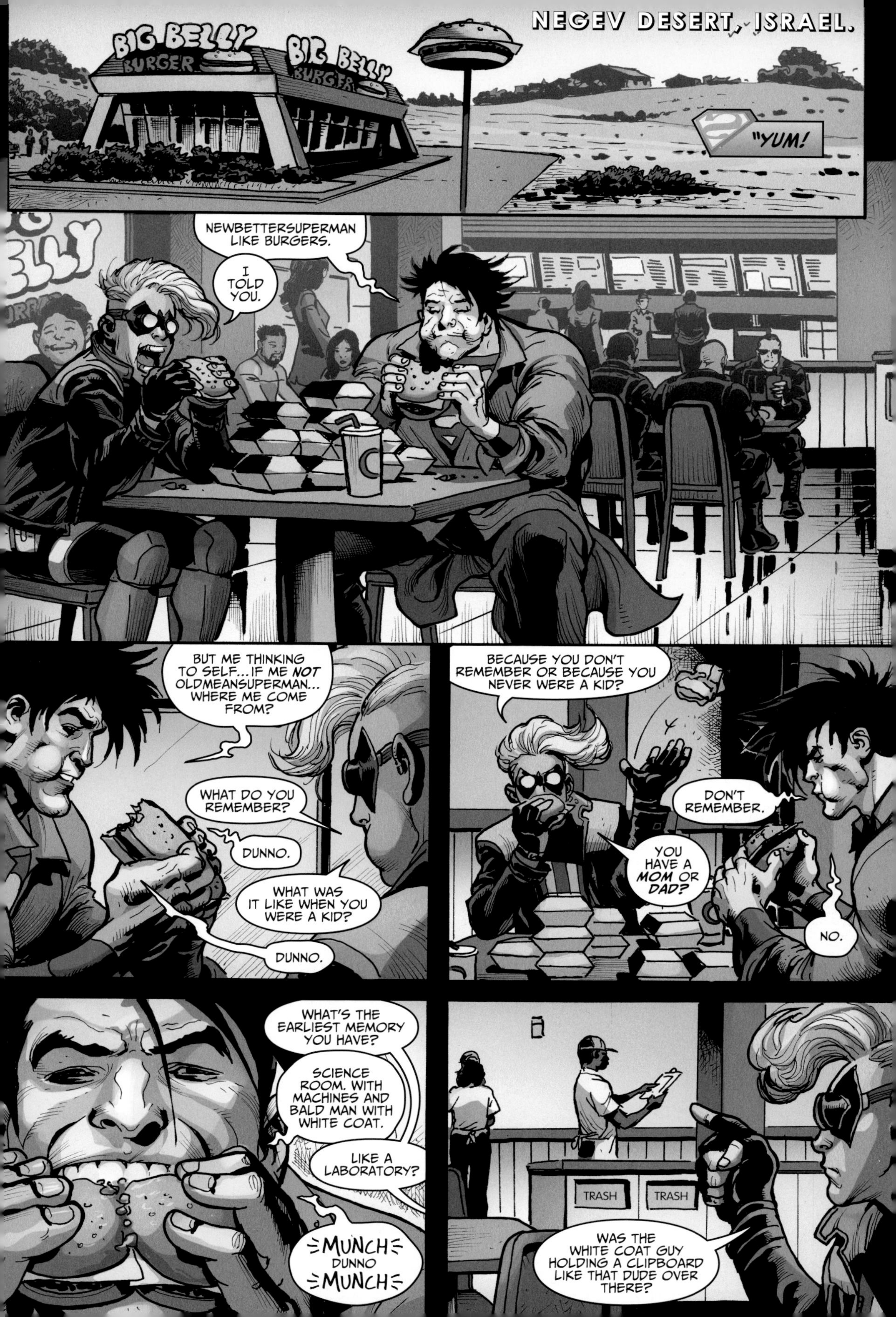
NEGEV DESERT, ISRAEL.
"YUM!
BIG BELLY BURGER
NEWBETTERSUPERMAN LIKE BURGERS.
I TOLD YOU.
BUT ME THINKING TO SELF...IF ME *NOT* OLDMEANSUPERMAN... WHERE ME COME FROM?
WHAT DO YOU REMEMBER?
DUNNO.
WHAT WAS IT LIKE WHEN YOU WERE A KID?
DUNNO.
BECAUSE YOU DON'T REMEMBER OR BECAUSE YOU NEVER WERE A KID?
DON'T REMEMBER.
YOU HAVE A *MOM* OR *DAD?*
NO.
WHAT'S THE EARLIEST MEMORY YOU HAVE?
SCIENCE ROOM. WITH MACHINES AND BALD MAN WITH WHITE COAT.
LIKE A LABORATORY?
MUNCH DUNNO MUNCH
TRASH
TRASH
WAS THE WHITE COAT GUY HOLDING A CLIPBOARD LIKE THAT DUDE OVER THERE?

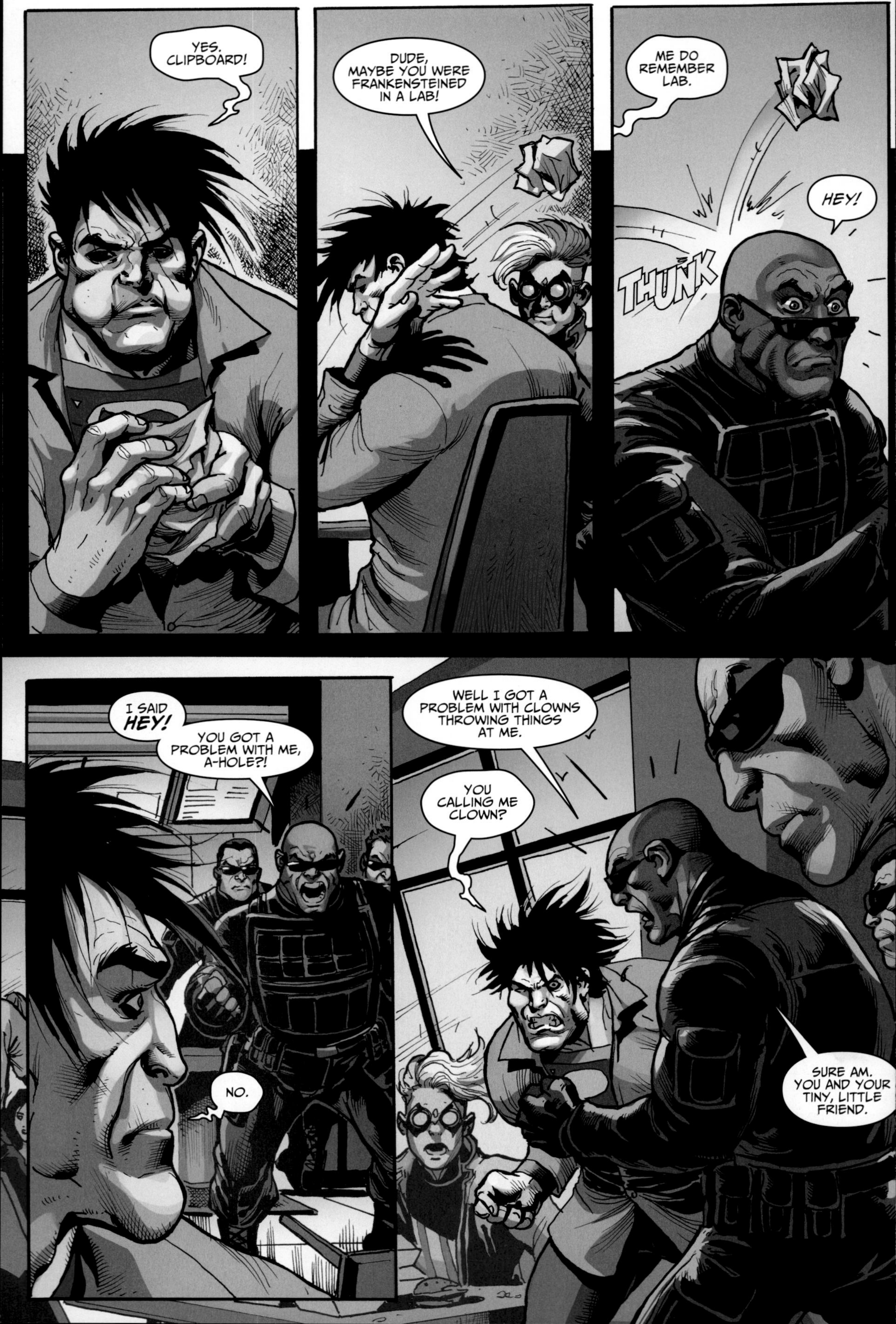
YES. CLIPBOARD!
DUDE, MAYBE YOU WERE FRANKENSTEINED IN A LAB!
ME DO REMEMBER LAB.
THUNK
HEY!
I SAID HEY!
YOU GOT A PROBLEM WITH ME, A-HOLE?!
NO.
WELL I GOT A PROBLEM WITH CLOWNS THROWING THINGS AT ME.
YOU CALLING ME CLOWN?
SURE AM. YOU AND YOUR TINY, LITTLE FRIEND.

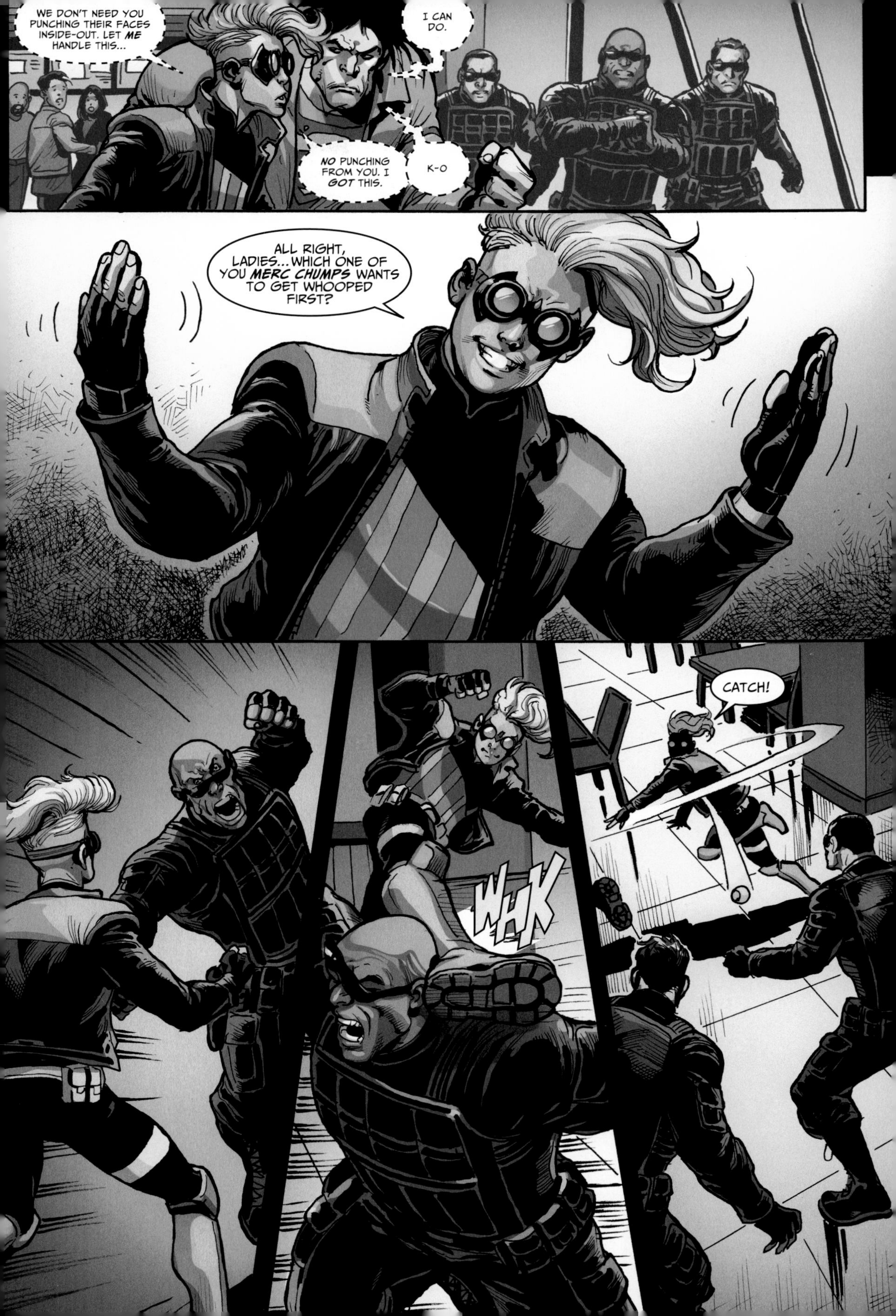
WE DON'T NEED YOU PUNCHING THEIR FACES INSIDE-OUT. LET ME HANDLE THIS...
I CAN DO.
NO PUNCHING FROM YOU. I GOT THIS.
K-O
ALL RIGHT, LADIES...WHICH ONE OF YOU MERC CHUMPS WANTS TO GET WHOOPED FIRST?
WHK
CATCH!

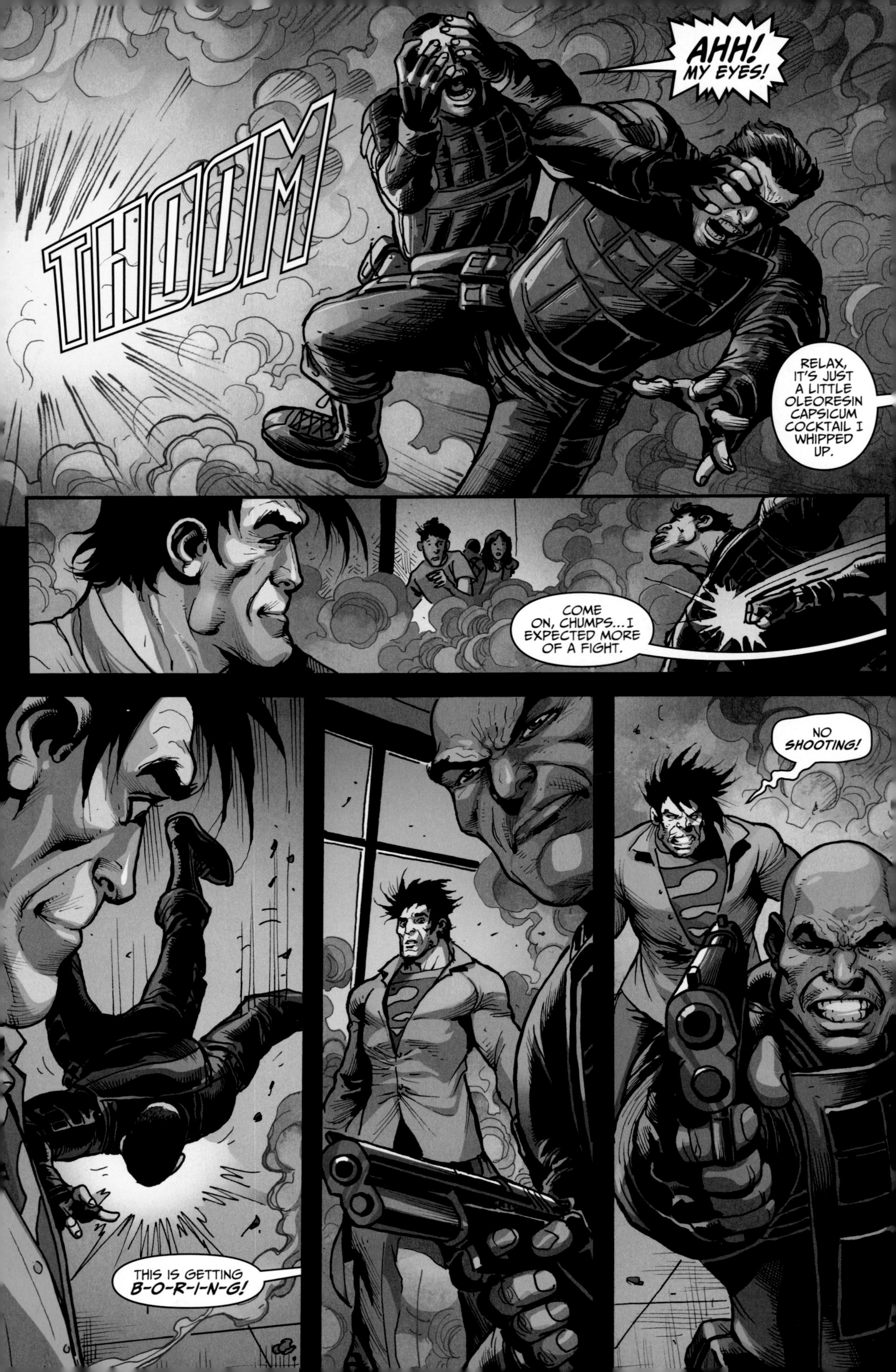
THOOM
AHH! MY EYES!
RELAX, IT'S JUST A LITTLE OLEORESIN CAPSICUM COCKTAIL I WHIPPED UP.
COME ON, CHUMPS... I EXPECTED MORE OF A FIGHT.
THIS IS GETTING B-O-R-I-N-G!
NO SHOOTING!

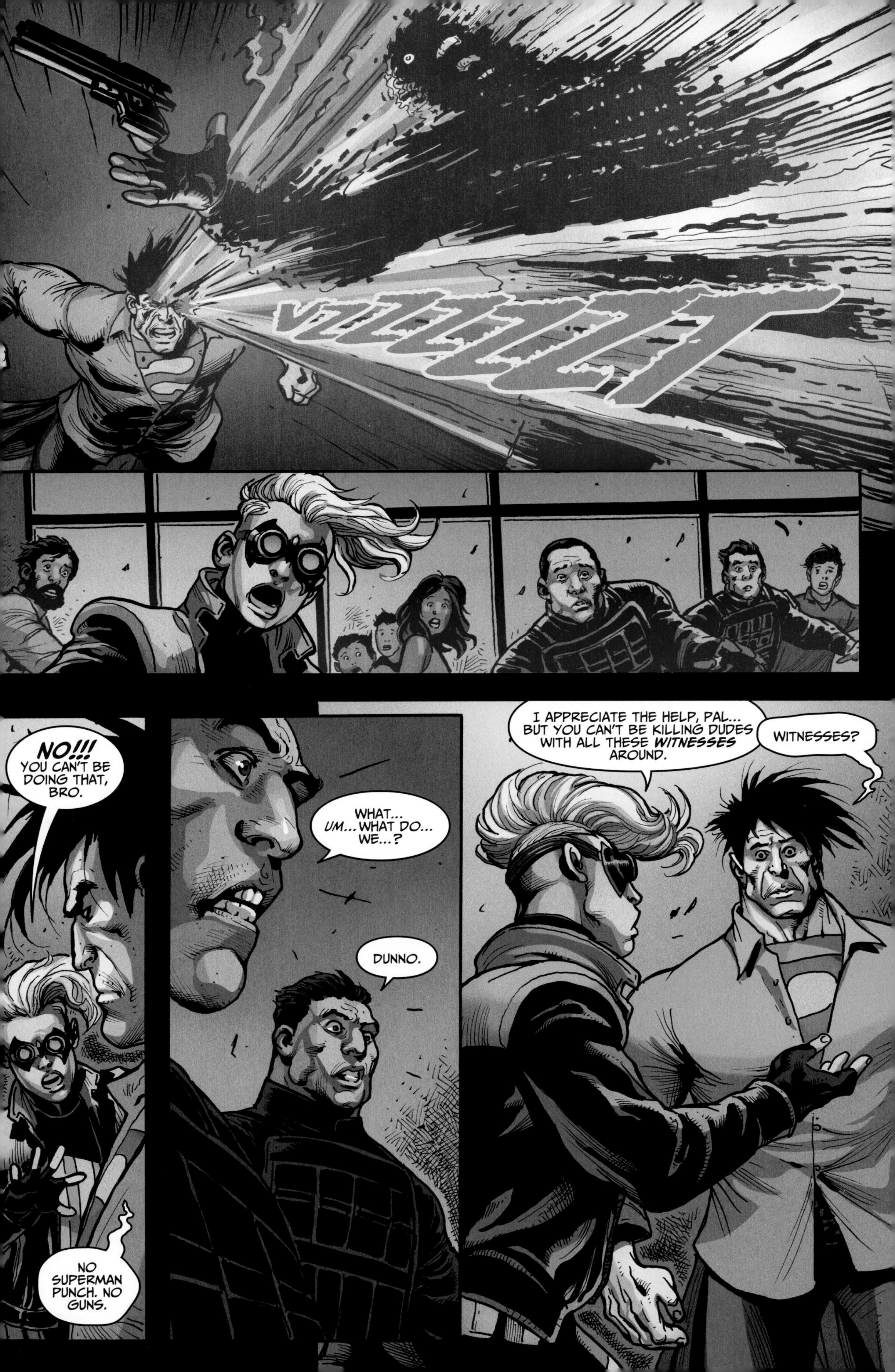

NO!!! YOU CAN'T BE DOING THAT, BRO.
NO SUPERMAN PUNCH. NO GUNS.
WHAT... UM... WHAT DO... WE...?
DUNNO.
I APPRECIATE THE HELP, PAL... BUT YOU CAN'T BE KILLING DUDES WITH ALL THESE WITNESSES AROUND.
WITNESSES?

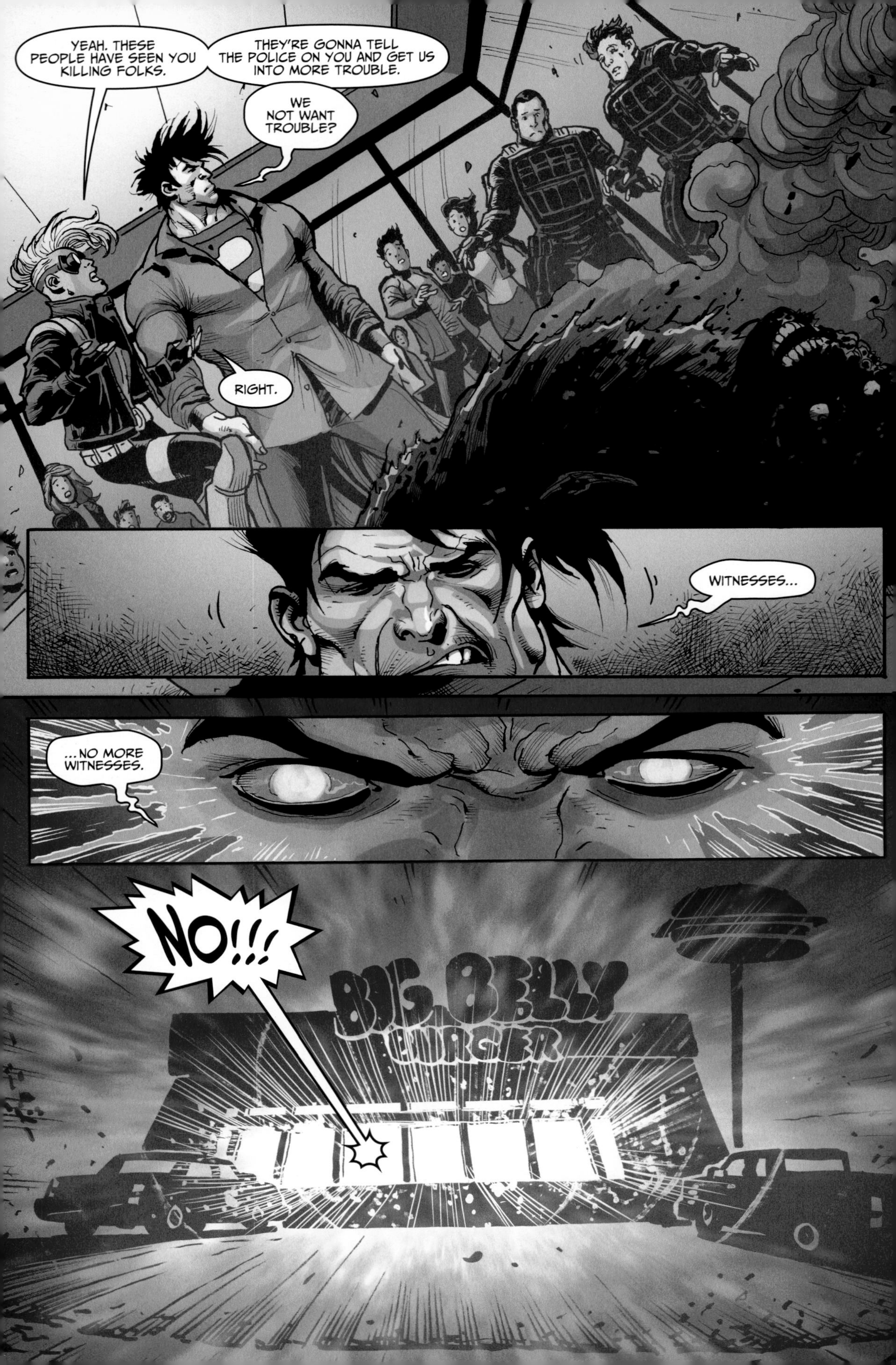
YEAH. THESE PEOPLE HAVE SEEN YOU KILLING FOLKS.
THEY'RE GONNA TELL THE POLICE ON YOU AND GET US INTO MORE TROUBLE.
WE NOT WANT TROUBLE?
RIGHT.
WITNESSES...
...NO MORE WITNESSES.
NO!!!
BIG BELLY BURGER

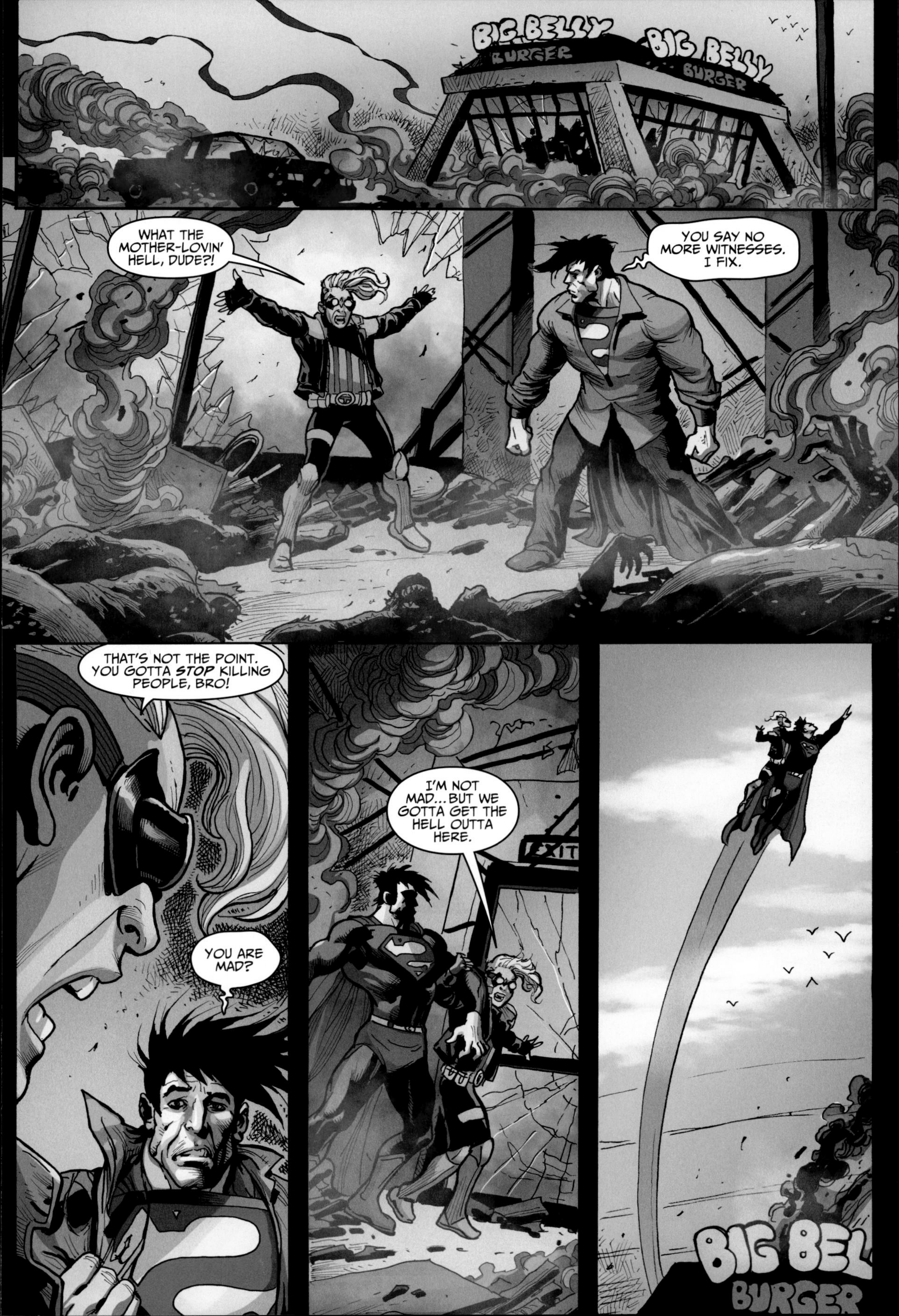
BIG BELLY BURGER
BIG BELLY BURGER
WHAT THE MOTHER-LOVIN' HELL, DUDE?!
YOU SAY NO MORE WITNESSES. I FIX.
THAT'S NOT THE POINT. YOU GOTTA *STOP* KILLING PEOPLE, BRO!
YOU ARE MAD?
I'M NOT MAD... BUT WE GOTTA GET THE HELL OUTTA HERE.
EXIT
BIG BEL
BURGER

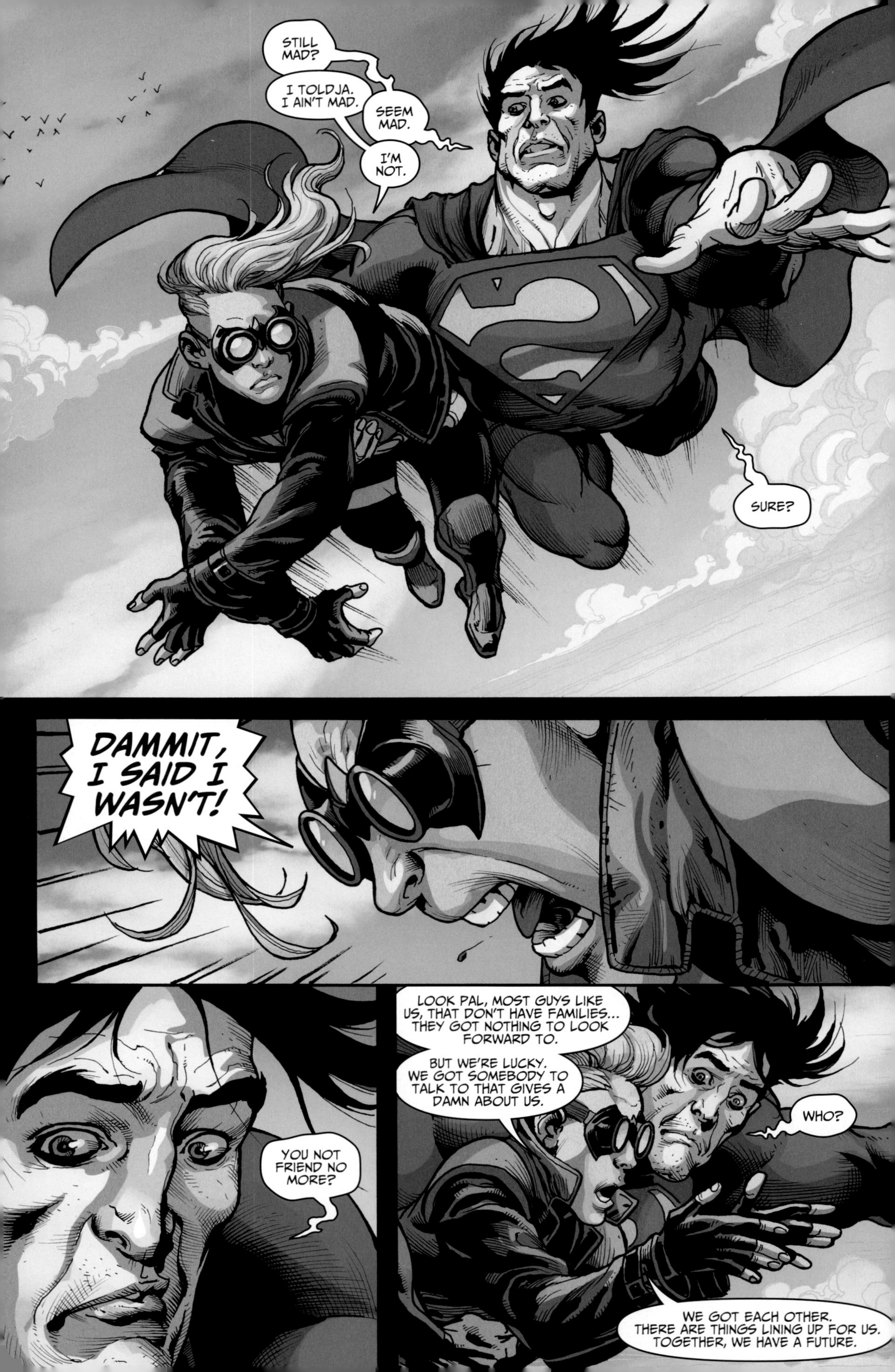
STILL MAD?
I TOLDJA. I AIN'T MAD.
SEEM MAD.
I'M NOT.
SURE?
DAMMIT, I SAID I WASN'T!
YOU NOT FRIEND NO MORE?
LOOK PAL, MOST GUYS LIKE US, THAT DON'T HAVE FAMILIES... THEY GOT NOTHING TO LOOK FORWARD TO.
BUT WE'RE LUCKY. WE GOT SOMEBODY TO TALK TO THAT GIVES A DAMN ABOUT US.
WHO?
WE GOT EACH OTHER. THERE ARE THINGS LINING UP FOR US. TOGETHER, WE HAVE A FUTURE.

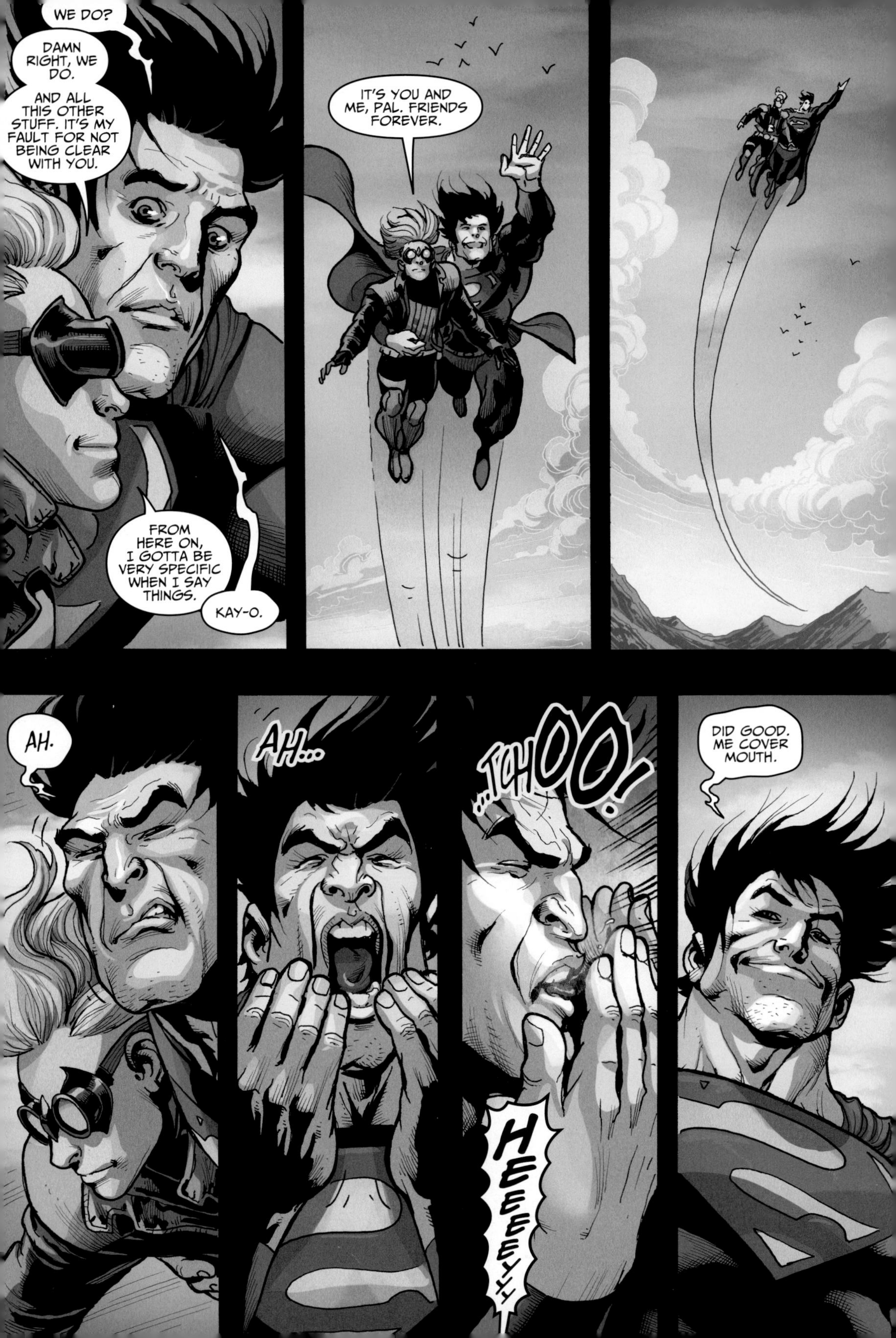
WE DO?
DAMN RIGHT, WE DO.
AND ALL THIS OTHER STUFF. IT'S MY FAULT FOR NOT BEING CLEAR WITH YOU.
FROM HERE ON, I GOTTA BE VERY SPECIFIC WHEN I SAY THINGS.
KAY-O.
IT'S YOU AND ME, PAL. FRIENDS FOREVER.
AH.
AH...
...TCHOO!
HEEEEYYY
DID GOOD. ME COVER MOUTH.

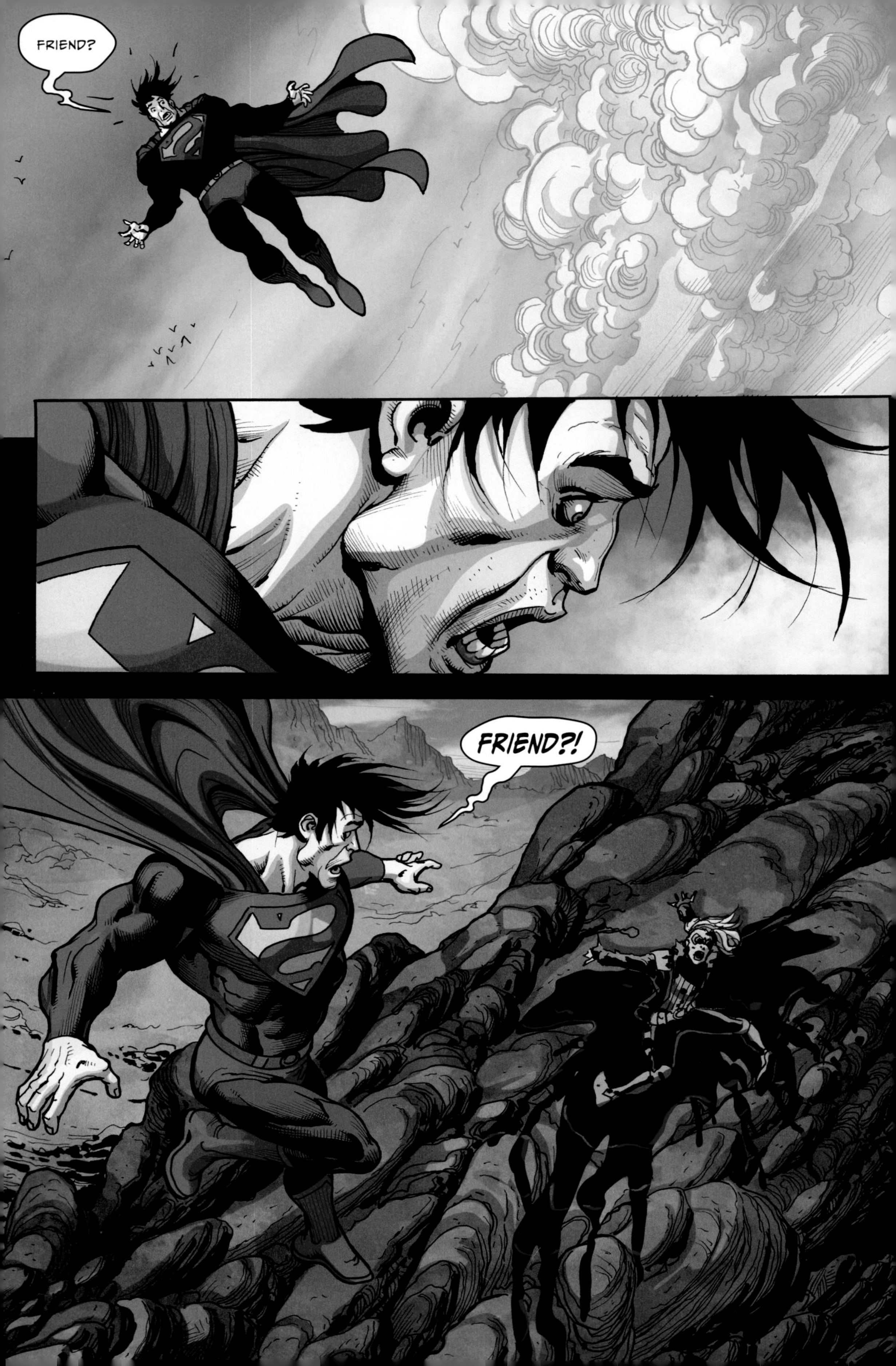
FRIEND?
FRIEND?!

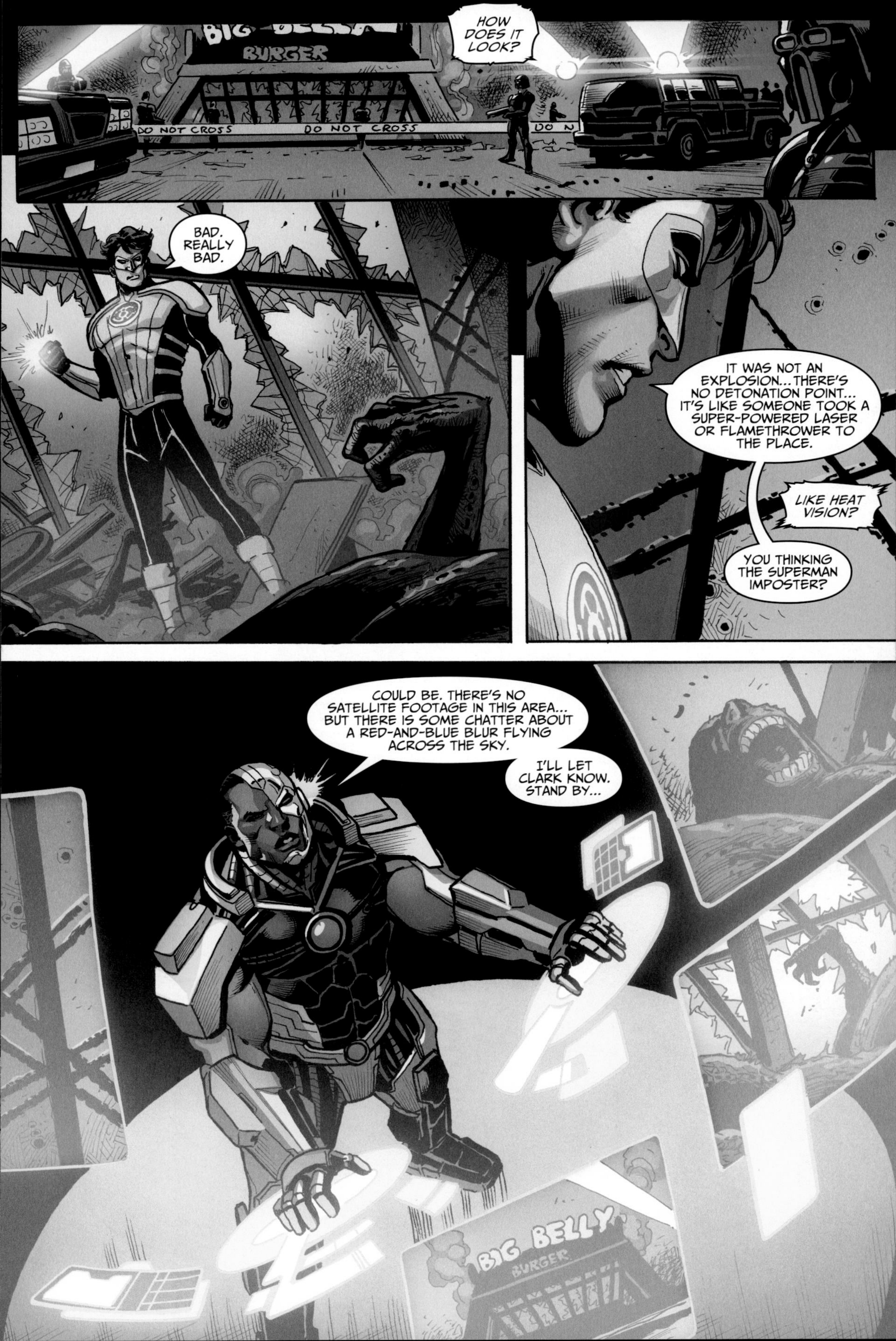
BIG BELLY
BURGER
HOW DOES IT LOOK?
DO NOT CROSS
DO NOT CROSS
BAD. REALLY BAD.
IT WAS NOT AN EXPLOSION...THERE'S NO DETONATION POINT... IT'S LIKE SOMEONE TOOK A SUPER-POWERED LASER OR FLAMETHROWER TO THE PLACE.
LIKE HEAT VISION?
YOU THINKING THE SUPERMAN IMPOSTER?
COULD BE. THERE'S NO SATELLITE FOOTAGE IN THIS AREA... BUT THERE IS SOME CHATTER ABOUT A RED-AND-BLUE BLUR FLYING ACROSS THE SKY.
I'LL LET CLARK KNOW. STAND BY...
BIG BELLY
BURGER

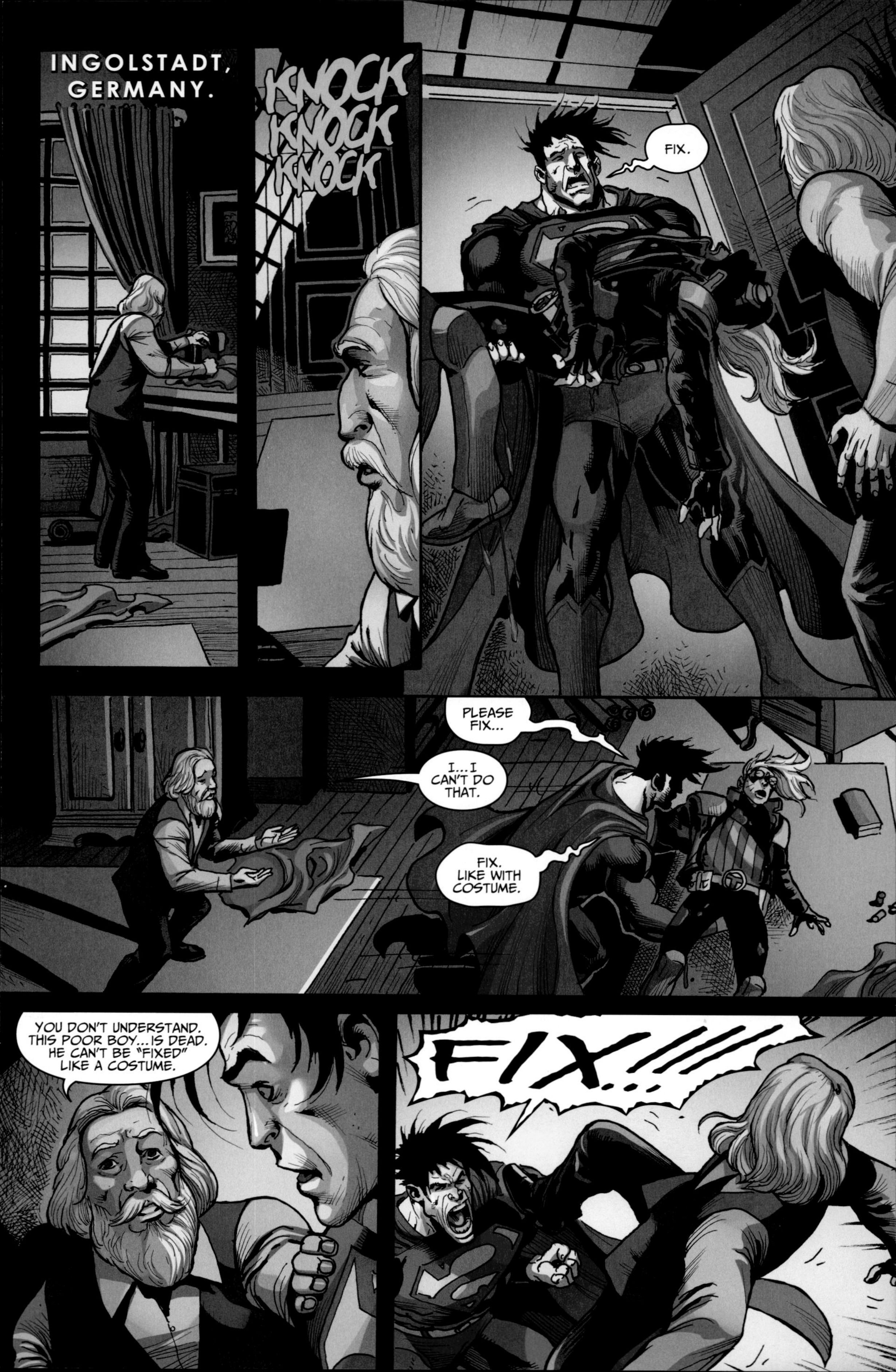
INGOLSTADT, GERMANY.
KNOCK KNOCK KNOCK
FIX.
PLEASE FIX...
I...I CAN'T DO THAT.
FIX. LIKE WITH COSTUME.
YOU DON'T UNDERSTAND. THIS POOR BOY...IS DEAD. HE CAN'T BE "FIXED" LIKE A COSTUME.
FIX..!!!

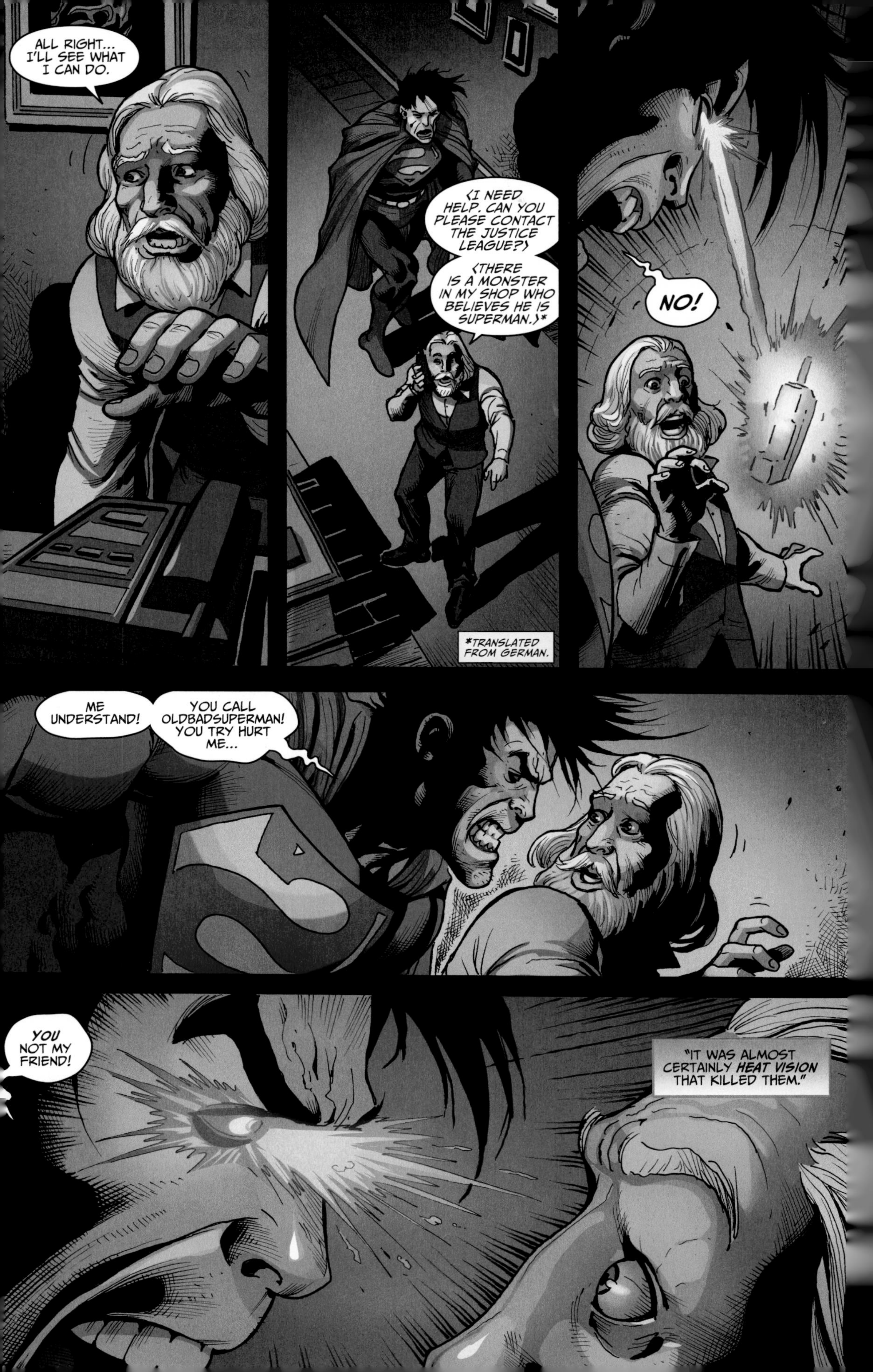
ALL RIGHT... I'LL SEE WHAT I CAN DO.
‹I NEED HELP. CAN YOU PLEASE CONTACT THE JUSTICE LEAGUE?›
‹THERE IS A MONSTER IN MY SHOP WHO BELIEVES HE IS SUPERMAN.›*
*TRANSLATED FROM GERMAN.
NO!
ME UNDERSTAND!
YOU CALL OLDBADSUPERMAN! YOU TRY HURT ME...
YOU NOT MY FRIEND!
"IT WAS ALMOST CERTAINLY HEAT VISION THAT KILLED THEM."

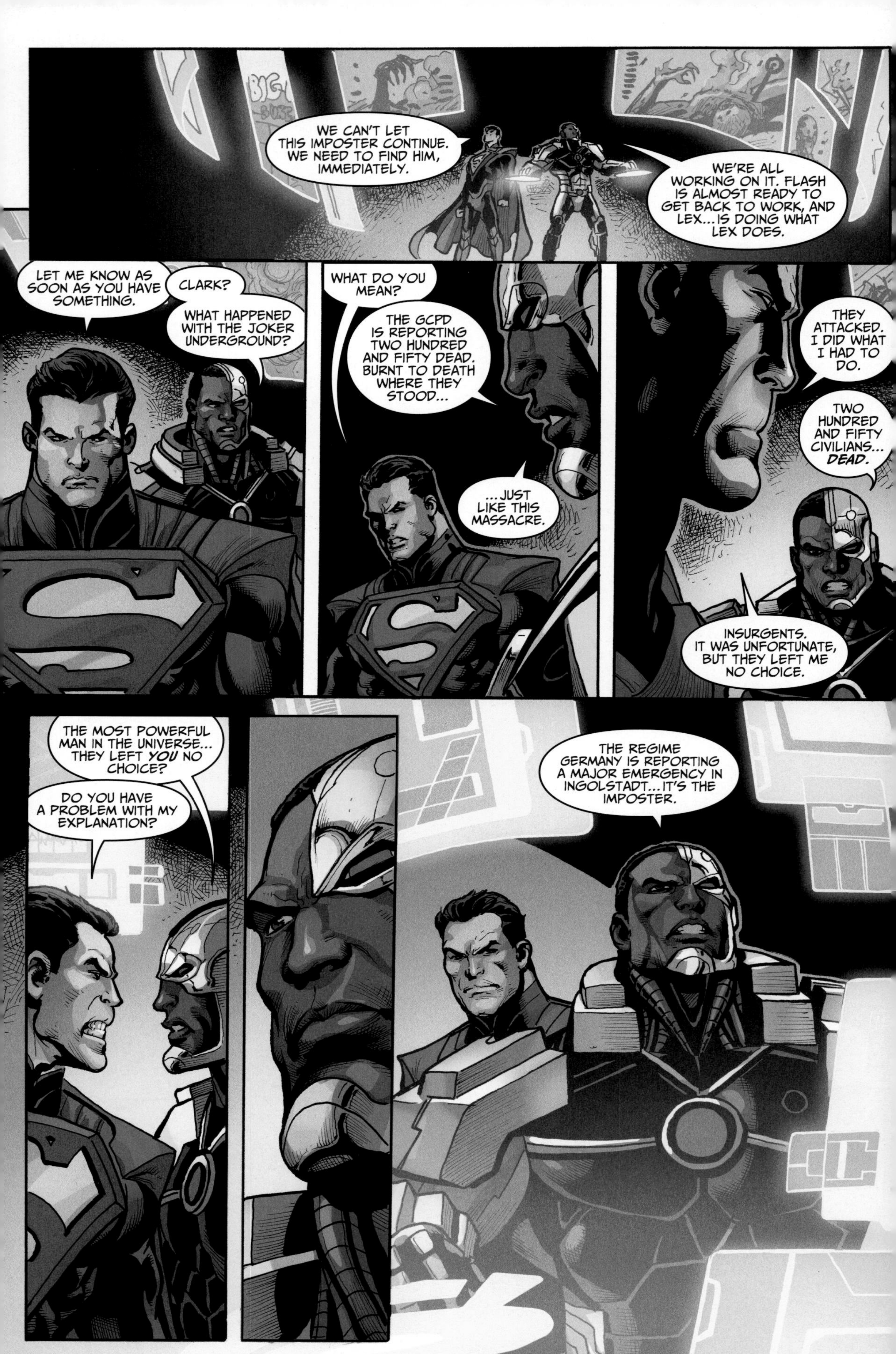
WE CAN'T LET THIS IMPOSTER CONTINUE. WE NEED TO FIND HIM, IMMEDIATELY.
WE'RE ALL WORKING ON IT. FLASH IS ALMOST READY TO GET BACK TO WORK, AND LEX...IS DOING WHAT LEX DOES.
LET ME KNOW AS SOON AS YOU HAVE SOMETHING.
CLARK?
WHAT HAPPENED WITH THE JOKER UNDERGROUND?
WHAT DO YOU MEAN?
THE GCPD IS REPORTING TWO HUNDRED AND FIFTY DEAD. BURNT TO DEATH WHERE THEY STOOD...
...JUST LIKE THIS MASSACRE.
THEY ATTACKED. I DID WHAT I HAD TO DO.
TWO HUNDRED AND FIFTY CIVILIANS... DEAD.
INSURGENTS. IT WAS UNFORTUNATE, BUT THEY LEFT ME NO CHOICE.
THE MOST POWERFUL MAN IN THE UNIVERSE... THEY LEFT YOU NO CHOICE?
DO YOU HAVE A PROBLEM WITH MY EXPLANATION?
THE REGIME GERMANY IS REPORTING A MAJOR EMERGENCY IN INGOLSTADT...IT'S THE IMPOSTER.

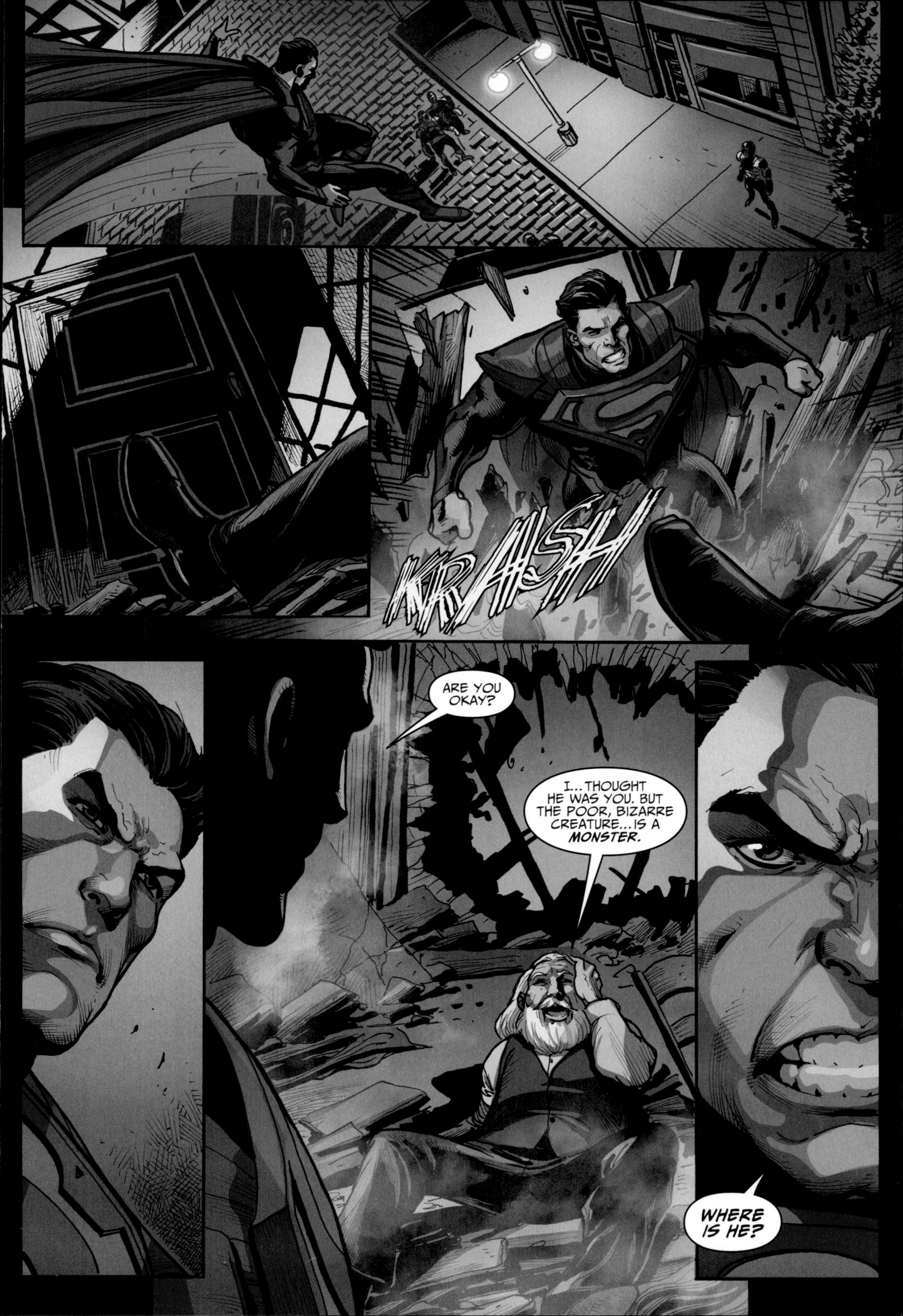

KRASH
ARE YOU OKAY?
I...THOUGHT HE WAS YOU. BUT THE POOR, BIZARRE CREATURE...IS A MONSTER.
WHERE IS HE?

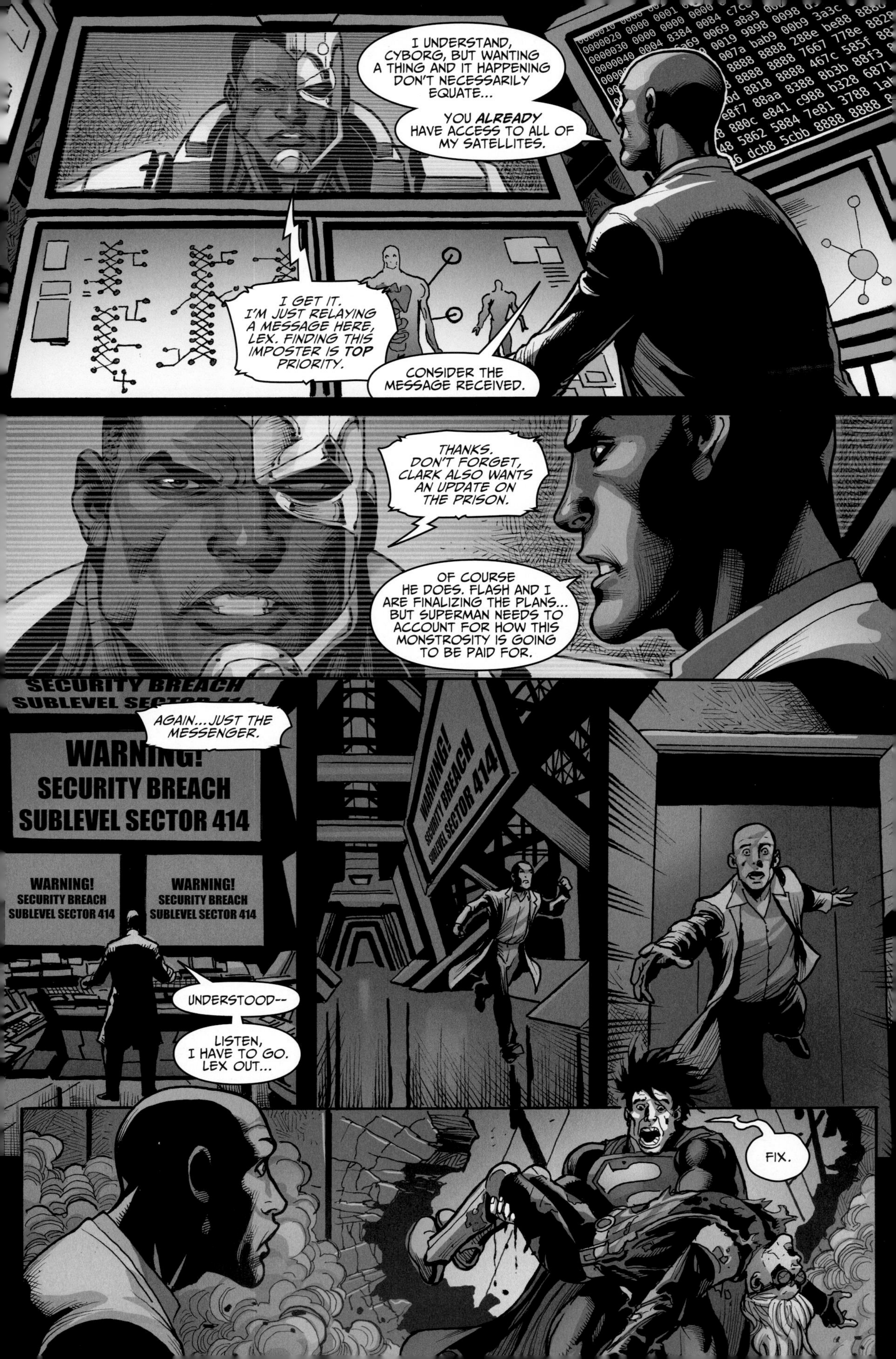
I UNDERSTAND, CYBORG, BUT WANTING A THING AND IT HAPPENING DON'T NECESSARILY EQUATE...
YOU ALREADY HAVE ACCESS TO ALL OF MY SATELLITES.
I GET IT. I'M JUST RELAYING A MESSAGE HERE, LEX. FINDING THIS IMPOSTER IS TOP PRIORITY.
CONSIDER THE MESSAGE RECEIVED.
THANKS. DON'T FORGET, CLARK ALSO WANTS AN UPDATE ON THE PRISON.
OF COURSE HE DOES. FLASH AND I ARE FINALIZING THE PLANS... BUT SUPERMAN NEEDS TO ACCOUNT FOR HOW THIS MONSTROSITY IS GOING TO BE PAID FOR.
SECURITY BREACH
SUBLEVEL SECTOR 414
AGAIN... JUST THE MESSENGER.
WARNING!
SECURITY BREACH
SUBLEVEL SECTOR 414
WARNING!
SECURITY BREACH
SUBLEVEL SECTOR 414
WARNING!
SECURITY BREACH
SUBLEVEL SECTOR 414
UNDERSTOOD--
LISTEN, I HAVE TO GO. LEX OUT...
WARNING!
SECURITY BREACH
SUBLEVEL SECTOR 414
FIX.

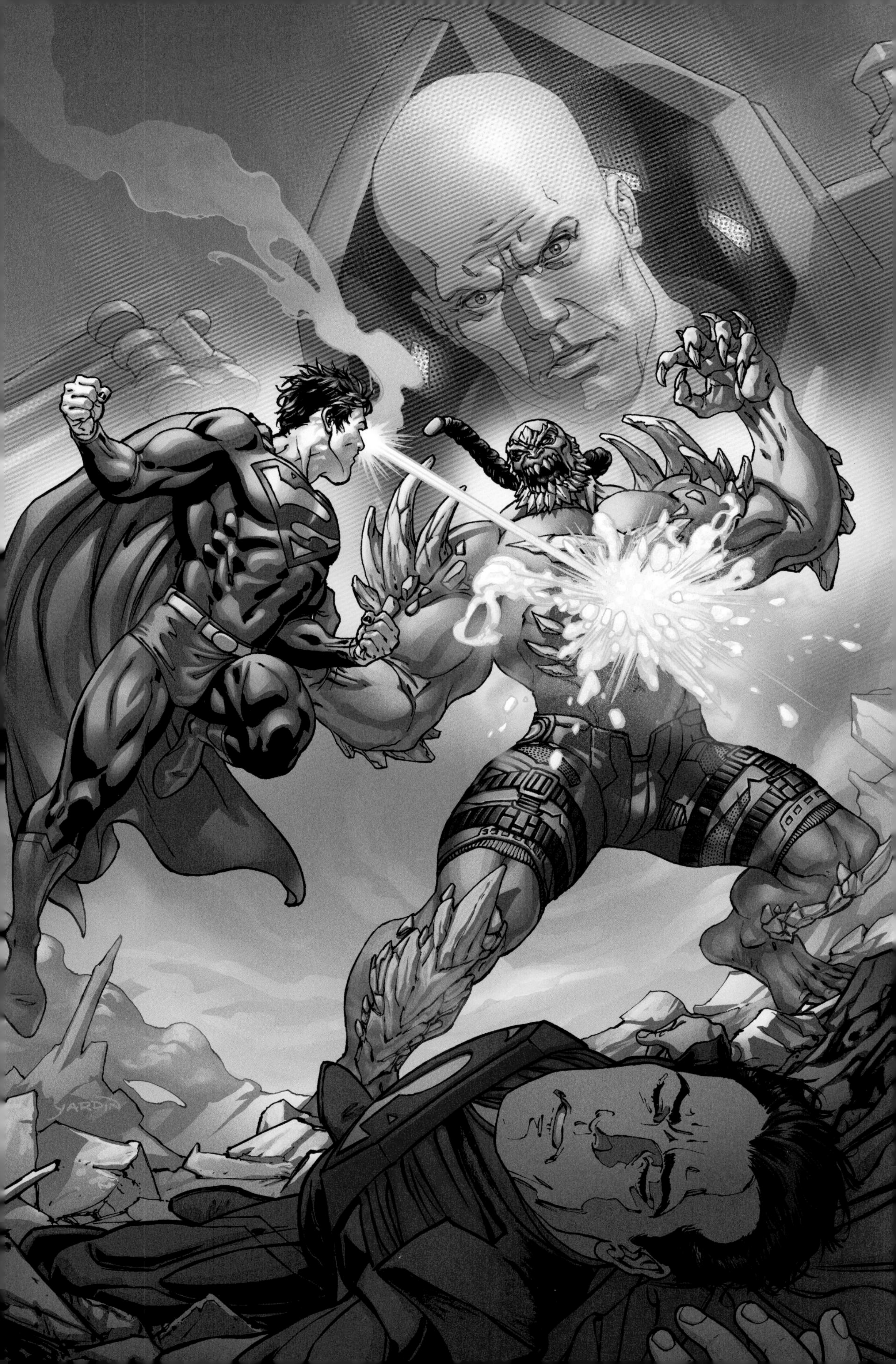
YARDIN

"Home to Roost" **Mike S. Miller** Artist **J. Nanjan** Colorist

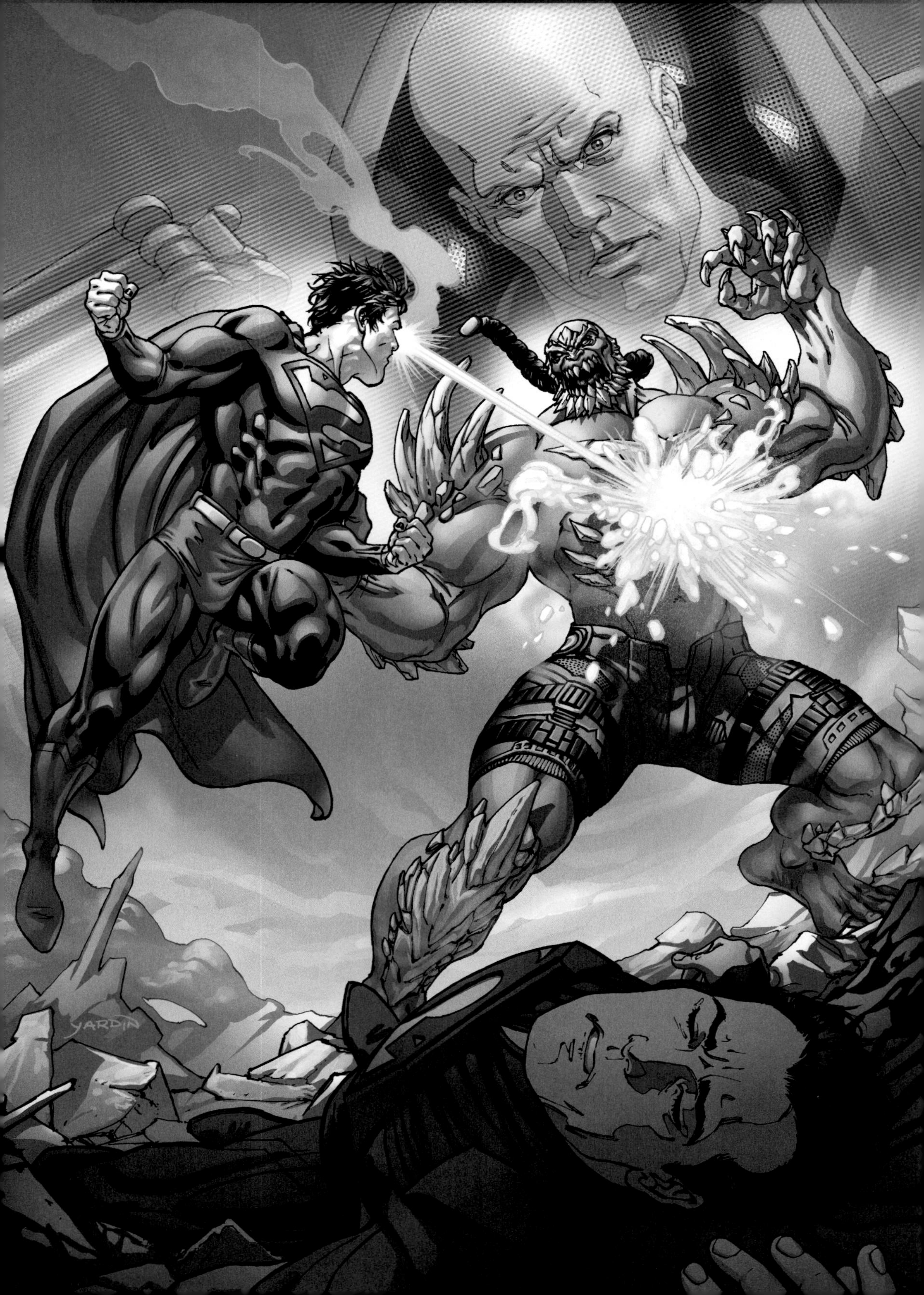
YARDIN

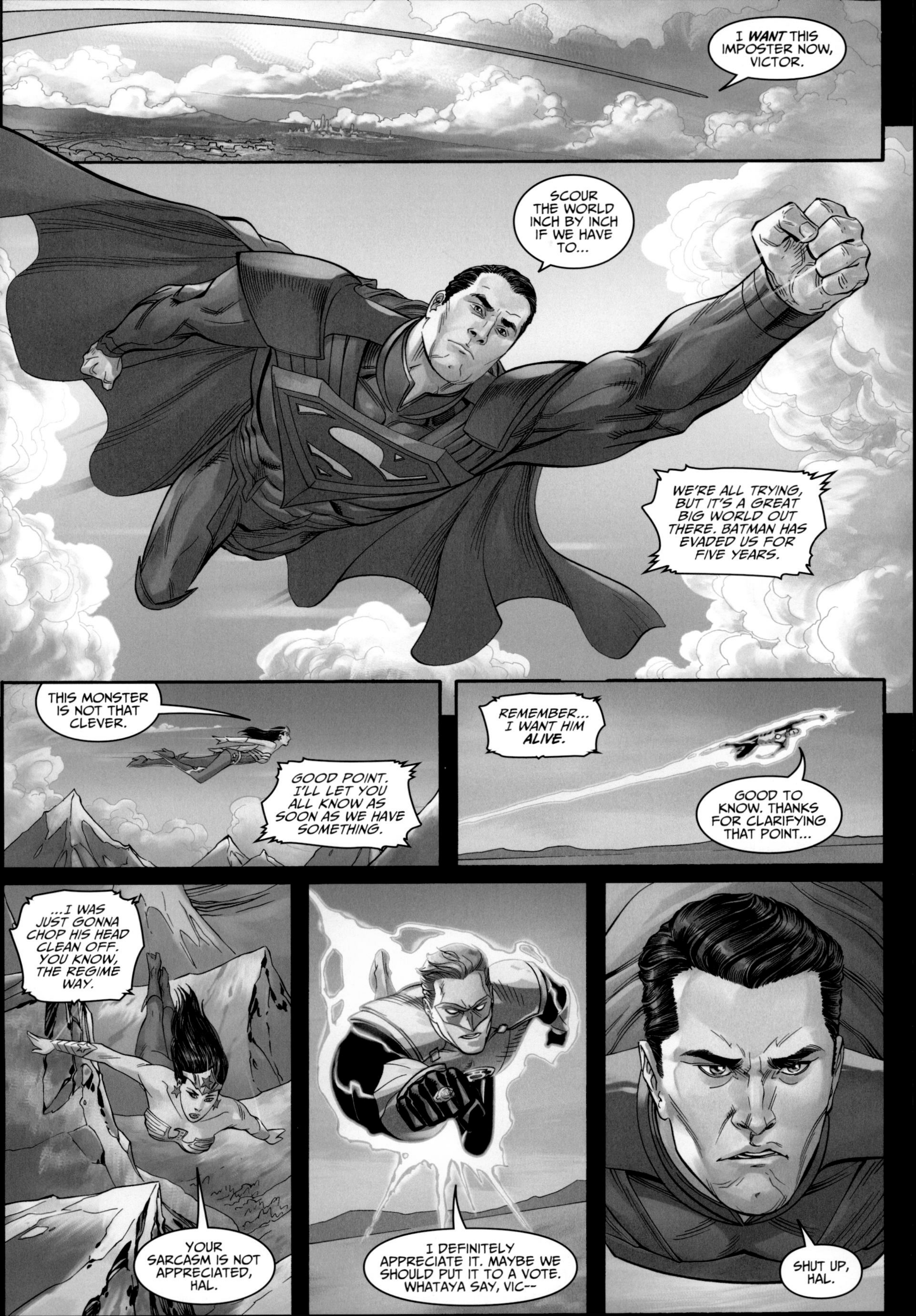
I **WANT** THIS IMPOSTER NOW, VICTOR.
SCOUR THE WORLD INCH BY INCH IF WE HAVE TO...
WE'RE ALL TRYING, BUT IT'S A GREAT BIG WORLD OUT THERE. BATMAN HAS EVADED US FOR FIVE YEARS.
THIS MONSTER IS NOT THAT CLEVER.
GOOD POINT. I'LL LET YOU ALL KNOW AS SOON AS WE HAVE SOMETHING.
*REMEMBER... I WANT HIM **ALIVE.***
GOOD TO KNOW. THANKS FOR CLARIFYING THAT POINT...
...I WAS JUST GONNA CHOP HIS HEAD CLEAN OFF. YOU KNOW, THE REGIME WAY.
YOUR SARCASM IS NOT APPRECIATED, HAL.
I DEFINITELY APPRECIATE IT. MAYBE WE SHOULD PUT IT TO A VOTE. WHATAYA SAY, VIC--
SHUT UP, HAL.

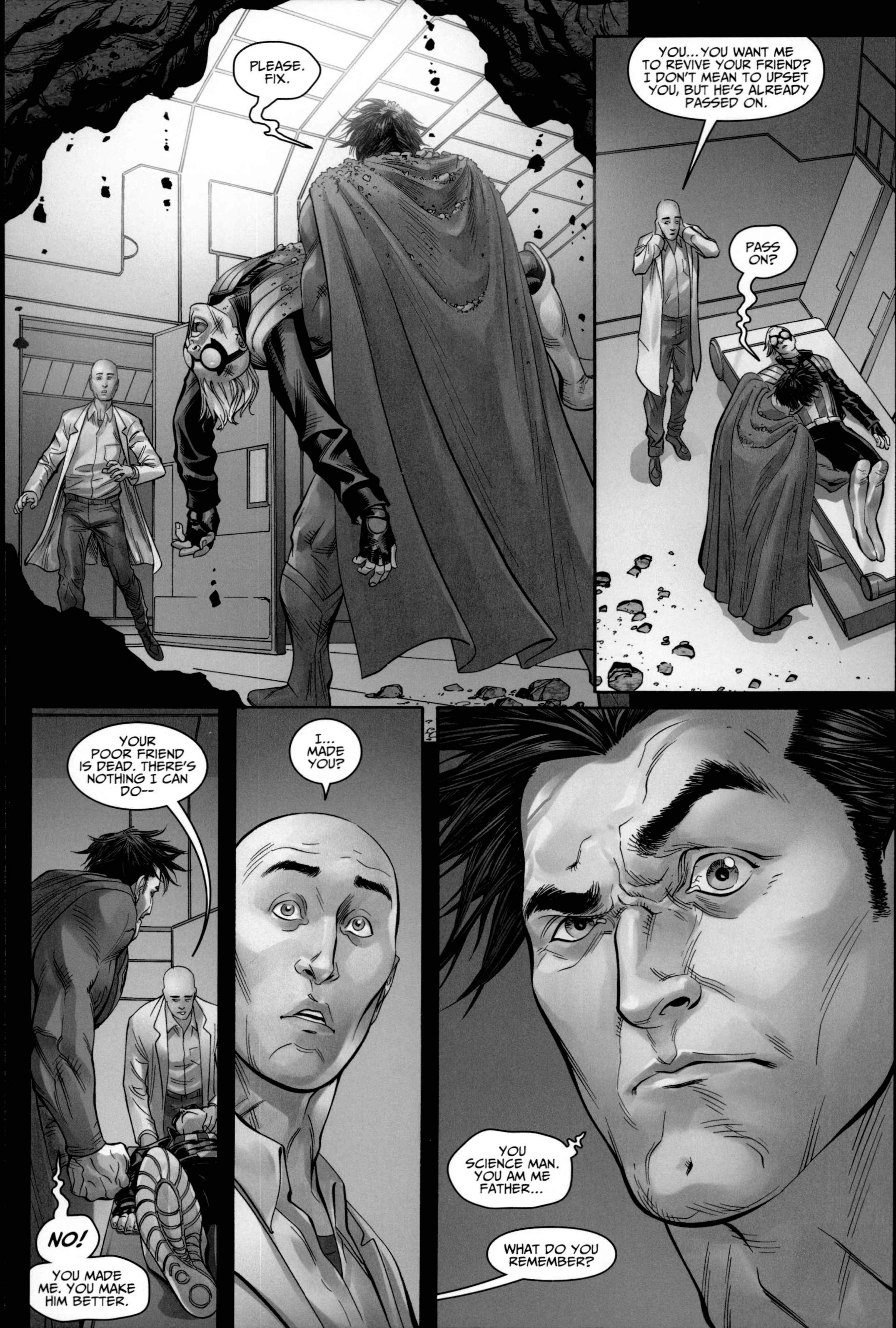
PLEASE. FIX.
YOU...YOU WANT ME TO REVIVE YOUR FRIEND? I DON'T MEAN TO UPSET YOU, BUT HE'S ALREADY PASSED ON.
PASS ON?
YOUR POOR FRIEND IS DEAD. THERE'S NOTHING I CAN DO--
NO!
YOU MADE ME. YOU MAKE HIM BETTER.
I... MADE YOU?
YOU SCIENCE MAN. YOU AM ME FATHER...
WHAT DO YOU REMEMBER?

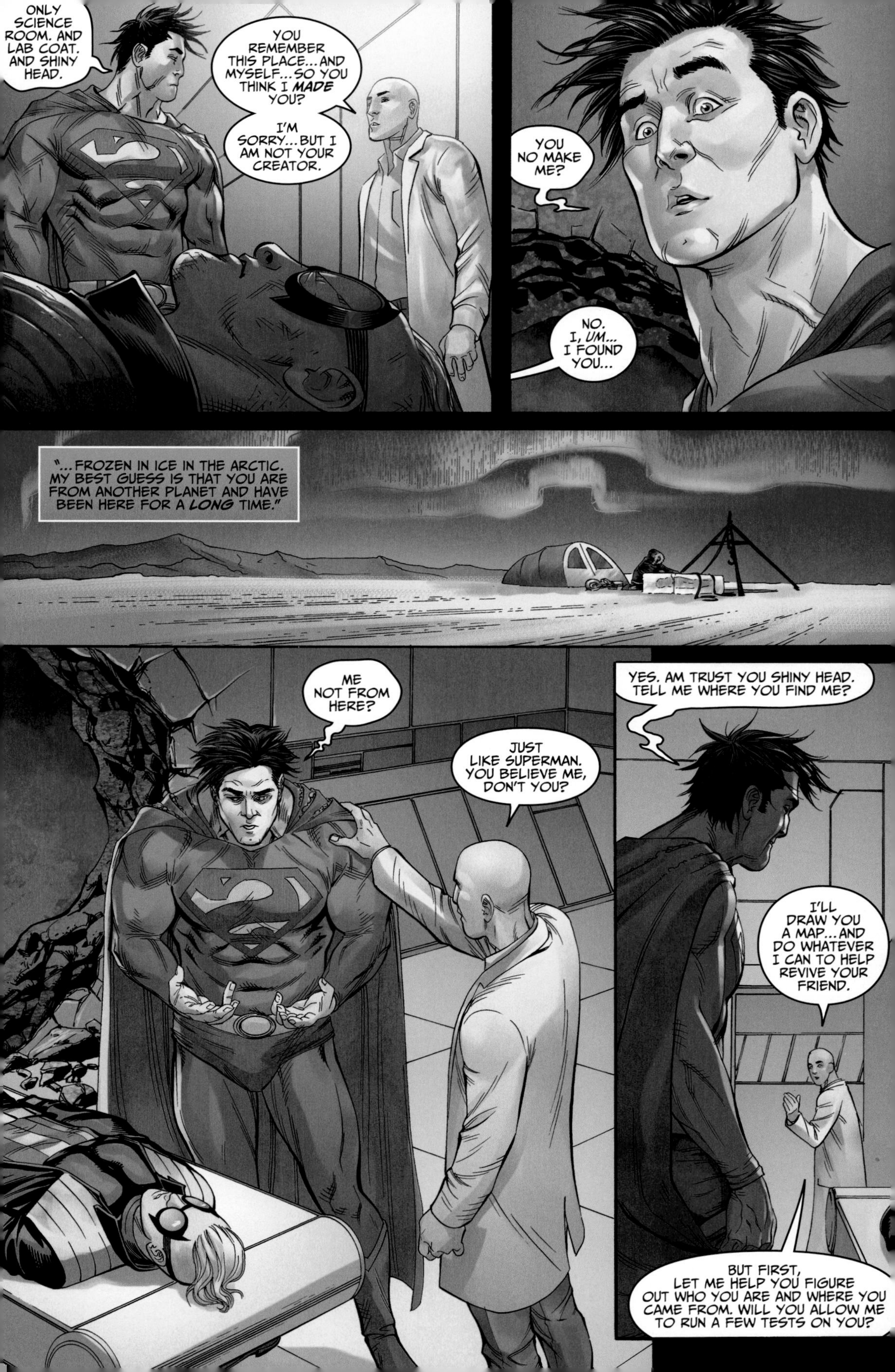
ONLY SCIENCE ROOM. AND LAB COAT. AND SHINY HEAD.
YOU REMEMBER THIS PLACE...AND MYSELF...SO YOU THINK I MADE YOU?
I'M SORRY...BUT I AM NOT YOUR CREATOR.
YOU NO MAKE ME?
NO. I, UM... I FOUND YOU...
"...FROZEN IN ICE IN THE ARCTIC. MY BEST GUESS IS THAT YOU ARE FROM ANOTHER PLANET AND HAVE BEEN HERE FOR A LONG TIME."
ME NOT FROM HERE?
JUST LIKE SUPERMAN. YOU BELIEVE ME, DON'T YOU?
YES. AM TRUST YOU SHINY HEAD. TELL ME WHERE YOU FIND ME?
I'LL DRAW YOU A MAP...AND DO WHATEVER I CAN TO HELP REVIVE YOUR FRIEND.
BUT FIRST, LET ME HELP YOU FIGURE OUT WHO YOU ARE AND WHERE YOU CAME FROM. WILL YOU ALLOW ME TO RUN A FEW TESTS ON YOU?

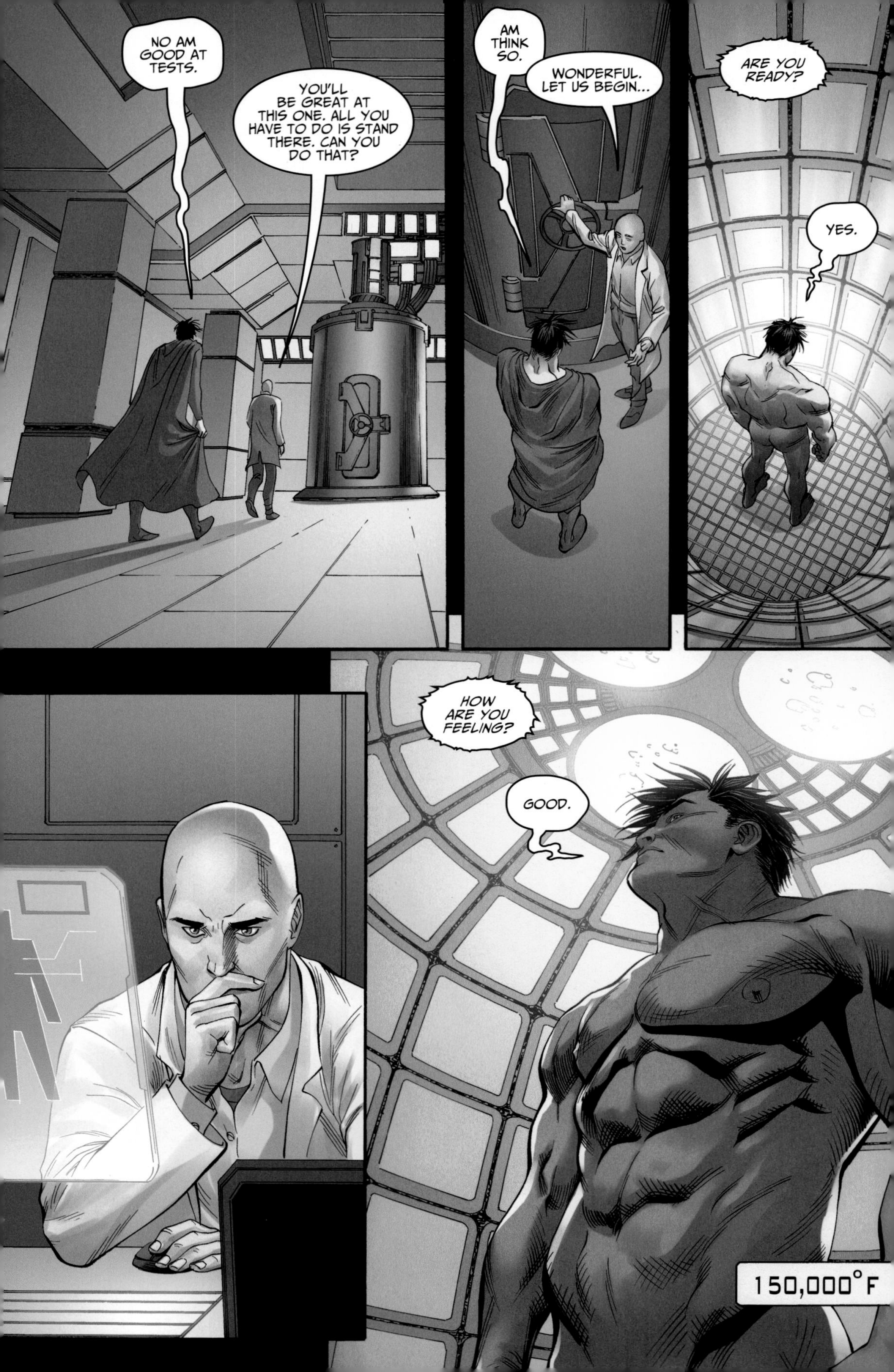
NO AM GOOD AT TESTS.
YOU'LL BE GREAT AT THIS ONE. ALL YOU HAVE TO DO IS STAND THERE. CAN YOU DO THAT?
AM THINK SO.
WONDERFUL. LET US BEGIN...
ARE YOU READY?
YES.
HOW ARE YOU FEELING?
GOOD.
150,000°F

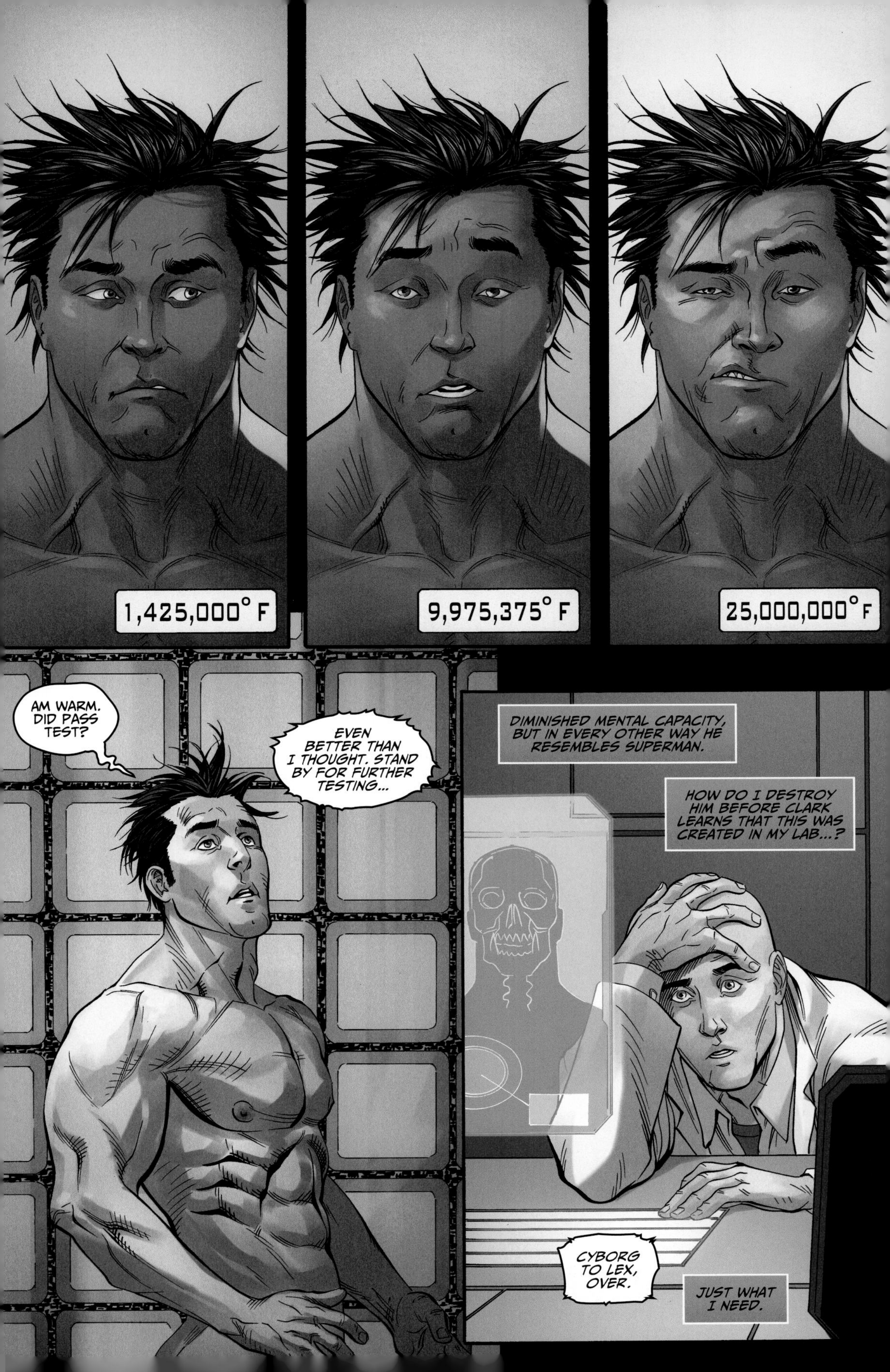
1,425,000° F
9,975,375° F
25,000,000° F
AM WARM. DID PASS TEST?
EVEN BETTER THAN I THOUGHT. STAND BY FOR FURTHER TESTING...
DIMINISHED MENTAL CAPACITY, BUT IN EVERY OTHER WAY HE RESEMBLES SUPERMAN.
HOW DO I DESTROY HIM BEFORE CLARK LEARNS THAT THIS WAS CREATED IN MY LAB...?
CYBORG TO LEX, OVER.
JUST WHAT I NEED.

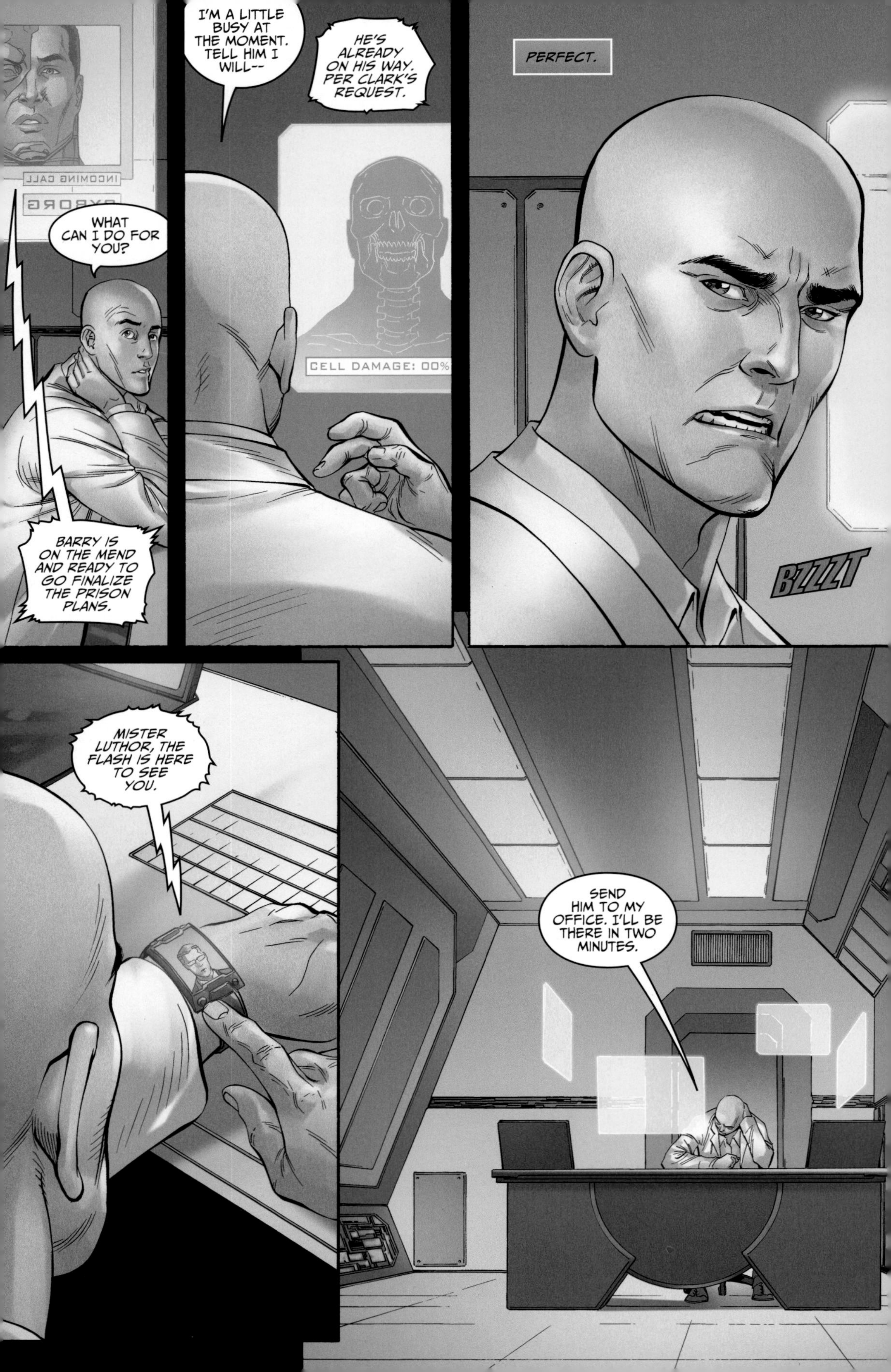
INCOMING CALL
CYBORG
WHAT CAN I DO FOR YOU?
BARRY IS ON THE MEND AND READY TO GO FINALIZE THE PRISON PLANS.
I'M A LITTLE BUSY AT THE MOMENT. TELL HIM I WILL--
HE'S ALREADY ON HIS WAY. PER CLARK'S REQUEST.
CELL DAMAGE: 00%
PERFECT.
BZZZT
MISTER LUTHOR, THE FLASH IS HERE TO SEE YOU.
SEND HIM TO MY OFFICE. I'LL BE THERE IN TWO MINUTES.

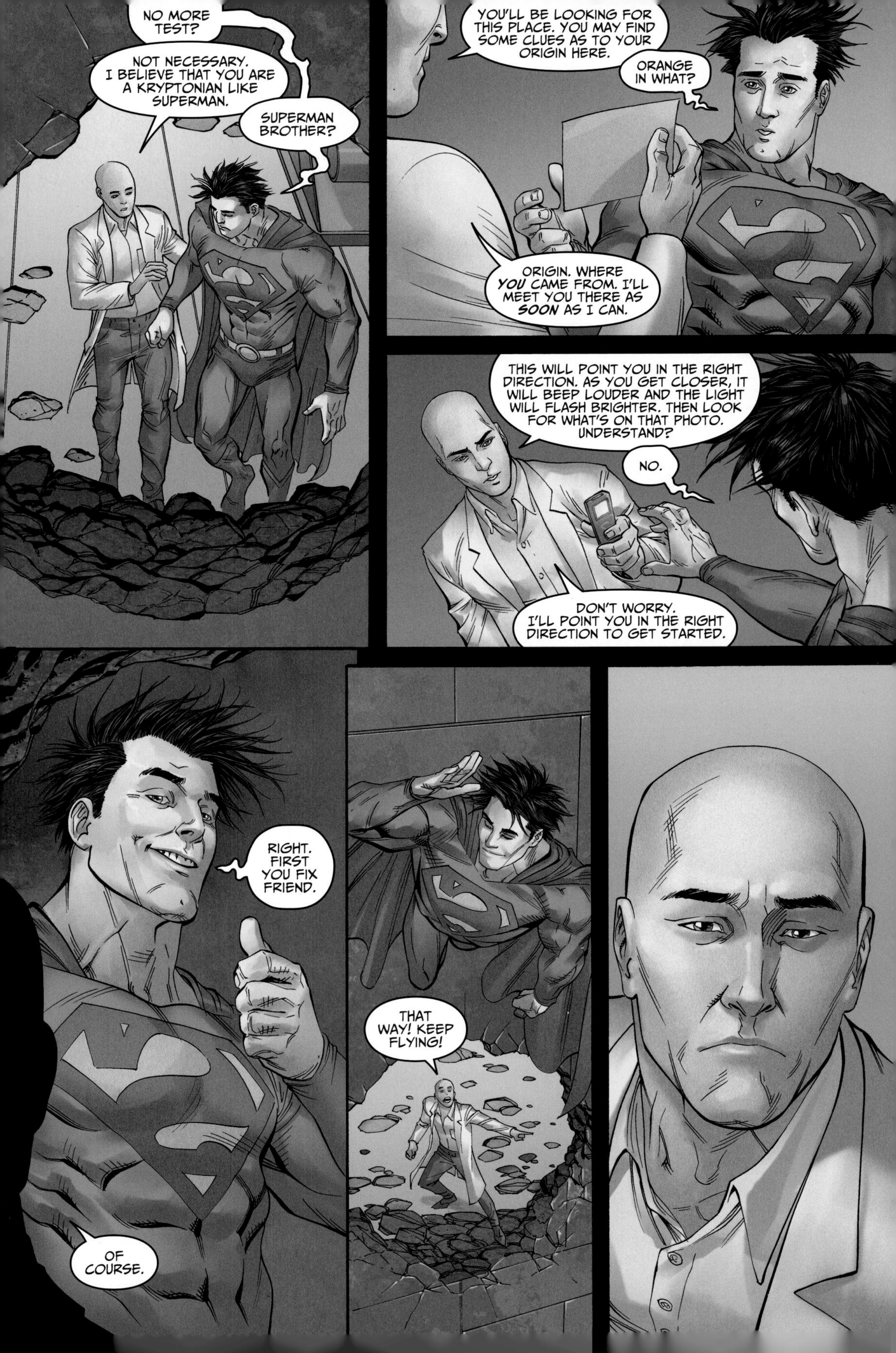
NO MORE TEST?
NOT NECESSARY. I BELIEVE THAT YOU ARE A KRYPTONIAN LIKE SUPERMAN.
SUPERMAN BROTHER?
YOU'LL BE LOOKING FOR THIS PLACE. YOU MAY FIND SOME CLUES AS TO YOUR ORIGIN HERE.
ORANGE IN WHAT?
ORIGIN. WHERE YOU CAME FROM. I'LL MEET YOU THERE AS SOON AS I CAN.
THIS WILL POINT YOU IN THE RIGHT DIRECTION. AS YOU GET CLOSER, IT WILL BEEP LOUDER AND THE LIGHT WILL FLASH BRIGHTER. THEN LOOK FOR WHAT'S ON THAT PHOTO. UNDERSTAND?
NO.
DON'T WORRY. I'LL POINT YOU IN THE RIGHT DIRECTION TO GET STARTED.
RIGHT. FIRST YOU FIX FRIEND.
OF COURSE.
THAT WAY! KEEP FLYING!

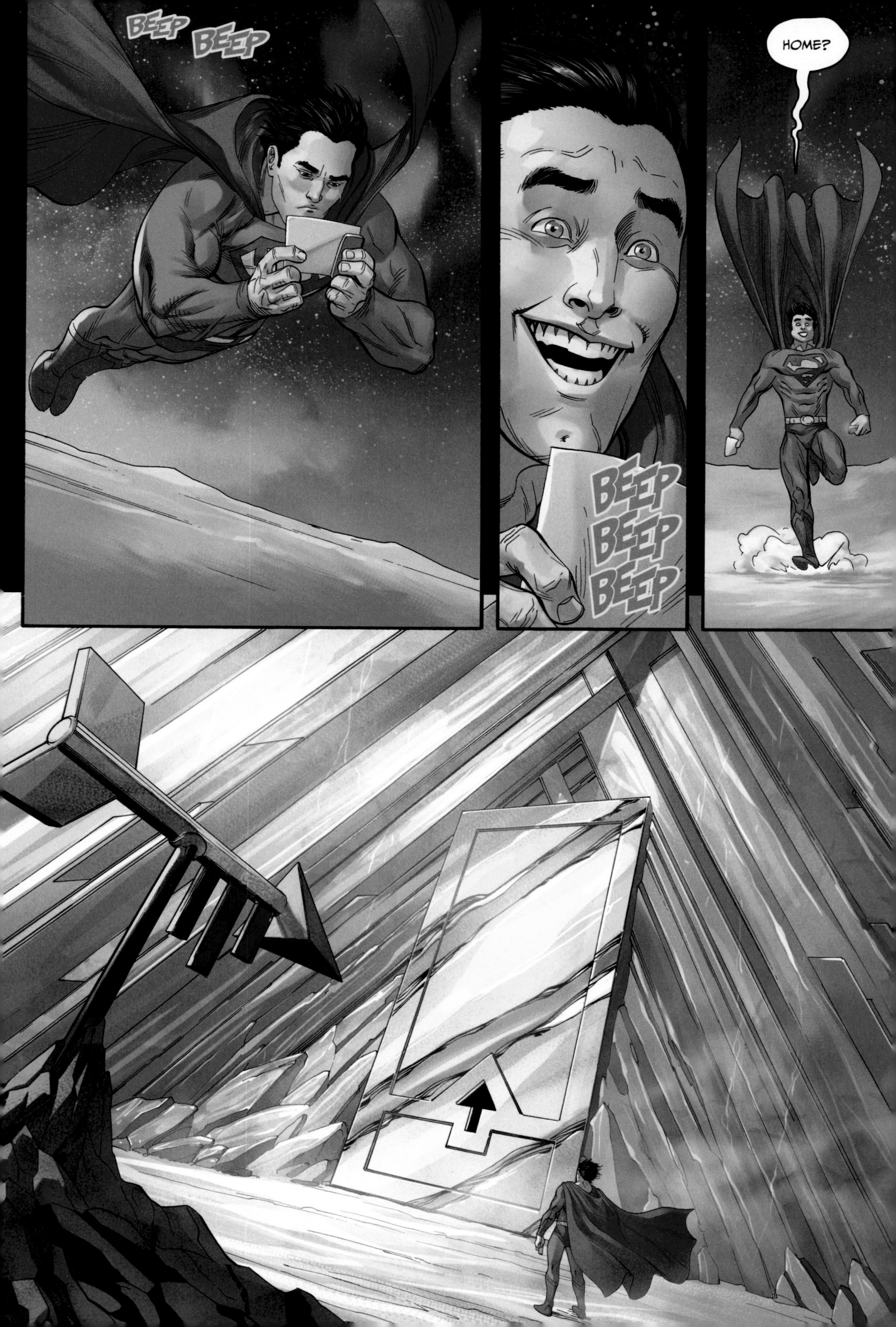
BEEP BEEP
BEEP BEEP BEEP
HOME?

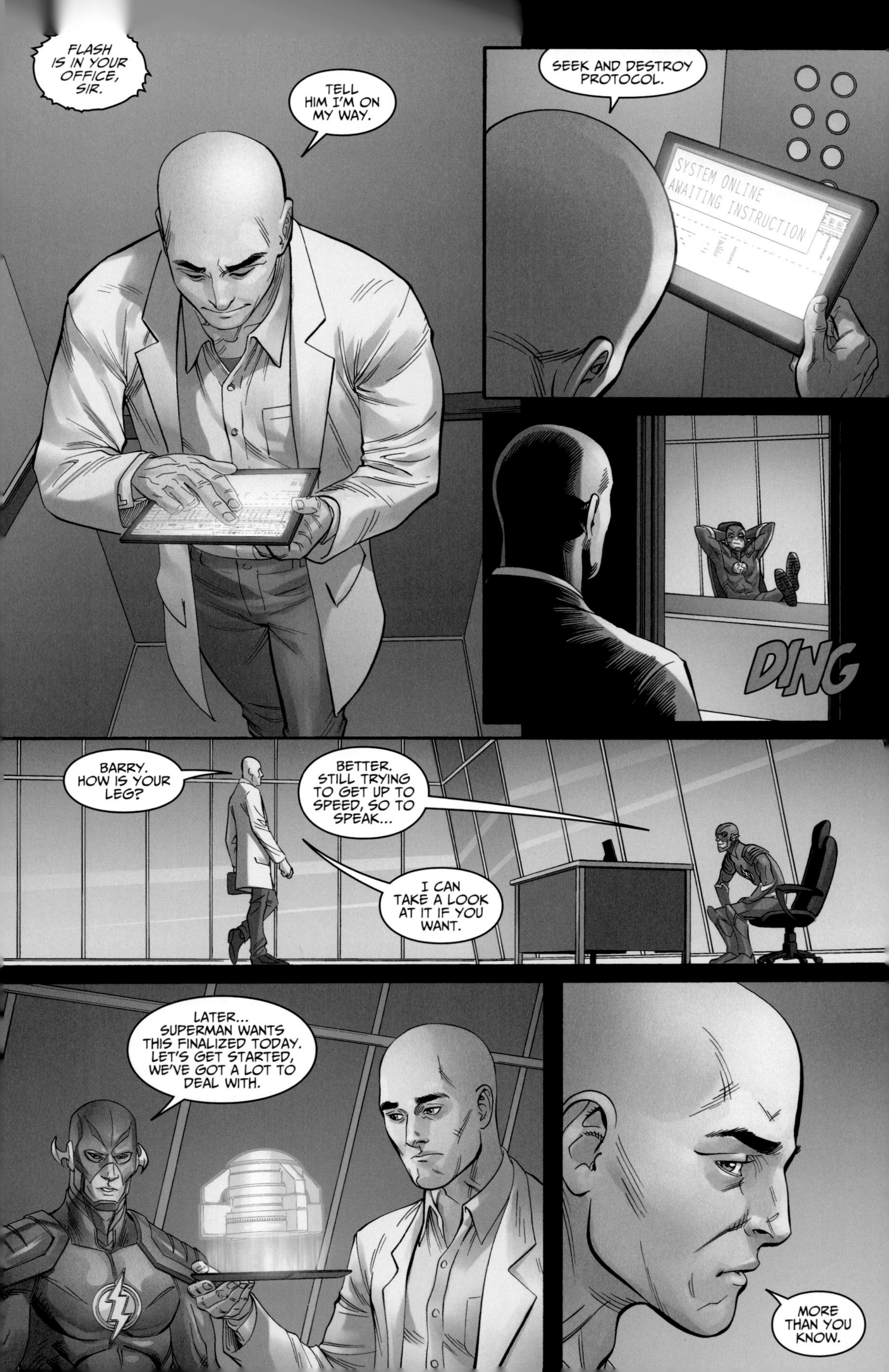
FLASH IS IN YOUR OFFICE, SIR.
TELL HIM I'M ON MY WAY.
SEEK AND DESTROY PROTOCOL.
SYSTEM ONLINE
AWAITING INSTRUCTION
DING
BARRY. HOW IS YOUR LEG?
BETTER. STILL TRYING TO GET UP TO SPEED, SO TO SPEAK...
I CAN TAKE A LOOK AT IT IF YOU WANT.
LATER... SUPERMAN WANTS THIS FINALIZED TODAY. LET'S GET STARTED, WE'VE GOT A LOT TO DEAL WITH.
MORE THAN YOU KNOW.

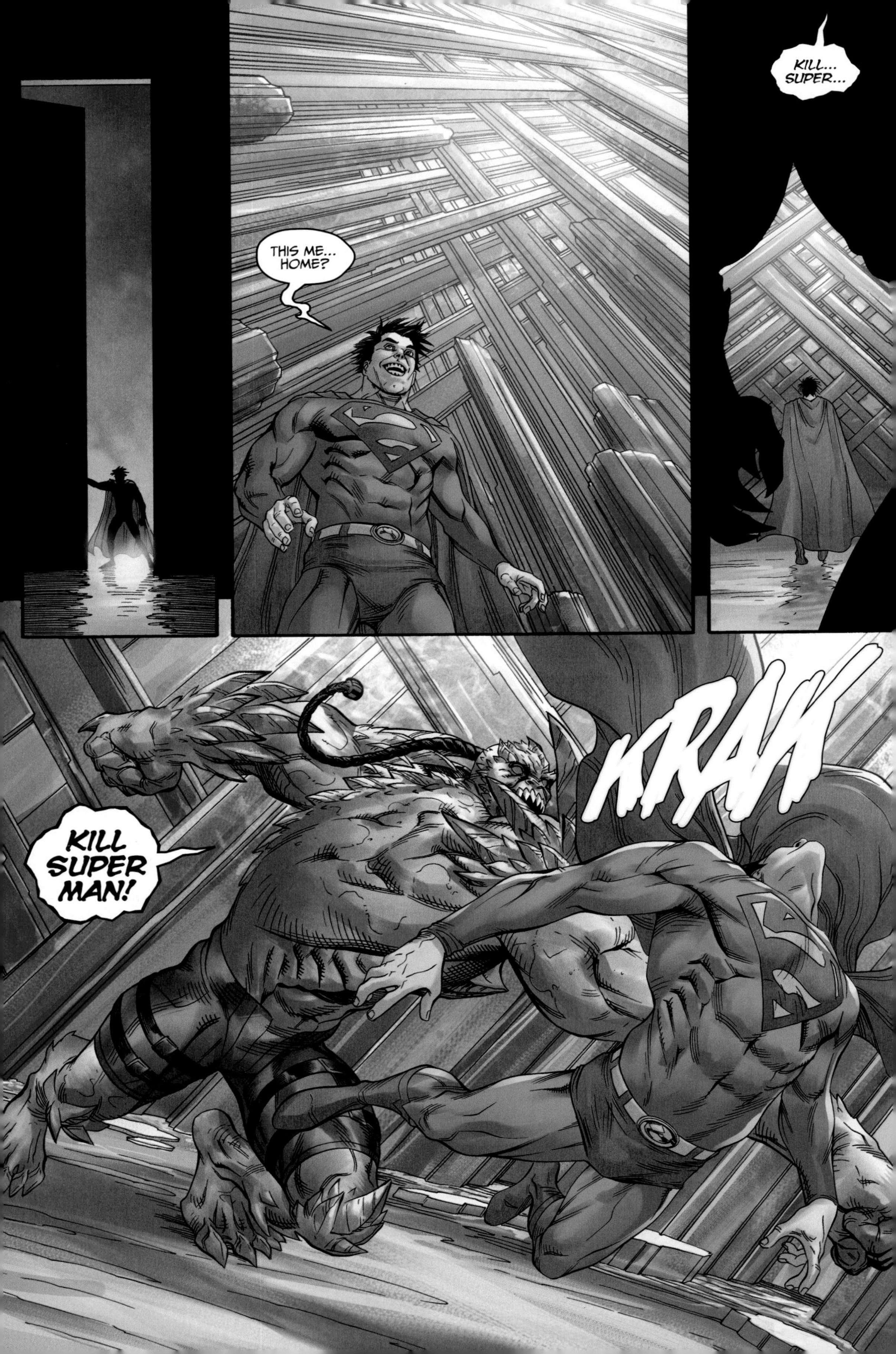
THIS ME... HOME?
KILL... SUPER...
KILL SUPER MAN!
KRAKK

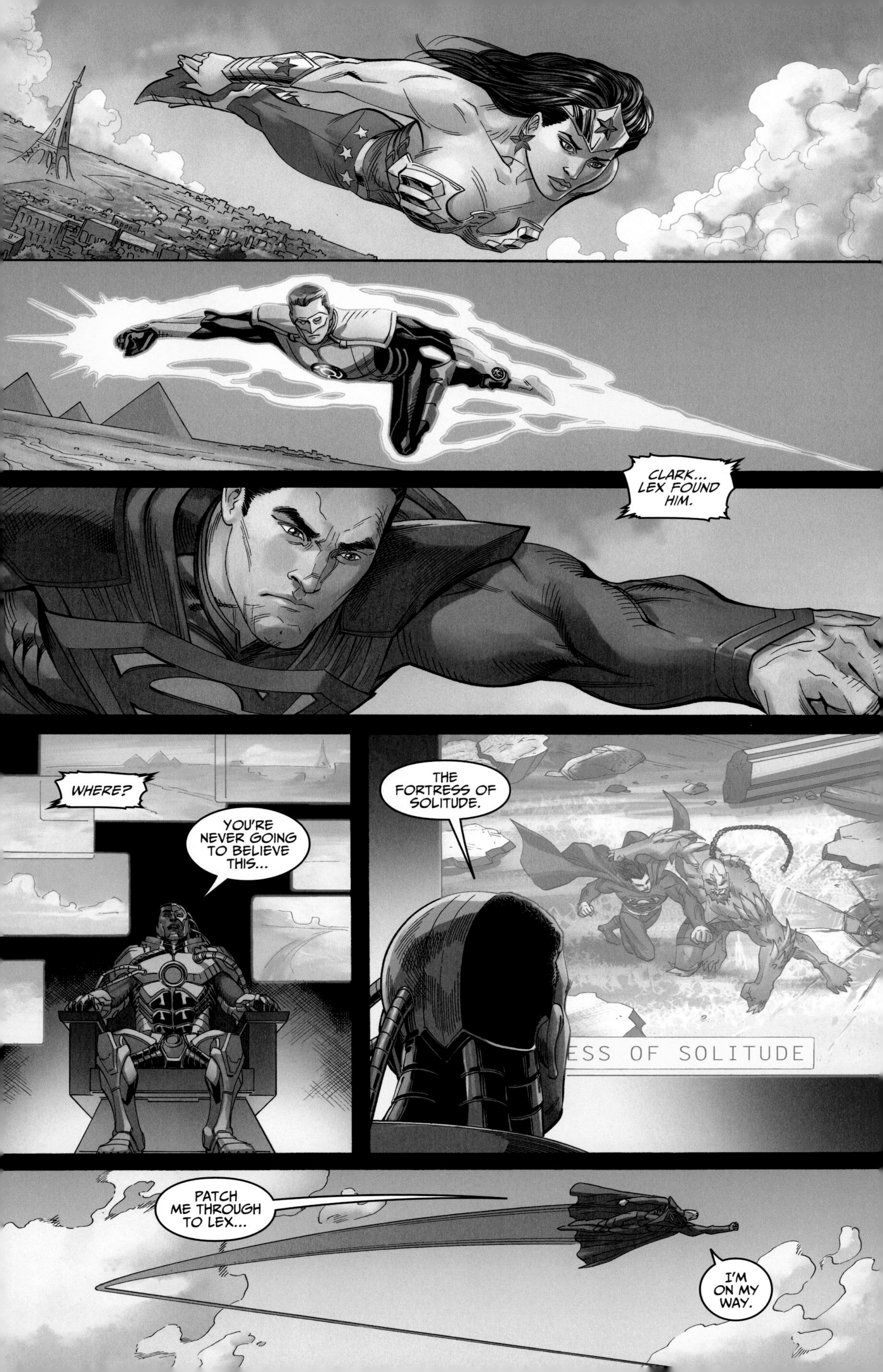
CLARK... LEX FOUND HIM.
WHERE?
YOU'RE NEVER GOING TO BELIEVE THIS...
THE FORTRESS OF SOLITUDE.
ESS OF SOLITUDE
PATCH ME THROUGH TO LEX...
I'M ON MY WAY.

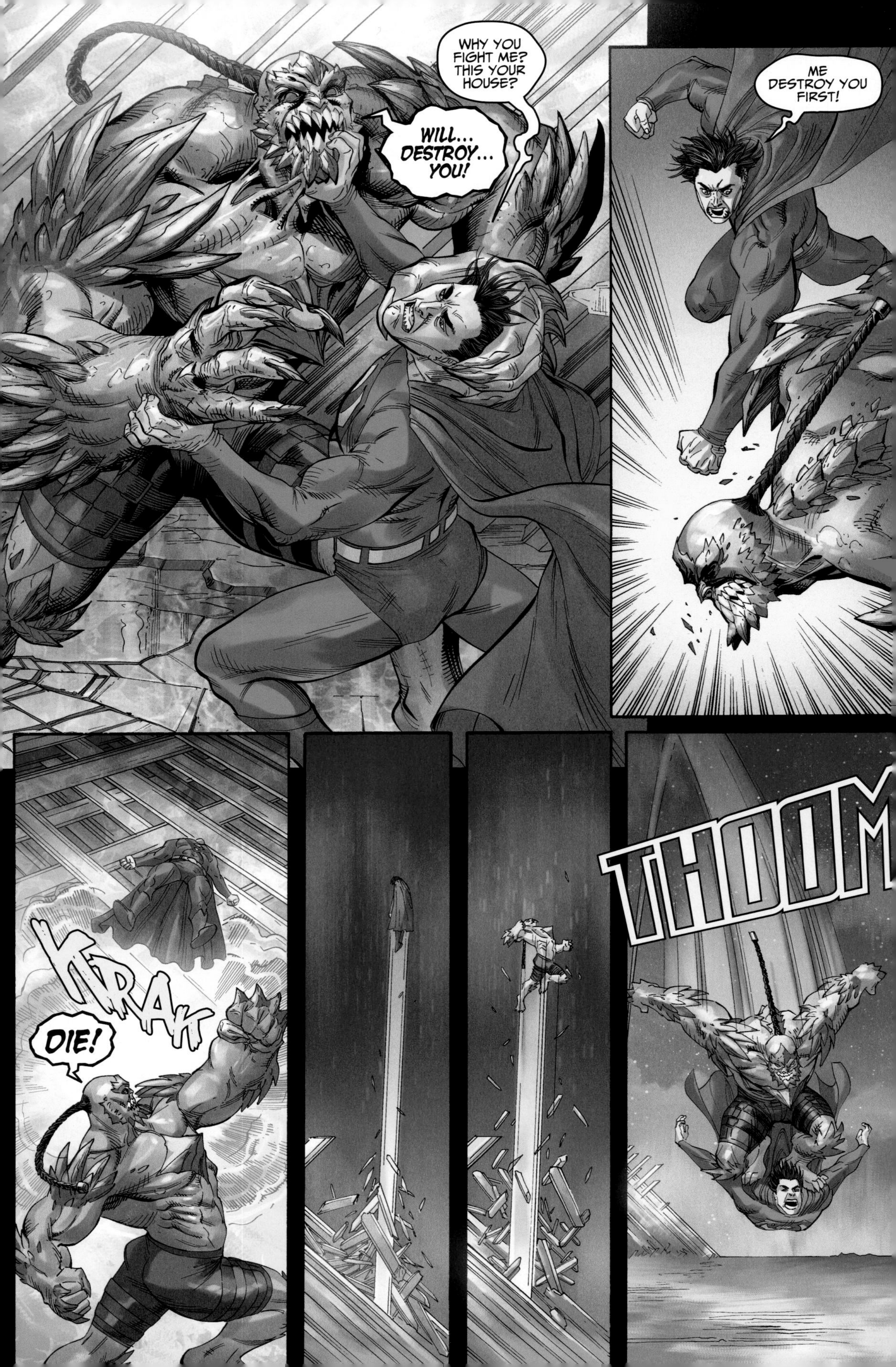
WHY YOU FIGHT ME? THIS YOUR HOUSE?
WILL... DESTROY... YOU!
ME DESTROY YOU FIRST!
KRAK
DIE!
THOOM

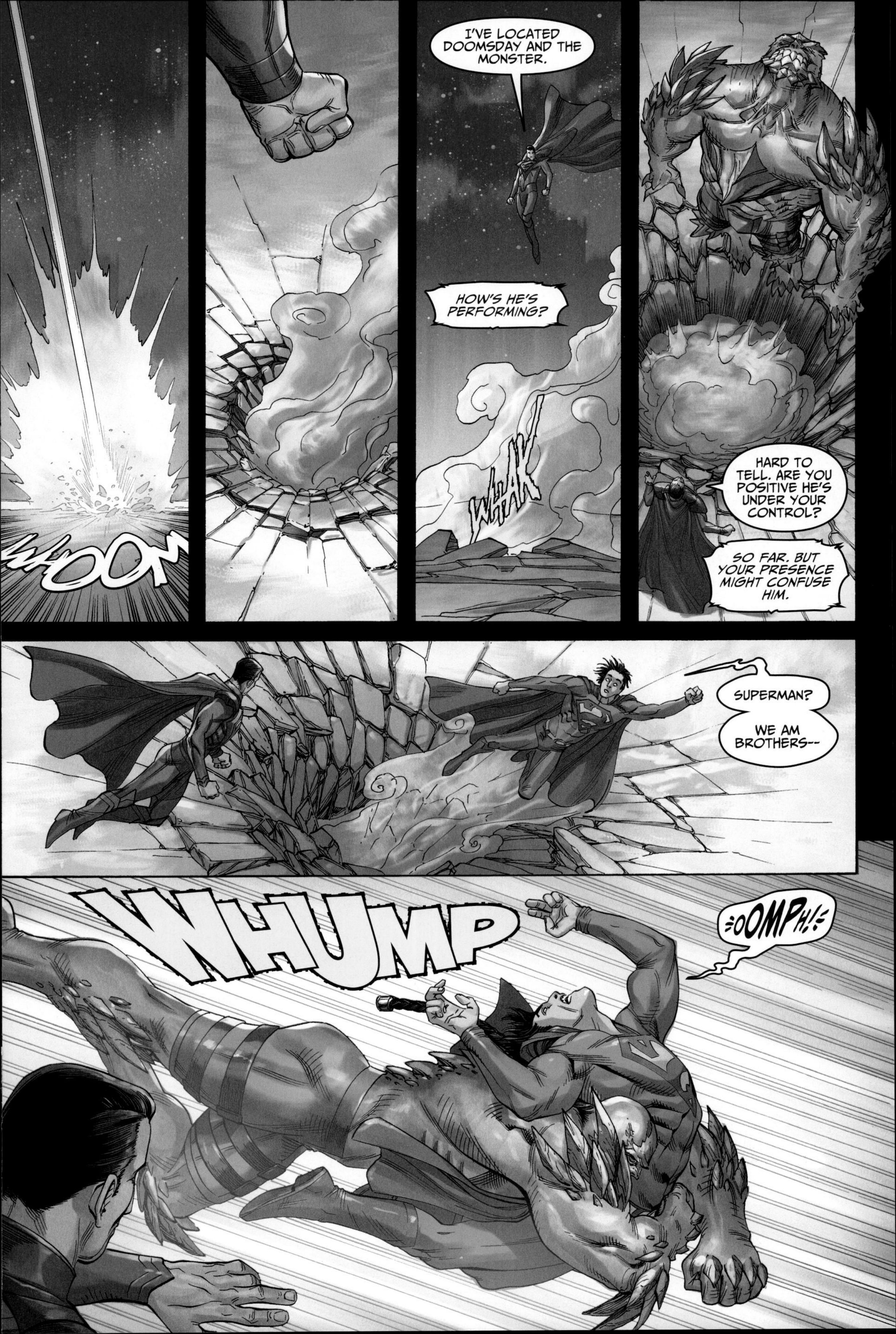
WHOOM
I'VE LOCATED DOOMSDAY AND THE MONSTER.
HOW'S HE'S PERFORMING?
WHAK
HARD TO TELL. ARE YOU POSITIVE HE'S UNDER YOUR CONTROL?
SO FAR. BUT YOUR PRESENCE MIGHT CONFUSE HIM.
SUPERMAN?
WE AM BROTHERS--
WHUMP
OOMPH!

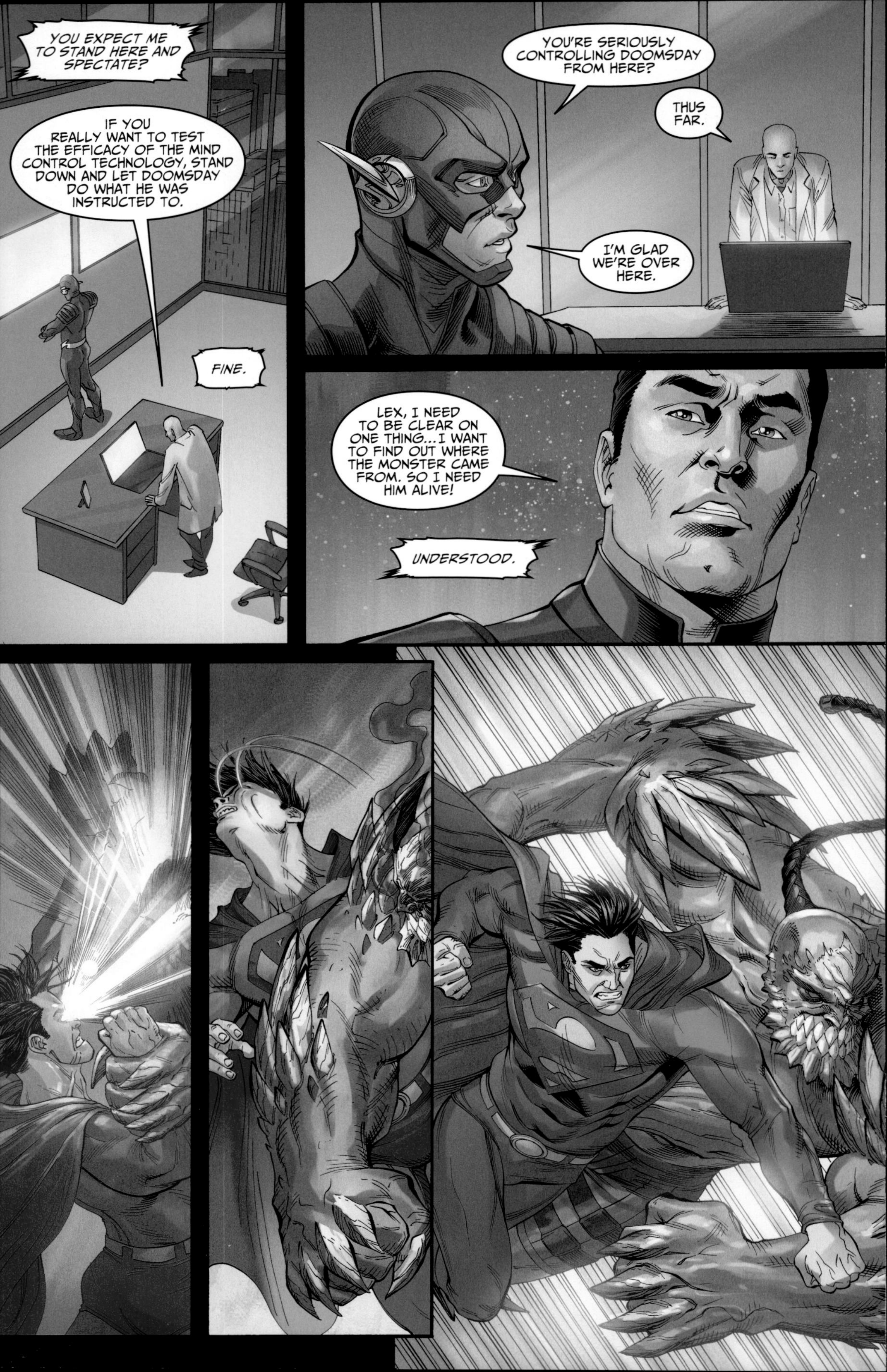
YOU EXPECT ME TO STAND HERE AND SPECTATE?
IF YOU REALLY WANT TO TEST THE EFFICACY OF THE MIND CONTROL TECHNOLOGY, STAND DOWN AND LET DOOMSDAY DO WHAT HE WAS INSTRUCTED TO.
FINE.
YOU'RE SERIOUSLY CONTROLLING DOOMSDAY FROM HERE?
THUS FAR.
I'M GLAD WE'RE OVER HERE.
LEX, I NEED TO BE CLEAR ON ONE THING...I WANT TO FIND OUT WHERE THE MONSTER CAME FROM. SO I NEED HIM ALIVE!
UNDERSTOOD.

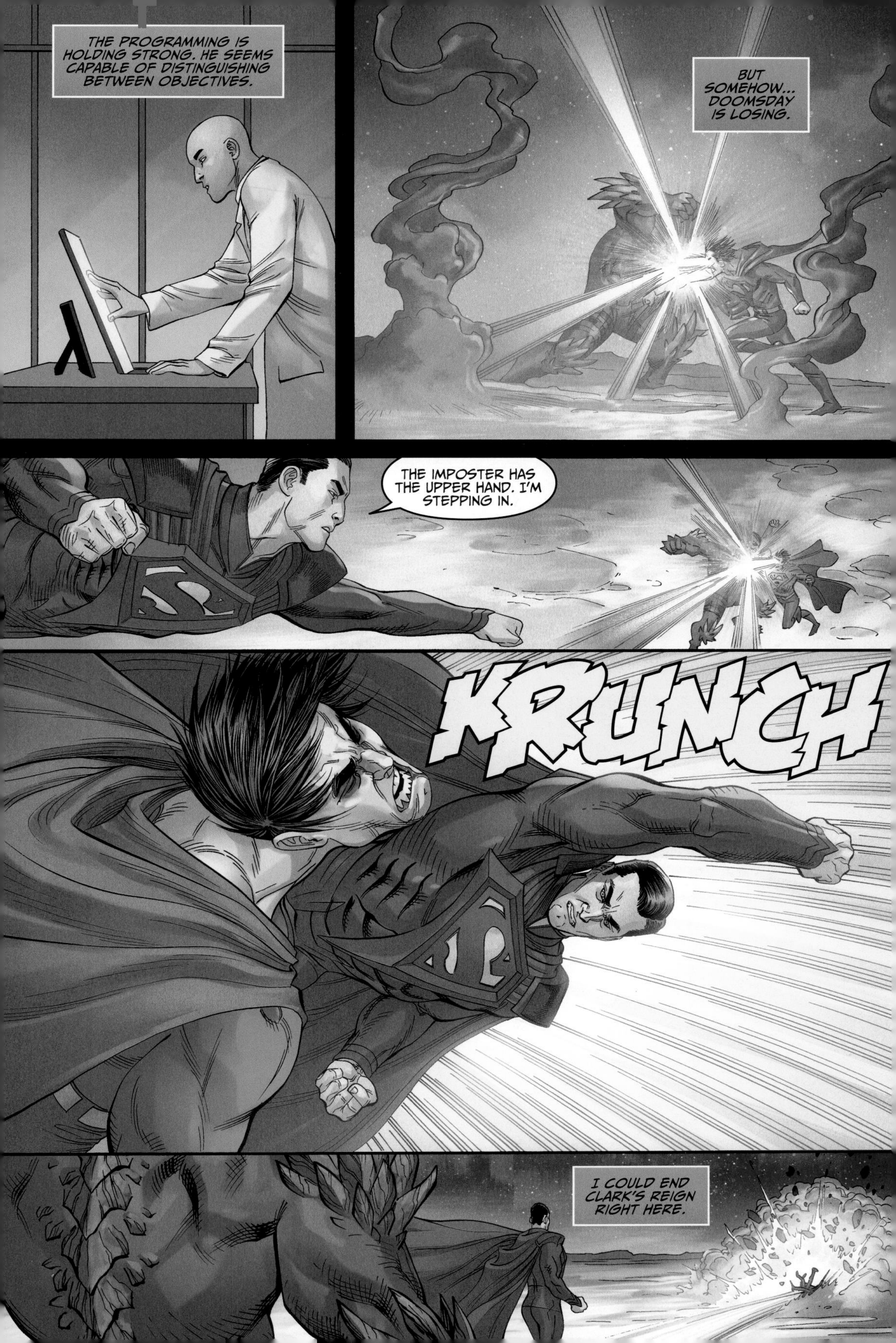
THE PROGRAMMING IS HOLDING STRONG. HE SEEMS CAPABLE OF DISTINGUISHING BETWEEN OBJECTIVES.
BUT SOMEHOW... DOOMSDAY IS LOSING.
THE IMPOSTER HAS THE UPPER HAND. I'M STEPPING IN.
KRUNCH
I COULD END CLARK'S REIGN RIGHT HERE.

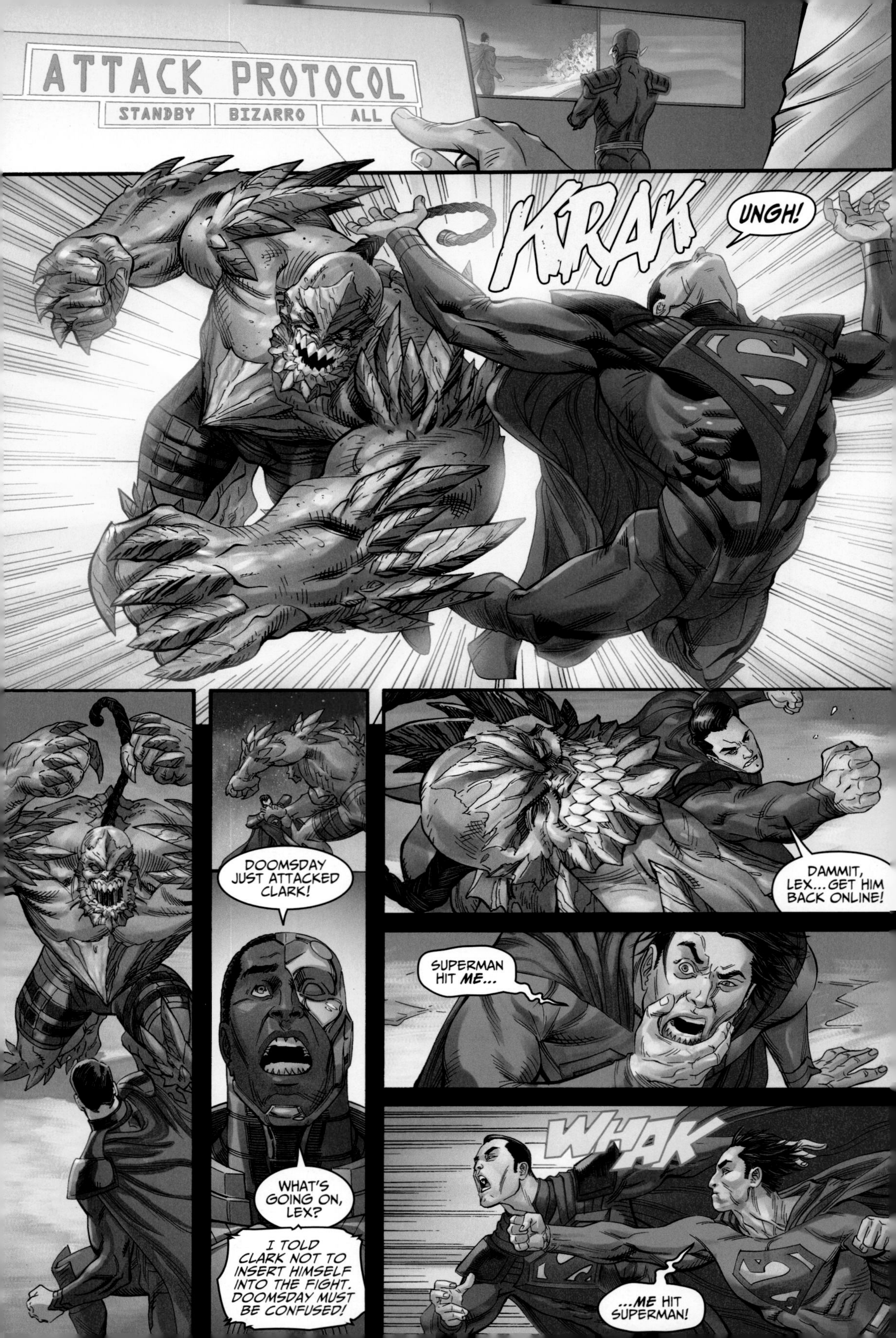

ATTACK PROTOCOL
STANDBY BIZARRO ALL
KRAK
UNGH!
DOOMSDAY JUST ATTACKED CLARK!
WHAT'S GOING ON, LEX?
I TOLD CLARK NOT TO INSERT HIMSELF INTO THE FIGHT. DOOMSDAY MUST BE CONFUSED!
DAMMIT, LEX... GET HIM BACK ONLINE!
SUPERMAN HIT ME...
WHAK
...ME HIT SUPERMAN!

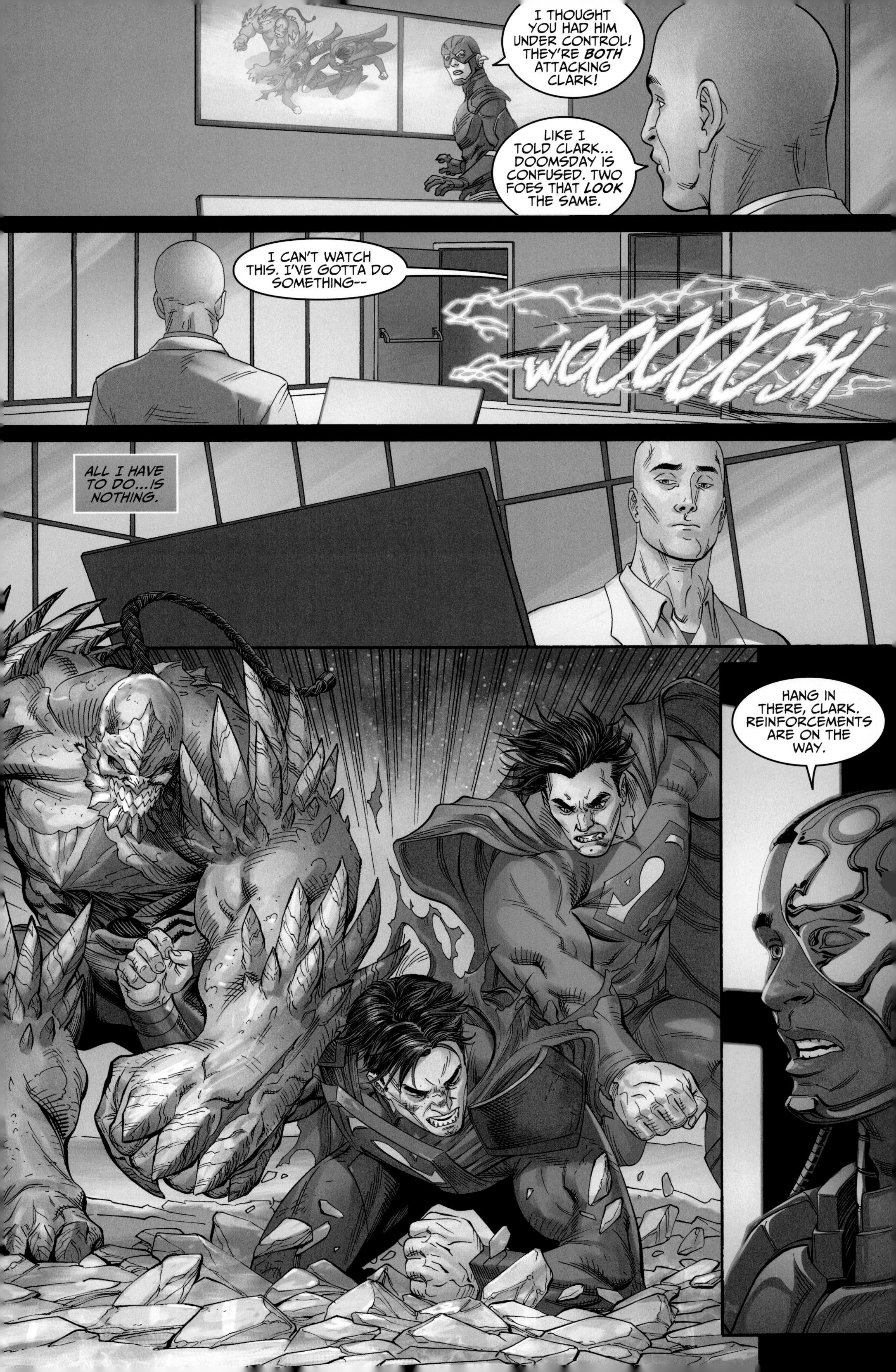
I THOUGHT YOU HAD HIM UNDER CONTROL! THEY'RE *BOTH* ATTACKING CLARK!
LIKE I TOLD CLARK... DOOMSDAY IS CONFUSED. TWO FOES THAT *LOOK* THE SAME.
I CAN'T WATCH THIS. I'VE GOTTA DO SOMETHING--
WOOOOOSH
ALL I HAVE TO DO...IS NOTHING.
HANG IN THERE, CLARK. REINFORCEMENTS ARE ON THE WAY.

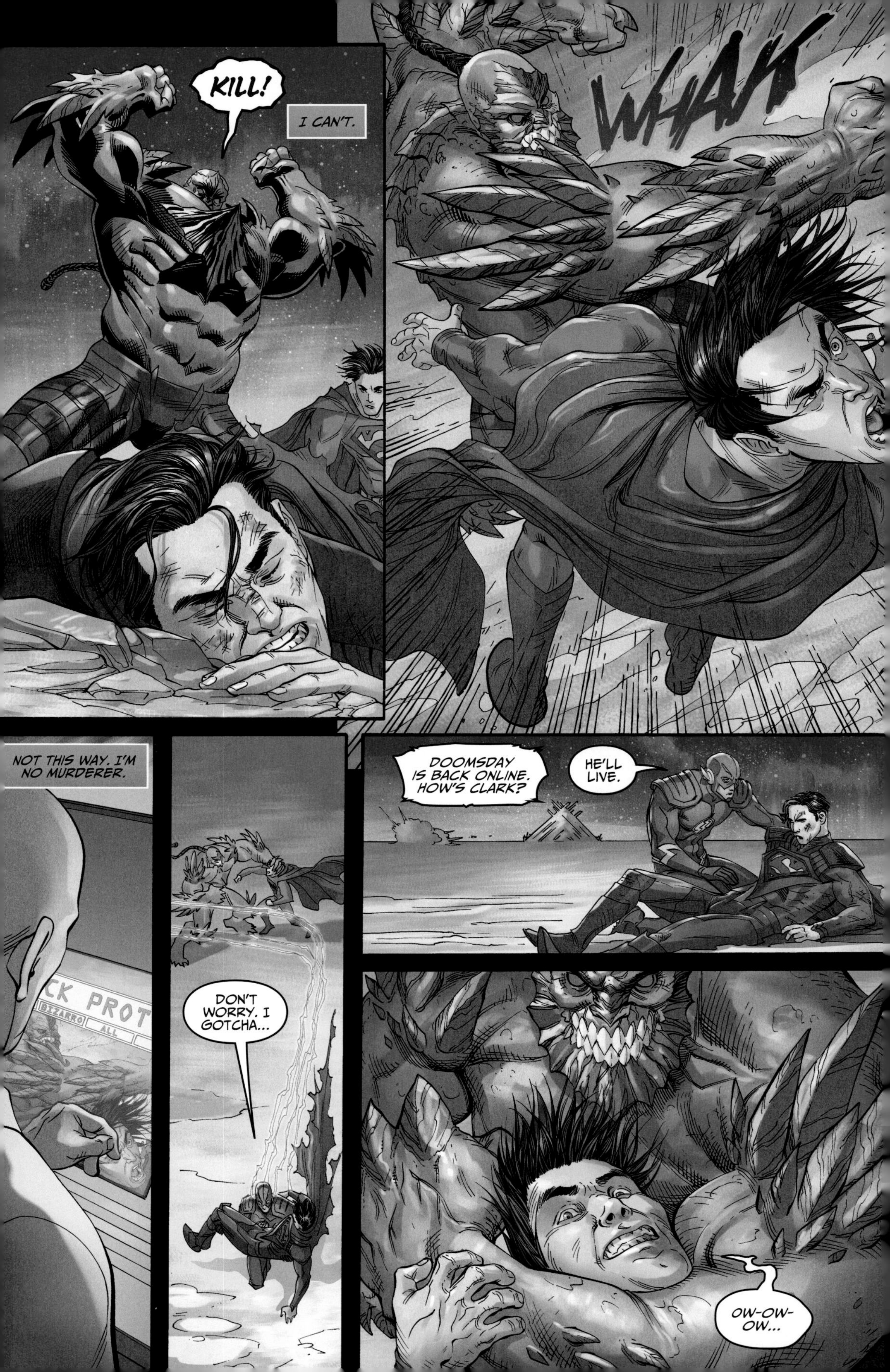
KILL!
I CAN'T.
WHAK
NOT THIS WAY. I'M NO MURDERER.
CK PROT
BIZARRO
ALL
DON'T WORRY. I GOTCHA...
DOOMSDAY IS BACK ONLINE. HOW'S CLARK?
HE'LL LIVE.
OW-OW-OW...

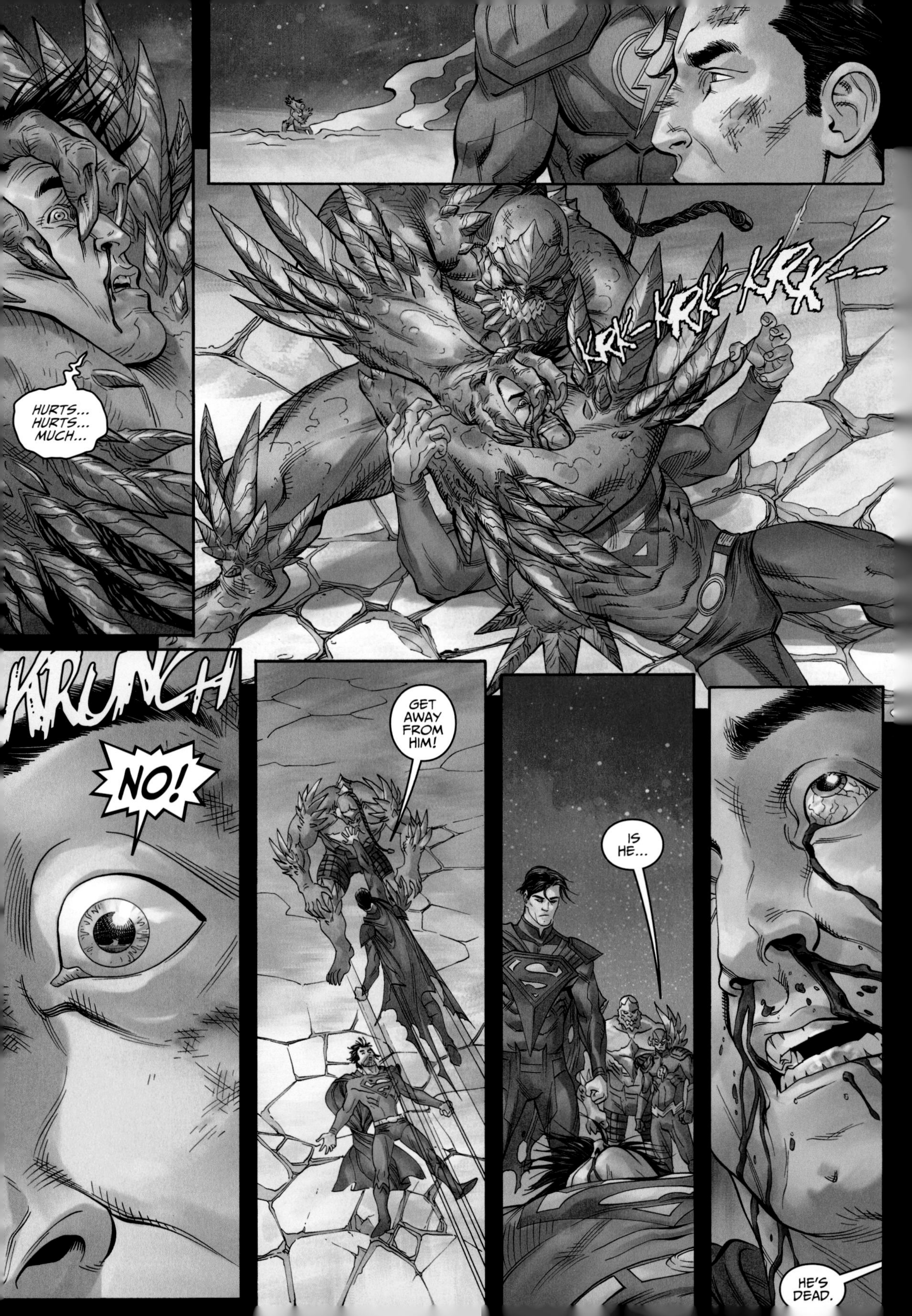
HURTS... HURTS... MUCH...
KRK-KRK-KRK--
KRUNCH
NO!
GET AWAY FROM HIM!
IS HE...
HE'S DEAD.

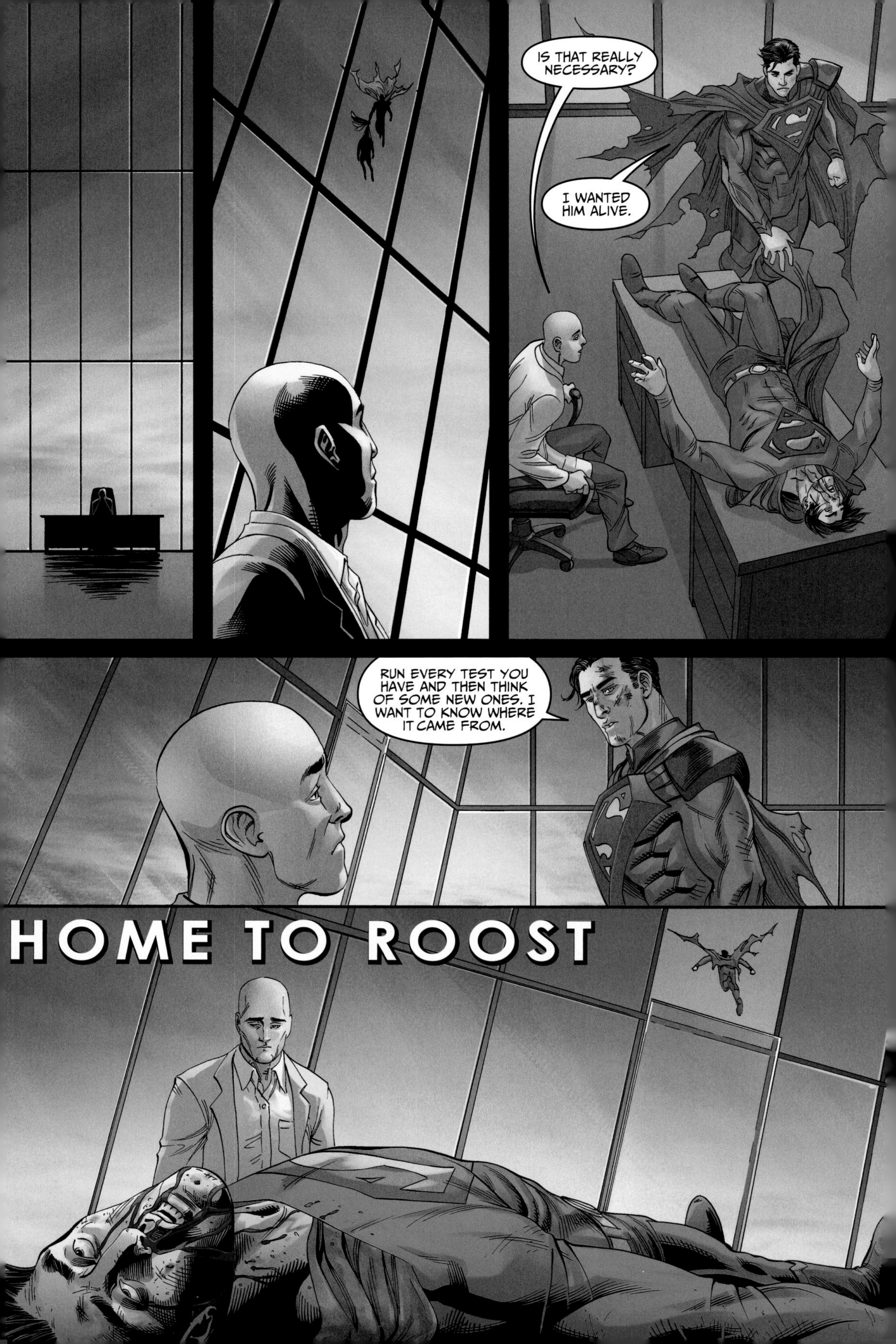

IS THAT REALLY NECESSARY?
I WANTED HIM ALIVE.
RUN EVERY TEST YOU HAVE AND THEN THINK OF SOME NEW ONES. I WANT TO KNOW WHERE IT CAME FROM.
HOME TO ROOST

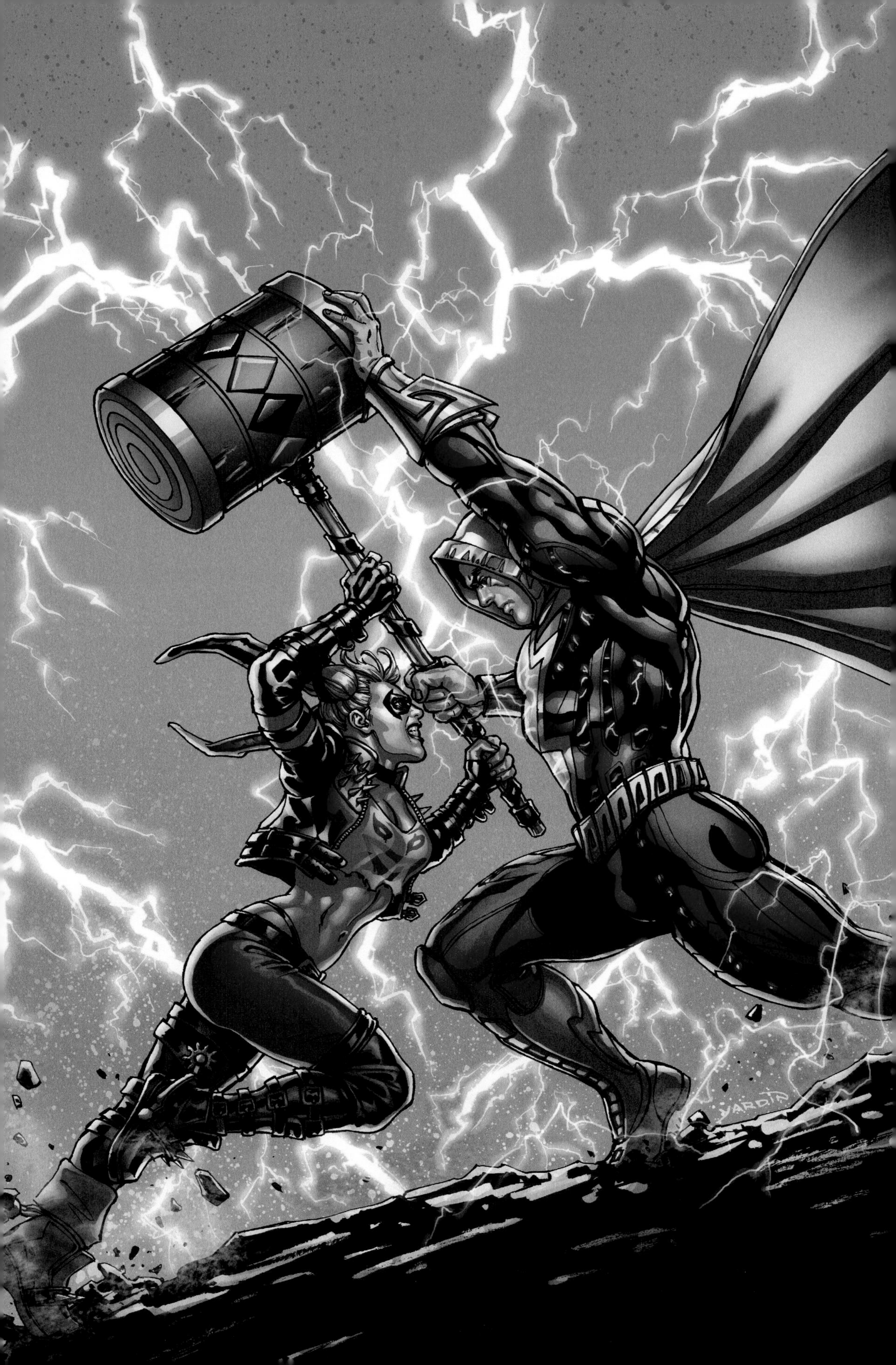
YARDIN

"Memorial" **Bruno Redondo** Penciller **Juan Albarrán** Inker **Rex Lokus** Colorist
"Tempers Flare" **Xermanico** Artist **Rex Lokus** Colorist

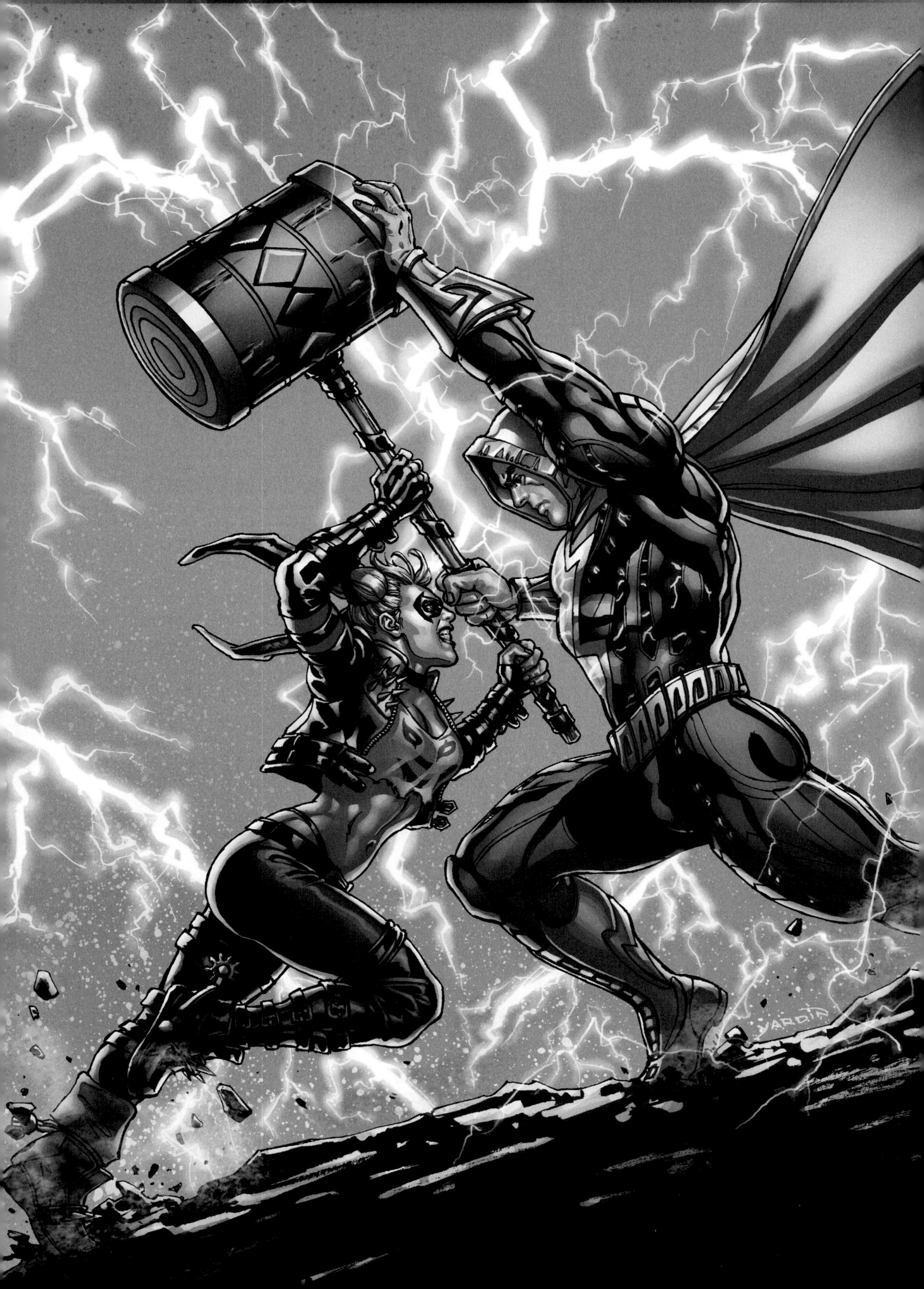

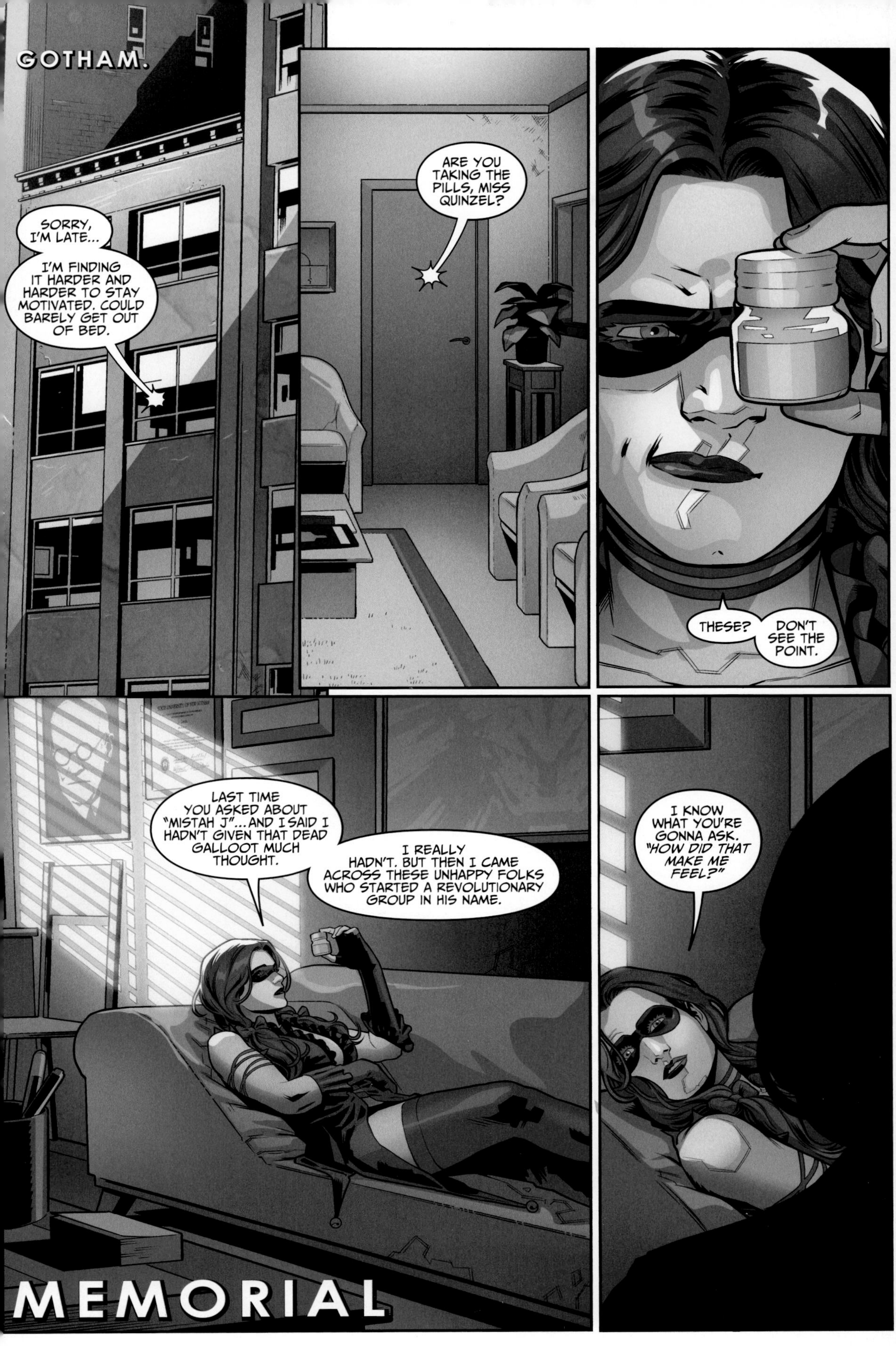
GOTHAM.
SORRY, I'M LATE...
I'M FINDING IT HARDER AND HARDER TO STAY MOTIVATED. COULD BARELY GET OUT OF BED.
ARE YOU TAKING THE PILLS, MISS QUINZEL?
THESE?
DON'T SEE THE POINT.
LAST TIME YOU ASKED ABOUT "MISTAH J"...AND I SAID I HADN'T GIVEN THAT DEAD GALLOOT MUCH THOUGHT.
I REALLY HADN'T. BUT THEN I CAME ACROSS THESE UNHAPPY FOLKS WHO STARTED A REVOLUTIONARY GROUP IN HIS NAME.
I KNOW WHAT YOU'RE GONNA ASK. "HOW DID THAT MAKE ME FEEL?"
MEMORIAL

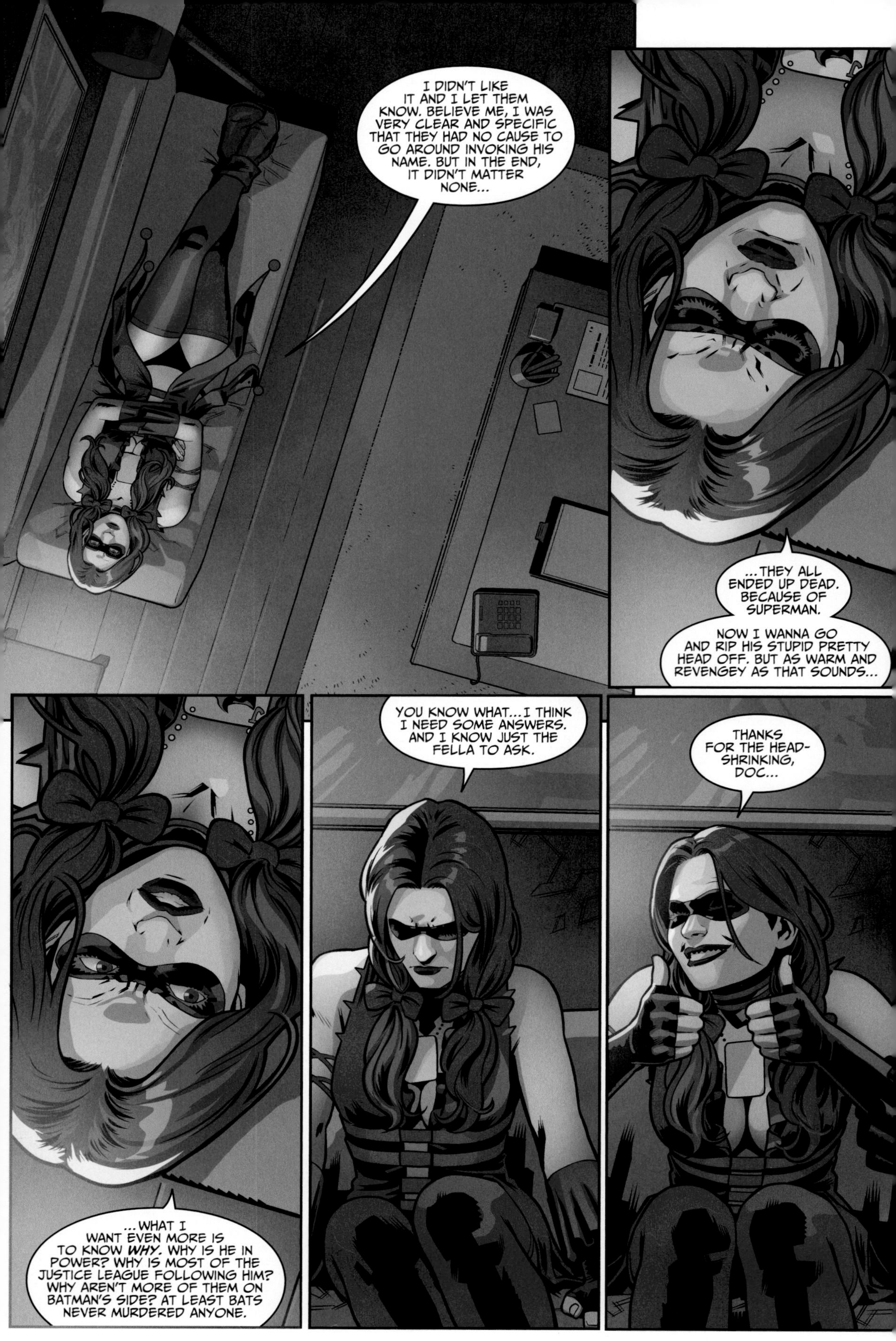
I DIDN'T LIKE IT AND I LET THEM KNOW. BELIEVE ME, I WAS VERY CLEAR AND SPECIFIC THAT THEY HAD NO CAUSE TO GO AROUND INVOKING HIS NAME. BUT IN THE END, IT DIDN'T MATTER NONE...
...THEY ALL ENDED UP DEAD. BECAUSE OF SUPERMAN.
NOW I WANNA GO AND RIP HIS STUPID PRETTY HEAD OFF. BUT AS WARM AND REVENGEY AS THAT SOUNDS...
...WHAT I WANT EVEN MORE IS TO KNOW *WHY*. WHY IS HE IN POWER? WHY IS MOST OF THE JUSTICE LEAGUE FOLLOWING HIM? WHY AREN'T MORE OF THEM ON BATMAN'S SIDE? AT LEAST BATS NEVER MURDERED ANYONE.
YOU KNOW WHAT...I THINK I NEED SOME ANSWERS. AND I KNOW JUST THE FELLA TO ASK.
THANKS FOR THE HEAD-SHRINKING, DOC...

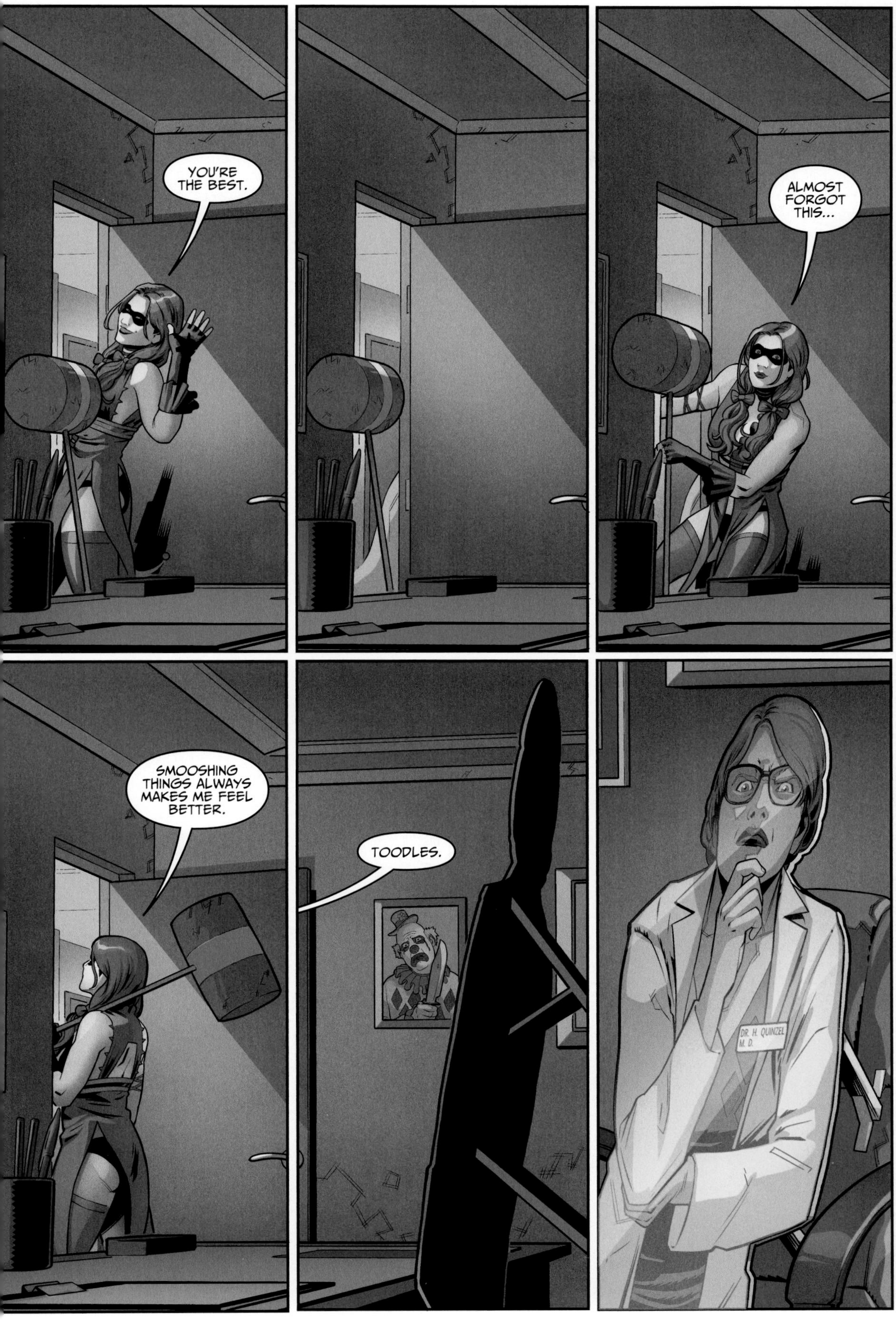
YOU'RE THE BEST.
ALMOST FORGOT THIS...
SMOOSHING THINGS ALWAYS MAKES ME FEEL BETTER.
TOODLES.
DR. H. QUINZEL M. D.

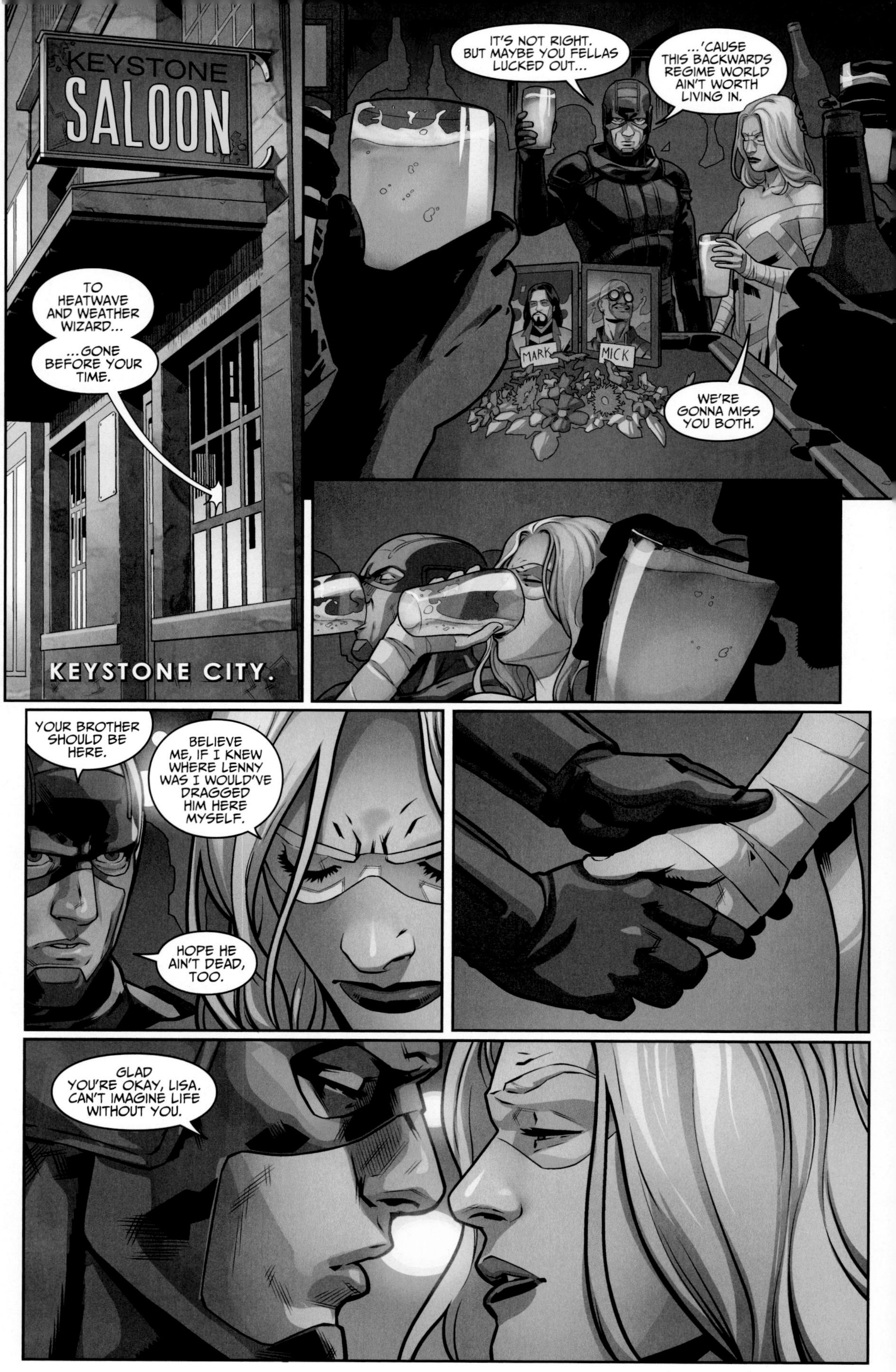
KEYSTONE
SALOON
TO HEATWAVE AND WEATHER WIZARD...
...GONE BEFORE YOUR TIME.
KEYSTONE CITY.
IT'S NOT RIGHT. BUT MAYBE YOU FELLAS LUCKED OUT...
...'CAUSE THIS BACKWARDS REGIME WORLD AIN'T WORTH LIVING IN.
MARK
MICK
WE'RE GONNA MISS YOU BOTH.
YOUR BROTHER SHOULD BE HERE.
BELIEVE ME, IF I KNEW WHERE LENNY WAS I WOULD'VE DRAGGED HIM HERE MYSELF.
HOPE HE AIN'T DEAD, TOO.
GLAD YOU'RE OKAY, LISA. CAN'T IMAGINE LIFE WITHOUT YOU.

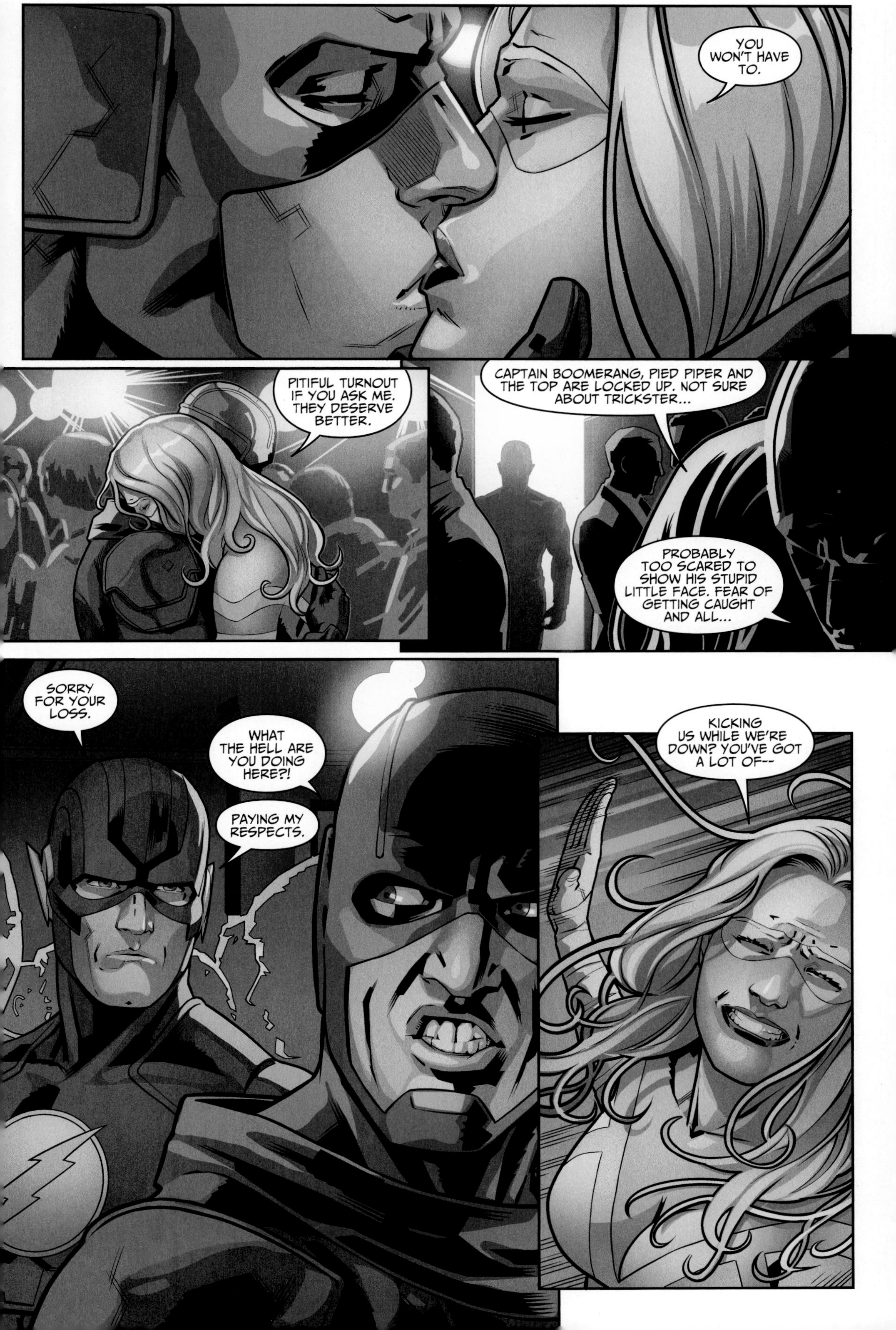
YOU WON'T HAVE TO.
PITIFUL TURNOUT IF YOU ASK ME. THEY DESERVE BETTER.
CAPTAIN BOOMERANG, PIED PIPER AND THE TOP ARE LOCKED UP. NOT SURE ABOUT TRICKSTER...
PROBABLY TOO SCARED TO SHOW HIS STUPID LITTLE FACE. FEAR OF GETTING CAUGHT AND ALL...
SORRY FOR YOUR LOSS.
WHAT THE HELL ARE YOU DOING HERE?!
PAYING MY RESPECTS.
KICKING US WHILE WE'RE DOWN? YOU'VE GOT A LOT OF--

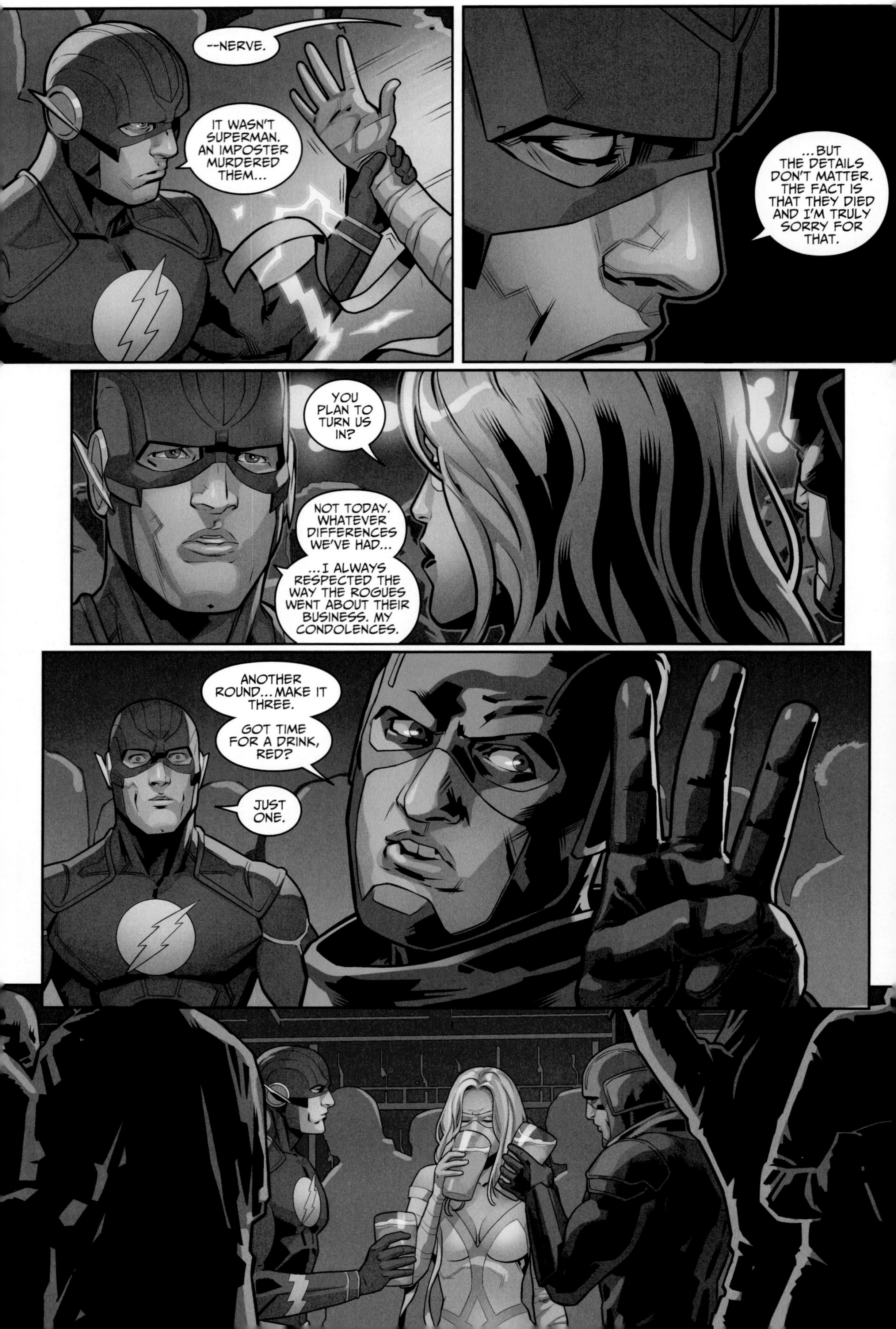
--NERVE.
IT WASN'T SUPERMAN. AN IMPOSTER MURDERED THEM...
...BUT THE DETAILS DON'T MATTER. THE FACT IS THAT THEY DIED AND I'M TRULY SORRY FOR THAT.
YOU PLAN TO TURN US IN?
NOT TODAY. WHATEVER DIFFERENCES WE'VE HAD...
...I ALWAYS RESPECTED THE WAY THE ROGUES WENT ABOUT THEIR BUSINESS. MY CONDOLENCES.
ANOTHER ROUND...MAKE IT THREE.
GOT TIME FOR A DRINK, RED?
JUST ONE.

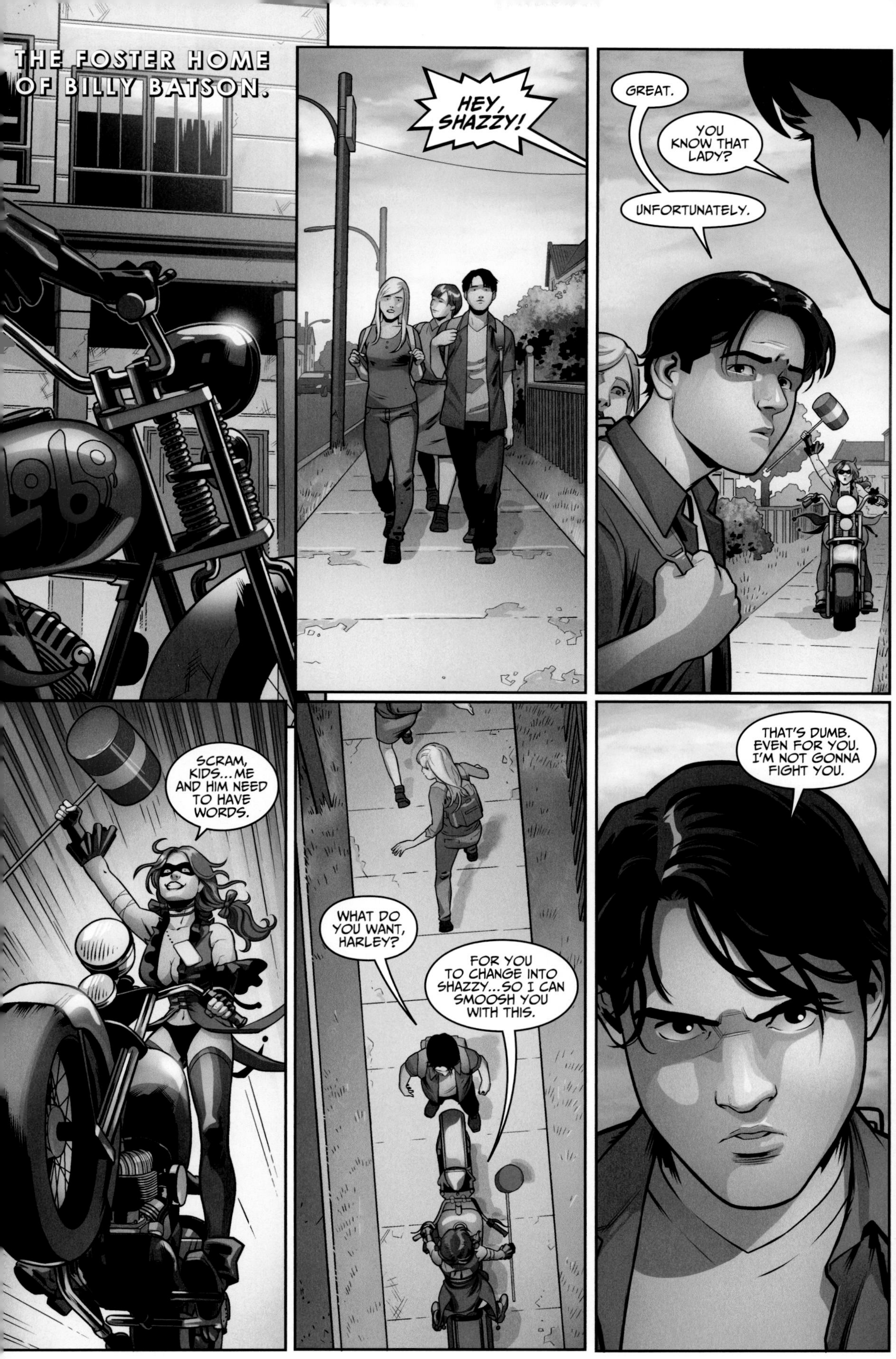
THE FOSTER HOME OF BILLY BATSON.
HEY, SHAZZY!
GREAT.
YOU KNOW THAT LADY?
UNFORTUNATELY.
SCRAM, KIDS...ME AND HIM NEED TO HAVE WORDS.
WHAT DO YOU WANT, HARLEY?
FOR YOU TO CHANGE INTO SHAZZY...SO I CAN SMOOSH YOU WITH THIS.
THAT'S DUMB. EVEN FOR YOU. I'M NOT GONNA FIGHT YOU.

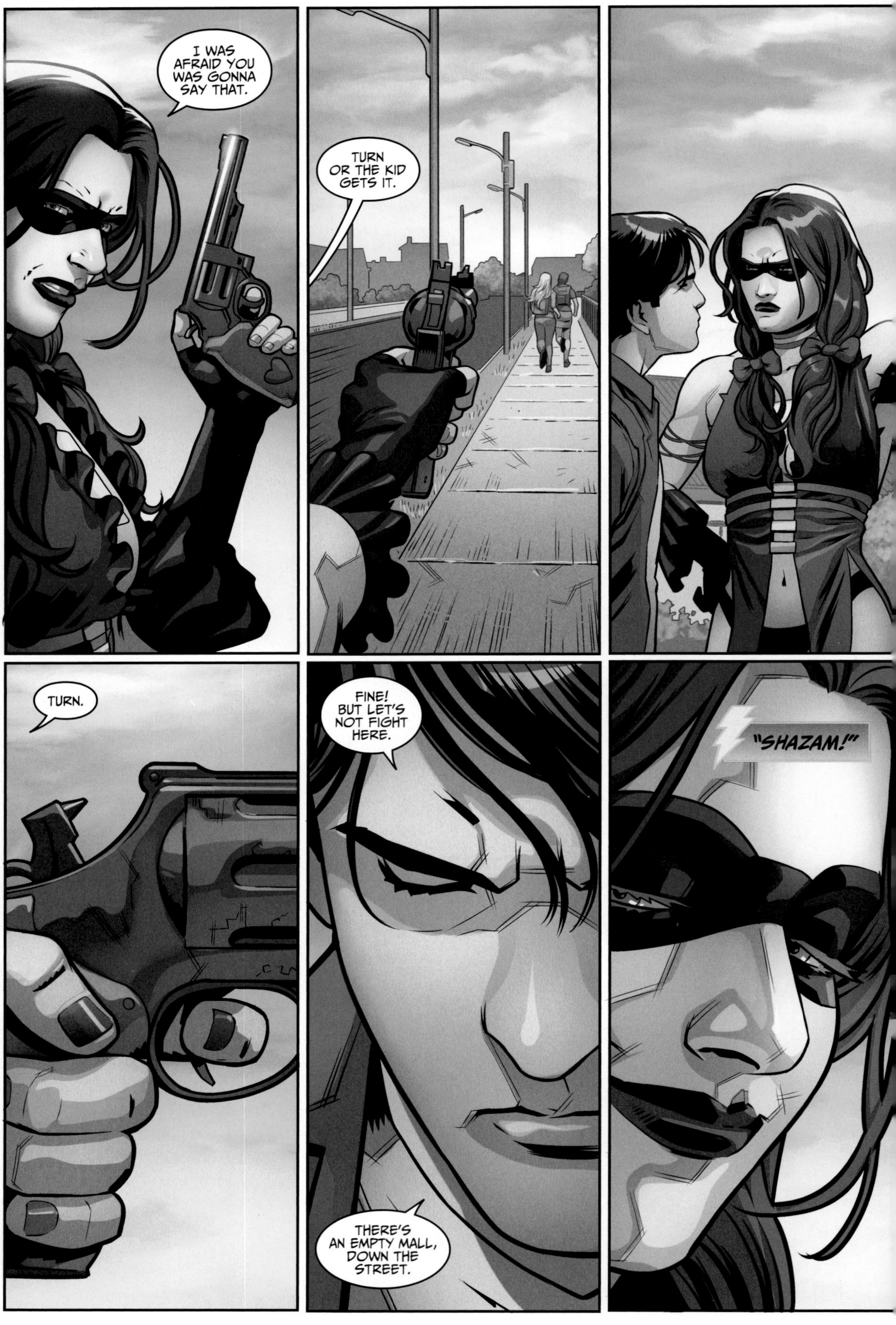
I WAS AFRAID YOU WAS GONNA SAY THAT.
TURN OR THE KID GETS IT.
TURN.
FINE! BUT LET'S NOT FIGHT HERE.
THERE'S AN EMPTY MALL, DOWN THE STREET.
"SHAZAM!"

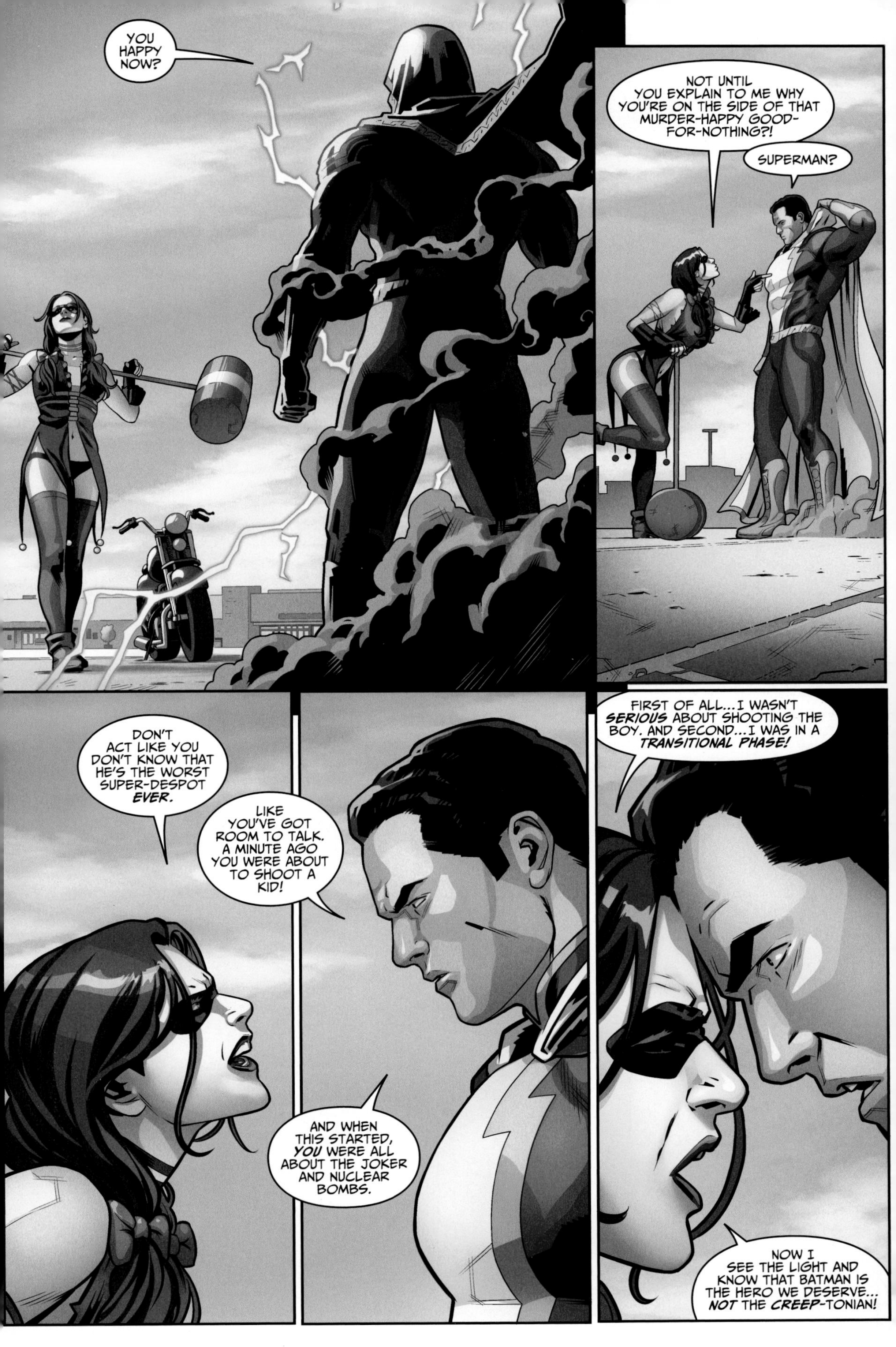

YOU HAPPY NOW?
NOT UNTIL YOU EXPLAIN TO ME WHY YOU'RE ON THE SIDE OF THAT MURDER-HAPPY GOOD-FOR-NOTHING?!
SUPERMAN?
DON'T ACT LIKE YOU DON'T KNOW THAT HE'S THE WORST SUPER-DESPOT EVER.
LIKE YOU'VE GOT ROOM TO TALK. A MINUTE AGO YOU WERE ABOUT TO SHOOT A KID!
AND WHEN THIS STARTED, YOU WERE ALL ABOUT THE JOKER AND NUCLEAR BOMBS.
FIRST OF ALL... I WASN'T SERIOUS ABOUT SHOOTING THE BOY. AND SECOND... I WAS IN A TRANSITIONAL PHASE!
NOW I SEE THE LIGHT AND KNOW THAT BATMAN IS THE HERO WE DESERVE... NOT THE CREEP-TONIAN!

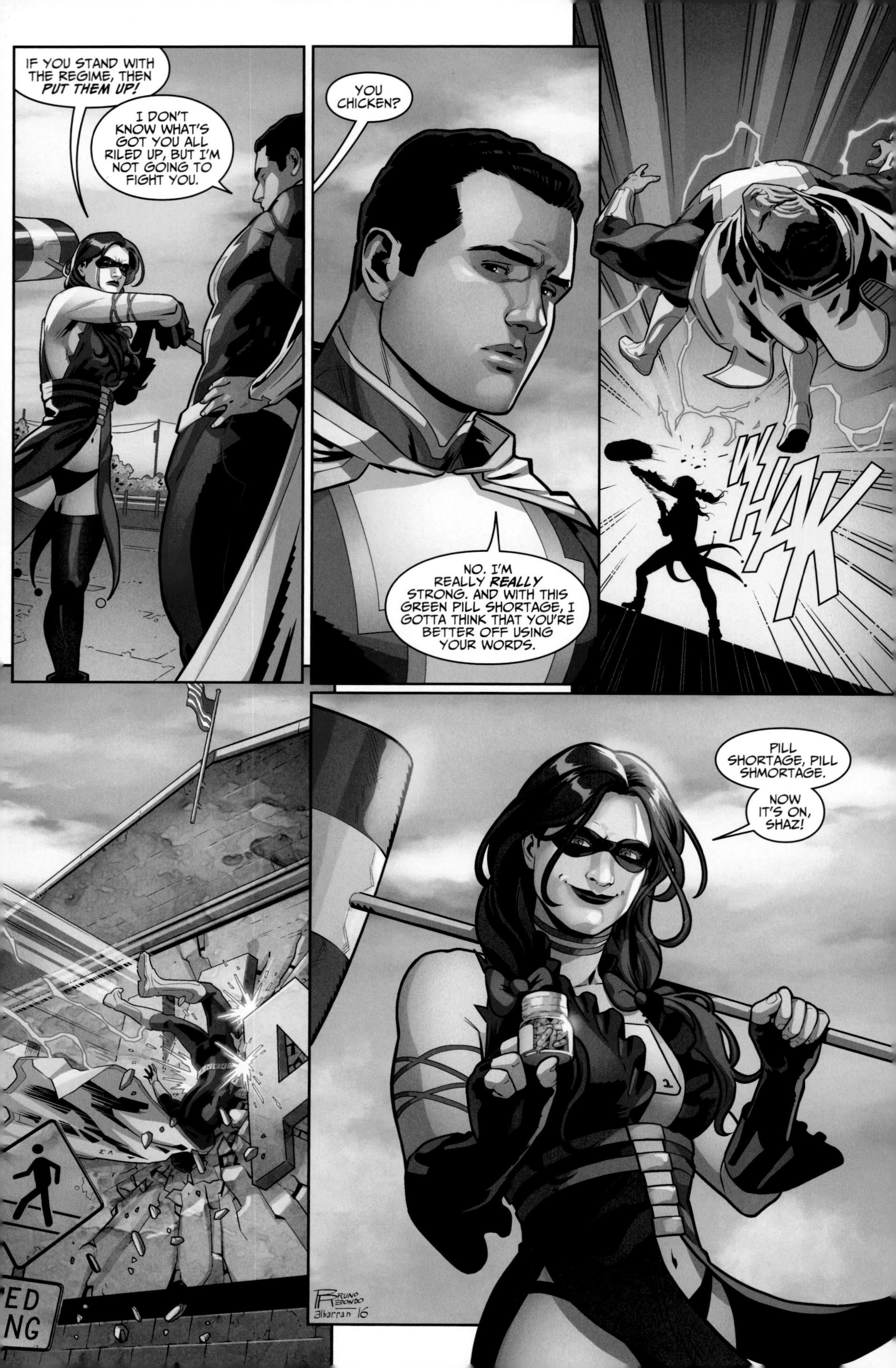
IF YOU STAND WITH THE REGIME, THEN PUT THEM UP!
I DON'T KNOW WHAT'S GOT YOU ALL RILED UP, BUT I'M NOT GOING TO FIGHT YOU.
YOU CHICKEN?
NO. I'M REALLY REALLY STRONG. AND WITH THIS GREEN PILL SHORTAGE, I GOTTA THINK THAT YOU'RE BETTER OFF USING YOUR WORDS.
WHAK
PILL SHORTAGE, PILL SHMORTAGE.
NOW IT'S ON, SHAZ!
BRUNO REDONDO
albarran '16

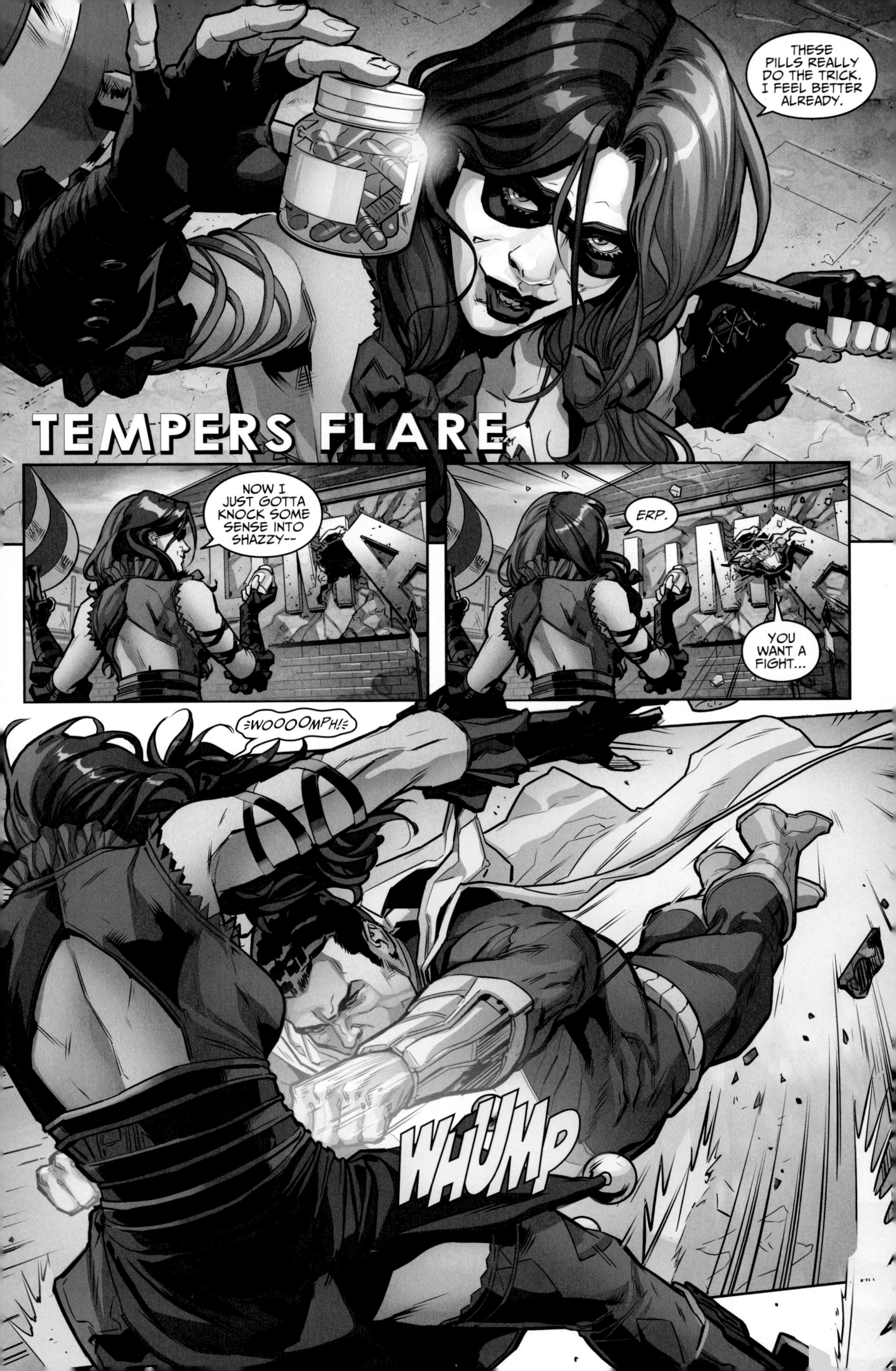

THESE PILLS REALLY DO THE TRICK. I FEEL BETTER ALREADY.
TEMPERS FLARE
NOW I JUST GOTTA KNOCK SOME SENSE INTO SHAZZY--
ERP.
YOU WANT A FIGHT...
WOOOOMPH!
WHUMP

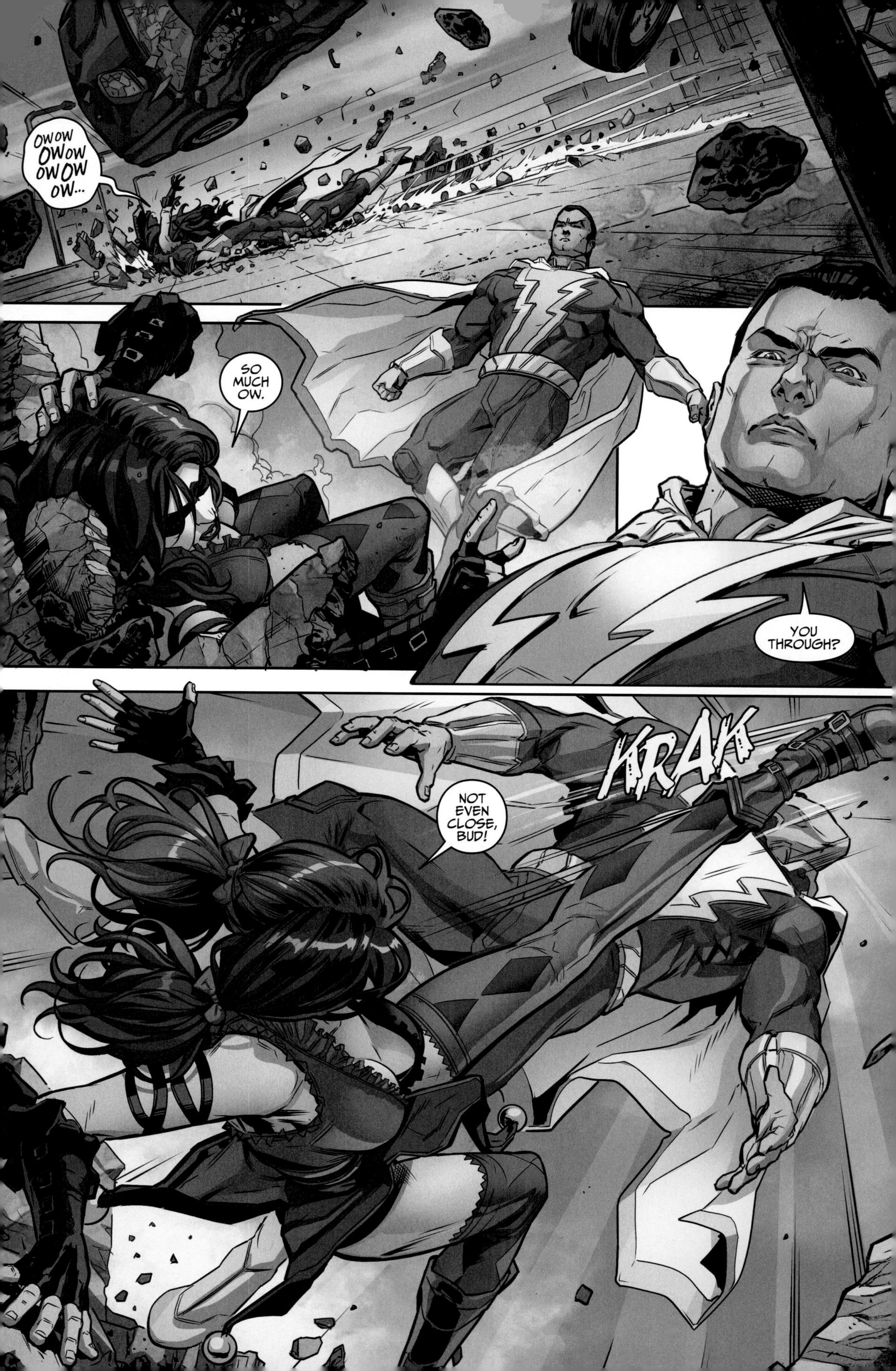
OWOW OWOW OWOW OW...
SO MUCH OW.
YOU THROUGH?
KRAK
NOT EVEN CLOSE, BUD!

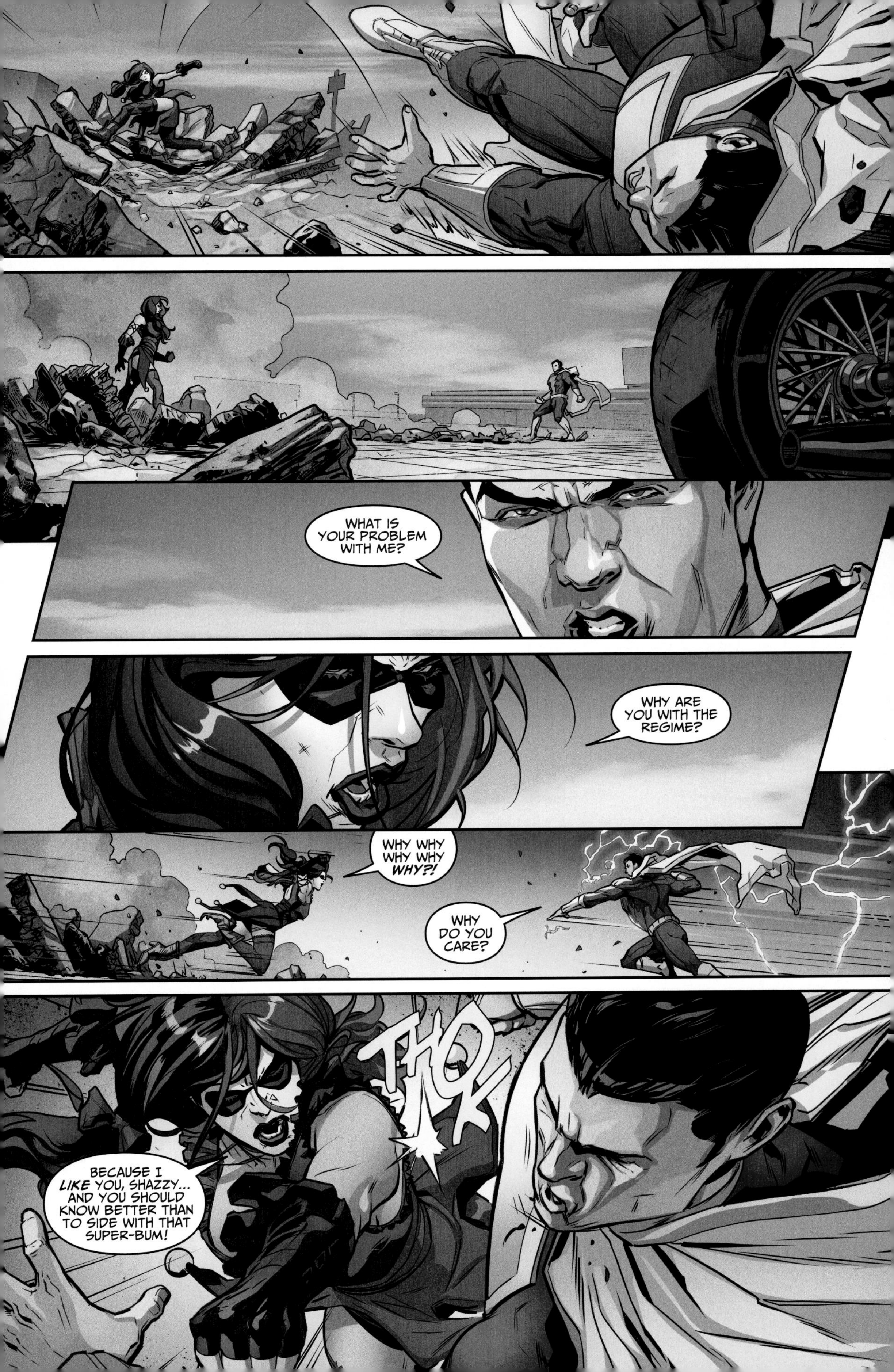
WHAT IS YOUR PROBLEM WITH ME?
WHY ARE YOU WITH THE REGIME?
WHY WHY WHY WHY WHY?!
WHY DO YOU CARE?
THOK
BECAUSE I LIKE YOU, SHAZZY... AND YOU SHOULD KNOW BETTER THAN TO SIDE WITH THAT SUPER-BUM!

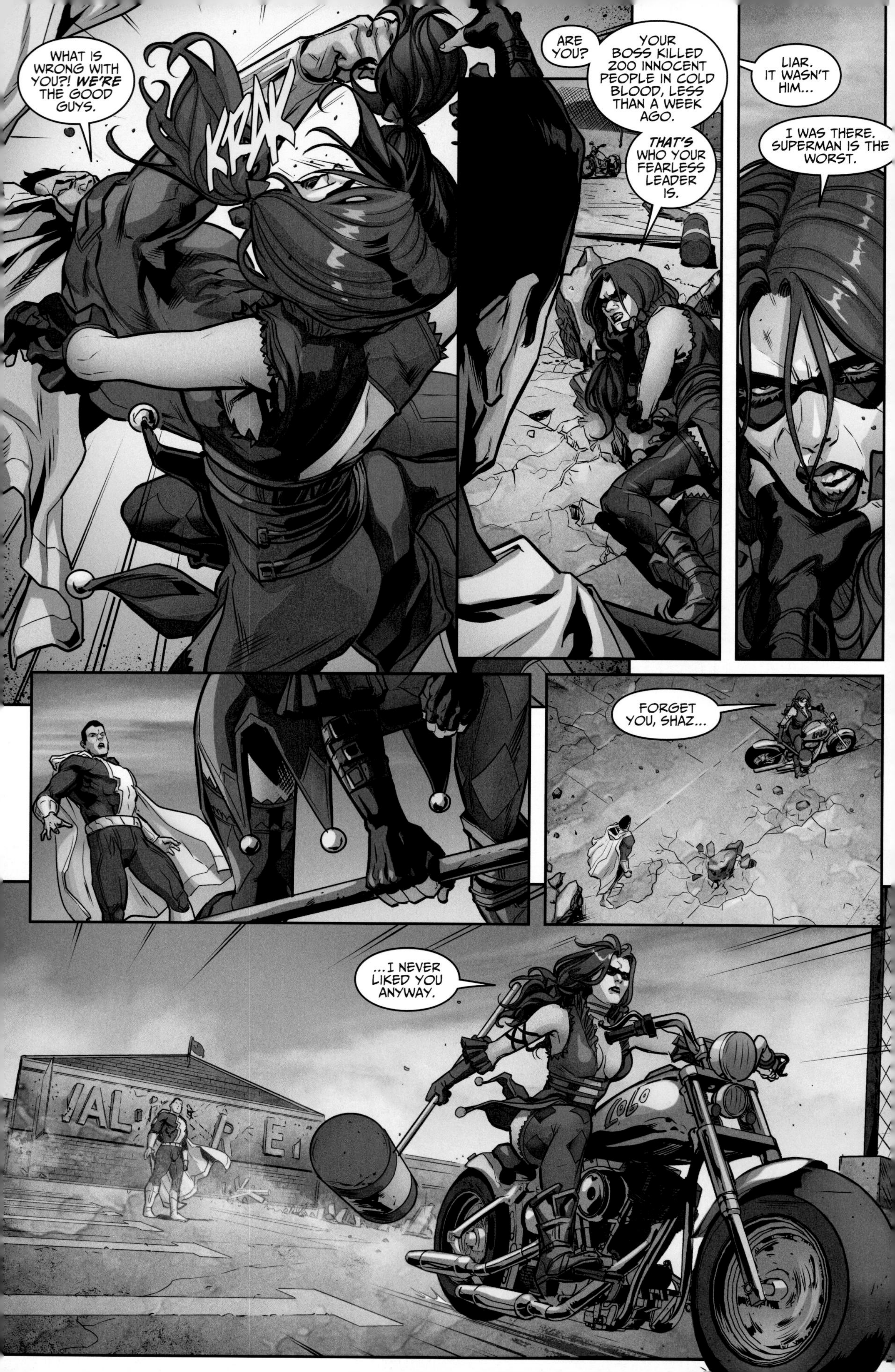
WHAT IS WRONG WITH YOU?! WE'RE THE GOOD GUYS.
KRAK
ARE YOU?
YOUR BOSS KILLED 200 INNOCENT PEOPLE IN COLD BLOOD, LESS THAN A WEEK AGO.
THAT'S WHO YOUR FEARLESS LEADER IS.
LIAR. IT WASN'T HIM...
I WAS THERE. SUPERMAN IS THE WORST.
FORGET YOU, SHAZ...
...I NEVER LIKED YOU ANYWAY.
LOBO

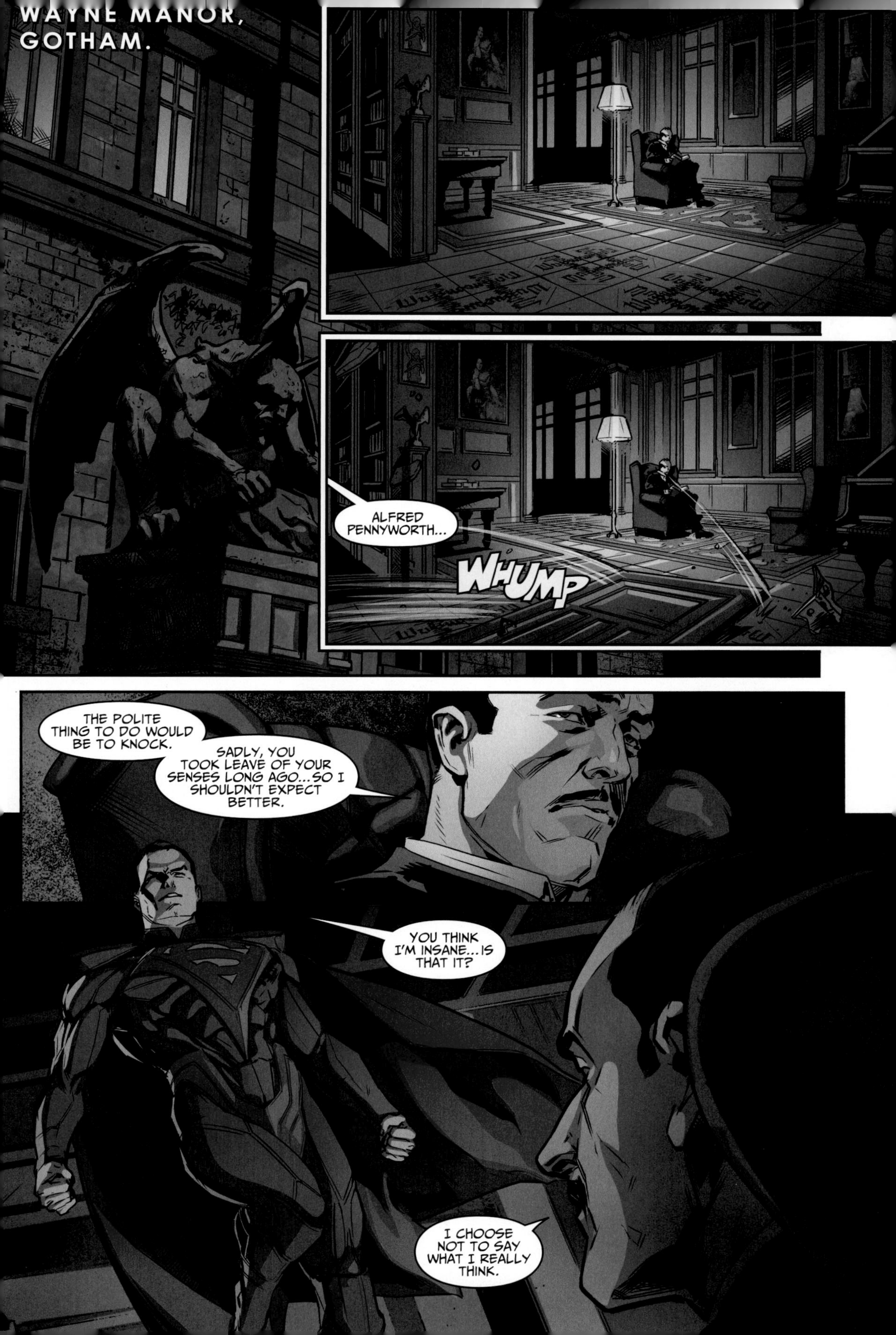
WAYNE MANOR, GOTHAM.
ALFRED PENNYWORTH...
WHUMP
THE POLITE THING TO DO WOULD BE TO KNOCK.
SADLY, YOU TOOK LEAVE OF YOUR SENSES LONG AGO...SO I SHOULDN'T EXPECT BETTER.
YOU THINK I'M INSANE...IS THAT IT?
I CHOOSE NOT TO SAY WHAT I REALLY THINK.

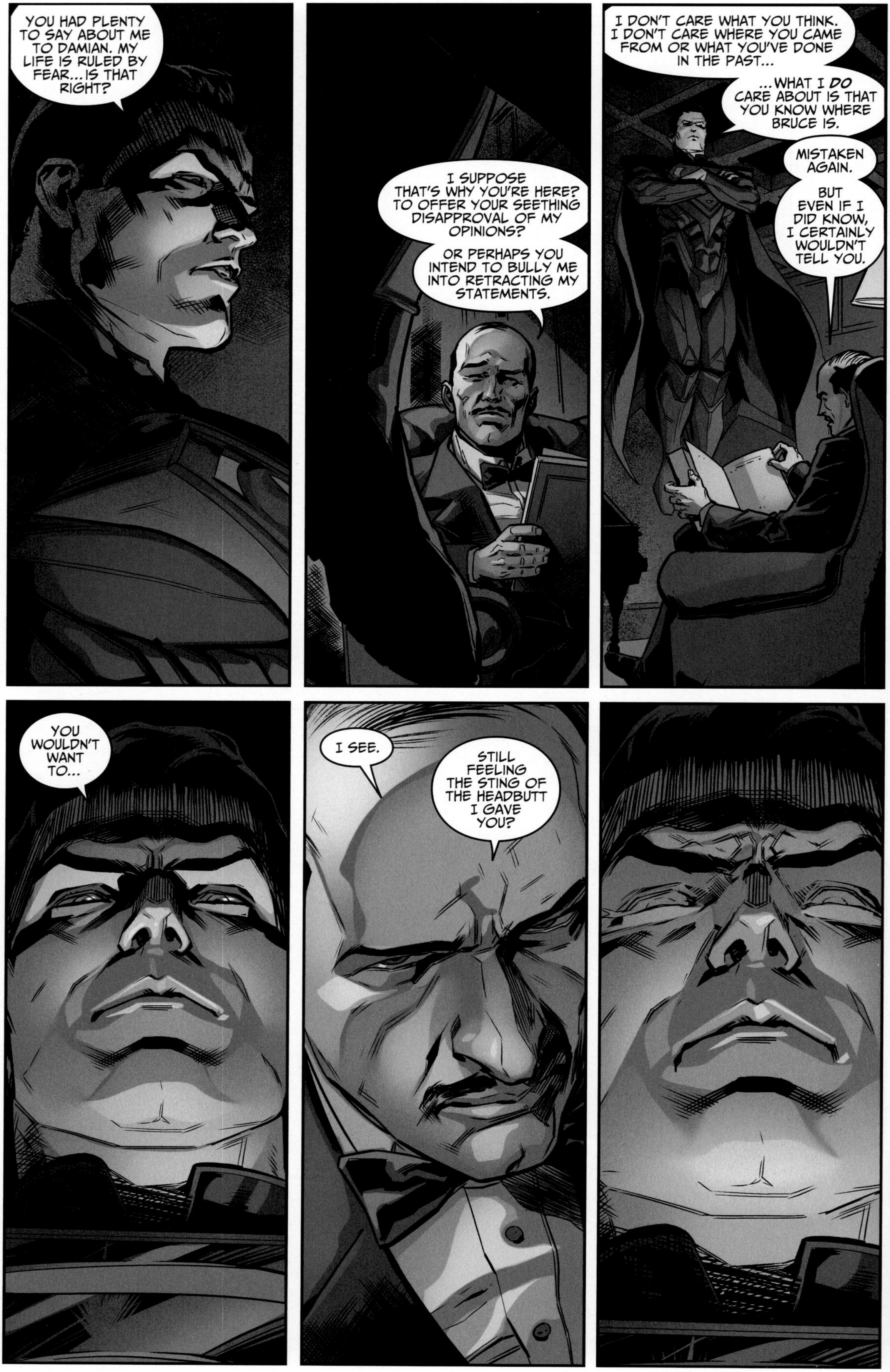

YOU HAD PLENTY TO SAY ABOUT ME TO DAMIAN. MY LIFE IS RULED BY FEAR...IS THAT RIGHT?
I SUPPOSE THAT'S WHY YOU'RE HERE? TO OFFER YOUR SEETHING DISAPPROVAL OF MY OPINIONS?
OR PERHAPS YOU INTEND TO BULLY ME INTO RETRACTING MY STATEMENTS.
I DON'T CARE WHAT YOU THINK. I DON'T CARE WHERE YOU CAME FROM OR WHAT YOU'VE DONE IN THE PAST...
...WHAT I DO CARE ABOUT IS THAT YOU KNOW WHERE BRUCE IS.
MISTAKEN AGAIN.
BUT EVEN IF I DID KNOW, I CERTAINLY WOULDN'T TELL YOU.
YOU WOULDN'T WANT TO...
I SEE.
STILL FEELING THE STING OF THE HEADBUTT I GAVE YOU?

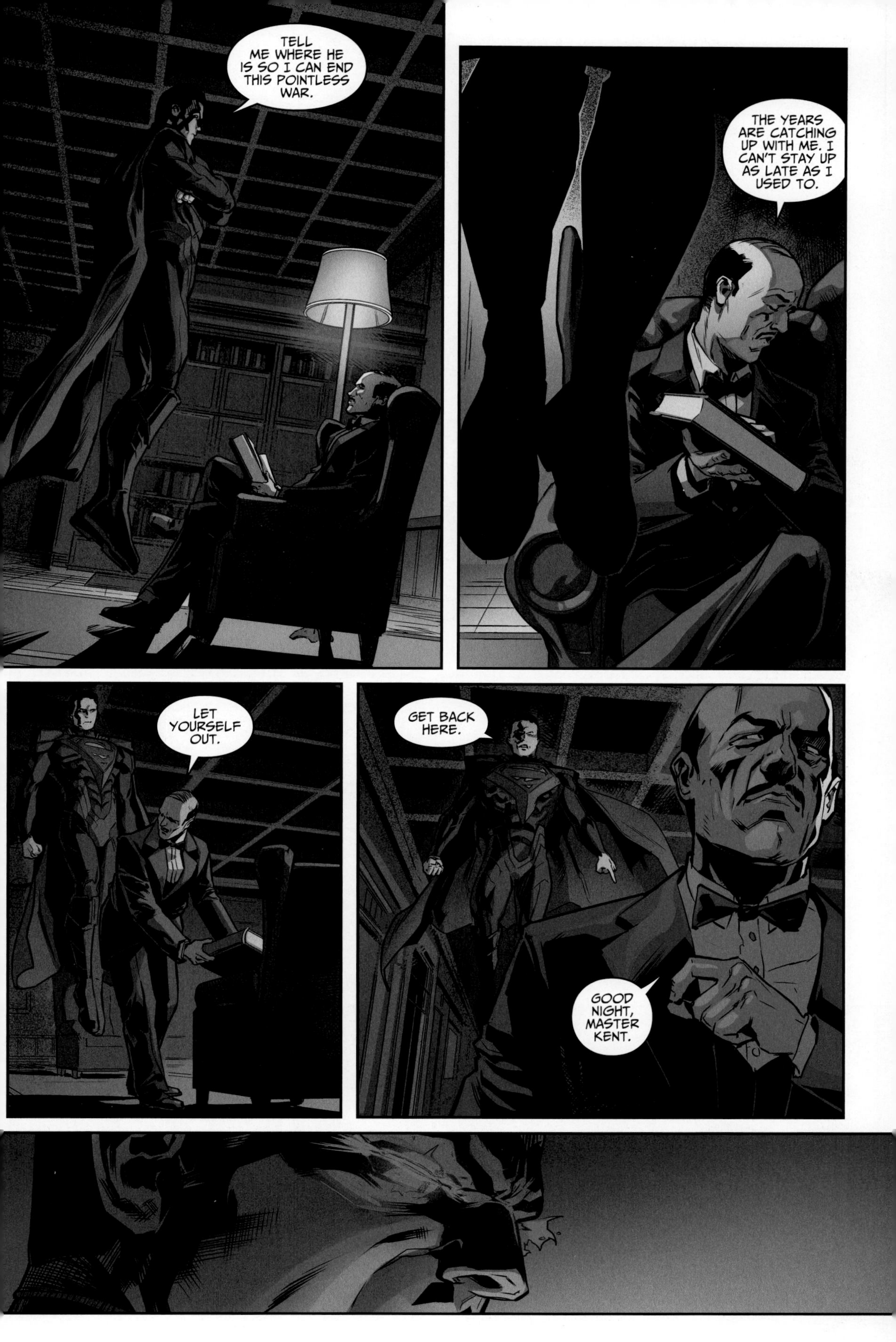
TELL ME WHERE HE IS SO I CAN END THIS POINTLESS WAR.
THE YEARS ARE CATCHING UP WITH ME. I CAN'T STAY UP AS LATE AS I USED TO.
LET YOURSELF OUT.
GET BACK HERE.
GOOD NIGHT, MASTER KENT.

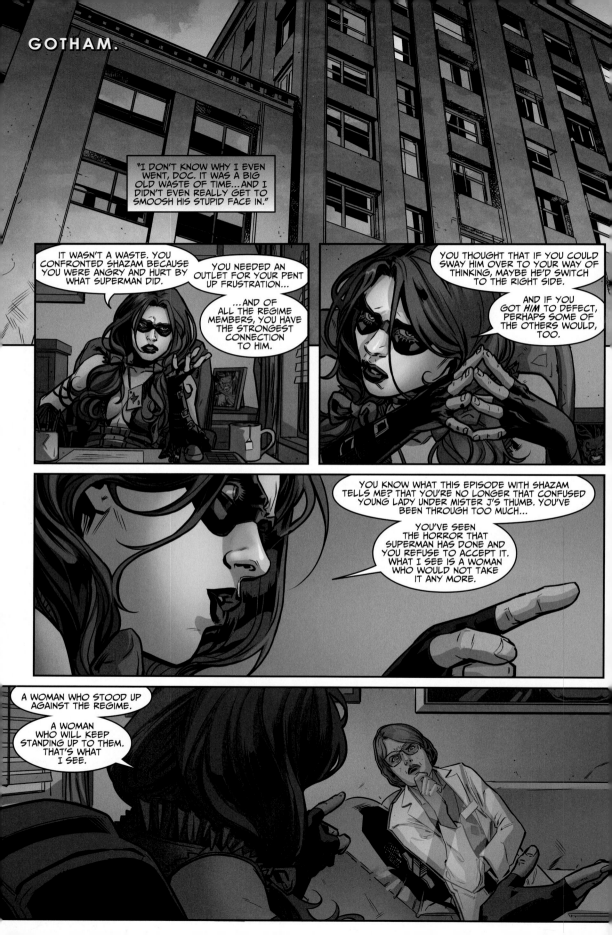

"I DON'T KNOW WHY I EVEN WENT, DOC. IT WAS A BIG OLD WASTE OF TIME... AND I DIDN'T EVEN REALLY GET TO SMOOSH HIS STUPID FACE IN."

IT WASN'T A WASTE. YOU CONFRONTED SHAZAM BECAUSE YOU WERE ANGRY AND HURT BY WHAT SUPERMAN DID.

YOU NEEDED AN OUTLET FOR YOUR PENT UP FRUSTRATION...

...AND OF ALL THE REGIME MEMBERS, YOU HAVE THE STRONGEST CONNECTION TO HIM.

YOU THOUGHT THAT IF YOU COULD SWAY HIM OVER TO YOUR WAY OF THINKING, MAYBE HE'D SWITCH TO THE RIGHT SIDE.

AND IF YOU GOT *HIM* TO DEFECT, PERHAPS SOME OF THE OTHERS WOULD, TOO.

YOU KNOW WHAT THIS EPISODE WITH SHAZAM TELLS ME? THAT YOU'RE NO LONGER THAT CONFUSED YOUNG LADY UNDER MISTER J'S THUMB. YOU'VE BEEN THROUGH TOO MUCH...

YOU'VE SEEN THE HORROR THAT SUPERMAN HAS DONE AND YOU REFUSE TO ACCEPT IT. WHAT I SEE IS A WOMAN WHO WOULD NOT TAKE IT ANY MORE.

A WOMAN WHO STOOD UP AGAINST THE REGIME.

A WOMAN WHO WILL KEEP STANDING UP TO THEM. THAT'S WHAT I SEE.

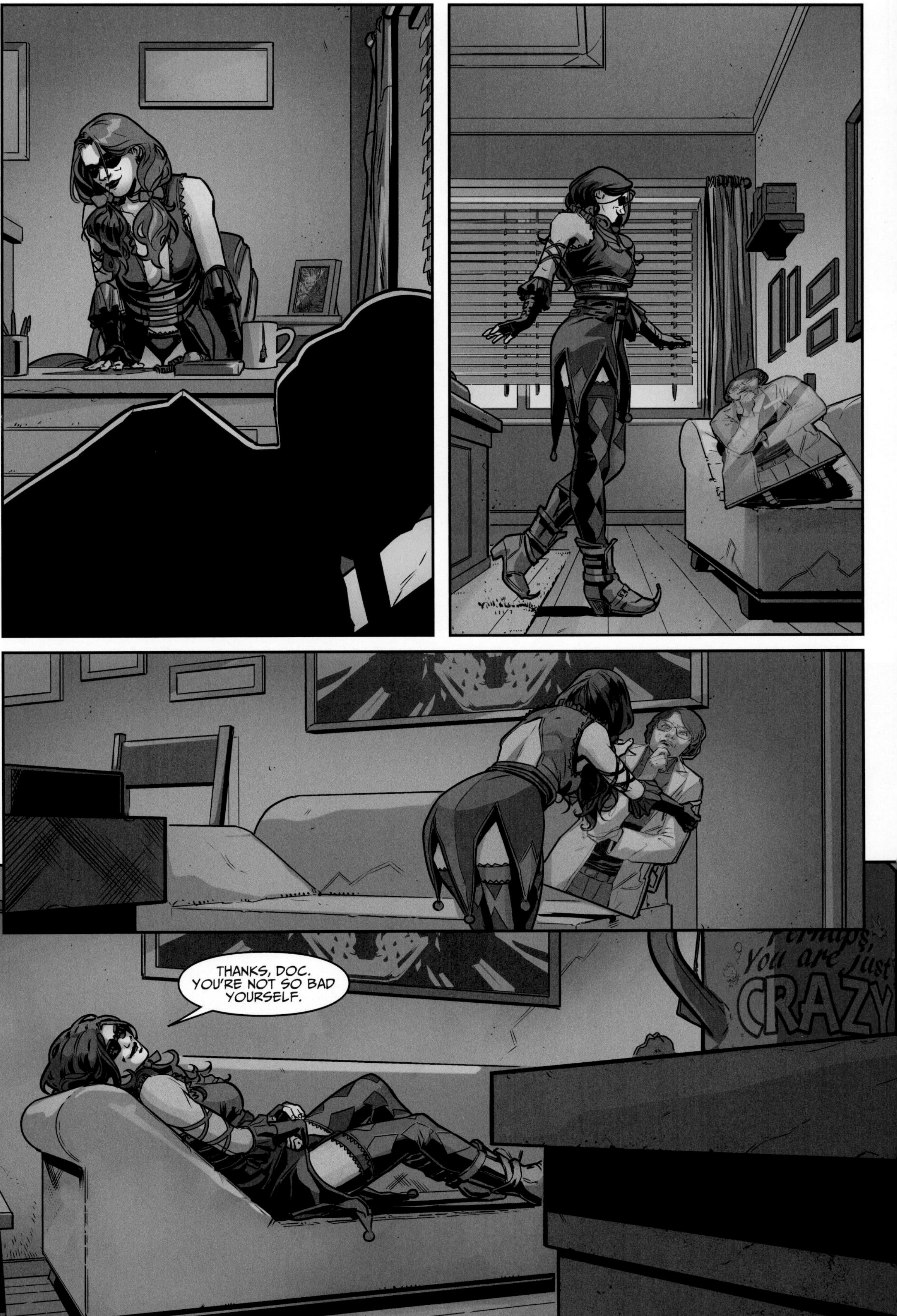
THANKS, DOC. YOU'RE NOT SO BAD YOURSELF.

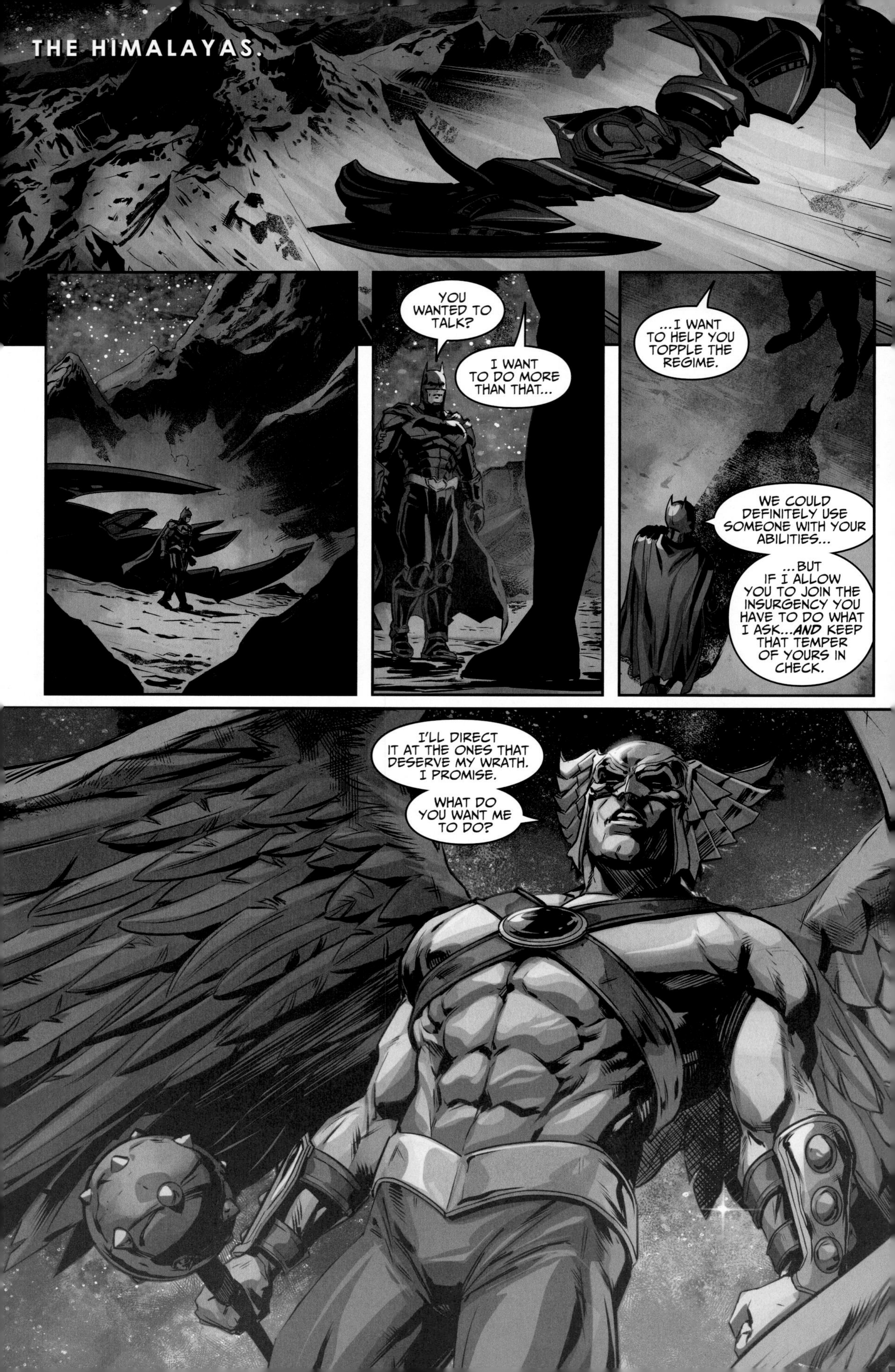
THE HIMALAYAS.
YOU WANTED TO TALK?
I WANT TO DO MORE THAN THAT...
...I WANT TO HELP YOU TOPPLE THE REGIME.
WE COULD DEFINITELY USE SOMEONE WITH YOUR ABILITIES...
...BUT IF I ALLOW YOU TO JOIN THE INSURGENCY YOU HAVE TO DO WHAT I ASK...AND KEEP THAT TEMPER OF YOURS IN CHECK.
I'LL DIRECT IT AT THE ONES THAT DESERVE MY WRATH. I PROMISE.
WHAT DO YOU WANT ME TO DO?

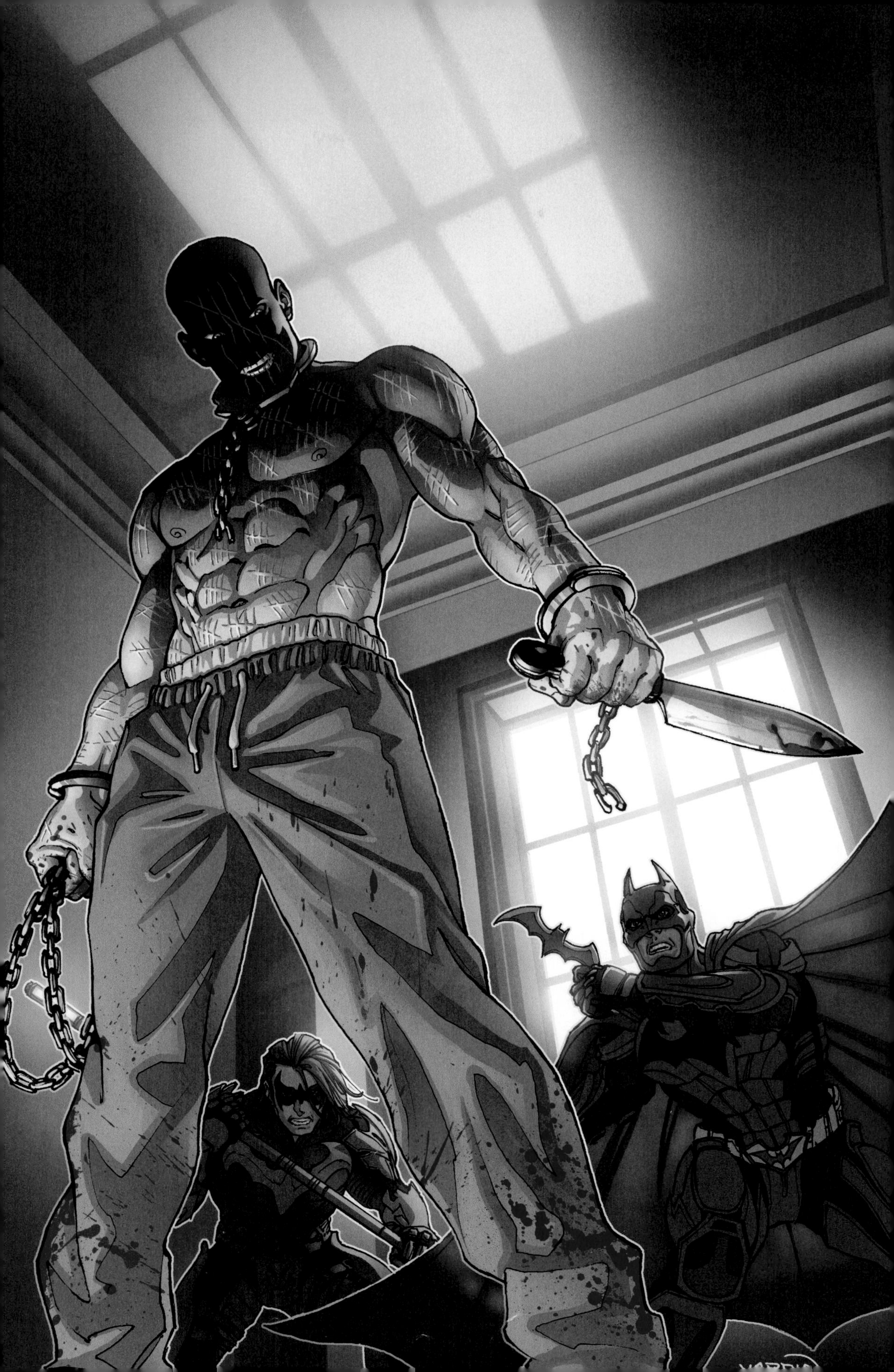

"Birthday" **Marco Santucci** Artist **Rex Lokus** Colorist

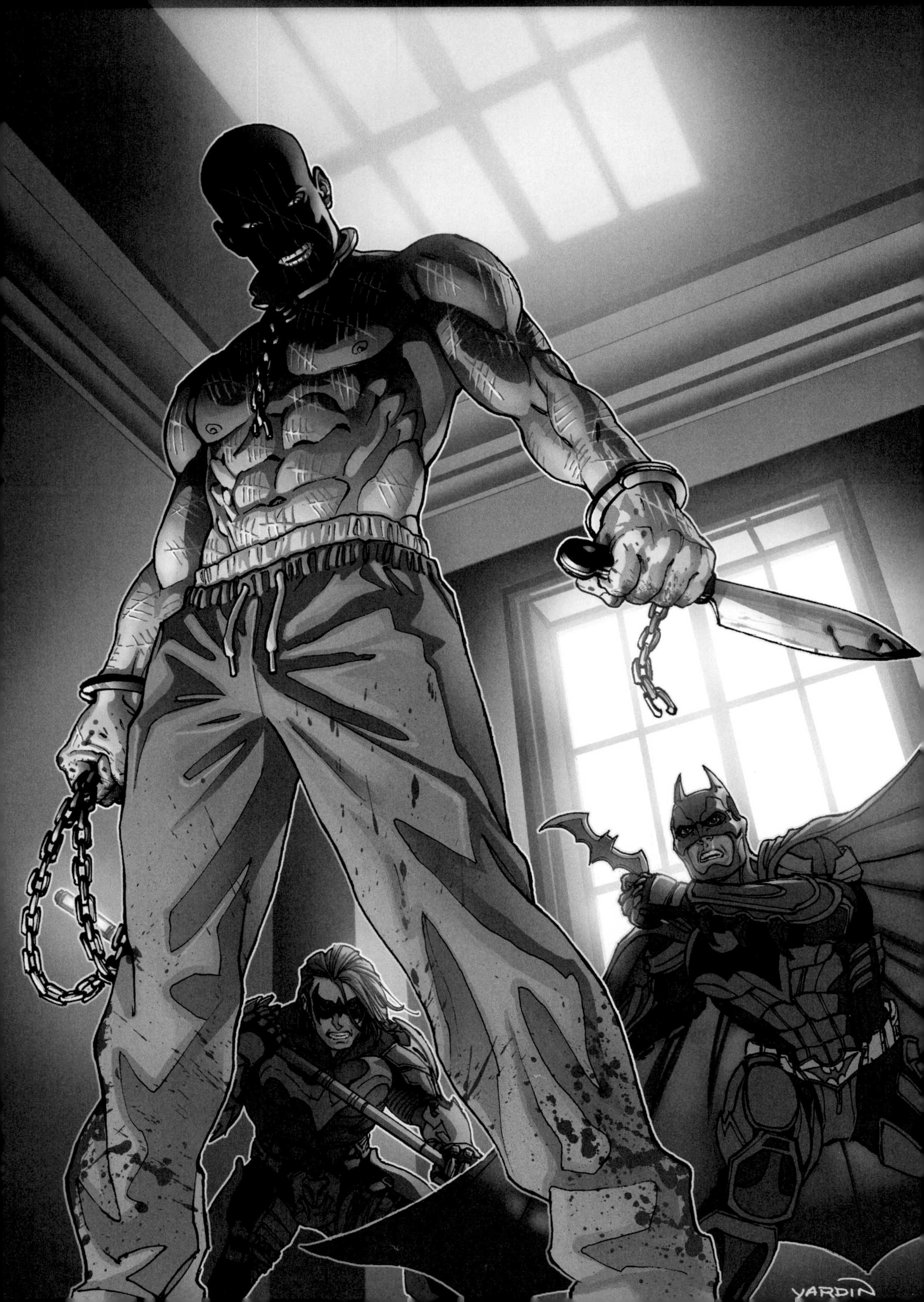
YARDIN

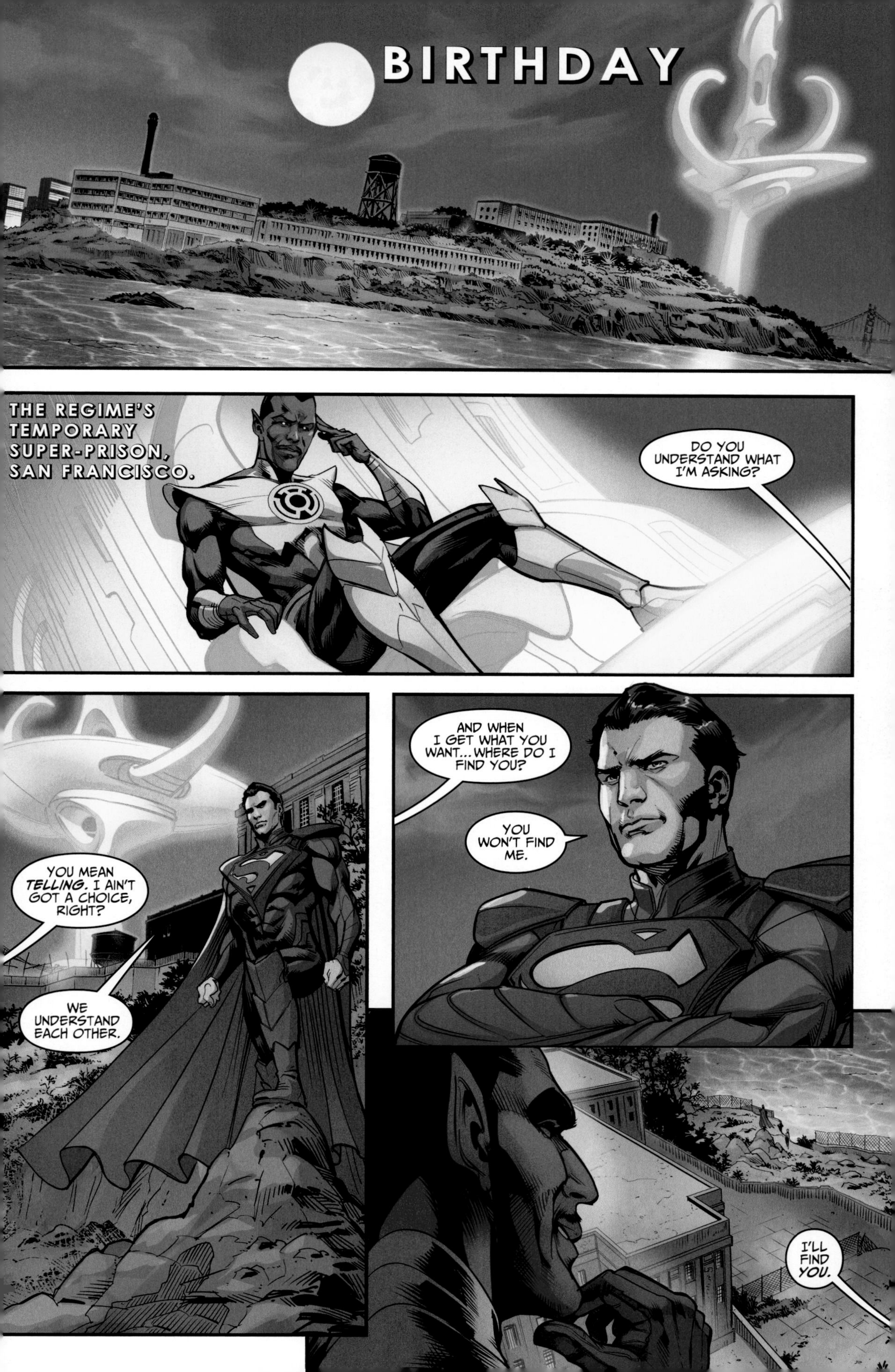
BIRTHDAY
THE REGIME'S TEMPORARY SUPER-PRISON, SAN FRANCISCO.
DO YOU UNDERSTAND WHAT I'M ASKING?
YOU MEAN *TELLING*. I AIN'T GOT A CHOICE, RIGHT?
WE UNDERSTAND EACH OTHER.
AND WHEN I GET WHAT YOU WANT... WHERE DO I FIND YOU?
YOU WON'T FIND ME.
I'LL FIND *YOU*.

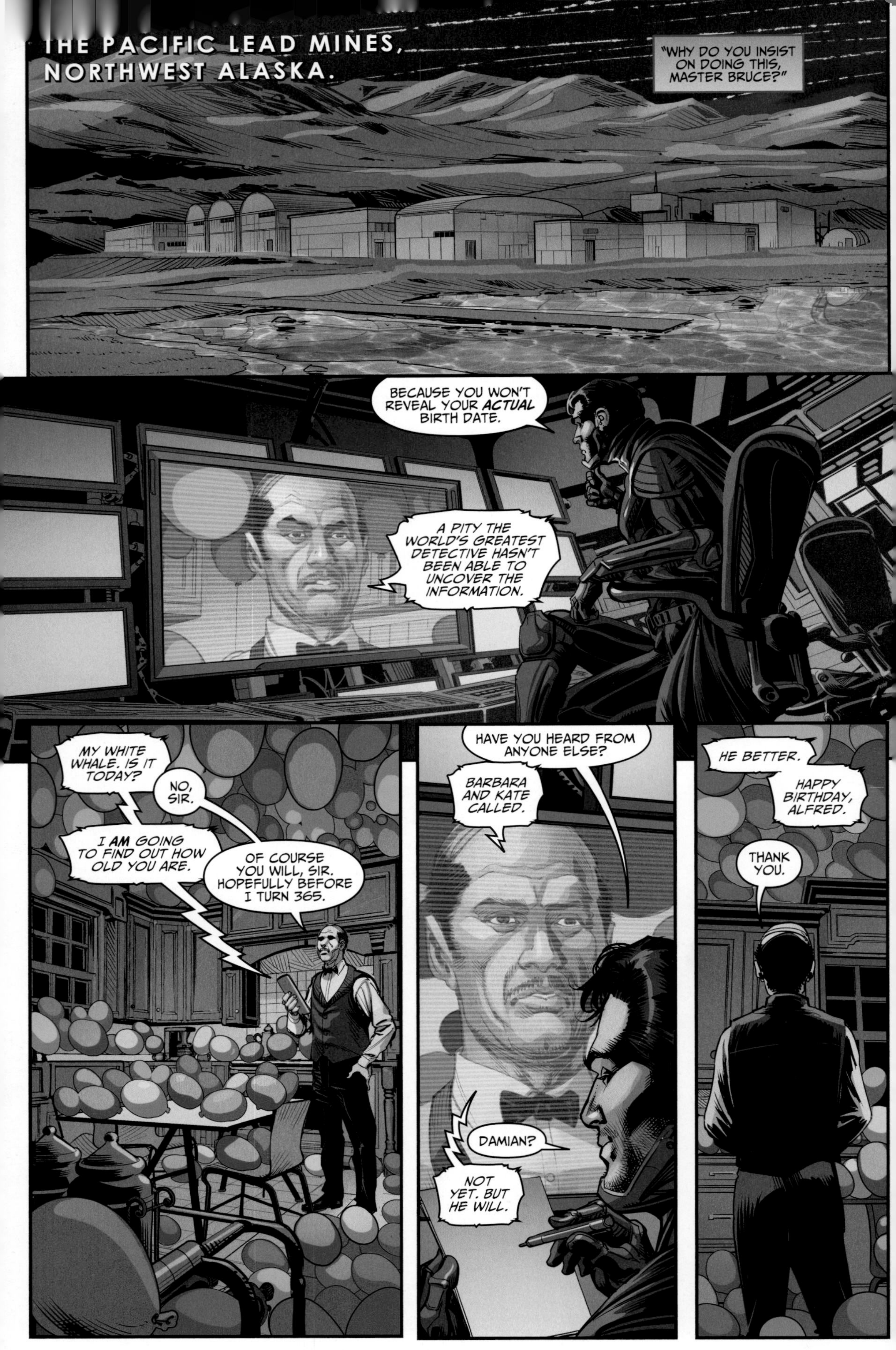
THE PACIFIC LEAD MINES, NORTHWEST ALASKA.
"WHY DO YOU INSIST ON DOING THIS, MASTER BRUCE?"
BECAUSE YOU WON'T REVEAL YOUR ACTUAL BIRTH DATE.
A PITY THE WORLD'S GREATEST DETECTIVE HASN'T BEEN ABLE TO UNCOVER THE INFORMATION.
MY WHITE WHALE. IS IT TODAY?
NO, SIR.
I AM GOING TO FIND OUT HOW OLD YOU ARE.
OF COURSE YOU WILL, SIR. HOPEFULLY BEFORE I TURN 365.
HAVE YOU HEARD FROM ANYONE ELSE?
BARBARA AND KATE CALLED.
DAMIAN?
NOT YET. BUT HE WILL.
HE BETTER.
HAPPY BIRTHDAY, ALFRED.
THANK YOU.

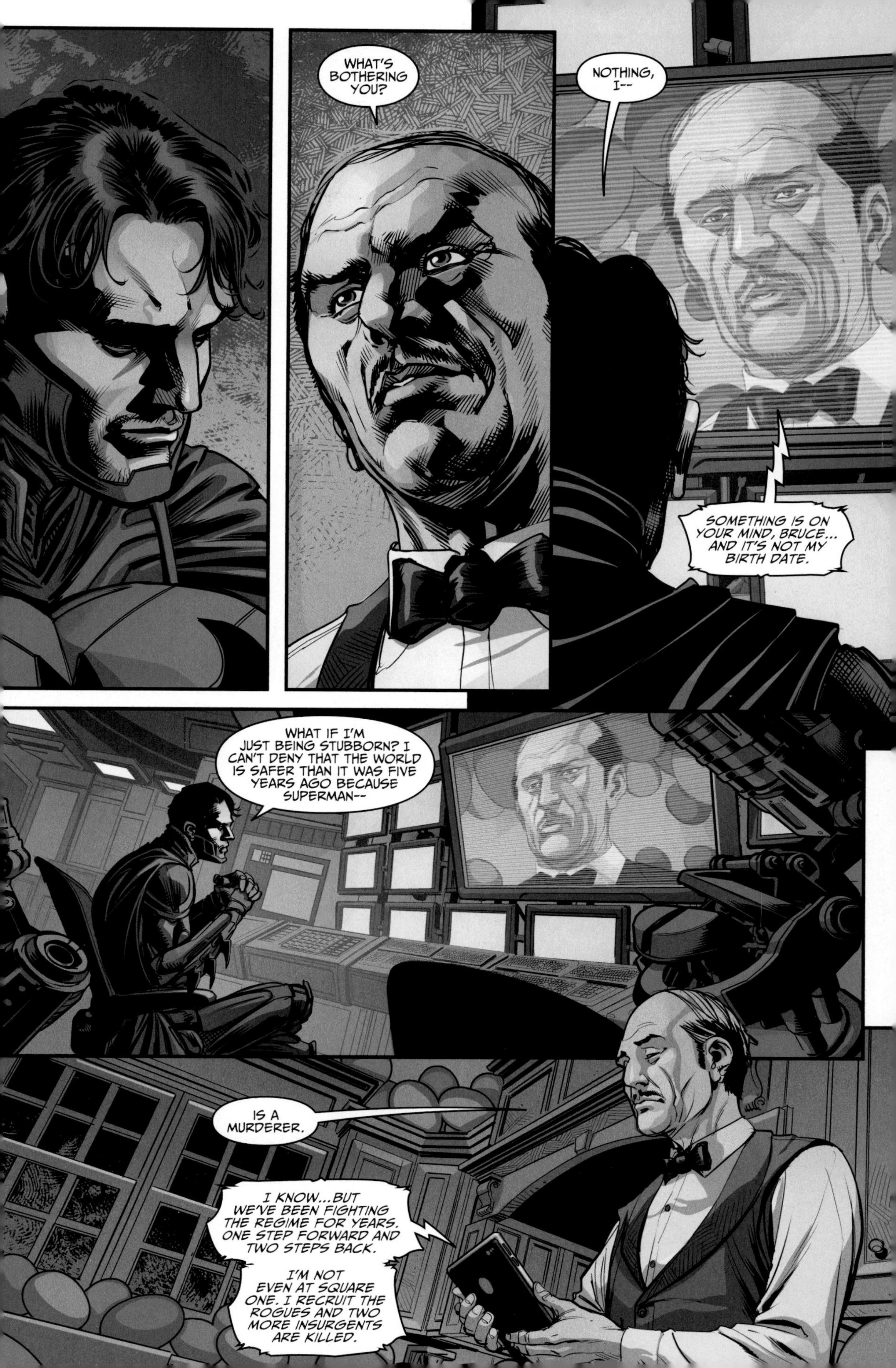
WHAT'S BOTHERING YOU?
NOTHING, I--
SOMETHING IS ON YOUR MIND, BRUCE... AND IT'S NOT MY BIRTH DATE.
WHAT IF I'M JUST BEING STUBBORN? I CAN'T DENY THAT THE WORLD IS SAFER THAN IT WAS FIVE YEARS AGO BECAUSE SUPERMAN--
IS A MURDERER.
I KNOW...BUT WE'VE BEEN FIGHTING THE REGIME FOR YEARS. ONE STEP FORWARD AND TWO STEPS BACK.
I'M NOT EVEN AT SQUARE ONE. I RECRUIT THE ROGUES AND TWO MORE INSURGENTS ARE KILLED.

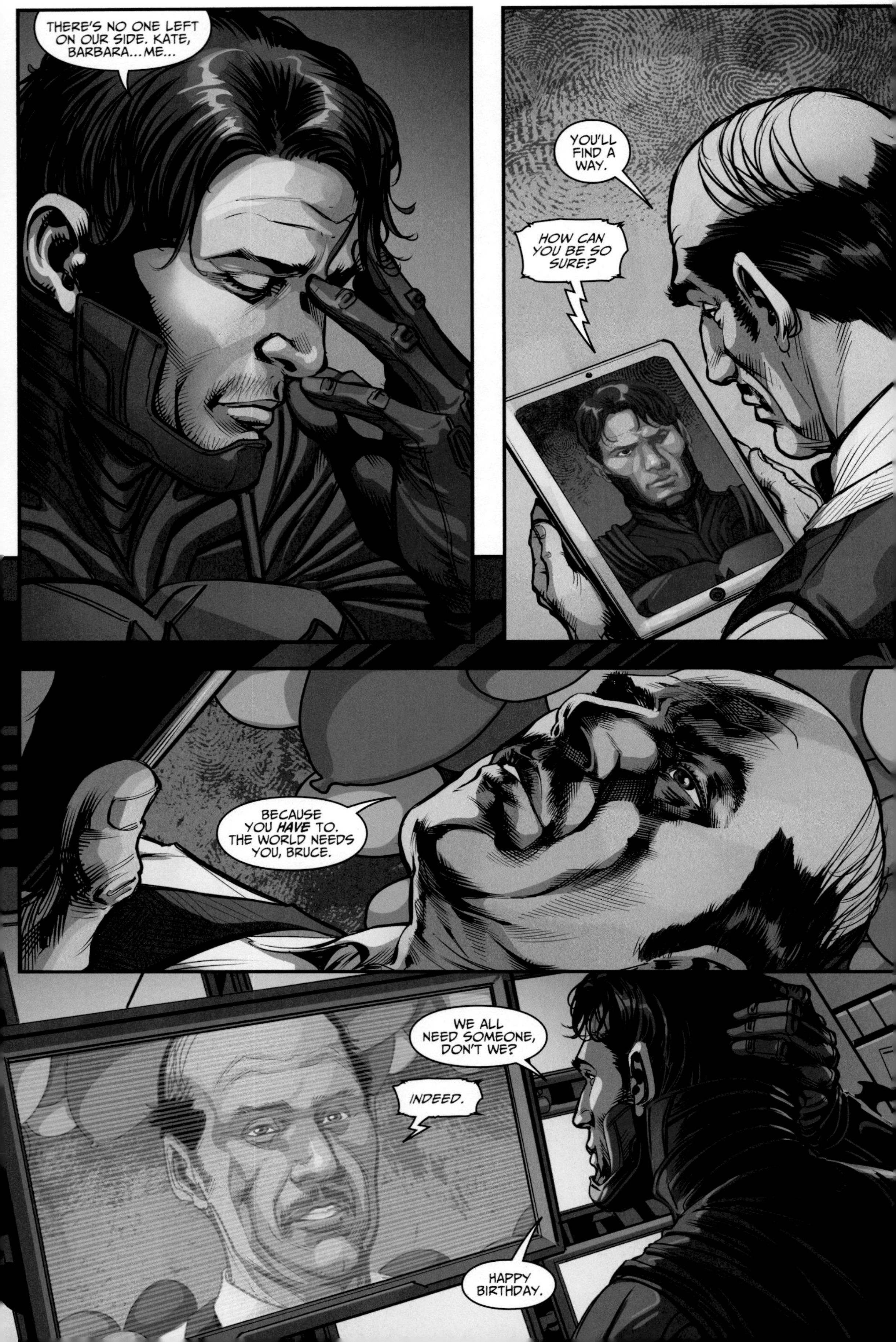
THERE'S NO ONE LEFT ON OUR SIDE. KATE, BARBARA...ME...
YOU'LL FIND A WAY.
HOW CAN YOU BE SO SURE?
BECAUSE YOU *HAVE* TO. THE WORLD NEEDS YOU, BRUCE.
WE ALL NEED SOMEONE, DON'T WE?
INDEED.
HAPPY BIRTHDAY.

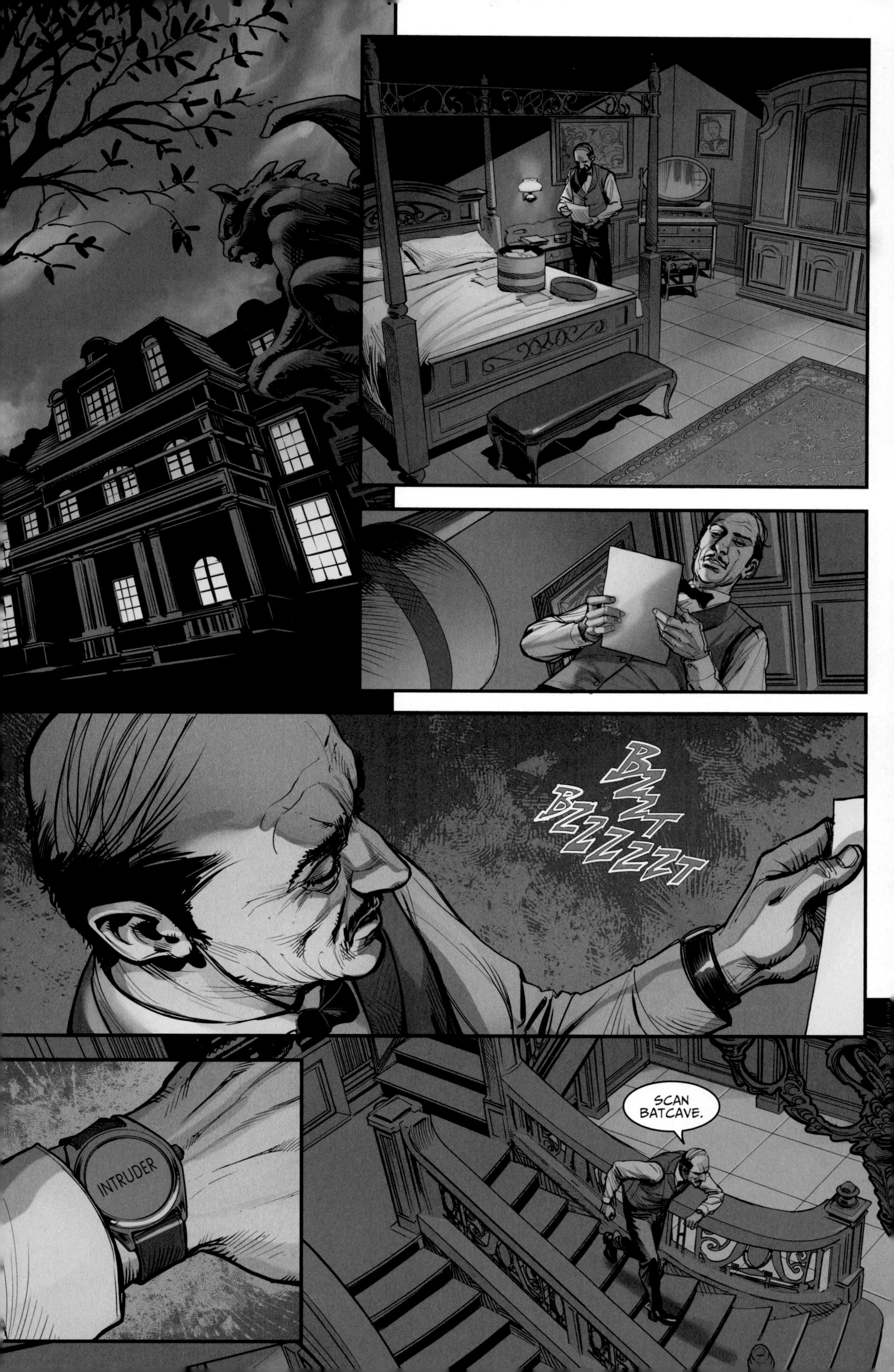
BZZT
BZZZZZZT
INTRUDER
SCAN BATCAVE.

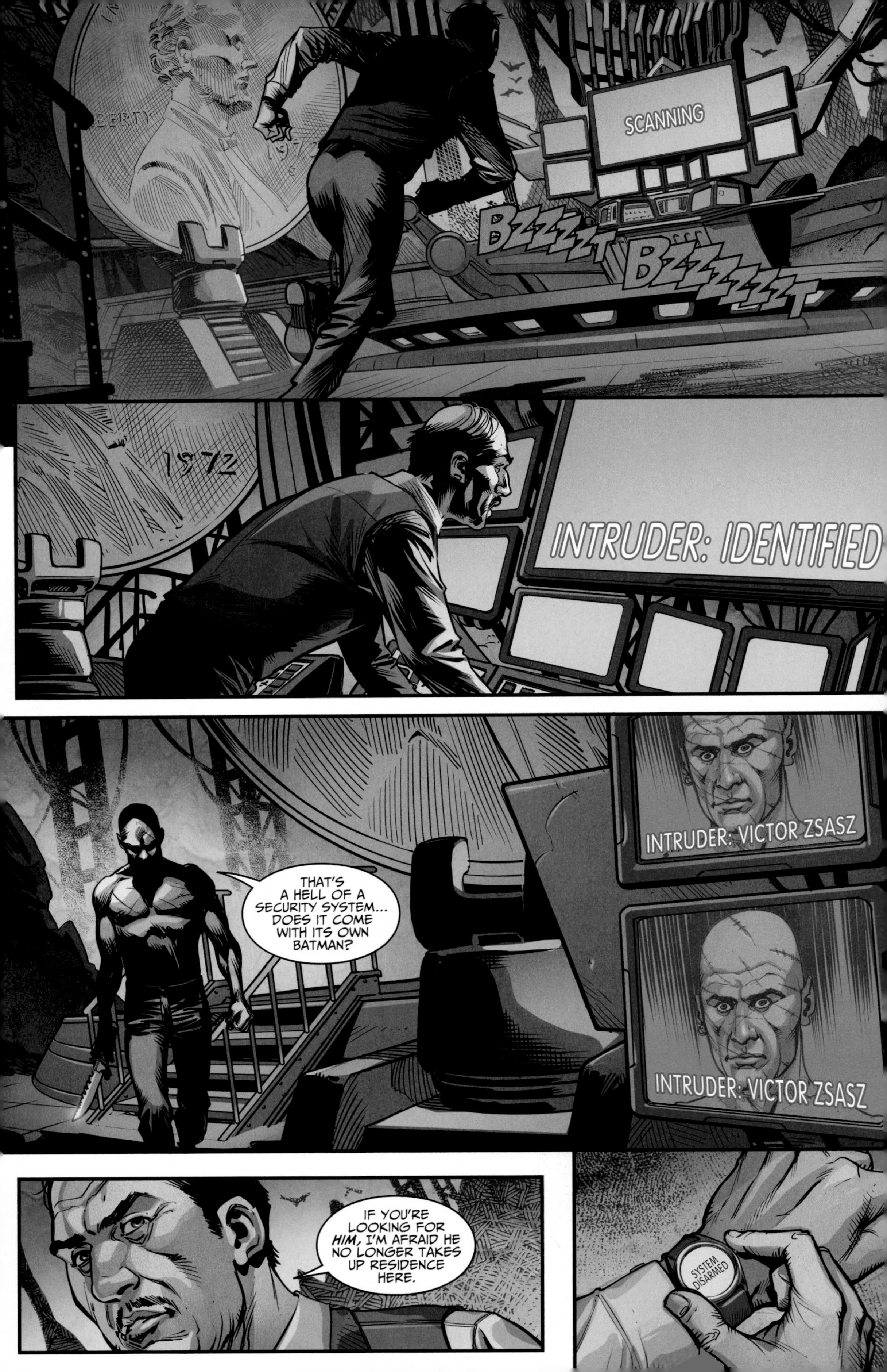
SCANNING
BZZZZT
BZZZZZZT
INTRUDER: IDENTIFIED
INTRUDER: VICTOR ZSASZ
INTRUDER: VICTOR ZSASZ
THAT'S A HELL OF A SECURITY SYSTEM... DOES IT COME WITH ITS OWN BATMAN?
IF YOU'RE LOOKING FOR *HIM*, I'M AFRAID HE NO LONGER TAKES UP RESIDENCE HERE.
SYSTEM DISARMED

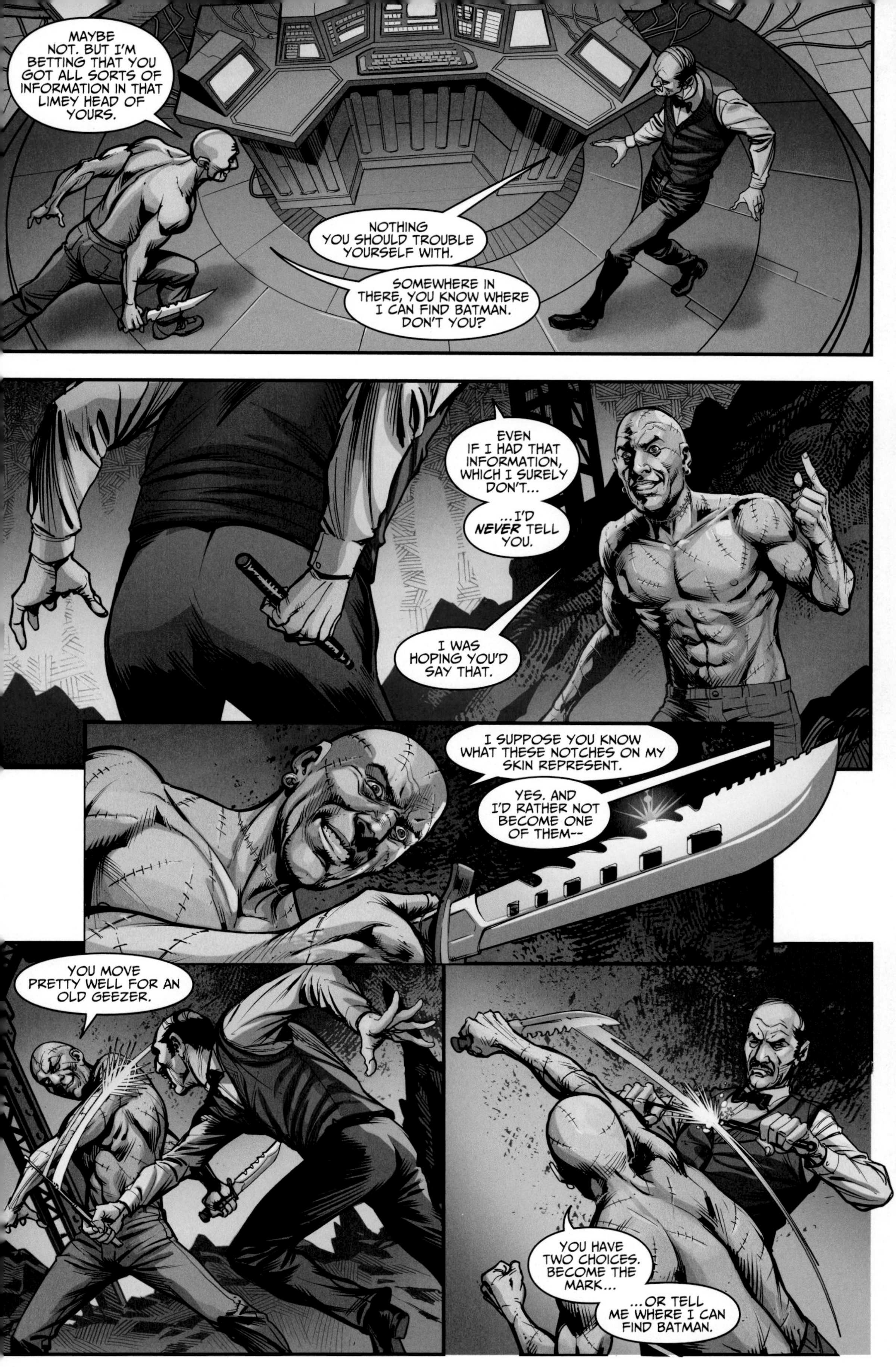
MAYBE NOT. BUT I'M BETTING THAT YOU GOT ALL SORTS OF INFORMATION IN THAT LIMEY HEAD OF YOURS.
NOTHING YOU SHOULD TROUBLE YOURSELF WITH.
SOMEWHERE IN THERE, YOU KNOW WHERE I CAN FIND BATMAN. DON'T YOU?
EVEN IF I HAD THAT INFORMATION, WHICH I SURELY DON'T...
...I'D NEVER TELL YOU.
I WAS HOPING YOU'D SAY THAT.
I SUPPOSE YOU KNOW WHAT THESE NOTCHES ON MY SKIN REPRESENT.
YES. AND I'D RATHER NOT BECOME ONE OF THEM--
YOU MOVE PRETTY WELL FOR AN OLD GEEZER.
YOU HAVE TWO CHOICES. BECOME THE MARK...
...OR TELL ME WHERE I CAN FIND BATMAN.

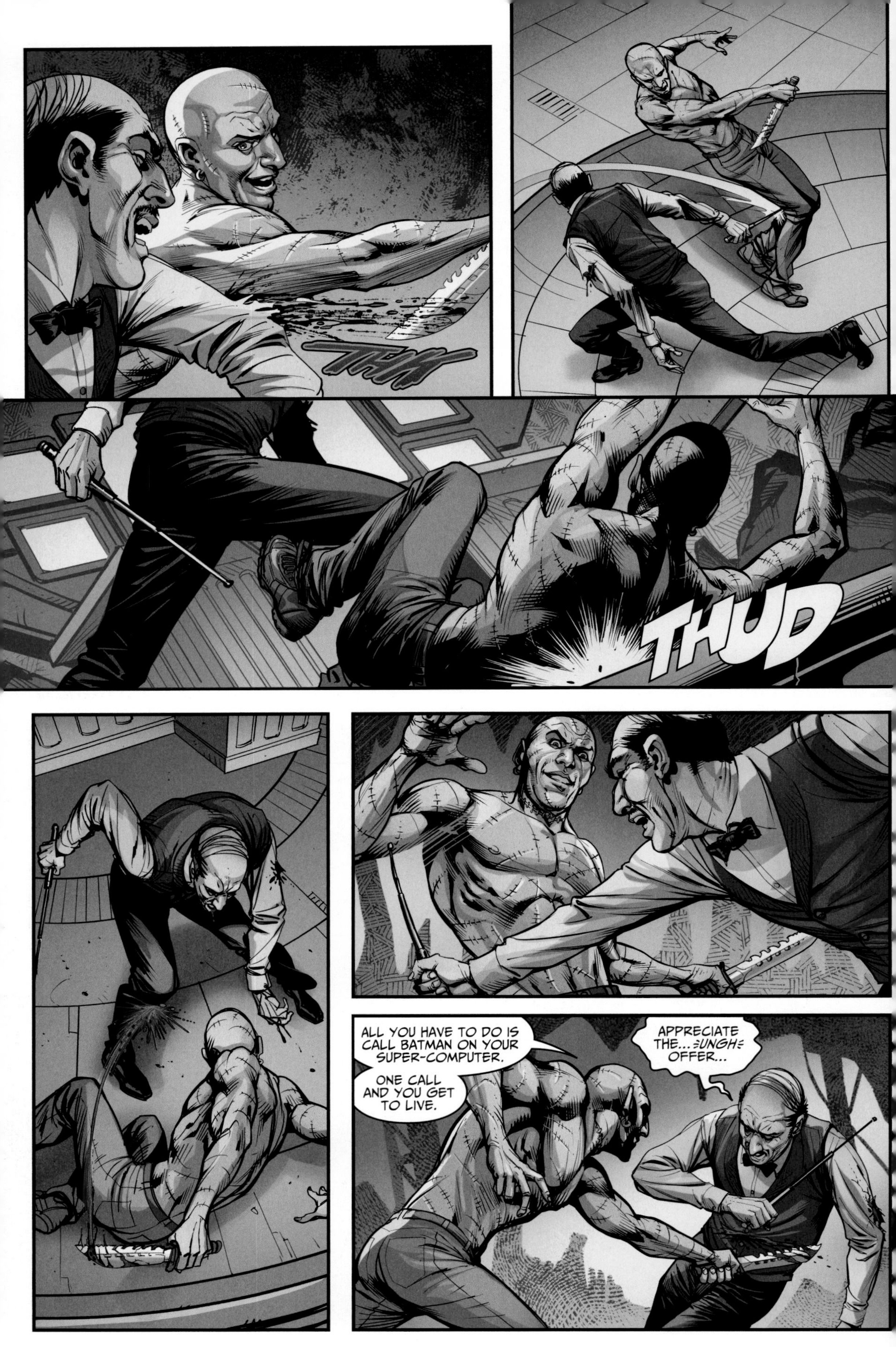
THK
THUD
ALL YOU HAVE TO DO IS CALL BATMAN ON YOUR SUPER-COMPUTER.
ONE CALL AND YOU GET TO LIVE.
APPRECIATE THE... =UNGH= OFFER...

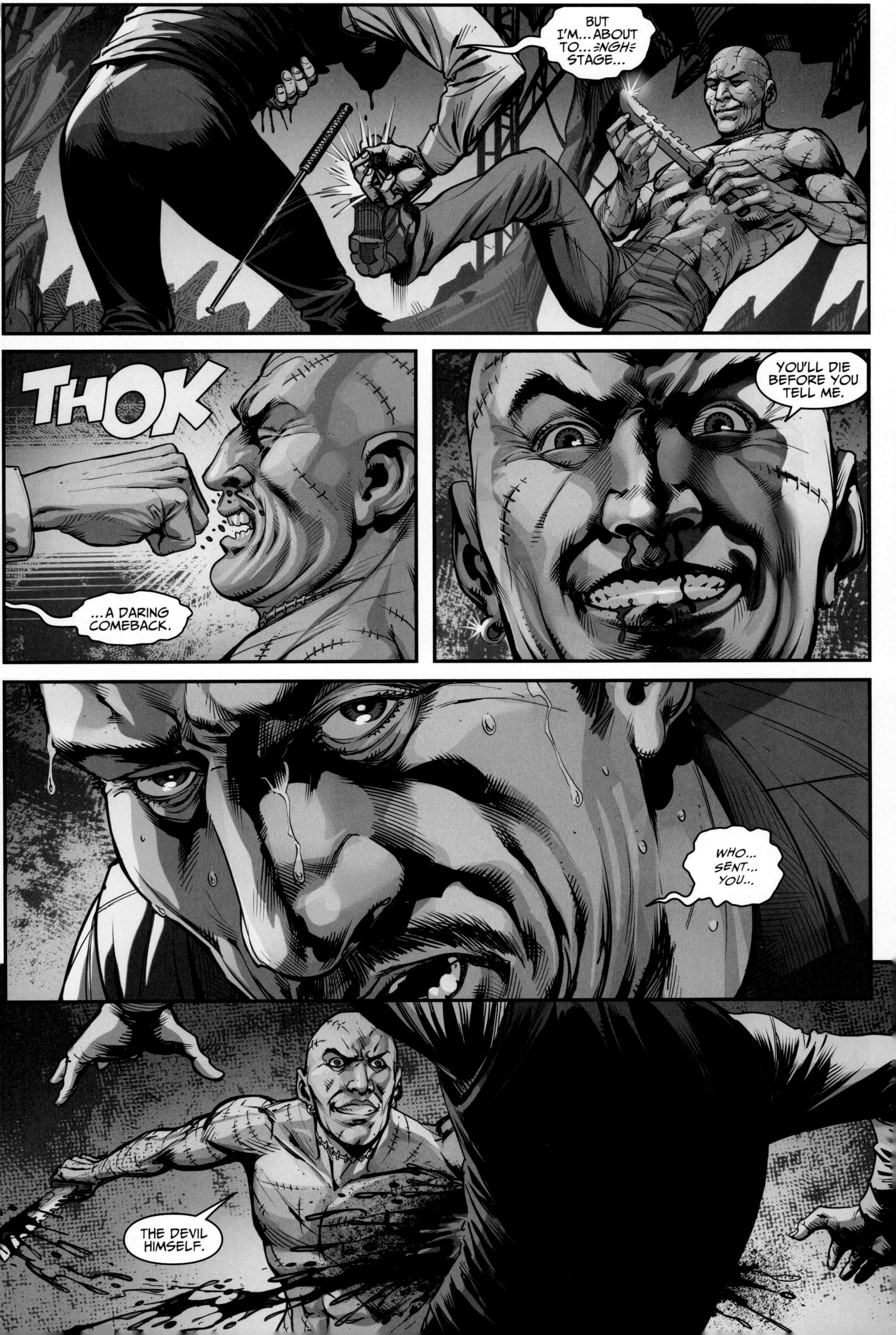
BUT I'M... ABOUT TO... NGH STAGE...
THOK
...A DARING COMEBACK.
YOU'LL DIE BEFORE YOU TELL ME.
WHO... SENT... YOU...
THE DEVIL HIMSELF.

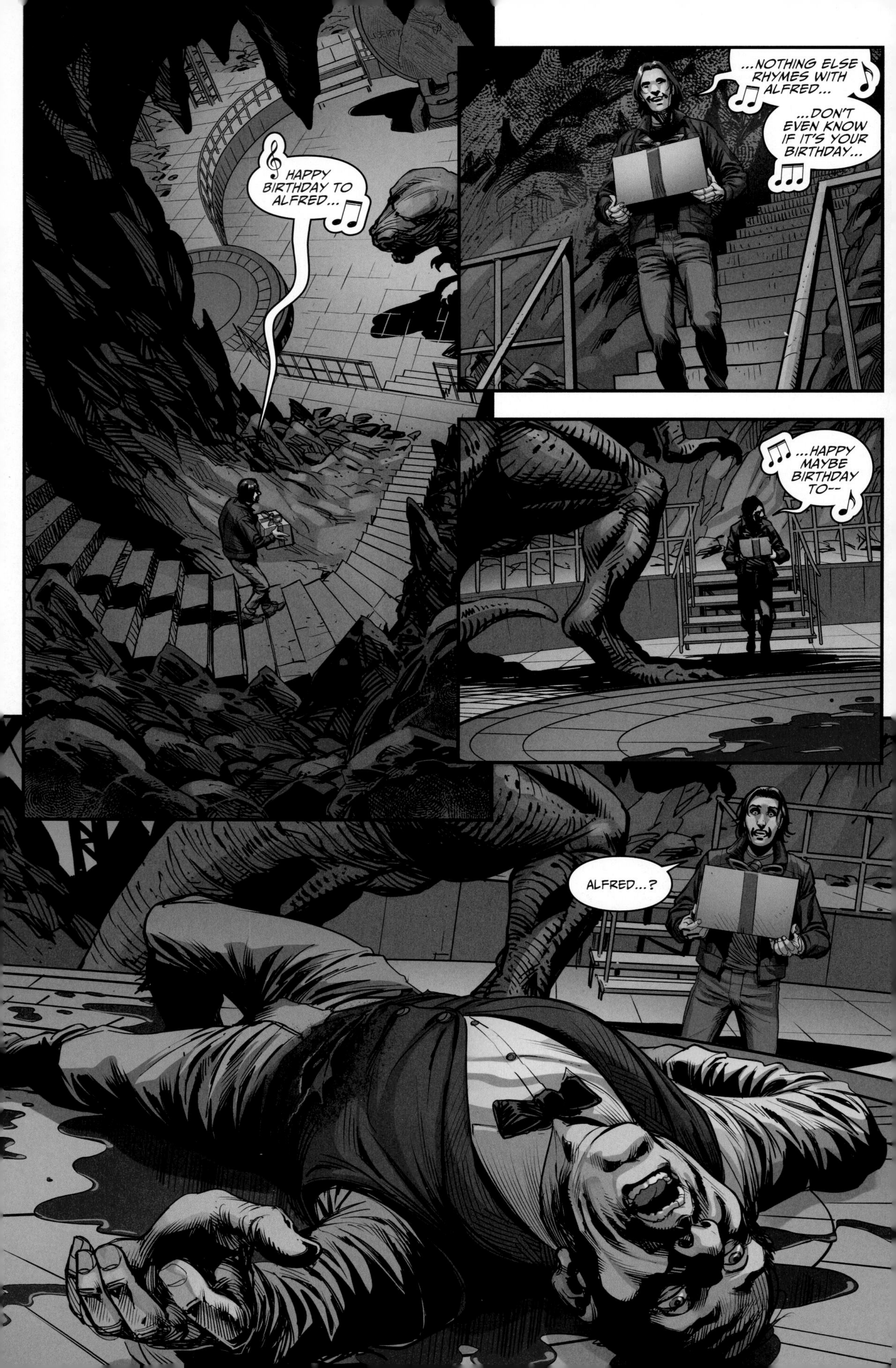
HAPPY BIRTHDAY TO ALFRED...
...NOTHING ELSE RHYMES WITH ALFRED...
...DON'T EVEN KNOW IF IT'S YOUR BIRTHDAY...
...HAPPY MAYBE BIRTHDAY TO--
ALFRED...?

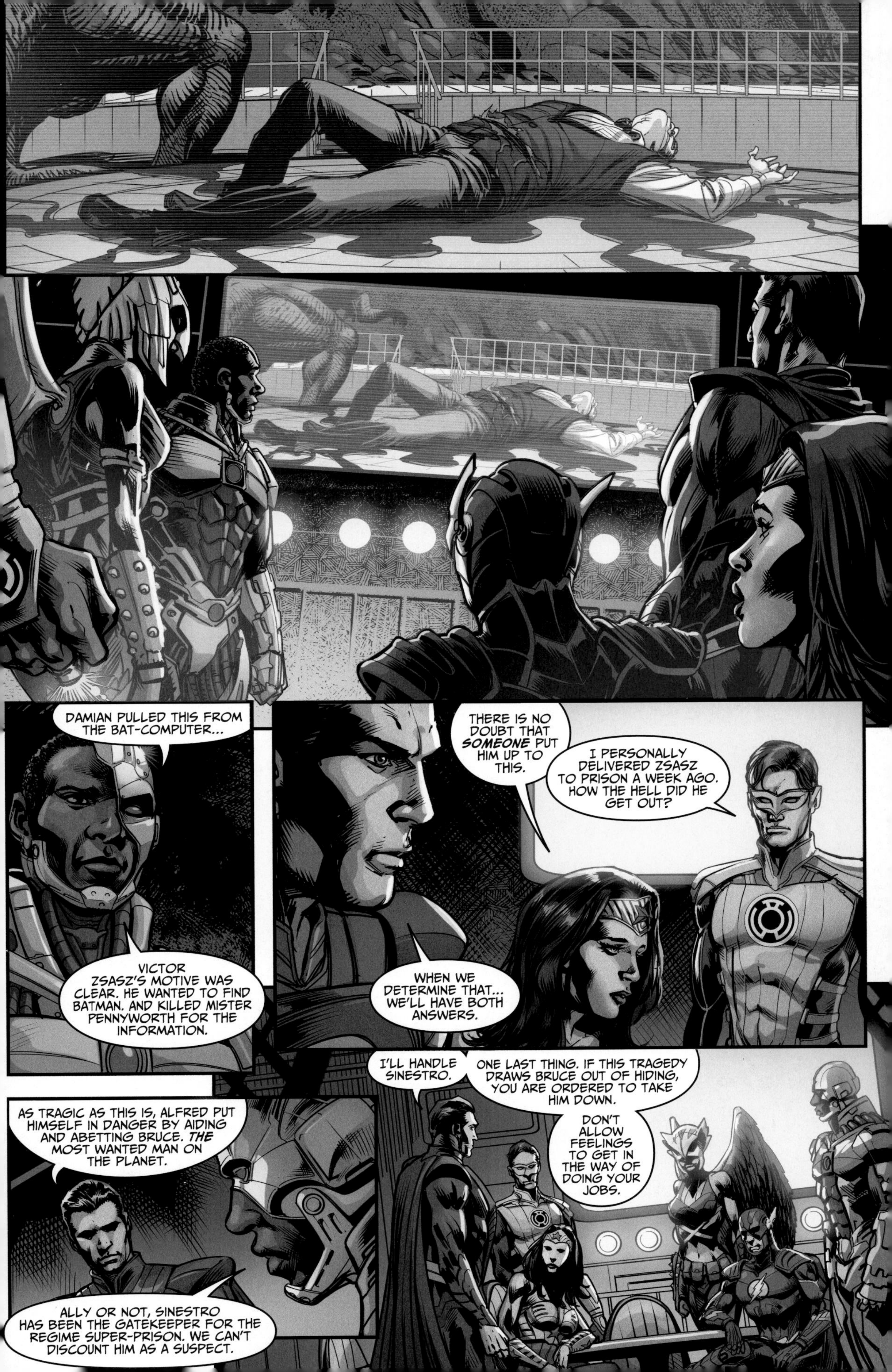
DAMIAN PULLED THIS FROM THE BAT-COMPUTER...
VICTOR ZSASZ'S MOTIVE WAS CLEAR. HE WANTED TO FIND BATMAN. AND KILLED MISTER PENNYWORTH FOR THE INFORMATION.
THERE IS NO DOUBT THAT *SOMEONE* PUT HIM UP TO THIS.
I PERSONALLY DELIVERED ZSASZ TO PRISON A WEEK AGO. HOW THE HELL DID HE GET OUT?
WHEN WE DETERMINE THAT... WE'LL HAVE BOTH ANSWERS.
AS TRAGIC AS THIS IS, ALFRED PUT HIMSELF IN DANGER BY AIDING AND ABETTING BRUCE. *THE* MOST WANTED MAN ON THE PLANET.
ALLY OR NOT, SINESTRO HAS BEEN THE GATEKEEPER FOR THE REGIME SUPER-PRISON. WE CAN'T DISCOUNT HIM AS A SUSPECT.
I'LL HANDLE SINESTRO.
ONE LAST THING. IF THIS TRAGEDY DRAWS BRUCE OUT OF HIDING, YOU ARE ORDERED TO TAKE HIM DOWN.
DON'T ALLOW FEELINGS TO GET IN THE WAY OF DOING YOUR JOBS.

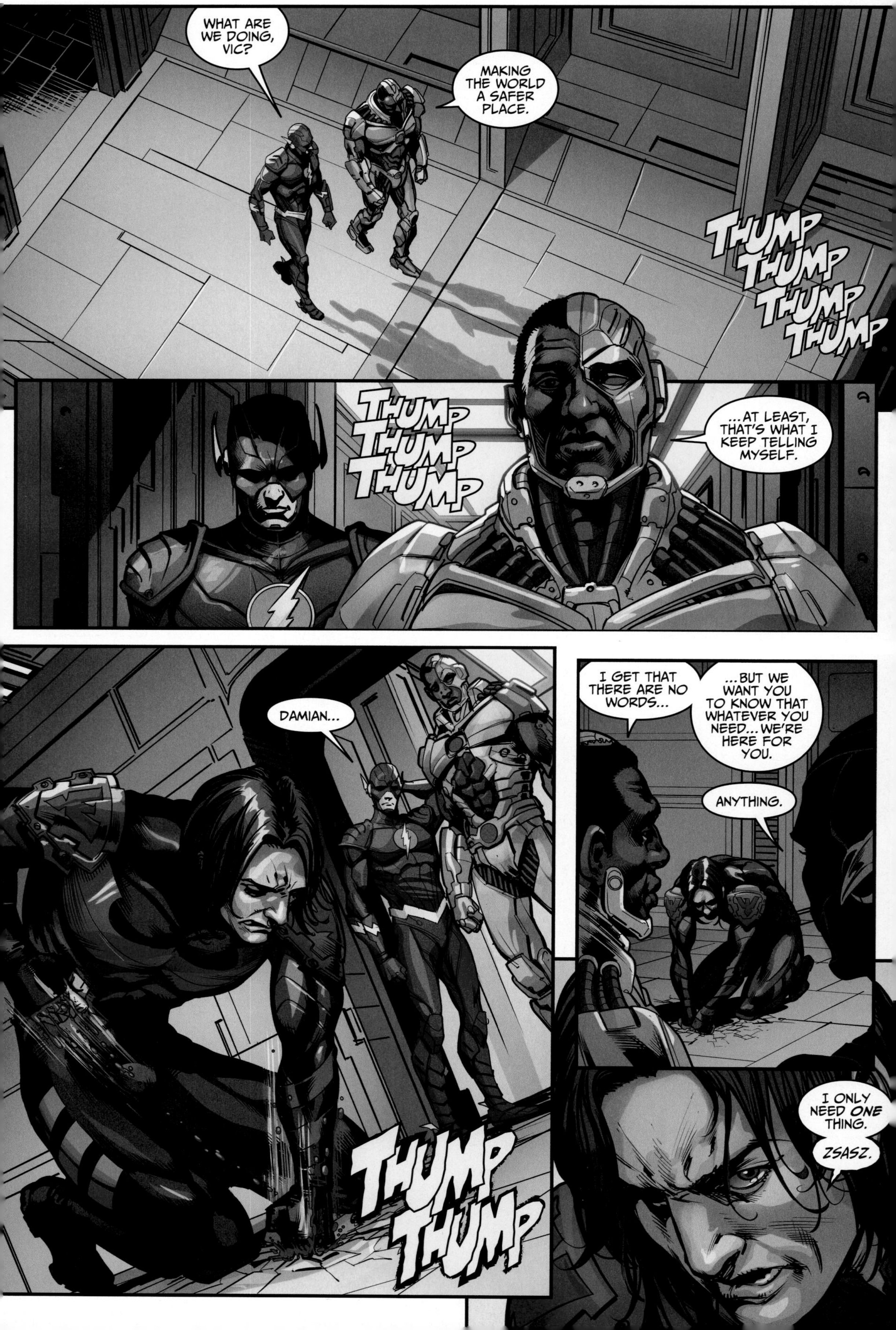
WHAT ARE WE DOING, VIC?
MAKING THE WORLD A SAFER PLACE.
THUMP THUMP THUMP THUMP
THUMP THUMP THUMP
...AT LEAST, THAT'S WHAT I KEEP TELLING MYSELF.
DAMIAN...
THUMP THUMP
I GET THAT THERE ARE NO WORDS...
...BUT WE WANT YOU TO KNOW THAT WHATEVER YOU NEED... WE'RE HERE FOR YOU.
ANYTHING.
I ONLY NEED ONE THING.
ZSASZ.

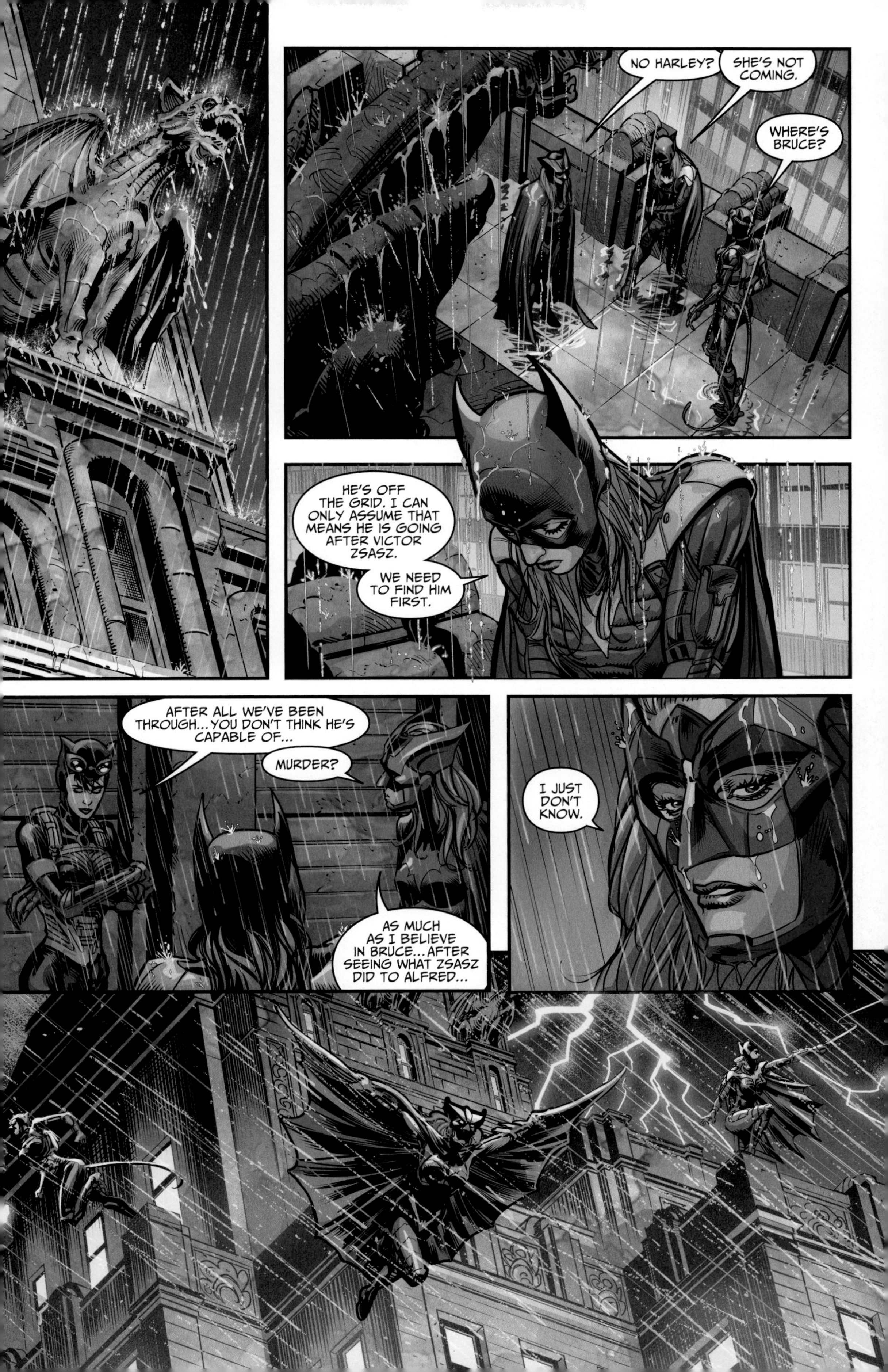

NO HARLEY?
SHE'S NOT COMING.
WHERE'S BRUCE?
HE'S OFF THE GRID. I CAN ONLY ASSUME THAT MEANS HE IS GOING AFTER VICTOR ZSASZ.
WE NEED TO FIND HIM FIRST.
AFTER ALL WE'VE BEEN THROUGH... YOU DON'T THINK HE'S CAPABLE OF...
MURDER?
AS MUCH AS I BELIEVE IN BRUCE... AFTER SEEING WHAT ZSASZ DID TO ALFRED...
I JUST DON'T KNOW.

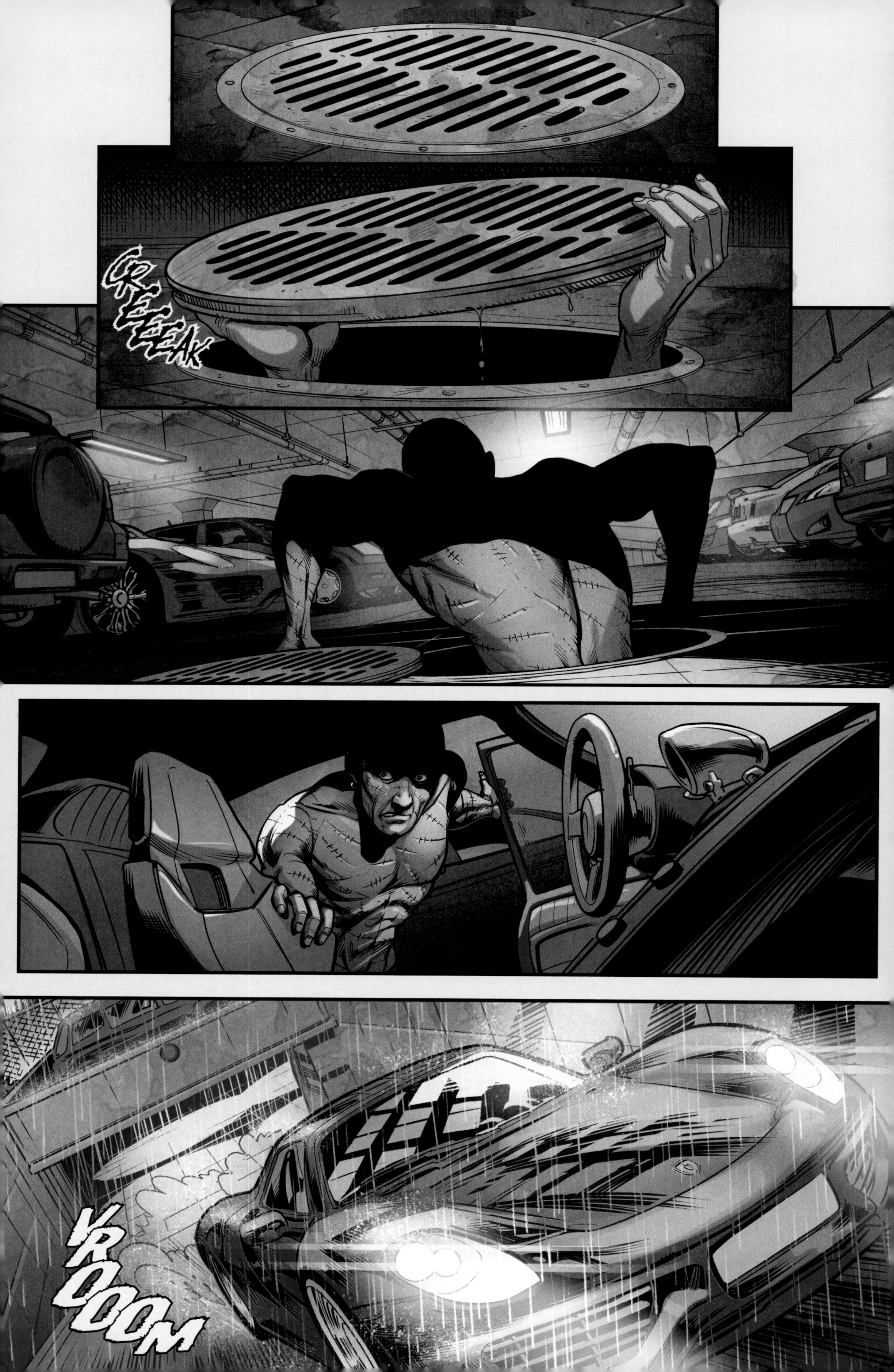
CREEEEAK
VROOOM

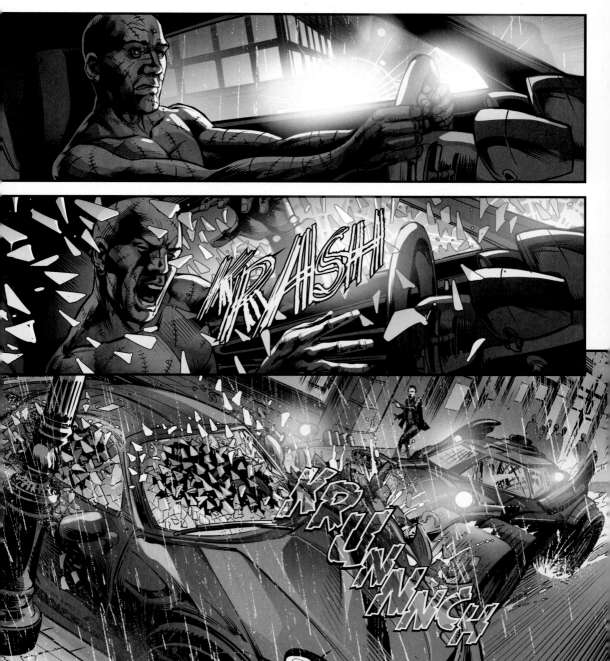

KRASH

KRUNNNNCH

=UNFH!=

NO!

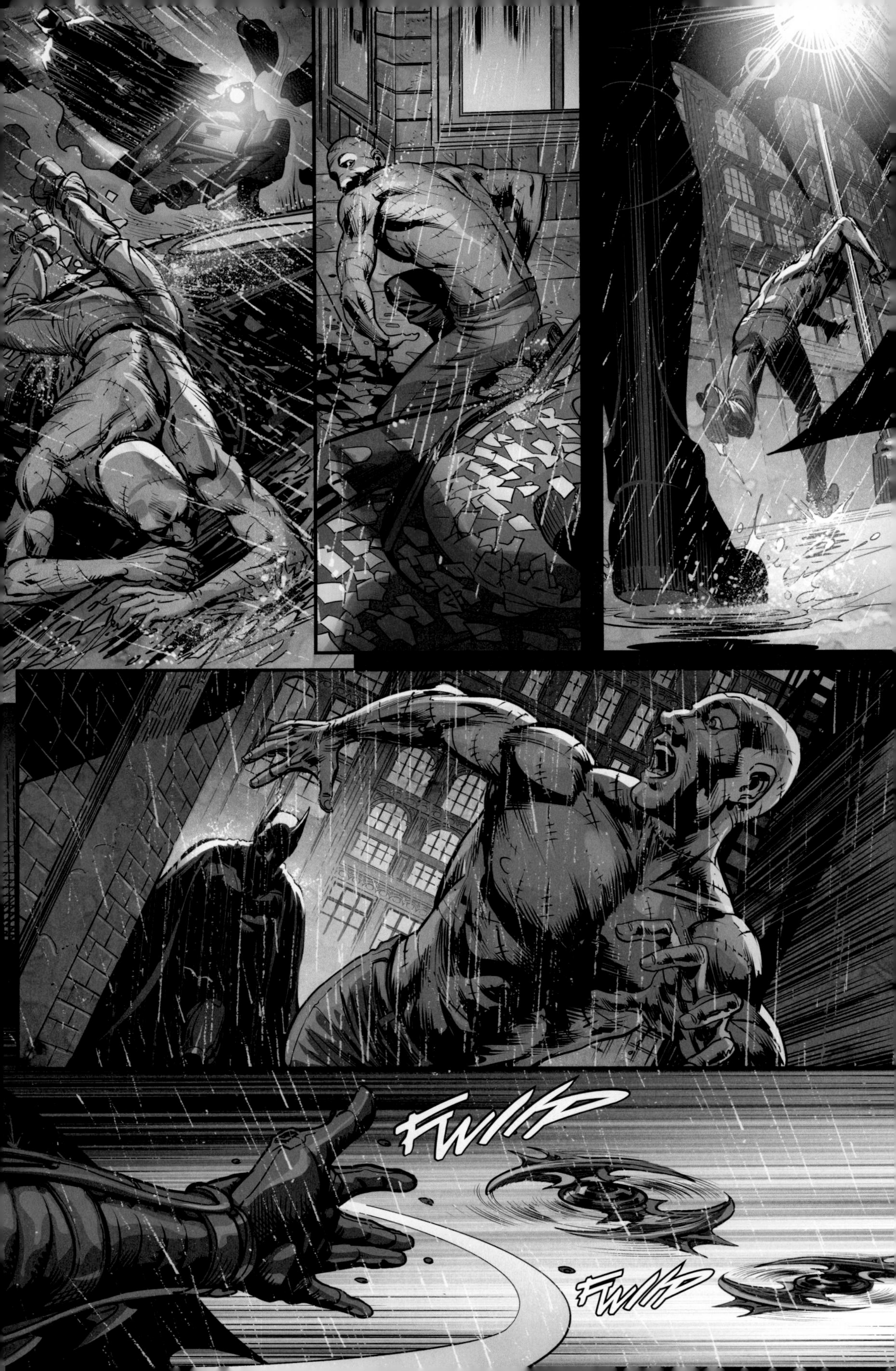
FWIP
FWIP

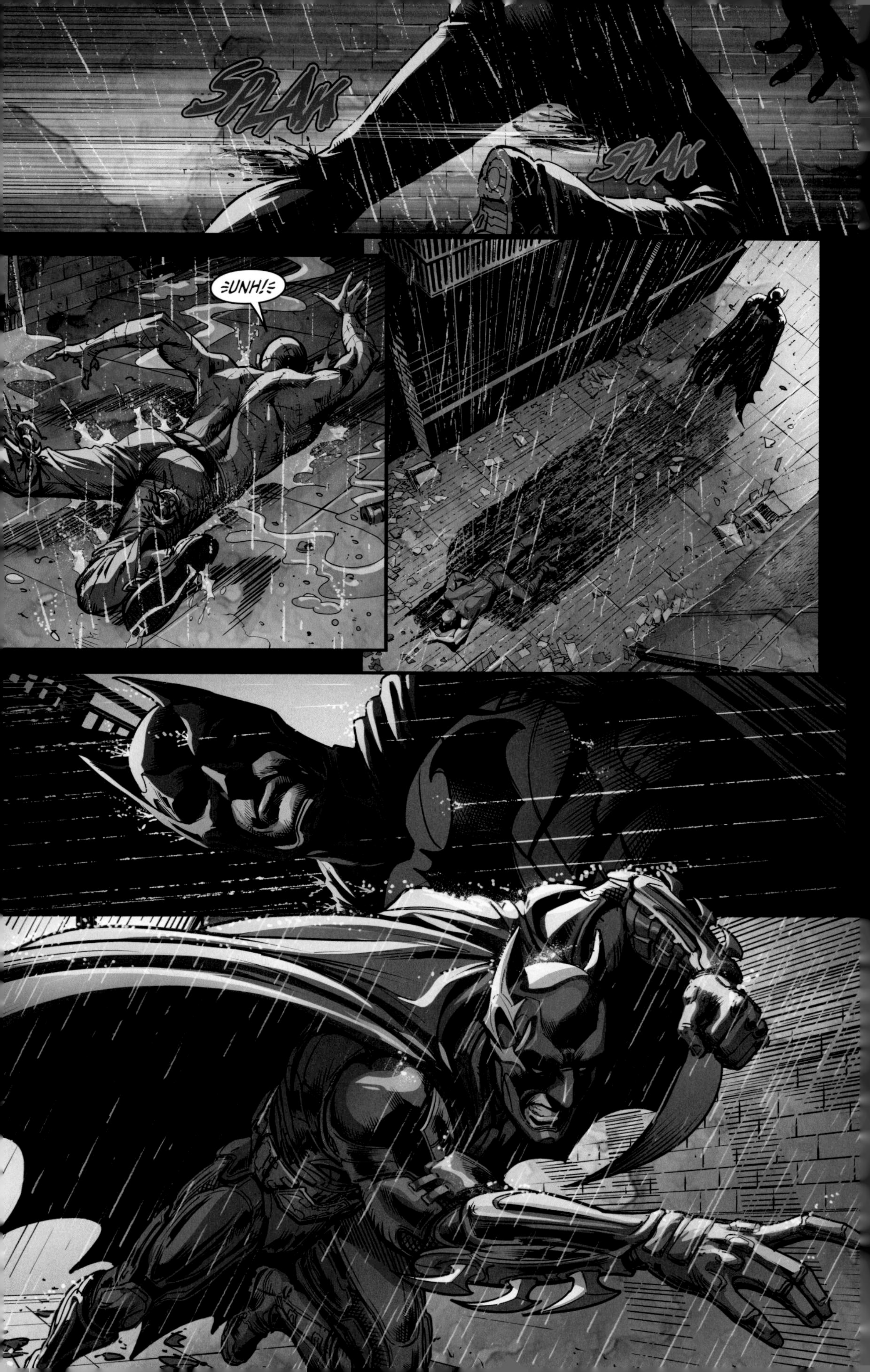
SPLAK
SPLAK
UNH!

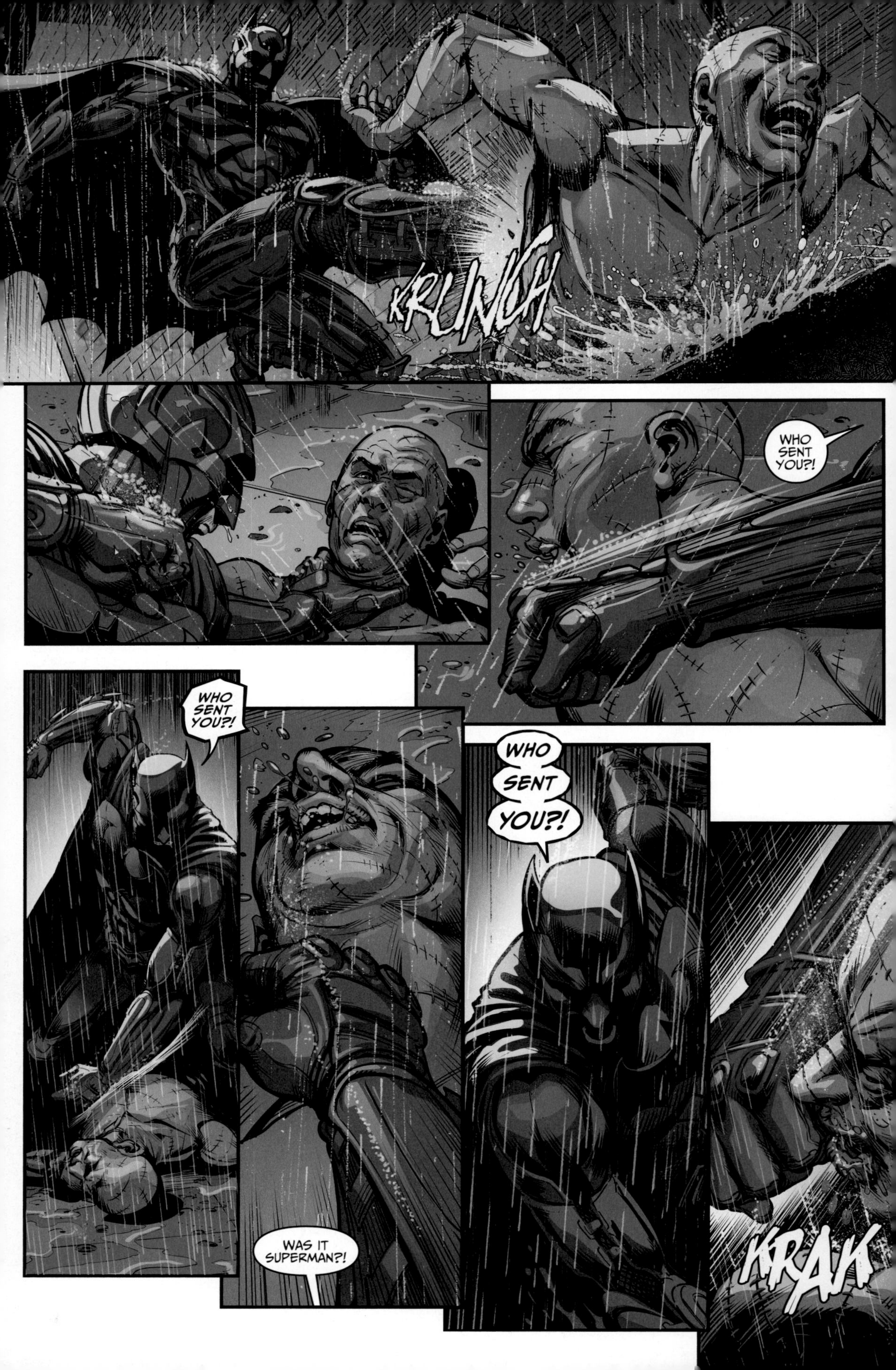
KRUNCH
WHO SENT YOU?!
WHO SENT YOU?!
WAS IT SUPERMAN?!
WHO SENT YOU?!
KRAK

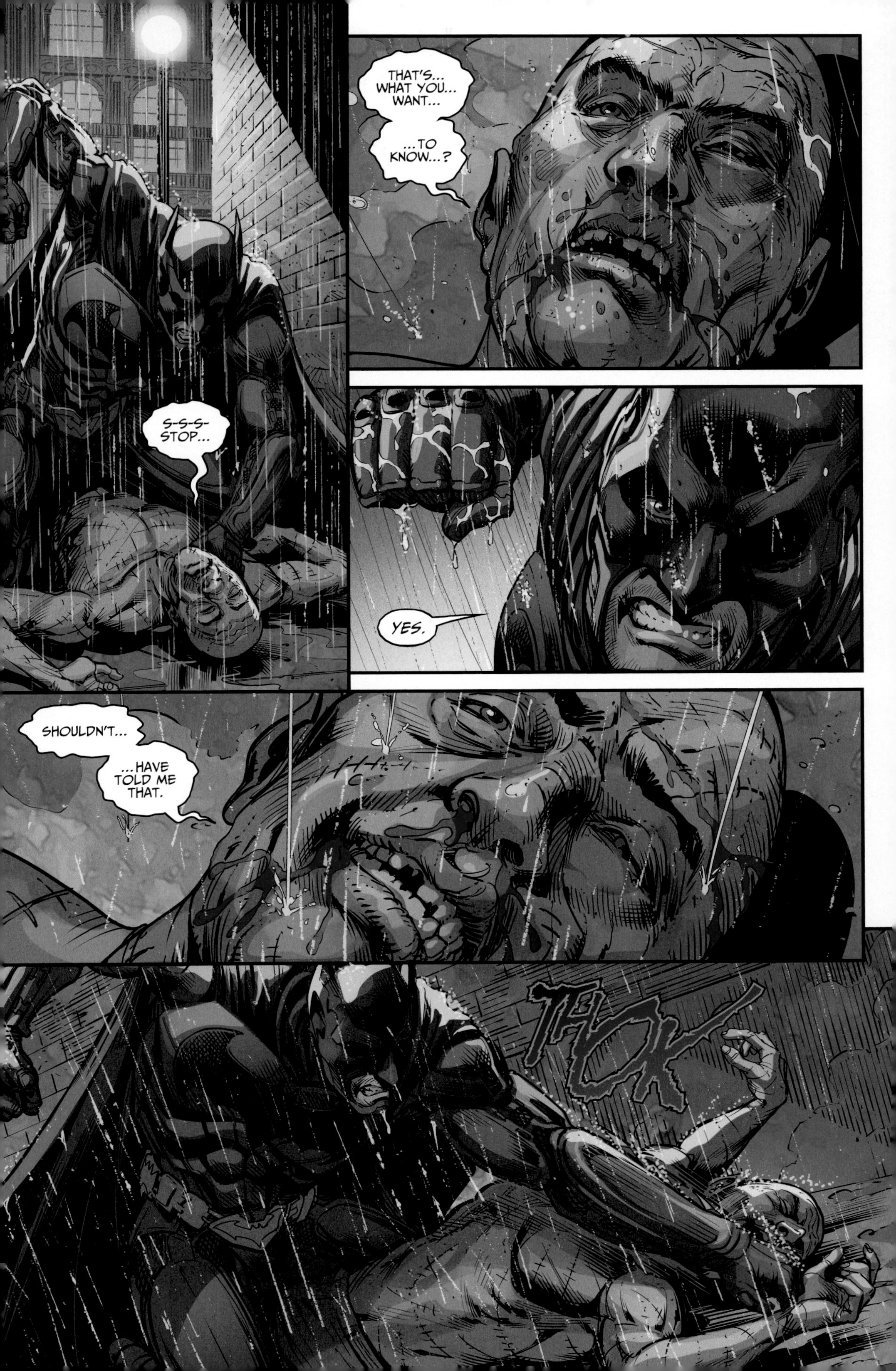
S-S-S-STOP...
THAT'S... WHAT YOU... WANT...
...TO KNOW...?
YES.
SHOULDN'T...
...HAVE TOLD ME THAT.
THOK

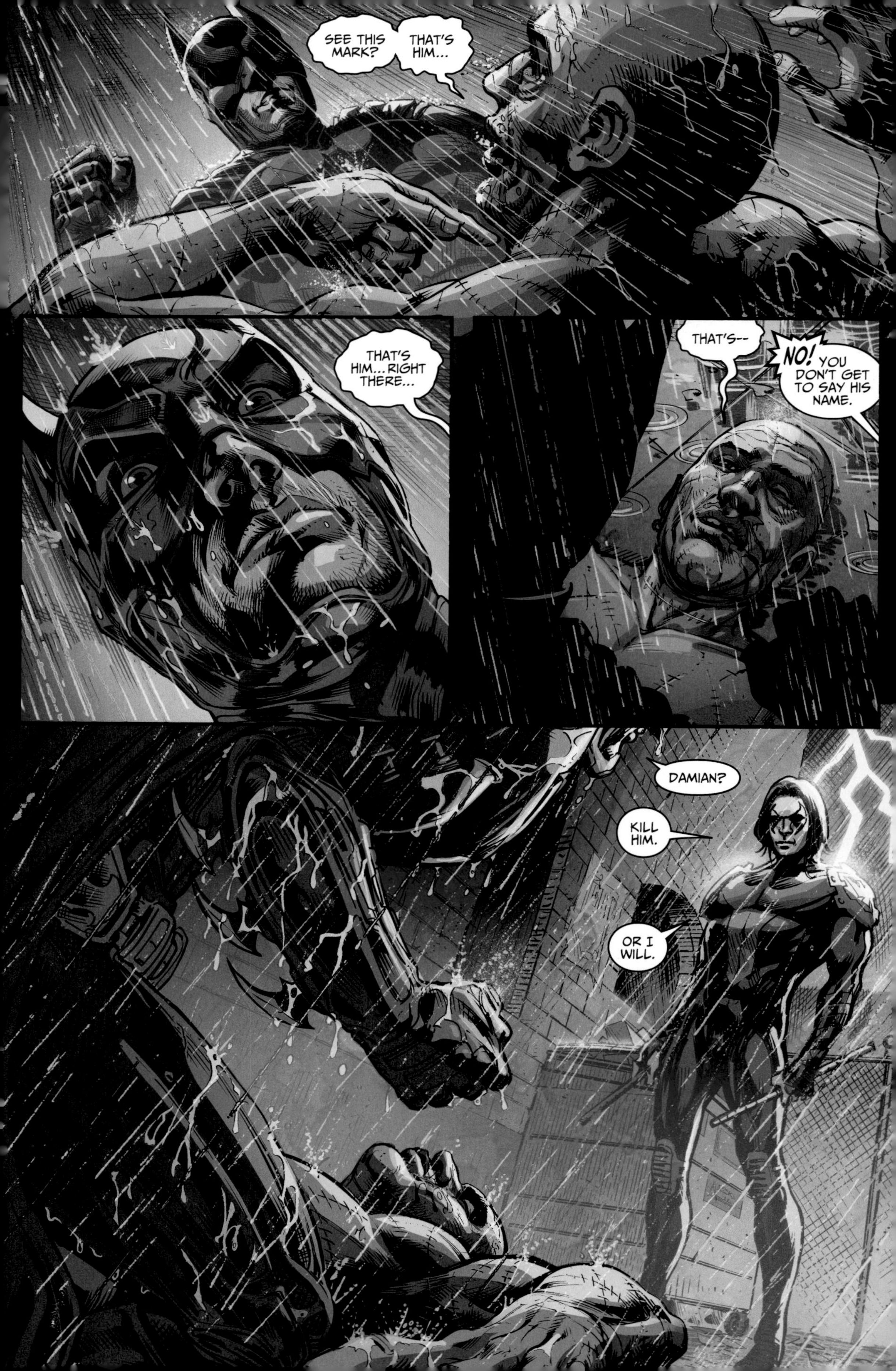
SEE THIS MARK?
THAT'S HIM...
THAT'S HIM... RIGHT THERE...
THAT'S--
NO! YOU DON'T GET TO SAY HIS NAME.
DAMIAN?
KILL HIM.
OR I WILL.

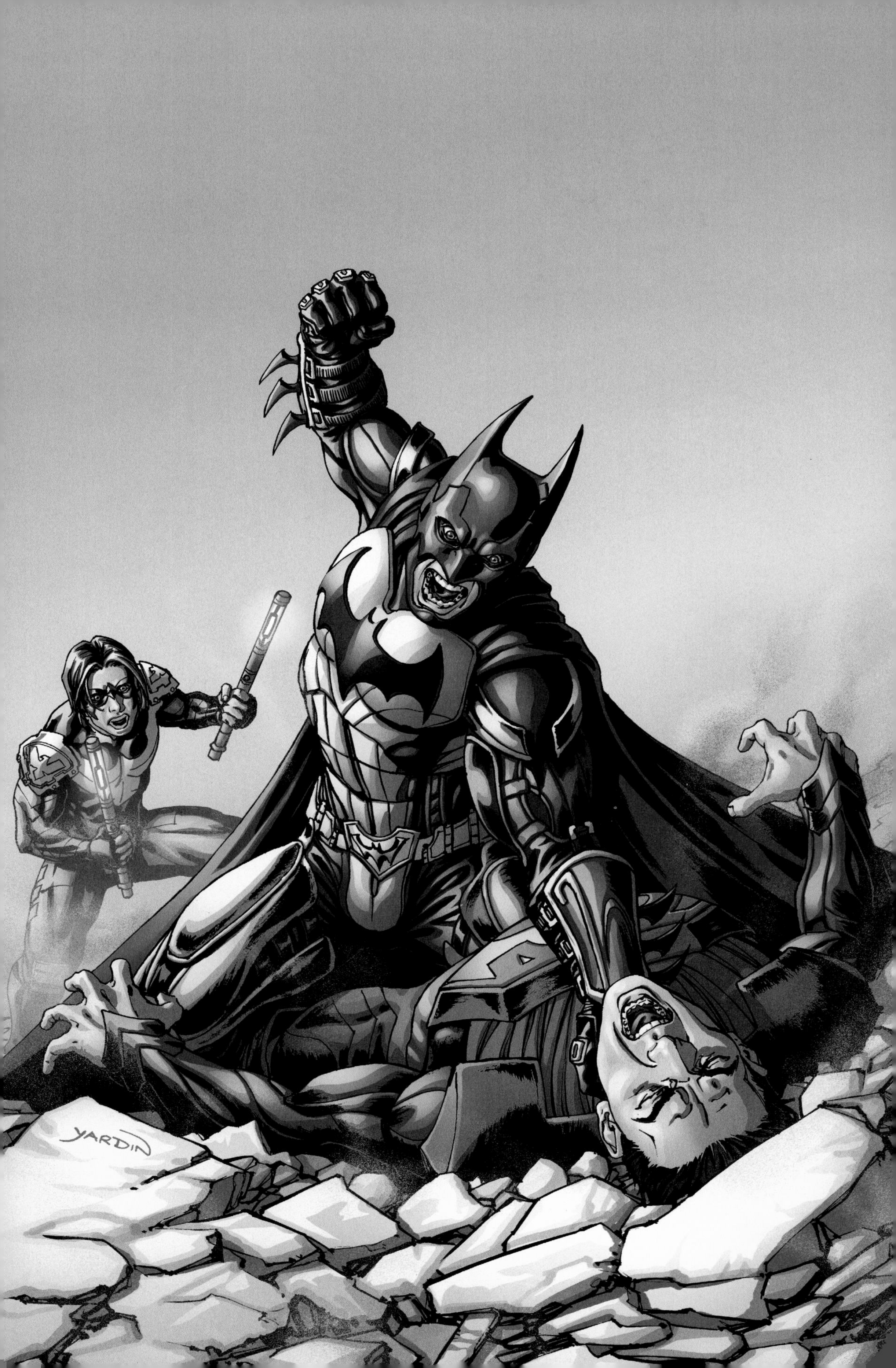
YARDIN

"Choices" **Mike S. Miller** Artist **J. Nanjan** Colorist

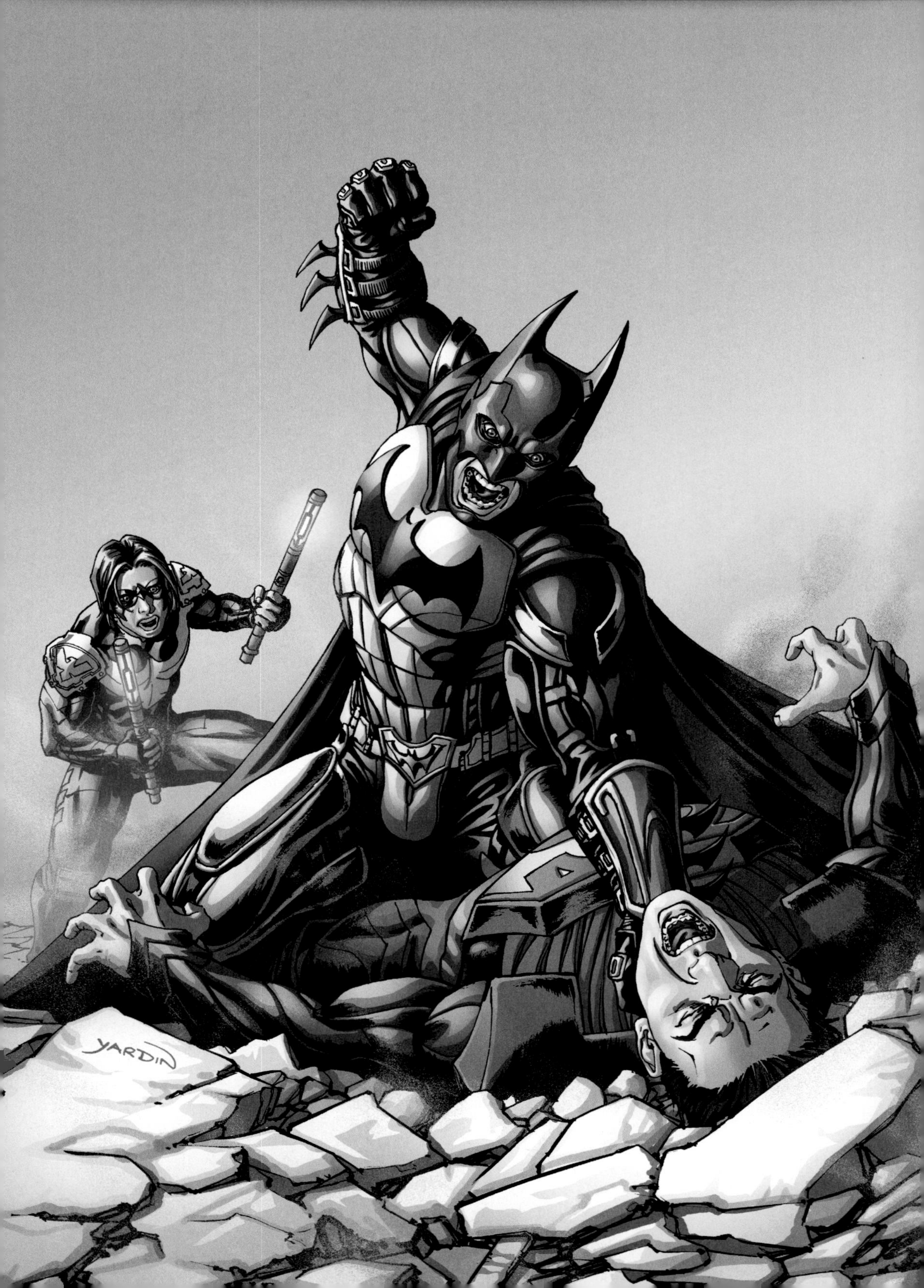

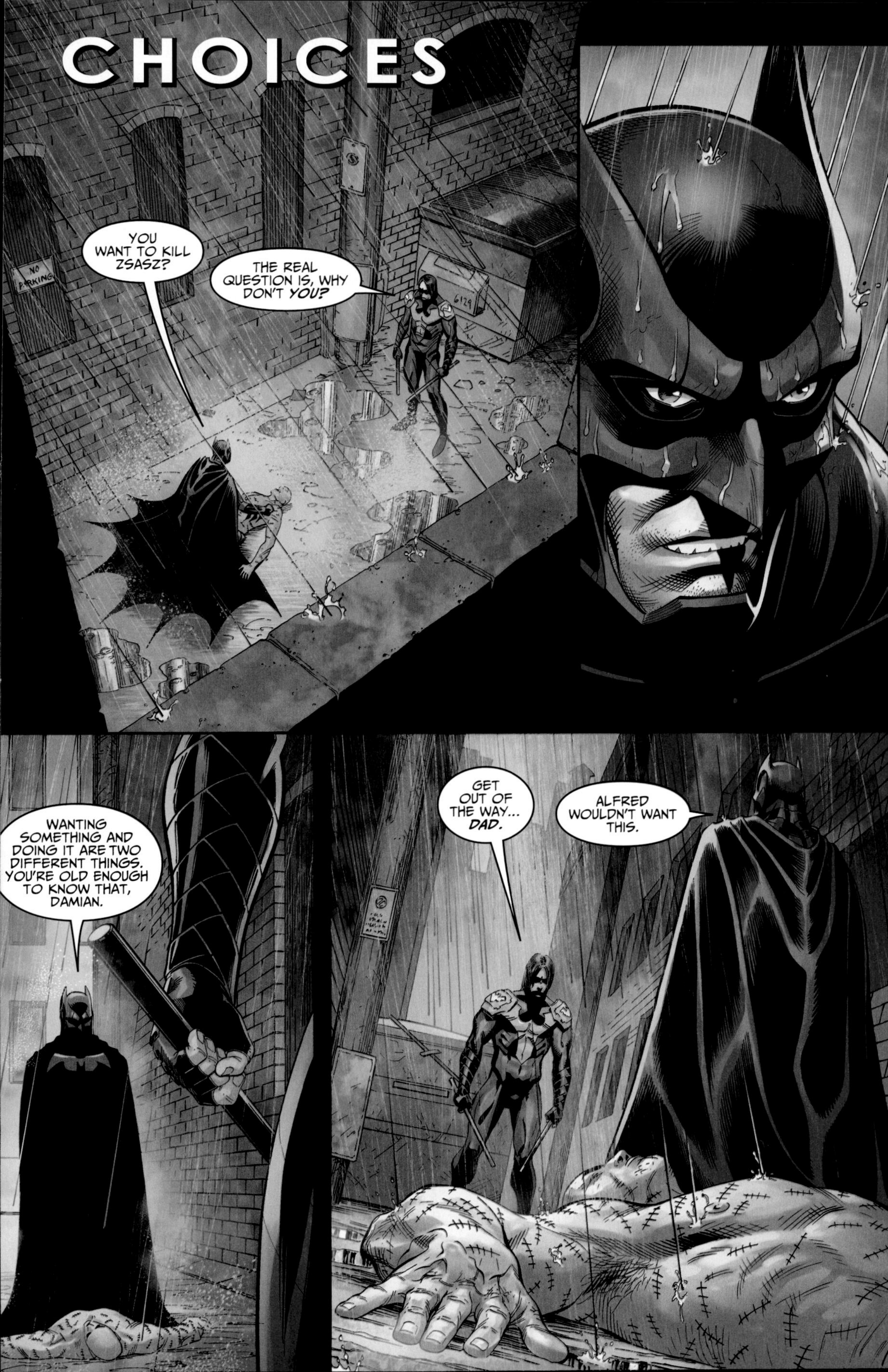
CHOICES
NO PARKING
YOU WANT TO KILL ZSASZ?
THE REAL QUESTION IS, WHY DON'T *YOU?*
WANTING SOMETHING AND DOING IT ARE TWO DIFFERENT THINGS. YOU'RE OLD ENOUGH TO KNOW THAT, DAMIAN.
GET OUT OF THE WAY... *DAD.*
ALFRED WOULDN'T WANT THIS.

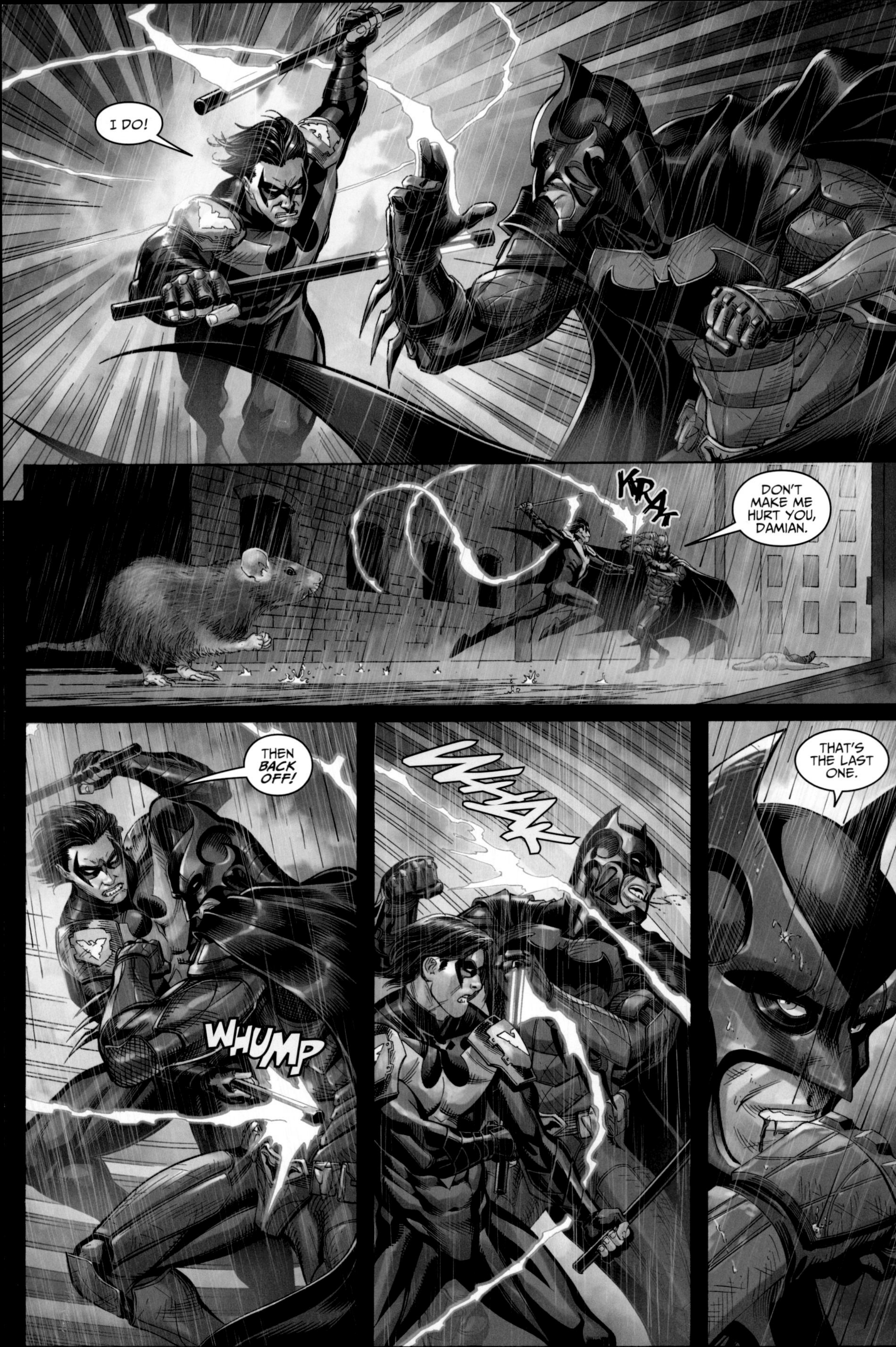
I DO!
KRAK
DON'T MAKE ME HURT YOU, DAMIAN.
THEN BACK OFF!
WHUMP
WHAK
THAT'S THE LAST ONE.

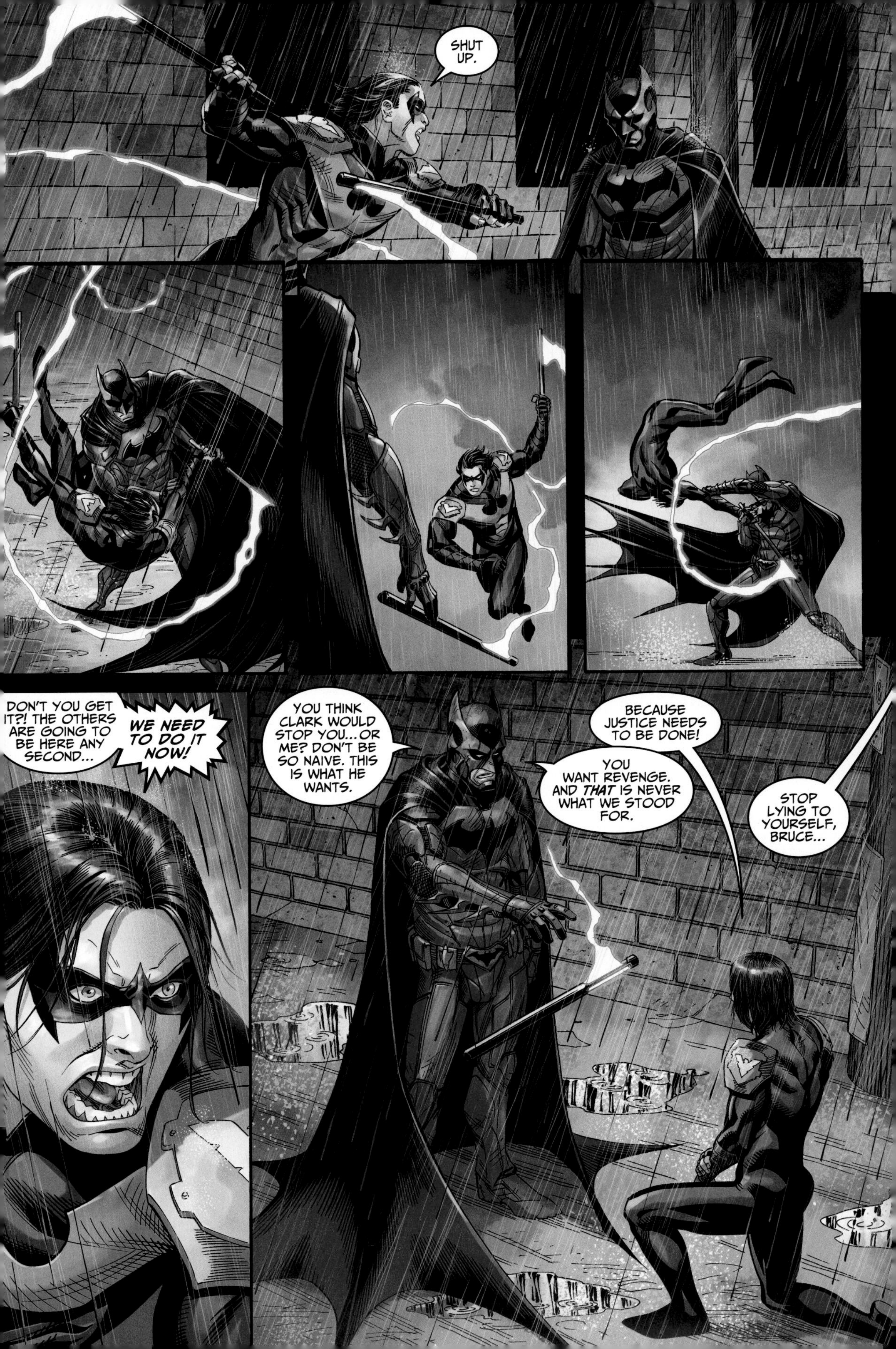

SHUT UP.
DON'T YOU GET IT?! THE OTHERS ARE GOING TO BE HERE ANY SECOND...
WE NEED TO DO IT NOW!
YOU THINK CLARK WOULD STOP YOU...OR ME? DON'T BE SO NAIVE. THIS IS WHAT HE WANTS.
BECAUSE JUSTICE NEEDS TO BE DONE!
YOU WANT REVENGE. AND THAT IS NEVER WHAT WE STOOD FOR.
STOP LYING TO YOURSELF, BRUCE...

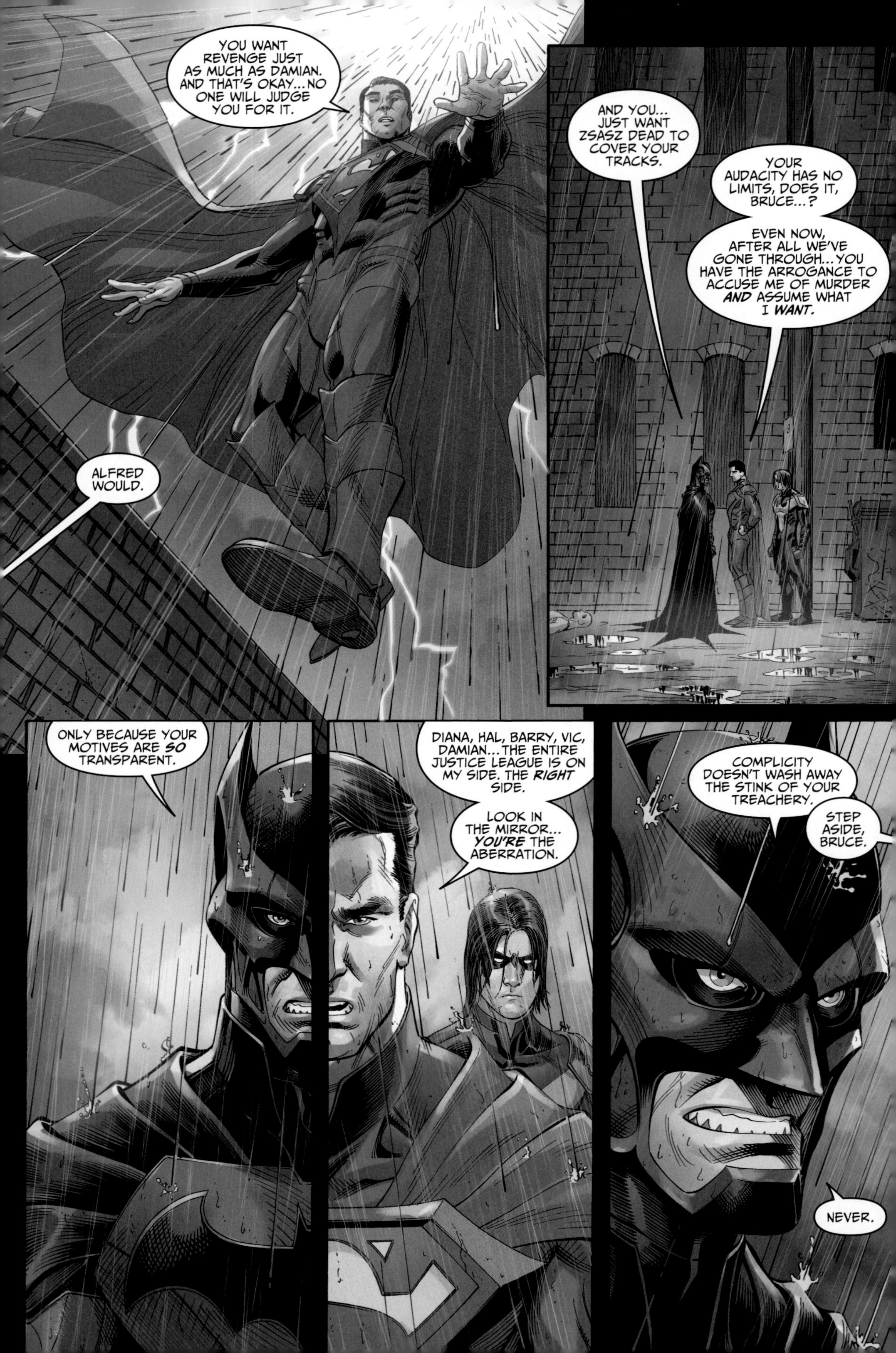
YOU WANT REVENGE JUST AS MUCH AS DAMIAN. AND THAT'S OKAY...NO ONE WILL JUDGE YOU FOR IT.
ALFRED WOULD.
AND YOU... JUST WANT ZSASZ DEAD TO COVER YOUR TRACKS.
YOUR AUDACITY HAS NO LIMITS, DOES IT, BRUCE...?
EVEN NOW, AFTER ALL WE'VE GONE THROUGH...YOU HAVE THE ARROGANCE TO ACCUSE ME OF MURDER AND ASSUME WHAT I WANT.
ONLY BECAUSE YOUR MOTIVES ARE SO TRANSPARENT.
DIANA, HAL, BARRY, VIC, DAMIAN...THE ENTIRE JUSTICE LEAGUE IS ON MY SIDE. THE RIGHT SIDE.
LOOK IN THE MIRROR... YOU'RE THE ABERRATION.
COMPLICITY DOESN'T WASH AWAY THE STINK OF YOUR TREACHERY.
STEP ASIDE, BRUCE.
NEVER.

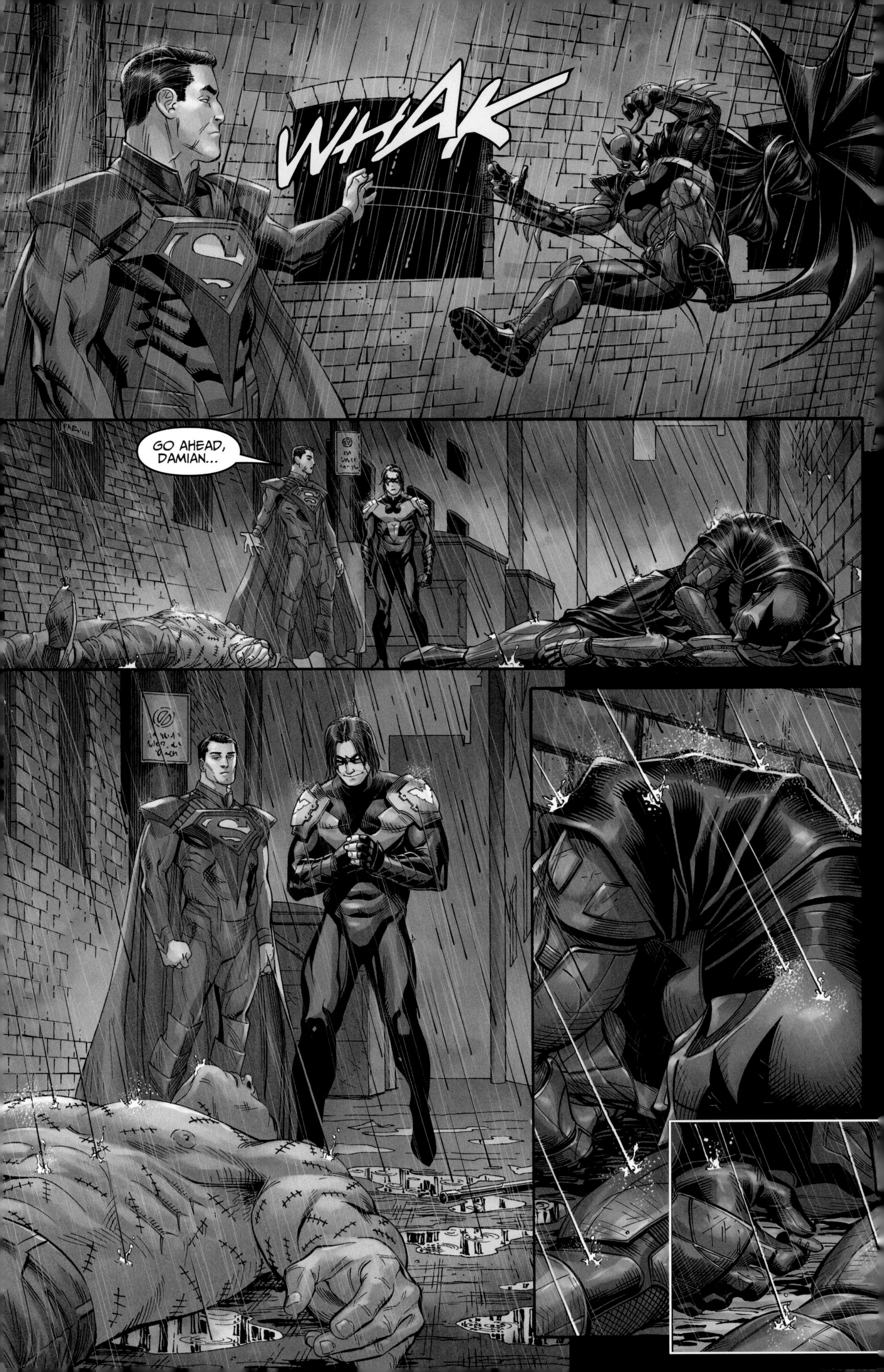
WHAK
GO AHEAD, DAMIAN...

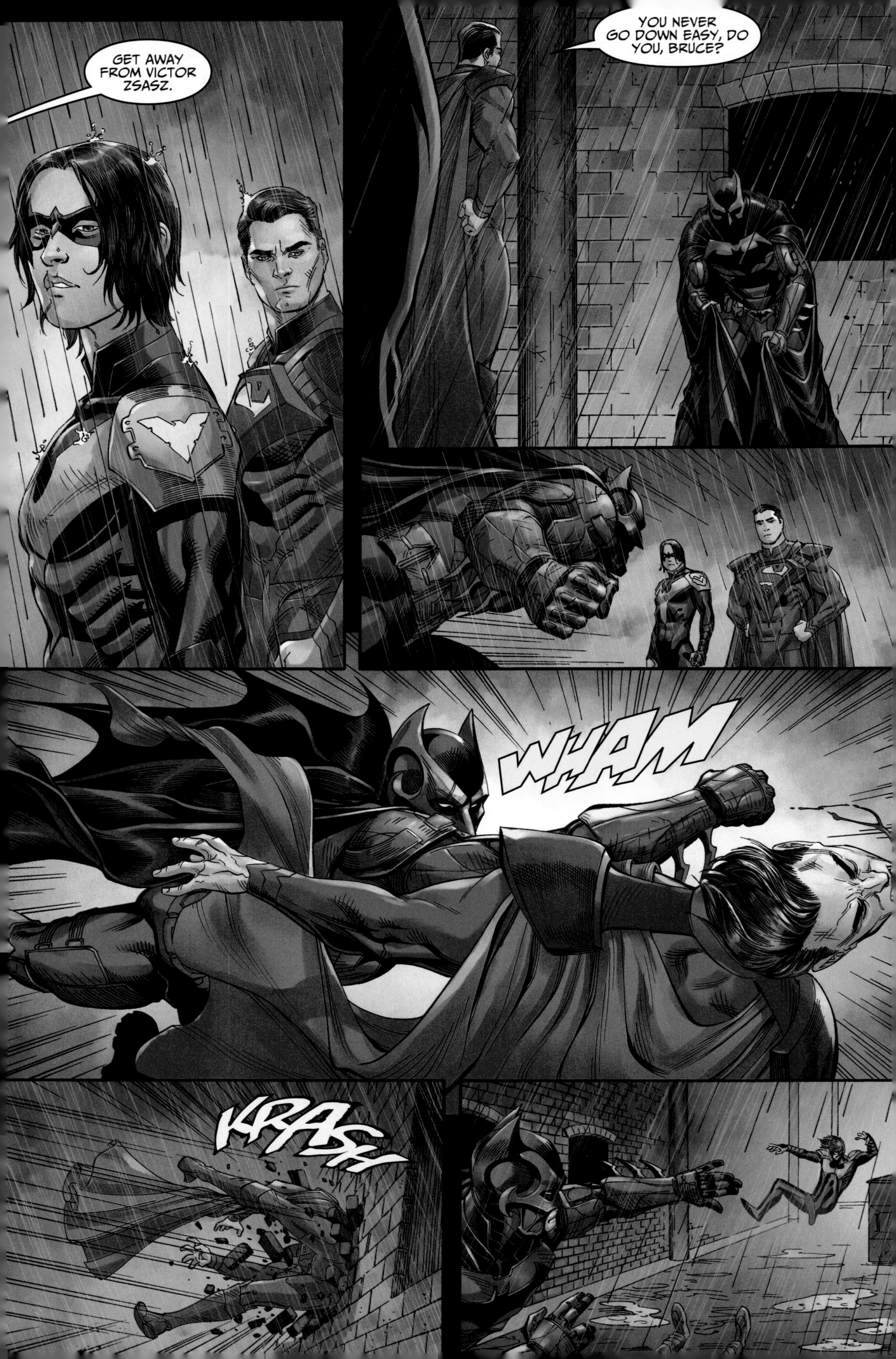
GET AWAY FROM VICTOR ZSASZ.
YOU NEVER GO DOWN EASY, DO YOU, BRUCE?
WHAM
KRASH

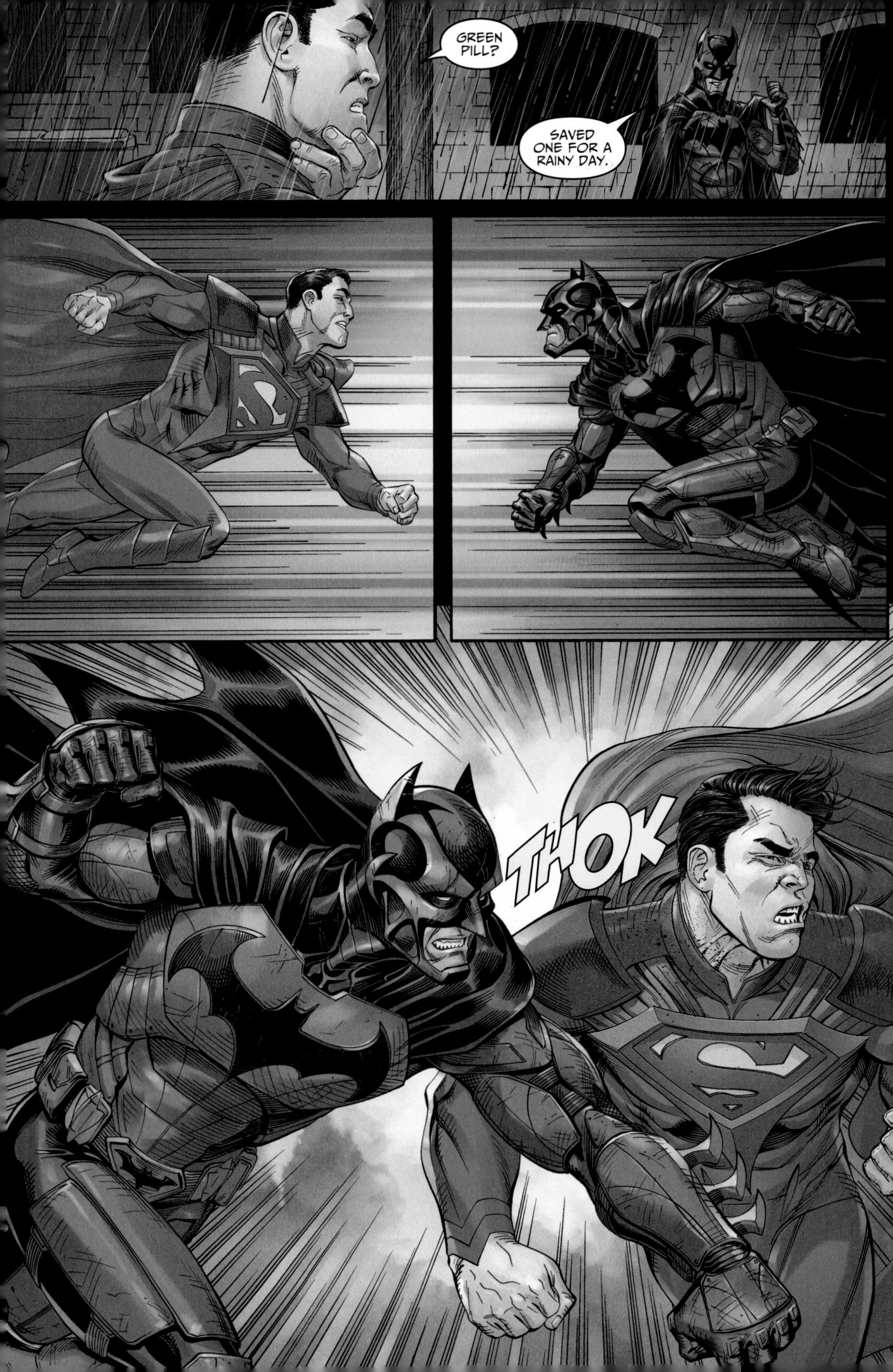
GREEN PILL?
SAVED ONE FOR A RAINY DAY.
THOK

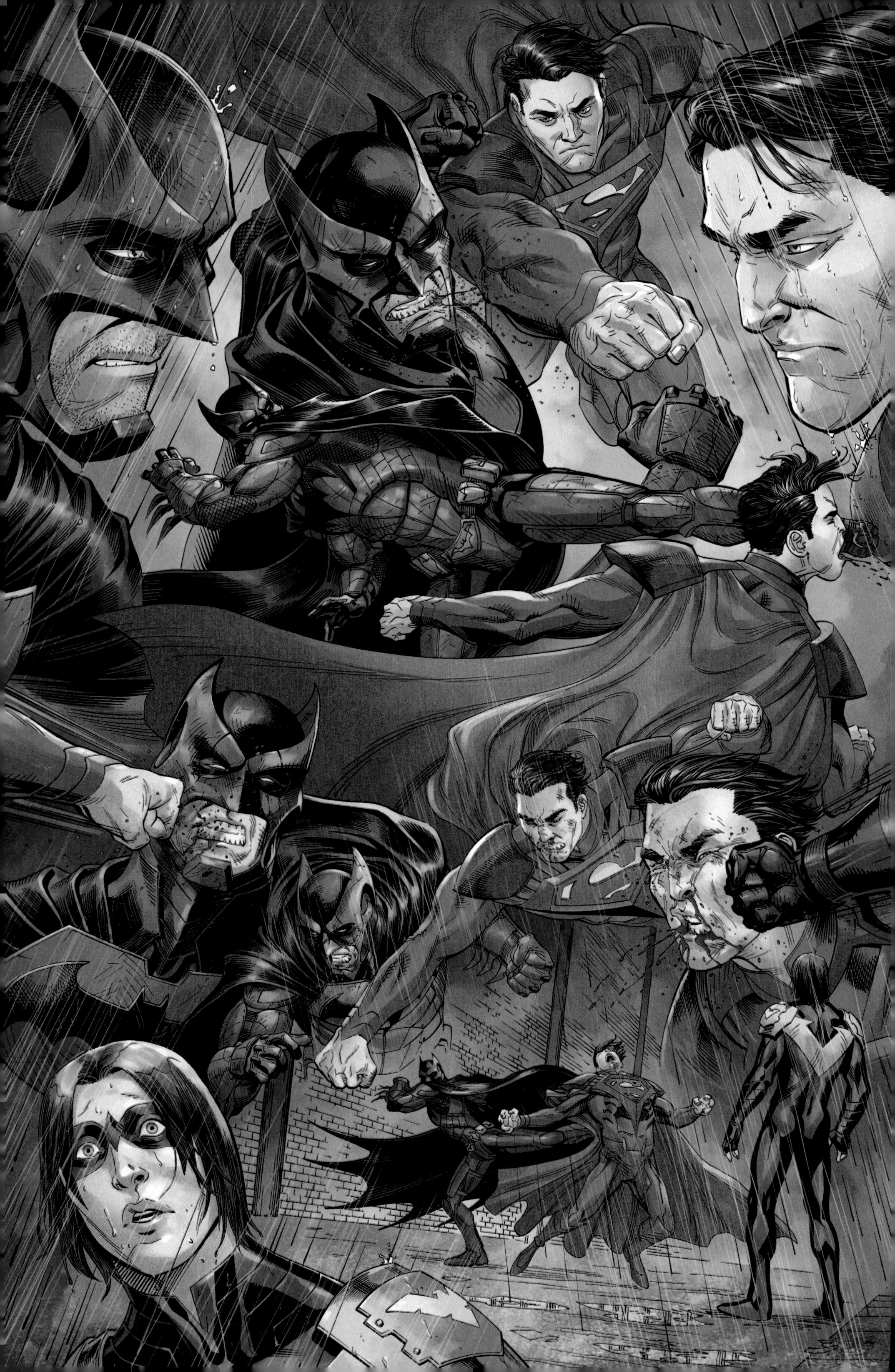

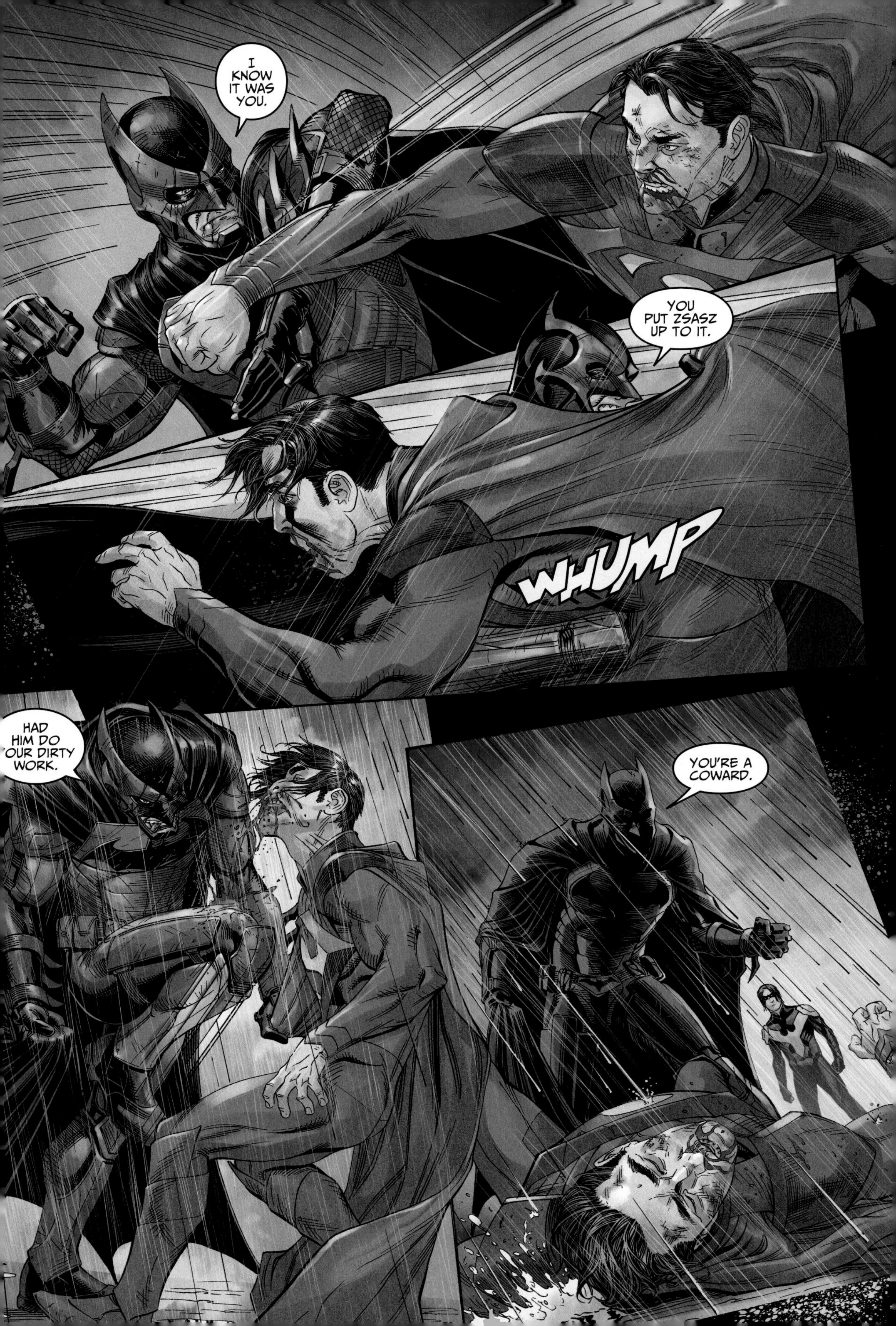
I KNOW IT WAS YOU.
YOU PUT ZSASZ UP TO IT.
WHUMP
HAD HIM DO OUR DIRTY WORK.
YOU'RE A COWARD.

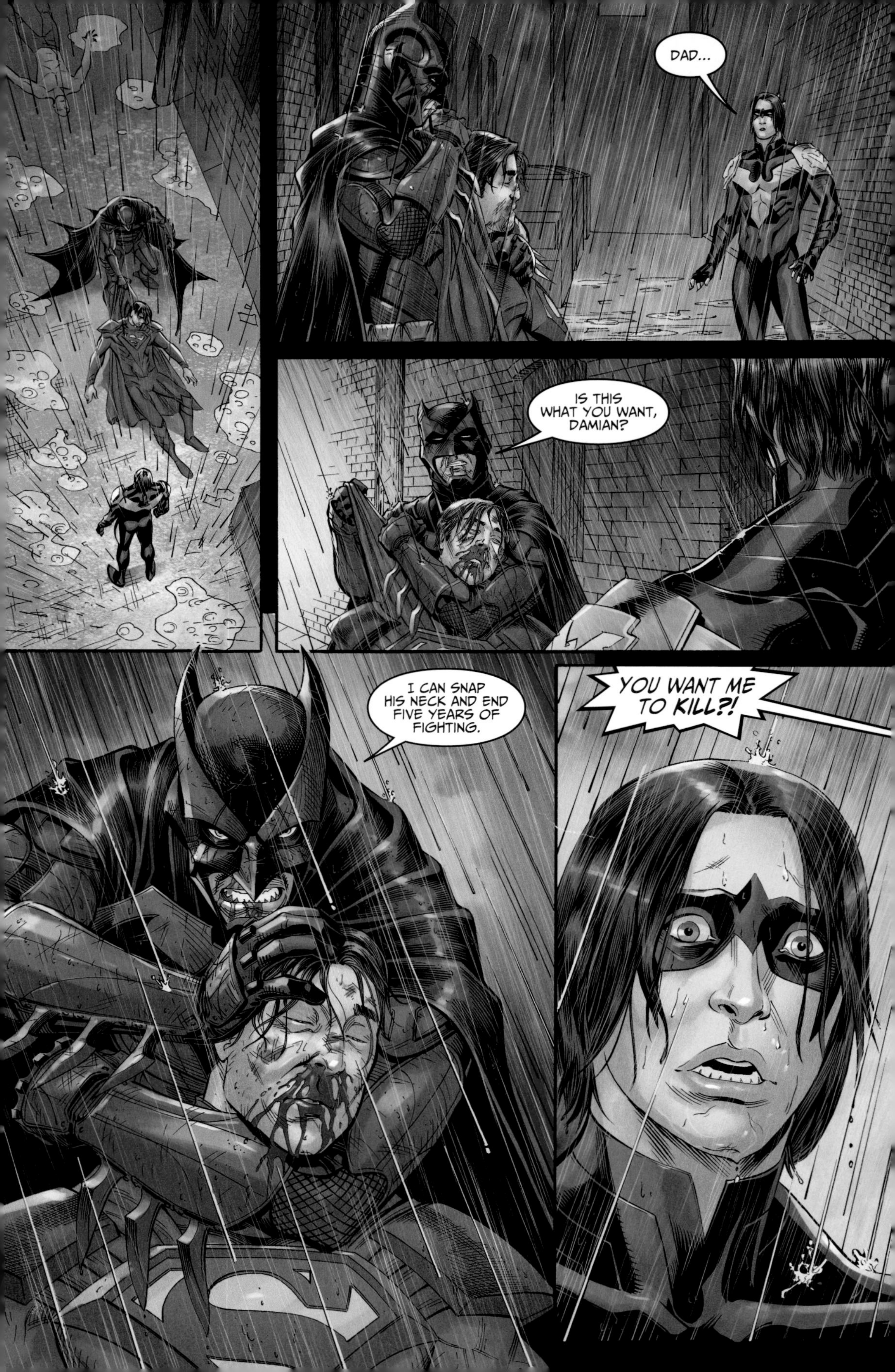
DAD...
IS THIS WHAT YOU WANT, DAMIAN?
I CAN SNAP HIS NECK AND END FIVE YEARS OF FIGHTING.
YOU WANT ME TO KILL?!

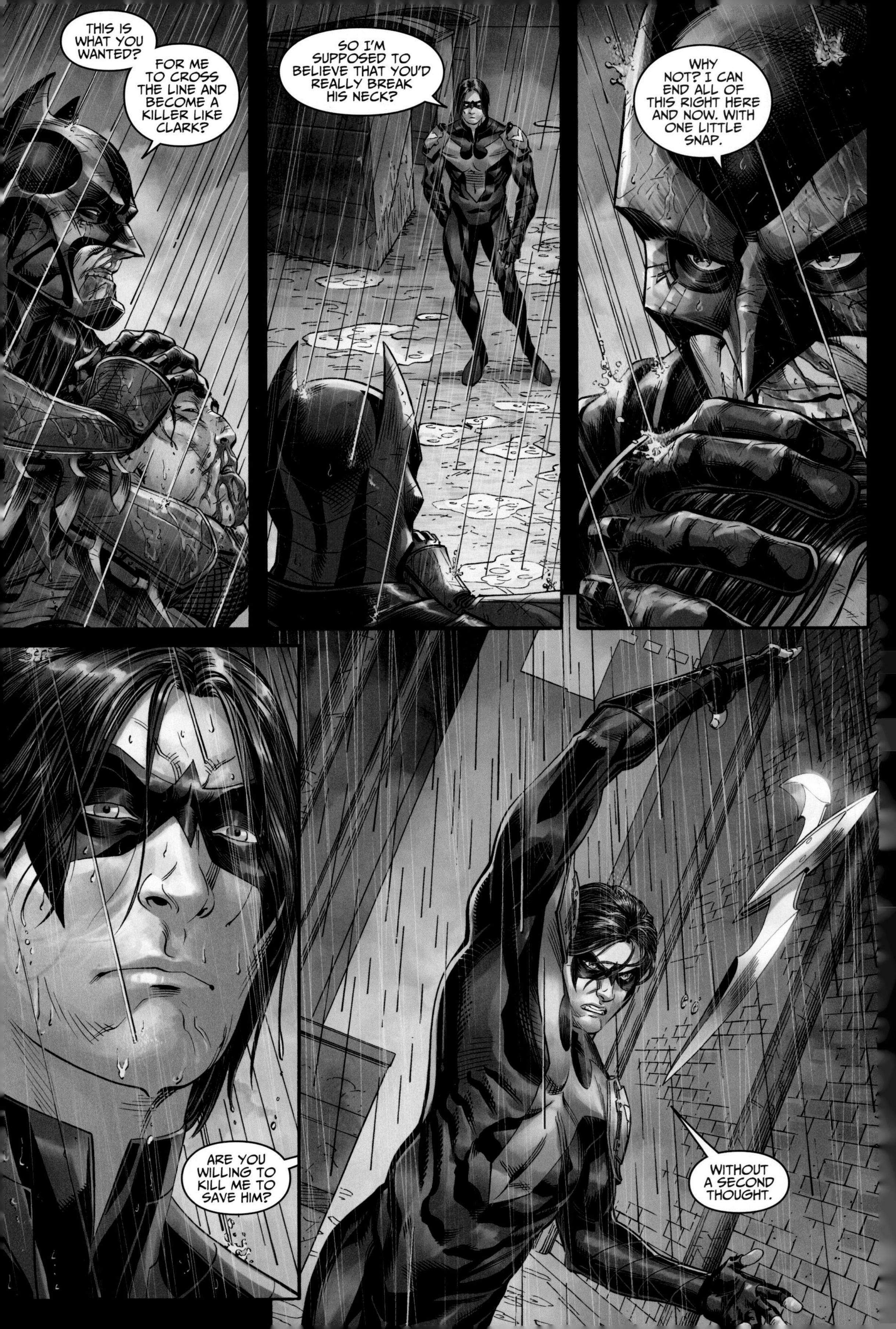
THIS IS WHAT YOU WANTED?
FOR ME TO CROSS THE LINE AND BECOME A KILLER LIKE CLARK?
SO I'M SUPPOSED TO BELIEVE THAT YOU'D REALLY BREAK HIS NECK?
WHY NOT? I CAN END ALL OF THIS RIGHT HERE AND NOW. WITH ONE LITTLE SNAP.
ARE YOU WILLING TO KILL ME TO SAVE HIM?
WITHOUT A SECOND THOUGHT.

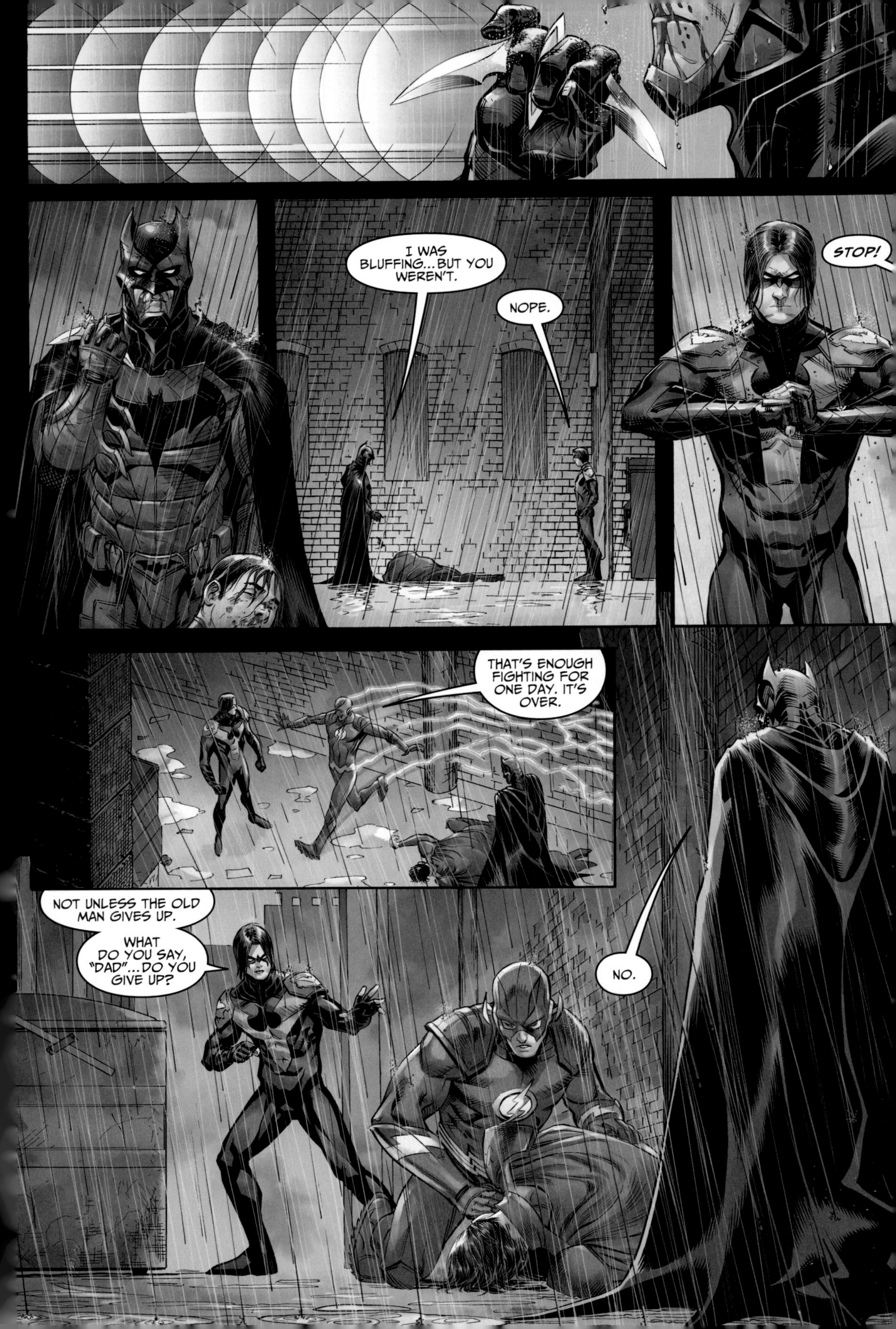
I WAS BLUFFING...BUT YOU WEREN'T.
NOPE.
STOP!
THAT'S ENOUGH FIGHTING FOR ONE DAY. IT'S OVER.
NOT UNLESS THE OLD MAN GIVES UP.
WHAT DO YOU SAY, "DAD"...DO YOU GIVE UP?
NO.

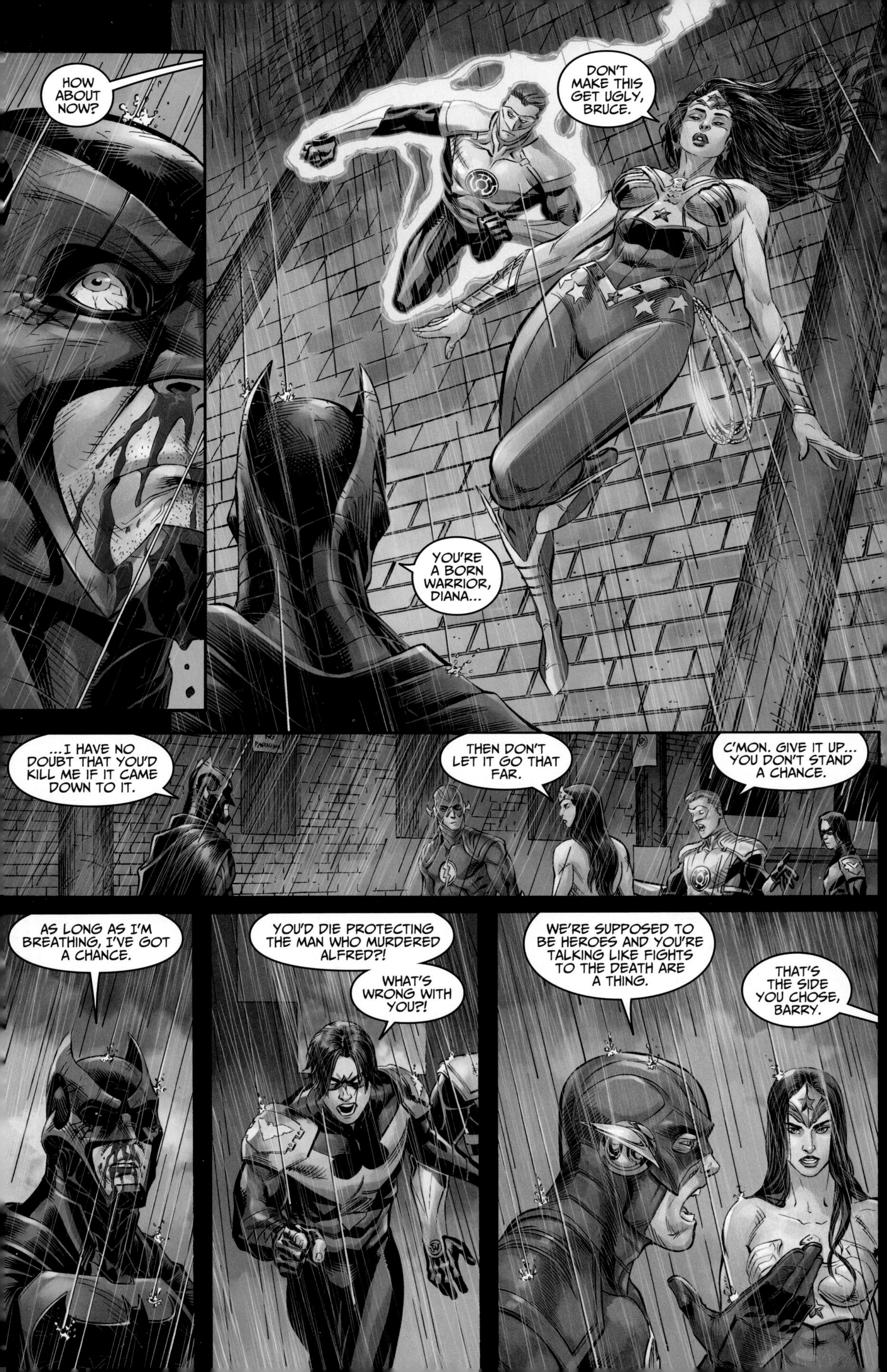
HOW ABOUT NOW?
DON'T MAKE THIS GET UGLY, BRUCE.
YOU'RE A BORN WARRIOR, DIANA...
...I HAVE NO DOUBT THAT YOU'D KILL ME IF IT CAME DOWN TO IT.
THEN DON'T LET IT GO THAT FAR.
C'MON. GIVE IT UP... YOU DON'T STAND A CHANCE.
AS LONG AS I'M BREATHING, I'VE GOT A CHANCE.
YOU'D DIE PROTECTING THE MAN WHO MURDERED ALFRED?!
WHAT'S WRONG WITH YOU?!
WE'RE SUPPOSED TO BE HEROES AND YOU'RE TALKING LIKE FIGHTS TO THE DEATH ARE A THING.
THAT'S THE SIDE YOU CHOSE, BARRY.

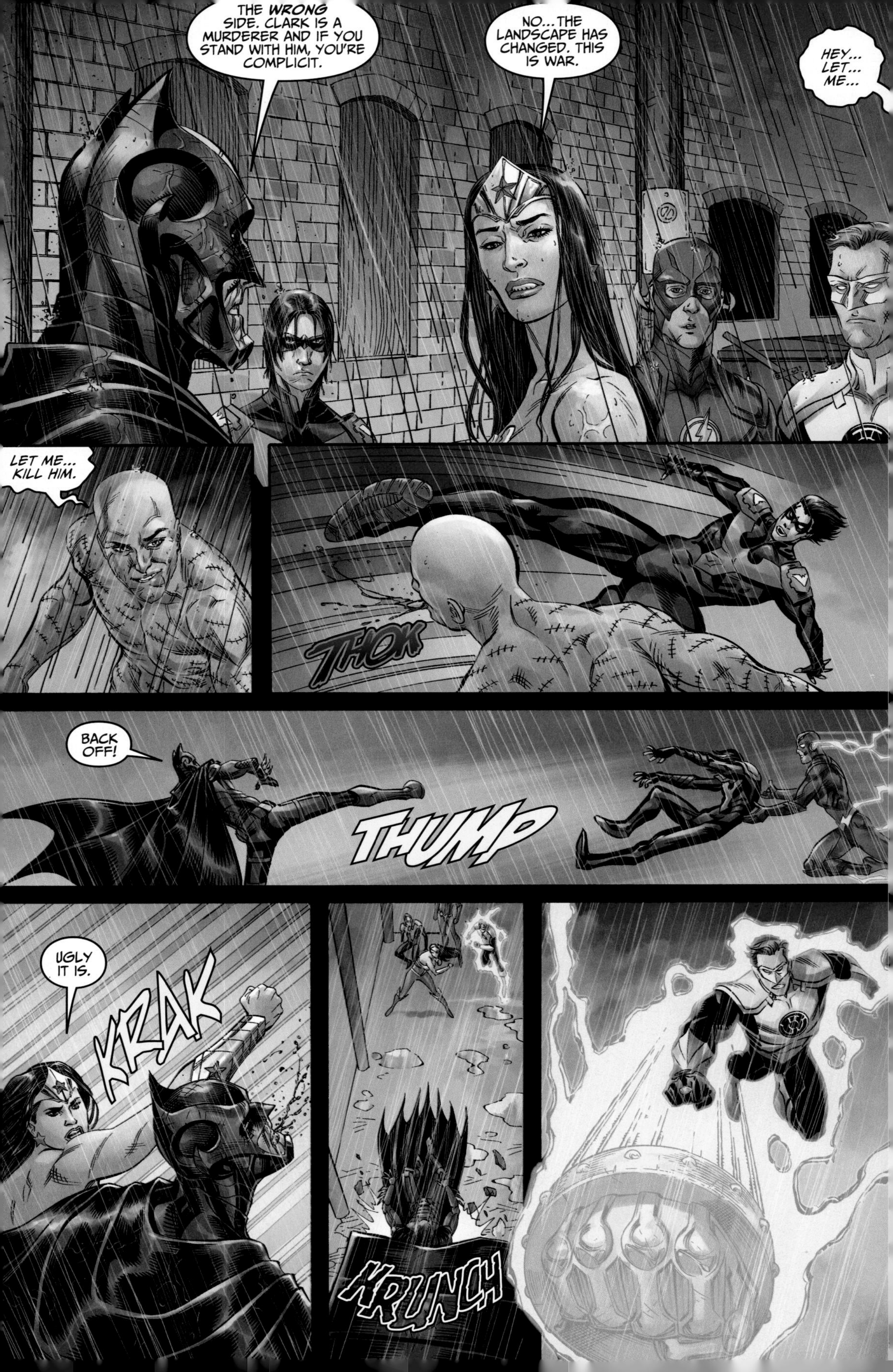
THE WRONG SIDE. CLARK IS A MURDERER AND IF YOU STAND WITH HIM, YOU'RE COMPLICIT.
NO... THE LANDSCAPE HAS CHANGED. THIS IS WAR.
HEY... LET... ME...
LET ME... KILL HIM.
THOK
BACK OFF!
THUMP
UGLY IT IS.
KRAK
KRUNCH

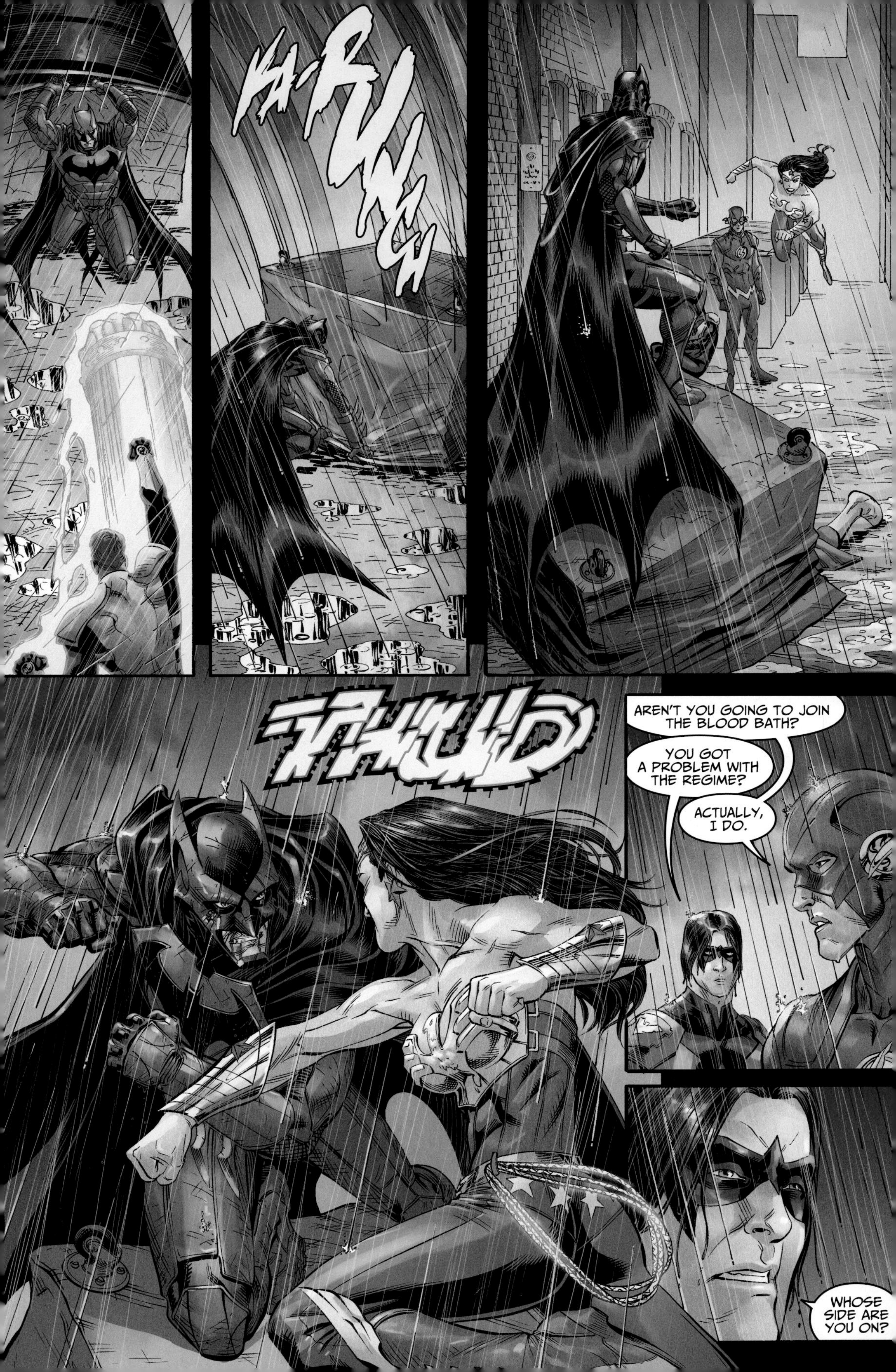
KA-RUNCH
THUD
AREN'T YOU GOING TO JOIN THE BLOOD BATH?
YOU GOT A PROBLEM WITH THE REGIME?
ACTUALLY, I DO.
WHOSE SIDE ARE YOU ON?

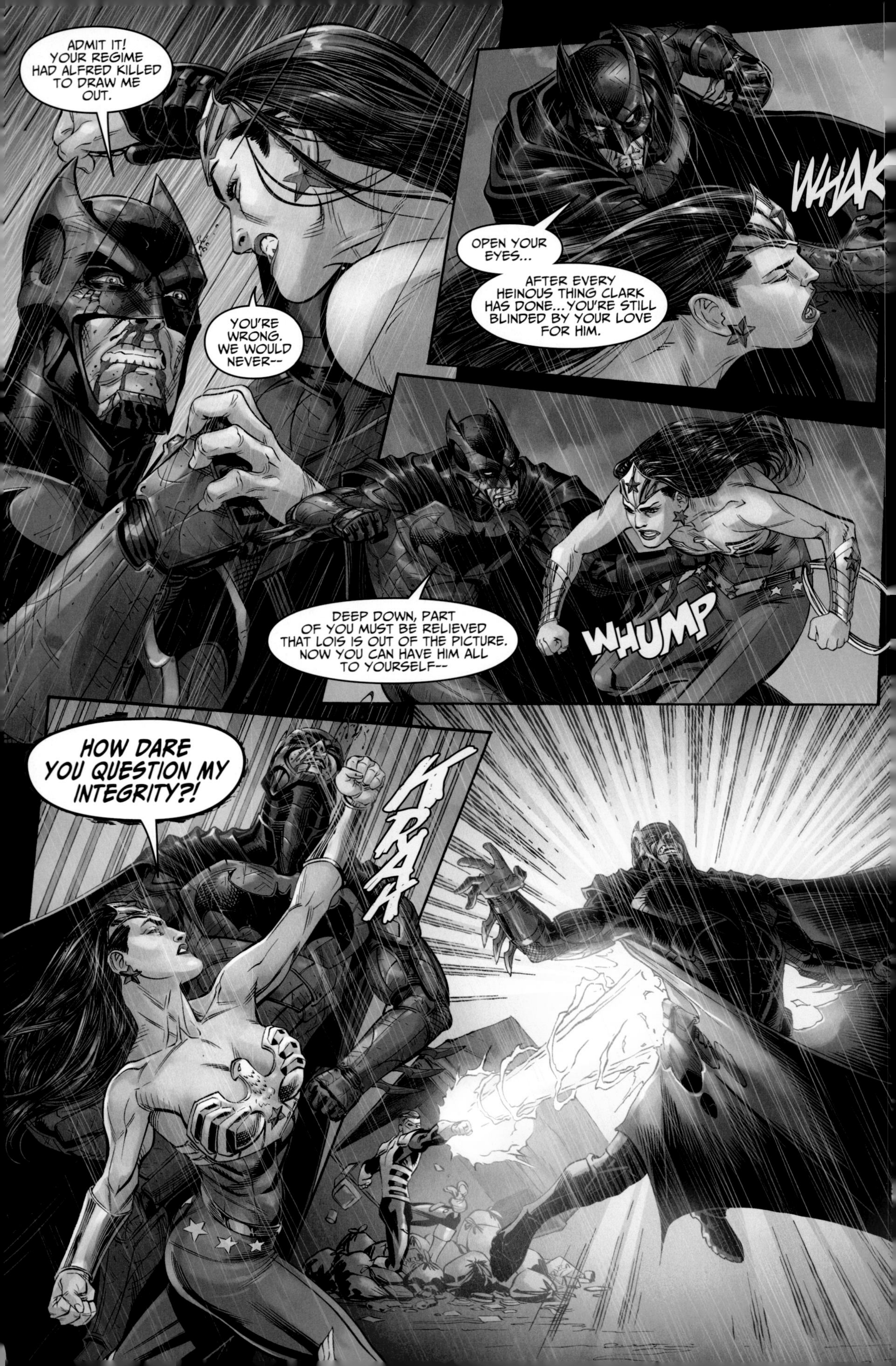
ADMIT IT! YOUR REGIME HAD ALFRED KILLED TO DRAW ME OUT.
YOU'RE WRONG. WE WOULD NEVER--
OPEN YOUR EYES...
AFTER EVERY HEINOUS THING CLARK HAS DONE...YOU'RE STILL BLINDED BY YOUR LOVE FOR HIM.
WHAK
DEEP DOWN, PART OF YOU MUST BE RELIEVED THAT LOIS IS OUT OF THE PICTURE. NOW YOU CAN HAVE HIM ALL TO YOURSELF--
WHUMP
HOW DARE YOU QUESTION MY INTEGRITY?!
KRAK

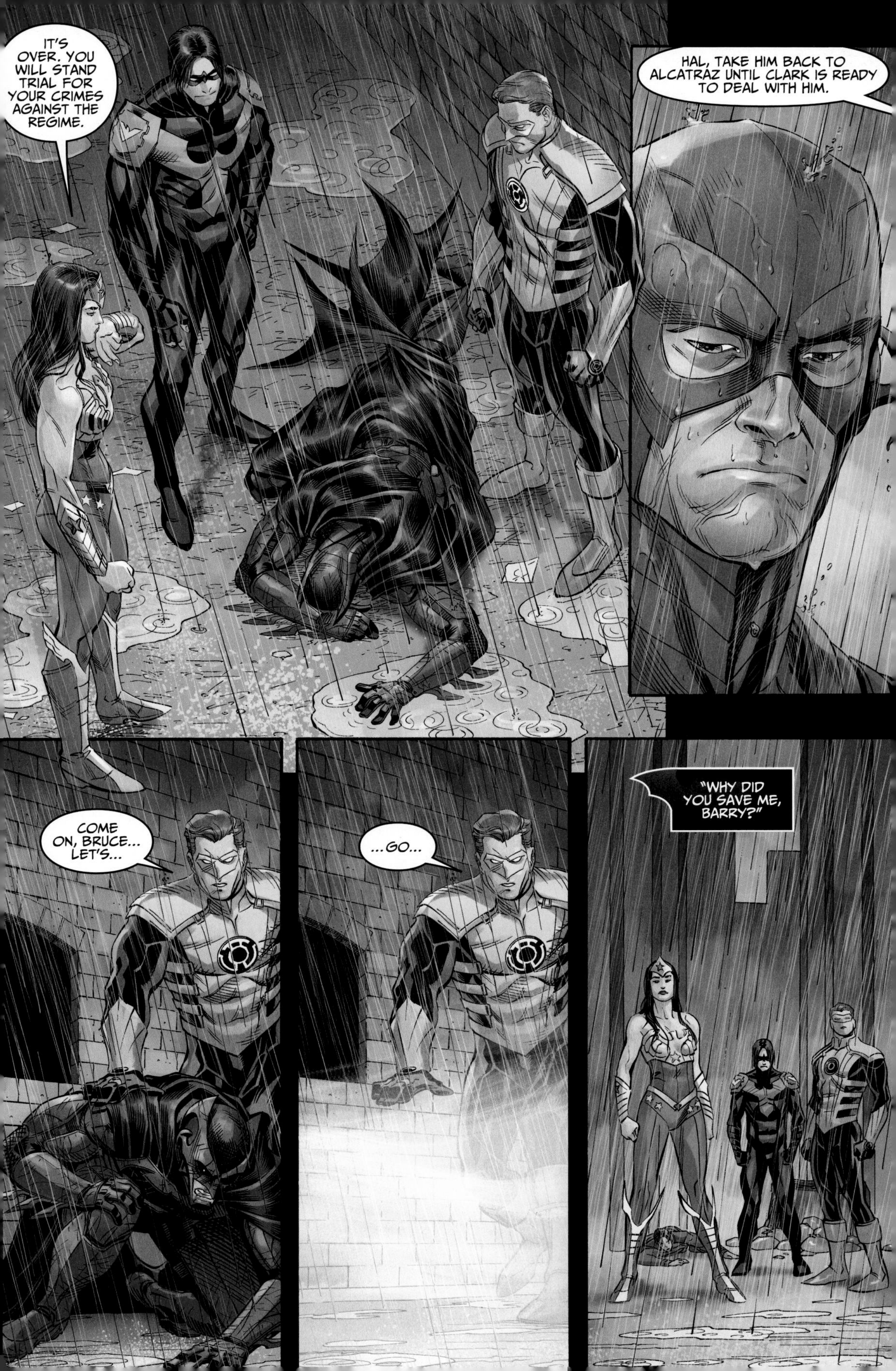
IT'S OVER. YOU WILL STAND TRIAL FOR YOUR CRIMES AGAINST THE REGIME.
HAL, TAKE HIM BACK TO ALCATRAZ UNTIL CLARK IS READY TO DEAL WITH HIM.
COME ON, BRUCE... LET'S...
...GO...
"WHY DID YOU SAVE ME, BARRY?"

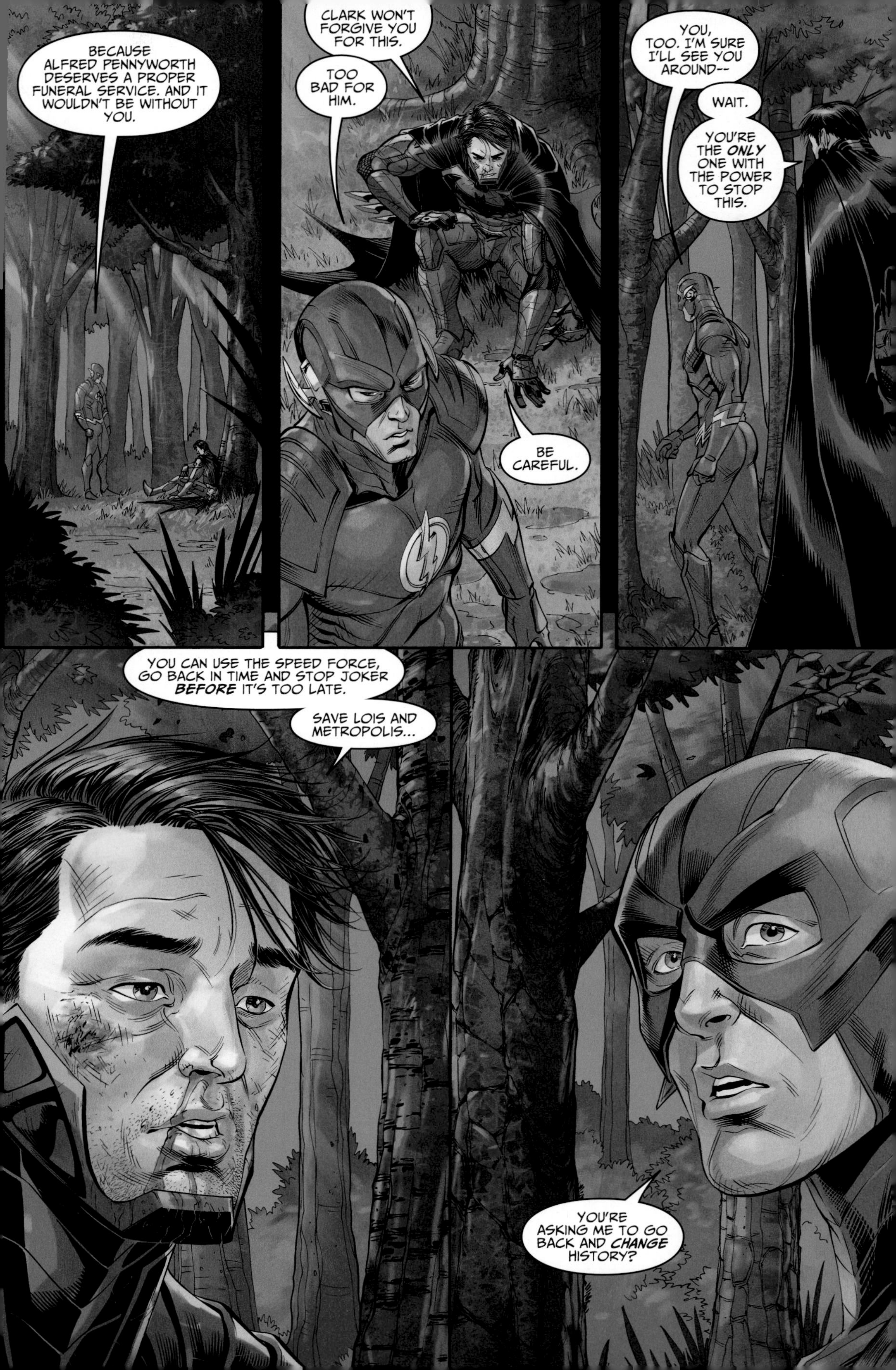
BECAUSE ALFRED PENNYWORTH DESERVES A PROPER FUNERAL SERVICE. AND IT WOULDN'T BE WITHOUT YOU.
CLARK WON'T FORGIVE YOU FOR THIS.
TOO BAD FOR HIM.
BE CAREFUL.
YOU, TOO. I'M SURE I'LL SEE YOU AROUND--
WAIT.
YOU'RE THE *ONLY* ONE WITH THE POWER TO STOP THIS.
YOU CAN USE THE SPEED FORCE, GO BACK IN TIME AND STOP JOKER *BEFORE* IT'S TOO LATE.
SAVE LOIS AND METROPOLIS...
YOU'RE ASKING ME TO GO BACK AND *CHANGE* HISTORY?

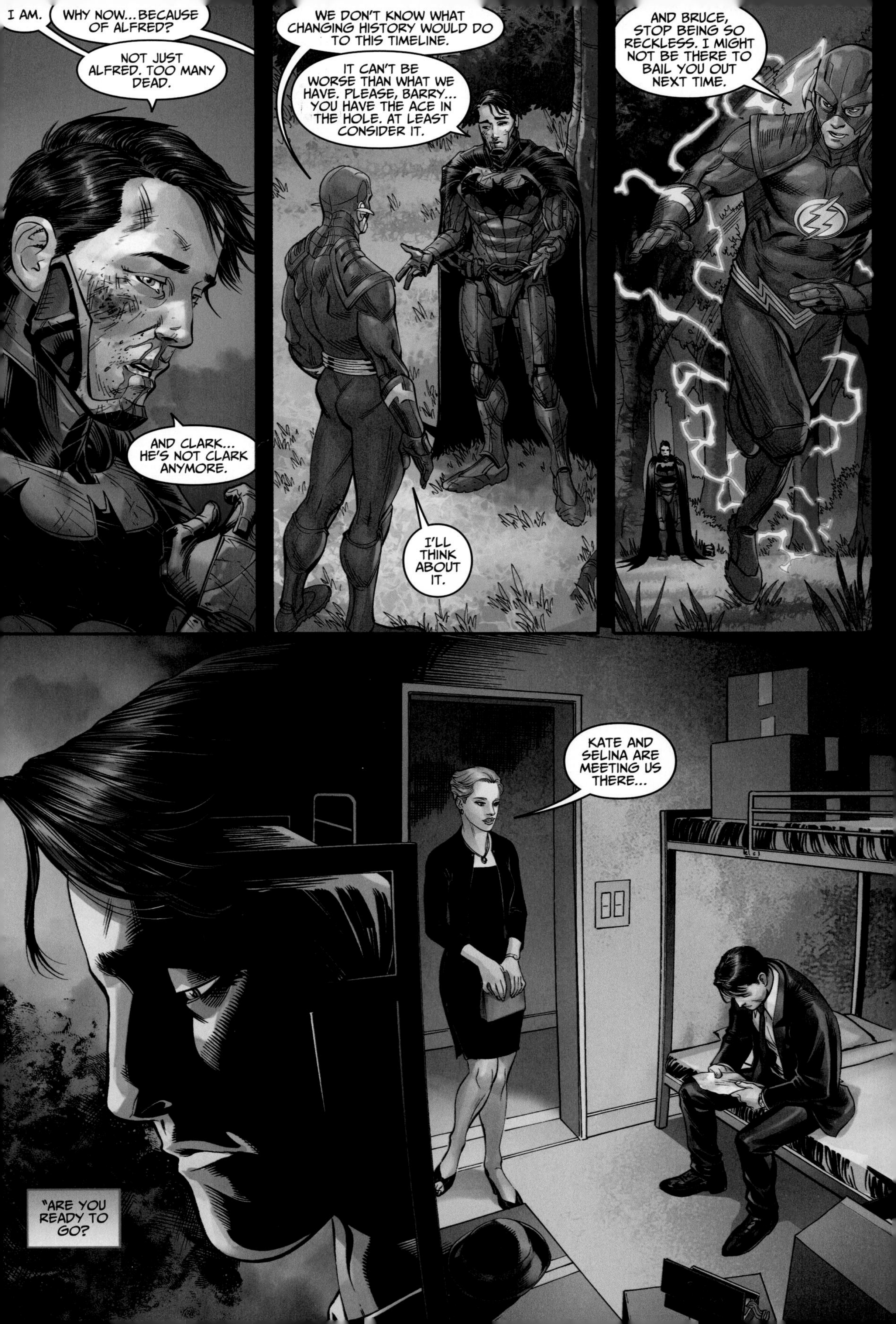
I AM.
WHY NOW...BECAUSE OF ALFRED?
NOT JUST ALFRED. TOO MANY DEAD.
AND CLARK... HE'S NOT CLARK ANYMORE.
WE DON'T KNOW WHAT CHANGING HISTORY WOULD DO TO THIS TIMELINE.
IT CAN'T BE WORSE THAN WHAT WE HAVE. PLEASE, BARRY... YOU HAVE THE ACE IN THE HOLE. AT LEAST CONSIDER IT.
I'LL THINK ABOUT IT.
AND BRUCE, STOP BEING SO RECKLESS. I MIGHT NOT BE THERE TO BAIL YOU OUT NEXT TIME.
KATE AND SELINA ARE MEETING US THERE...
"ARE YOU READY TO GO?

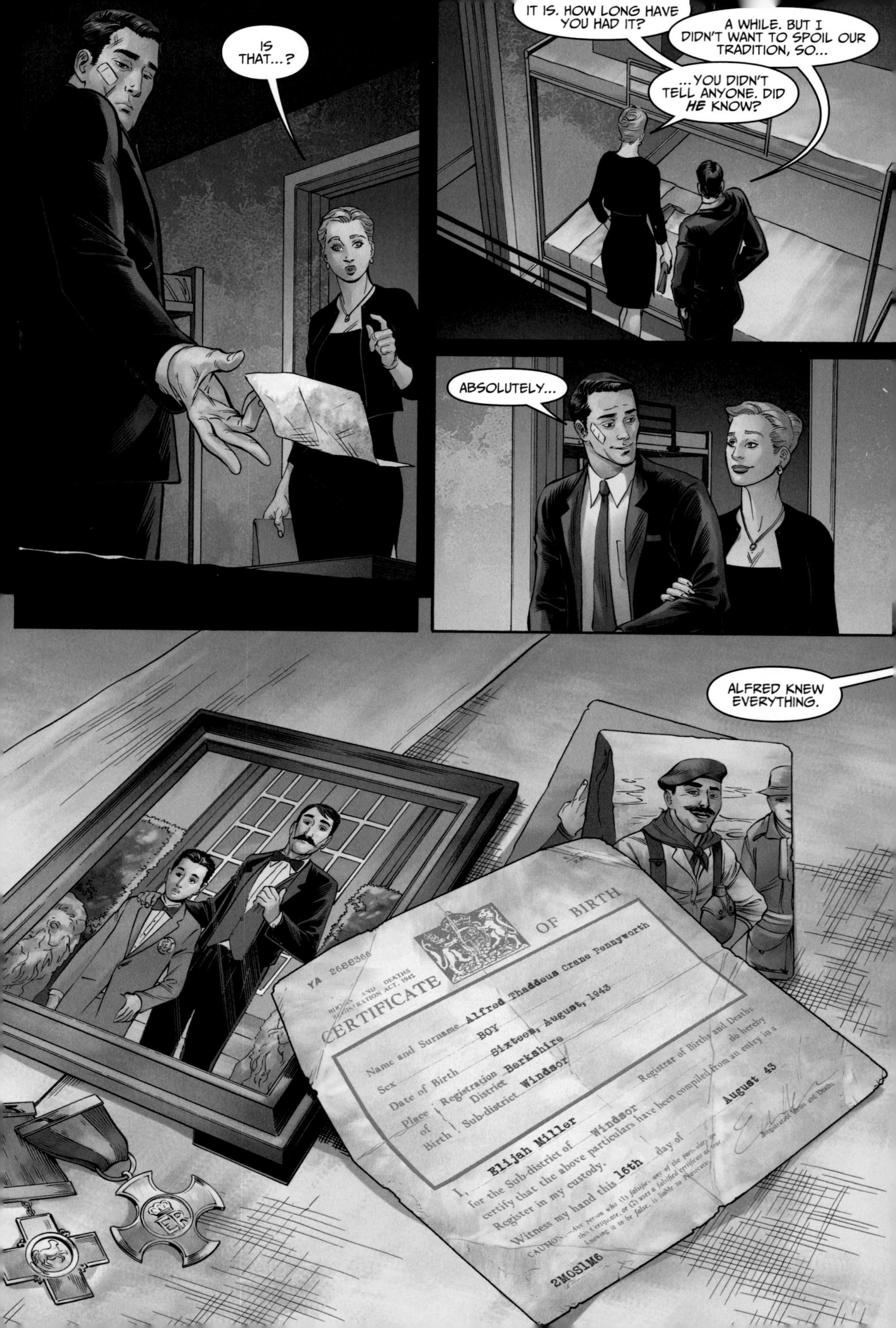
IS THAT...?
IT IS. HOW LONG HAVE YOU HAD IT?
A WHILE. BUT I DIDN'T WANT TO SPOIL OUR TRADITION, SO...
...YOU DIDN'T TELL ANYONE. DID *HE* KNOW?
ABSOLUTELY...
ALFRED KNEW EVERYTHING.
YA 2688366
CERTIFICATE OF BIRTH
Name and Surname Alfred Thaddeus Crane Pennyworth
Sex BOY
Date of Birth Sixteen, August, 1943
Place of Birth Registration District Berkshire
Sub-district Windsor
I, Elijah Miller Registrar of Births and Deaths for the Sub-district of Windsor do hereby certify that the above particulars have been compiled from an entry in a Register in my custody.
Witness my hand this 16th day of August 43
Registrar of Births and Deaths
2MOSLM6

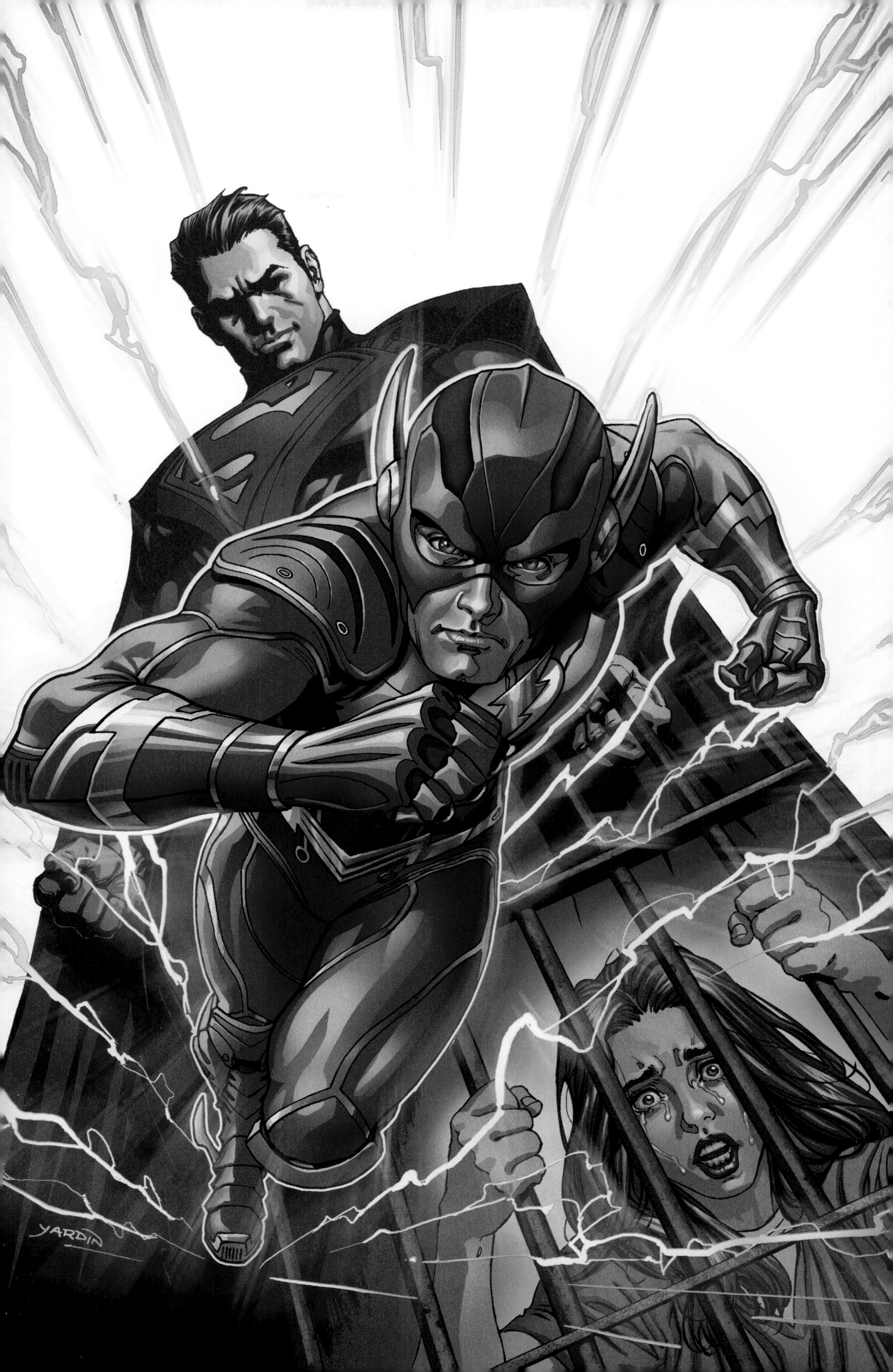
YARDIN

"Barry" **Tom Derenick** Artist **Rex Lokus** Colorist

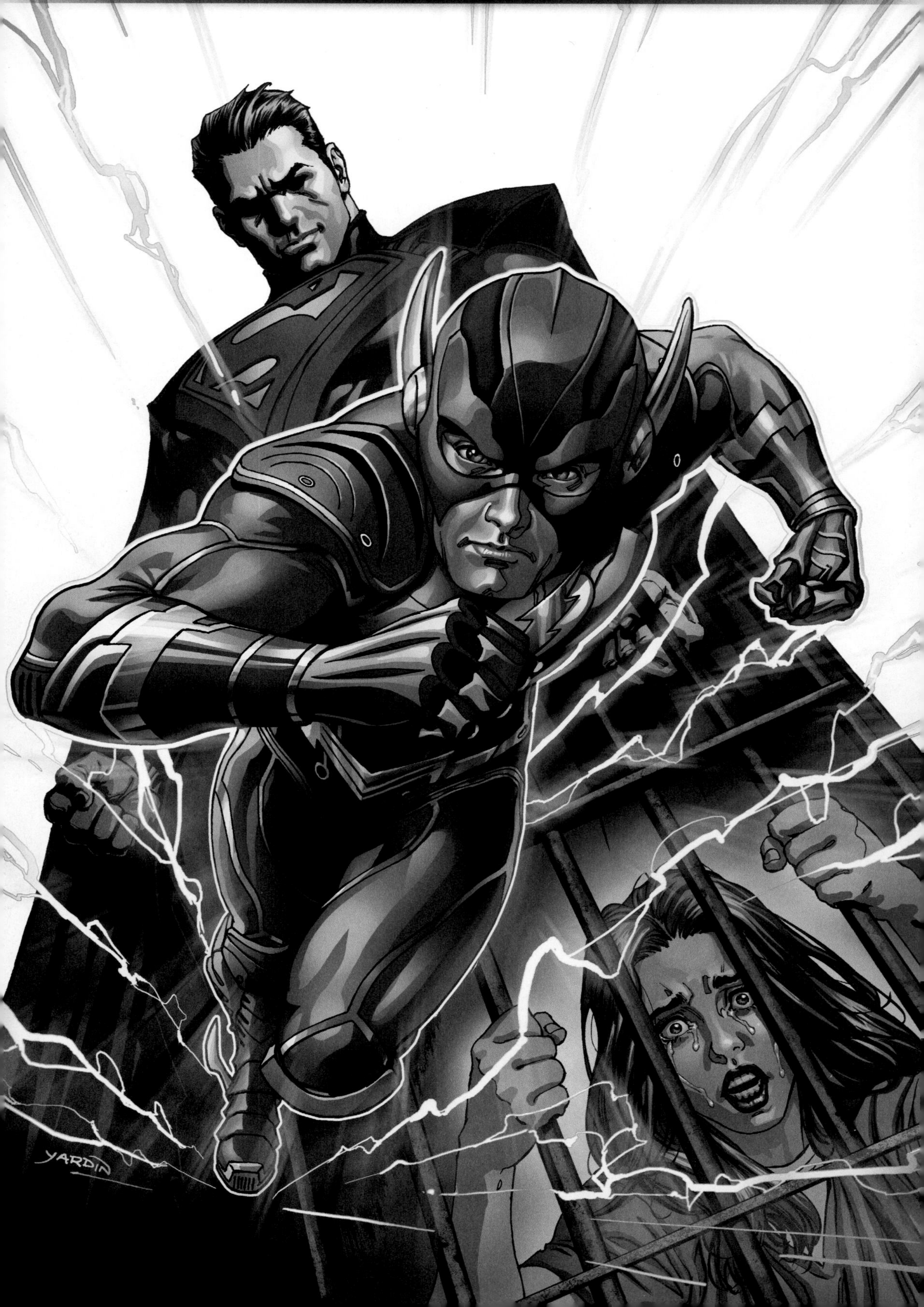
YARDIN

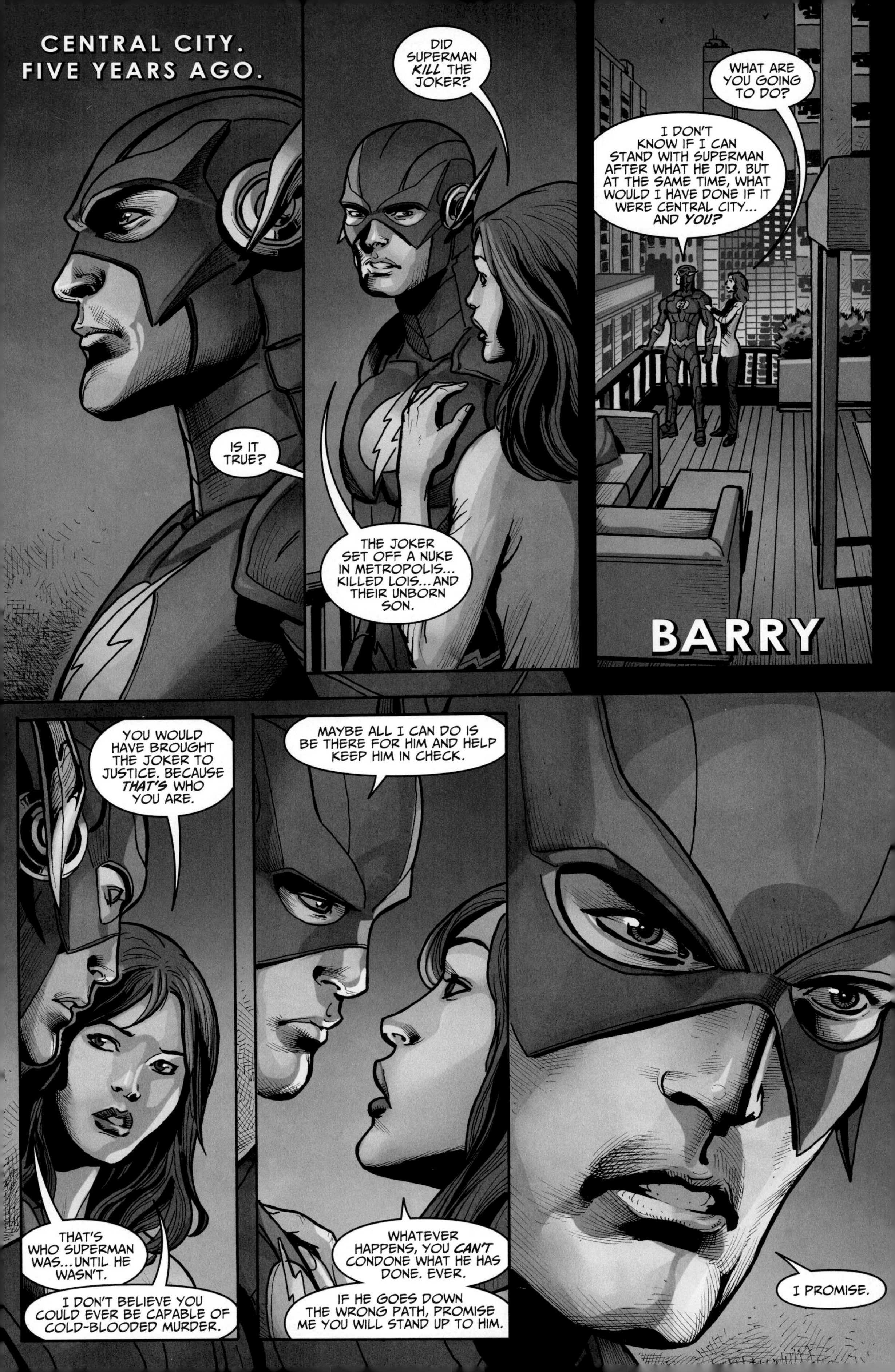
CENTRAL CITY. FIVE YEARS AGO.
IS IT TRUE?
DID SUPERMAN KILL THE JOKER?
THE JOKER SET OFF A NUKE IN METROPOLIS... KILLED LOIS...AND THEIR UNBORN SON.
WHAT ARE YOU GOING TO DO?
I DON'T KNOW IF I CAN STAND WITH SUPERMAN AFTER WHAT HE DID. BUT AT THE SAME TIME, WHAT WOULD I HAVE DONE IF IT WERE CENTRAL CITY... AND YOU?
BARRY
YOU WOULD HAVE BROUGHT THE JOKER TO JUSTICE. BECAUSE THAT'S WHO YOU ARE.
THAT'S WHO SUPERMAN WAS...UNTIL HE WASN'T.
I DON'T BELIEVE YOU COULD EVER BE CAPABLE OF COLD-BLOODED MURDER.
MAYBE ALL I CAN DO IS BE THERE FOR HIM AND HELP KEEP HIM IN CHECK.
WHATEVER HAPPENS, YOU CAN'T CONDONE WHAT HE HAS DONE. EVER.
IF HE GOES DOWN THE WRONG PATH, PROMISE ME YOU WILL STAND UP TO HIM.
I PROMISE.

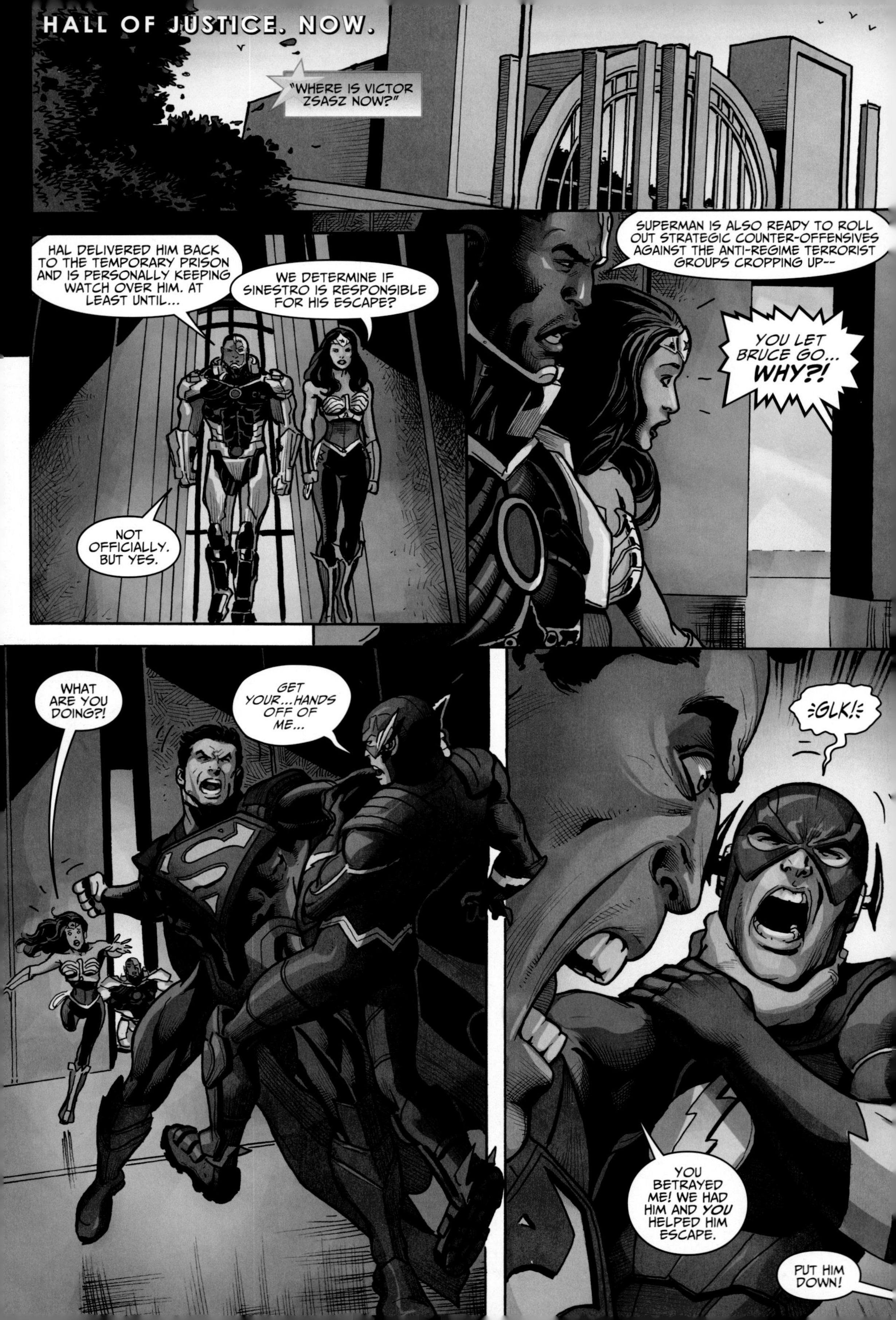
HALL OF JUSTICE. NOW.
"WHERE IS VICTOR ZSASZ NOW?"
HAL DELIVERED HIM BACK TO THE TEMPORARY PRISON AND IS PERSONALLY KEEPING WATCH OVER HIM. AT LEAST UNTIL...
WE DETERMINE IF SINESTRO IS RESPONSIBLE FOR HIS ESCAPE?
NOT OFFICIALLY. BUT YES.
SUPERMAN IS ALSO READY TO ROLL OUT STRATEGIC COUNTER-OFFENSIVES AGAINST THE ANTI-REGIME TERRORIST GROUPS CROPPING UP--
YOU LET BRUCE GO... WHY?!
WHAT ARE YOU DOING?!
GET YOUR...HANDS OFF OF ME...
GLK!
YOU BETRAYED ME! WE HAD HIM AND YOU HELPED HIM ESCAPE.
PUT HIM DOWN!

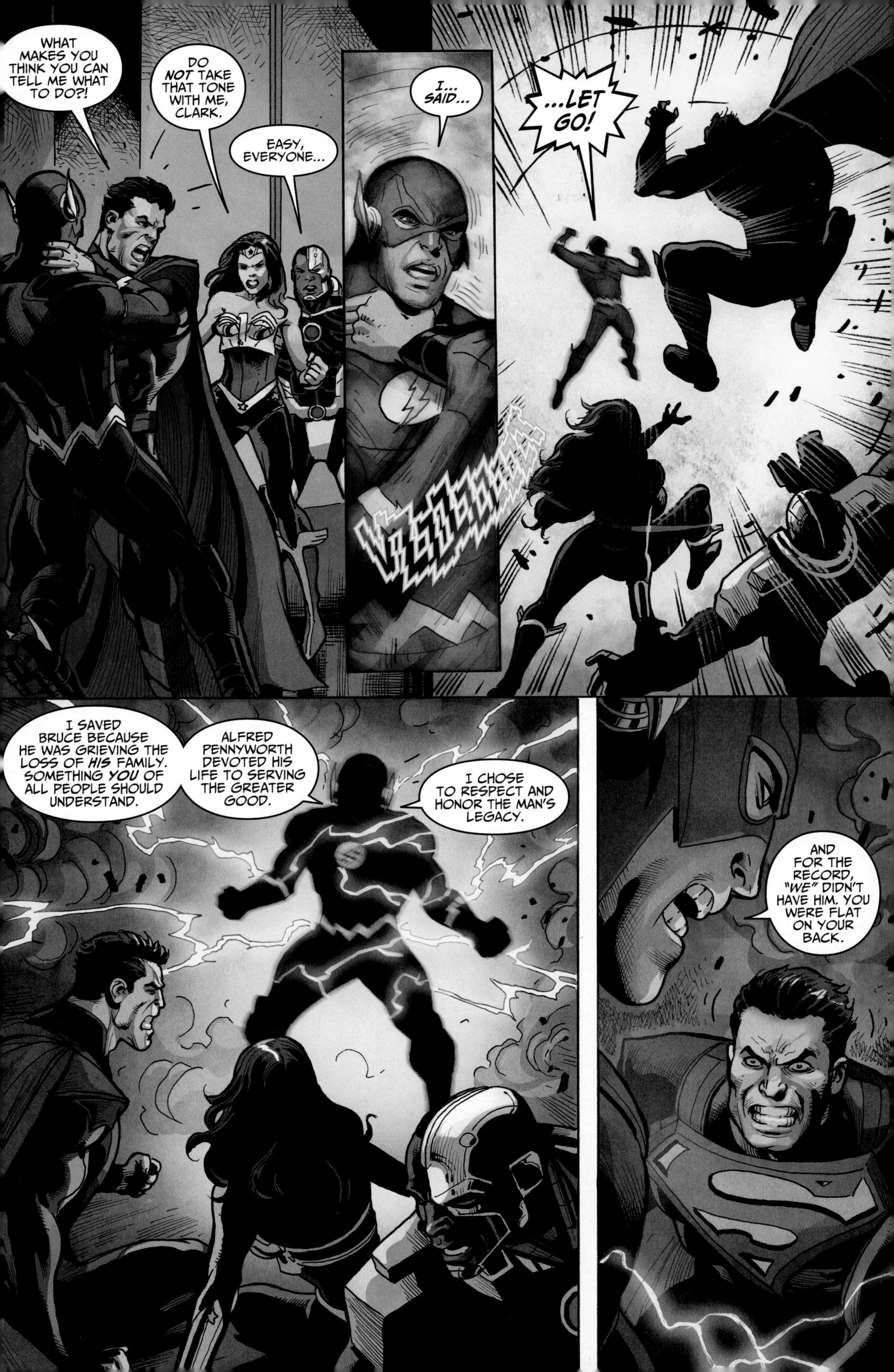
WHAT MAKES YOU THINK YOU CAN TELL ME WHAT TO DO?!
DO NOT TAKE THAT TONE WITH ME, CLARK.
EASY, EVERYONE...
I... SAID...
...LET GO!
I SAVED BRUCE BECAUSE HE WAS GRIEVING THE LOSS OF HIS FAMILY. SOMETHING YOU OF ALL PEOPLE SHOULD UNDERSTAND.
ALFRED PENNYWORTH DEVOTED HIS LIFE TO SERVING THE GREATER GOOD.
I CHOSE TO RESPECT AND HONOR THE MAN'S LEGACY.
AND FOR THE RECORD, "WE" DIDN'T HAVE HIM. YOU WERE FLAT ON YOUR BACK.

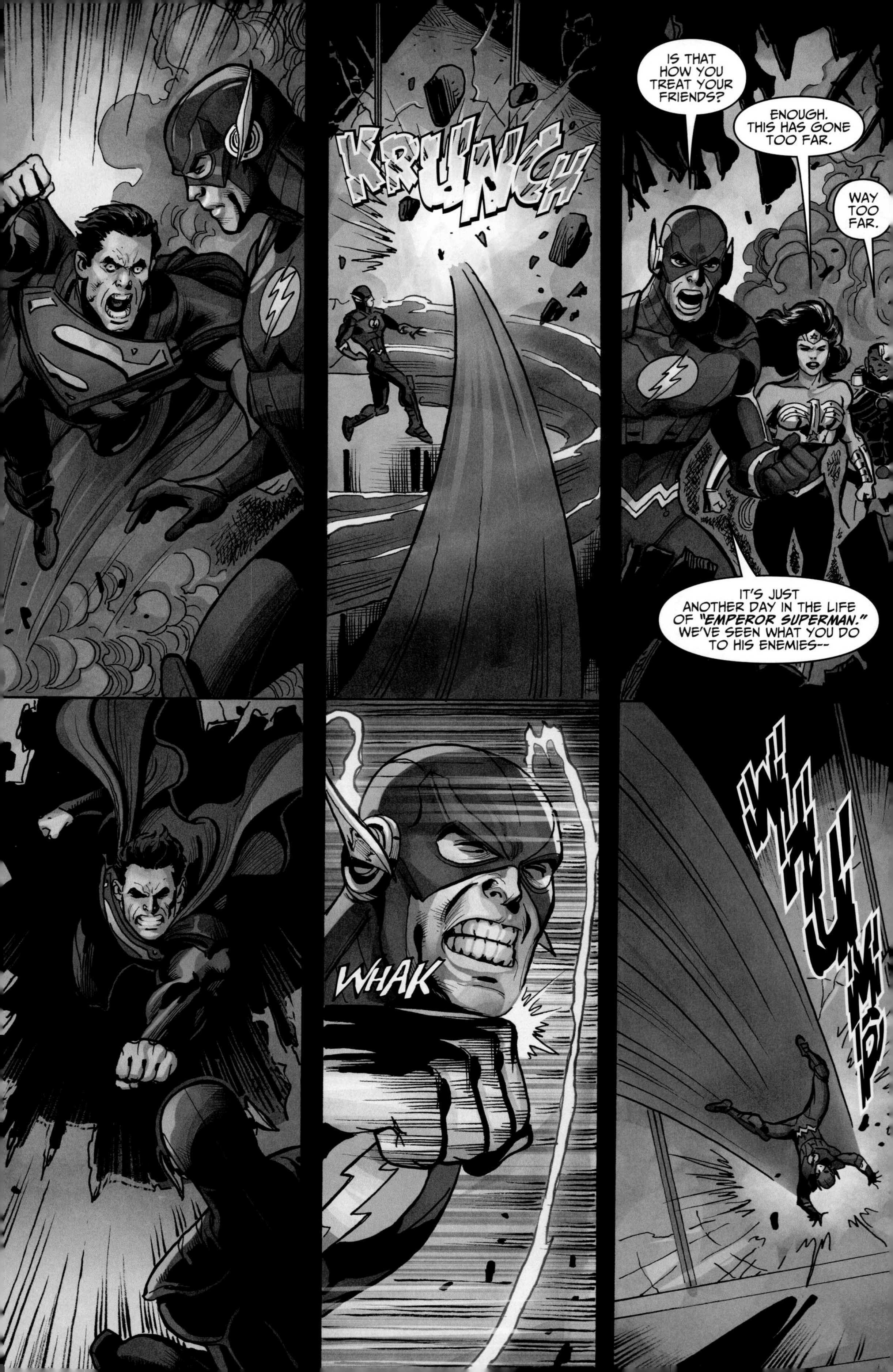
KRUNCH
IS THAT HOW YOU TREAT YOUR FRIENDS?
ENOUGH. THIS HAS GONE TOO FAR.
WAY TOO FAR.
IT'S JUST ANOTHER DAY IN THE LIFE OF "EMPEROR SUPERMAN." WE'VE SEEN WHAT YOU DO TO HIS ENEMIES--
WHAK
WHUMP

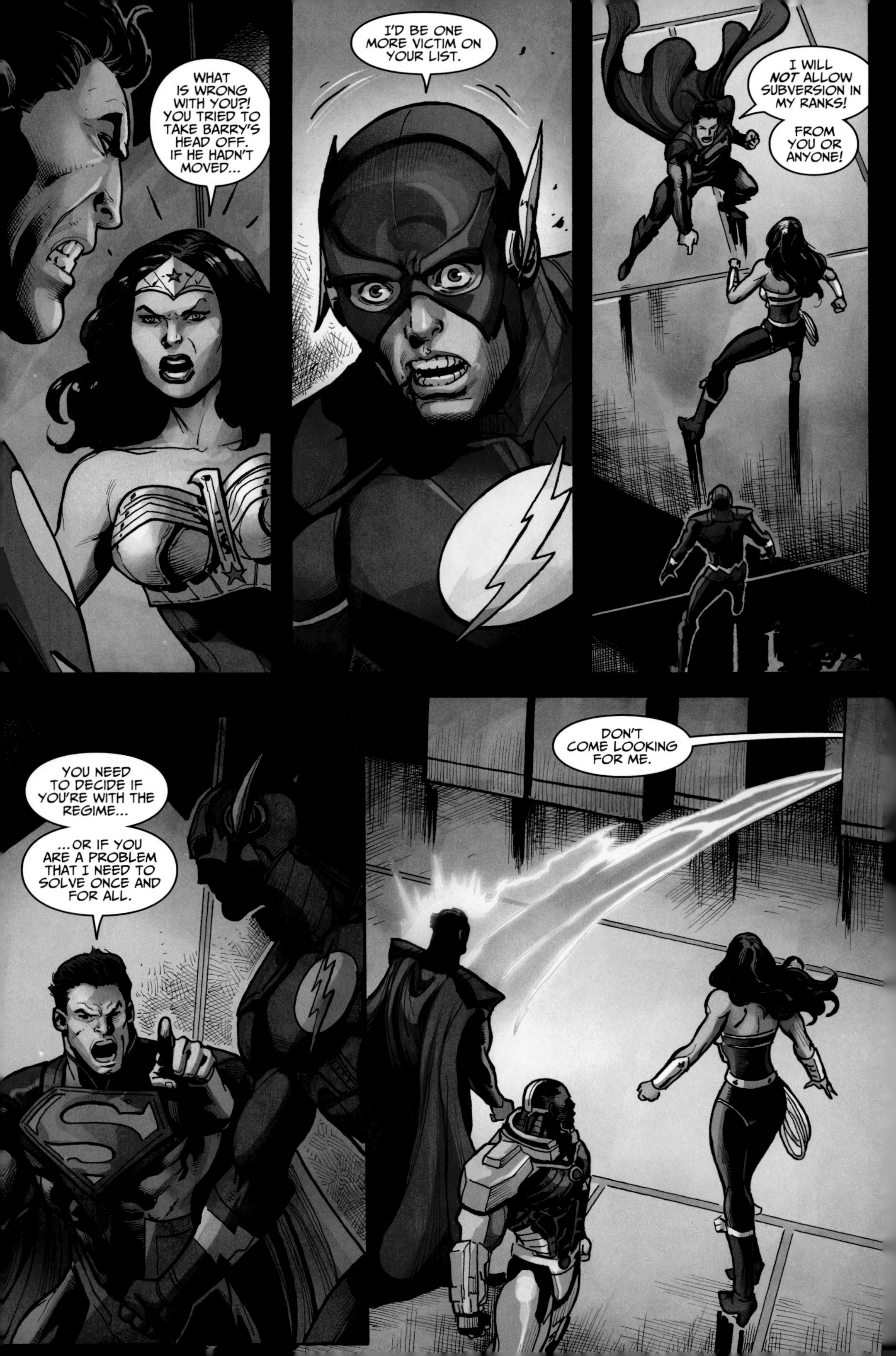
WHAT IS WRONG WITH YOU?! YOU TRIED TO TAKE BARRY'S HEAD OFF. IF HE HADN'T MOVED...
I'D BE ONE MORE VICTIM ON YOUR LIST.
I WILL *NOT* ALLOW SUBVERSION IN MY RANKS!
FROM YOU OR ANYONE!
YOU NEED TO DECIDE IF YOU'RE WITH THE REGIME...
...OR IF YOU ARE A PROBLEM THAT I NEED TO SOLVE ONCE AND FOR ALL.
DON'T COME LOOKING FOR ME.

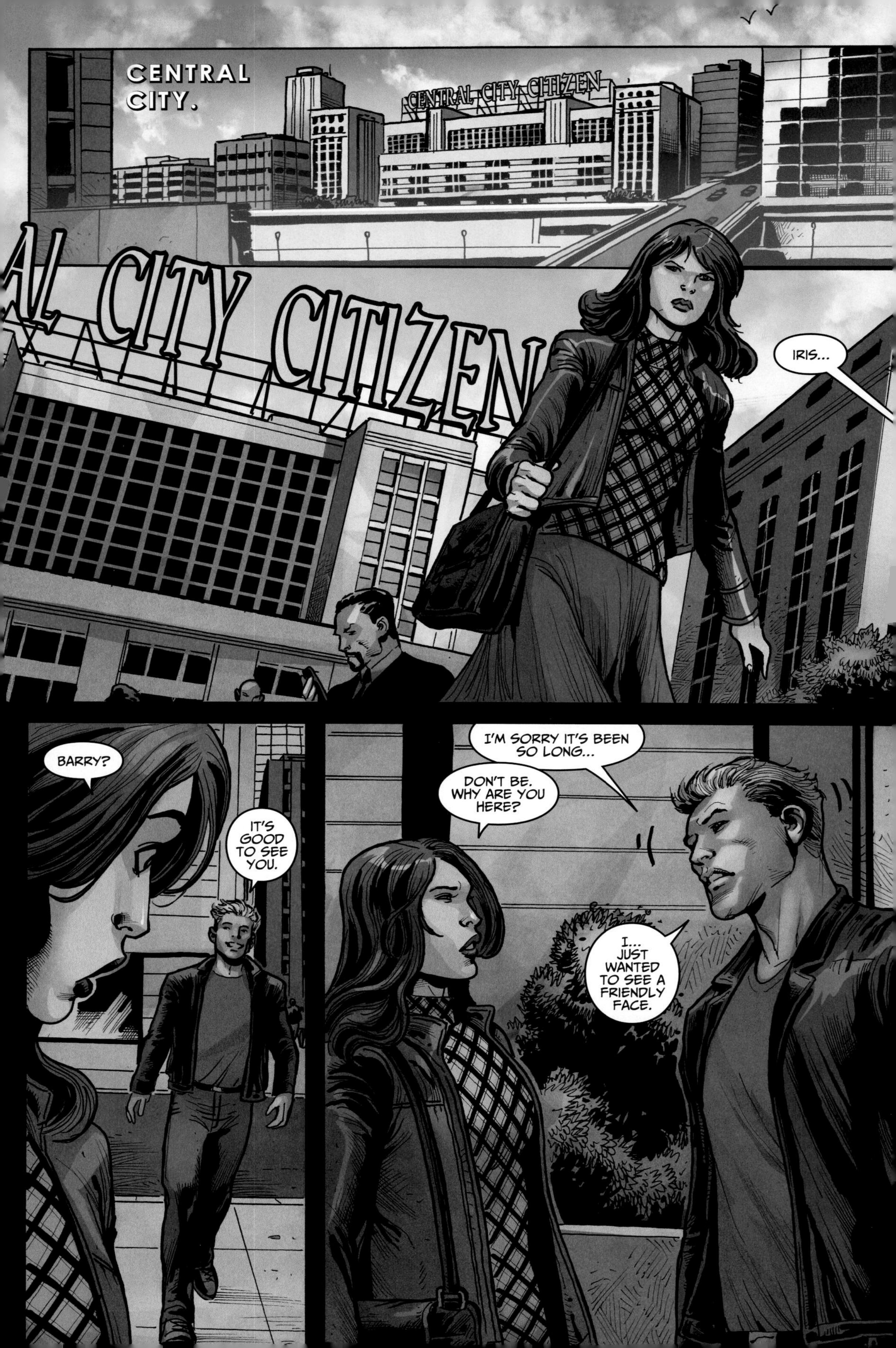
CENTRAL CITY.
CENTRAL CITY CITIZEN
AL CITY CITIZEN
IRIS...
BARRY?
IT'S GOOD TO SEE YOU.
I'M SORRY IT'S BEEN SO LONG...
DON'T BE. WHY ARE YOU HERE?
I... JUST WANTED TO SEE A FRIENDLY FACE.

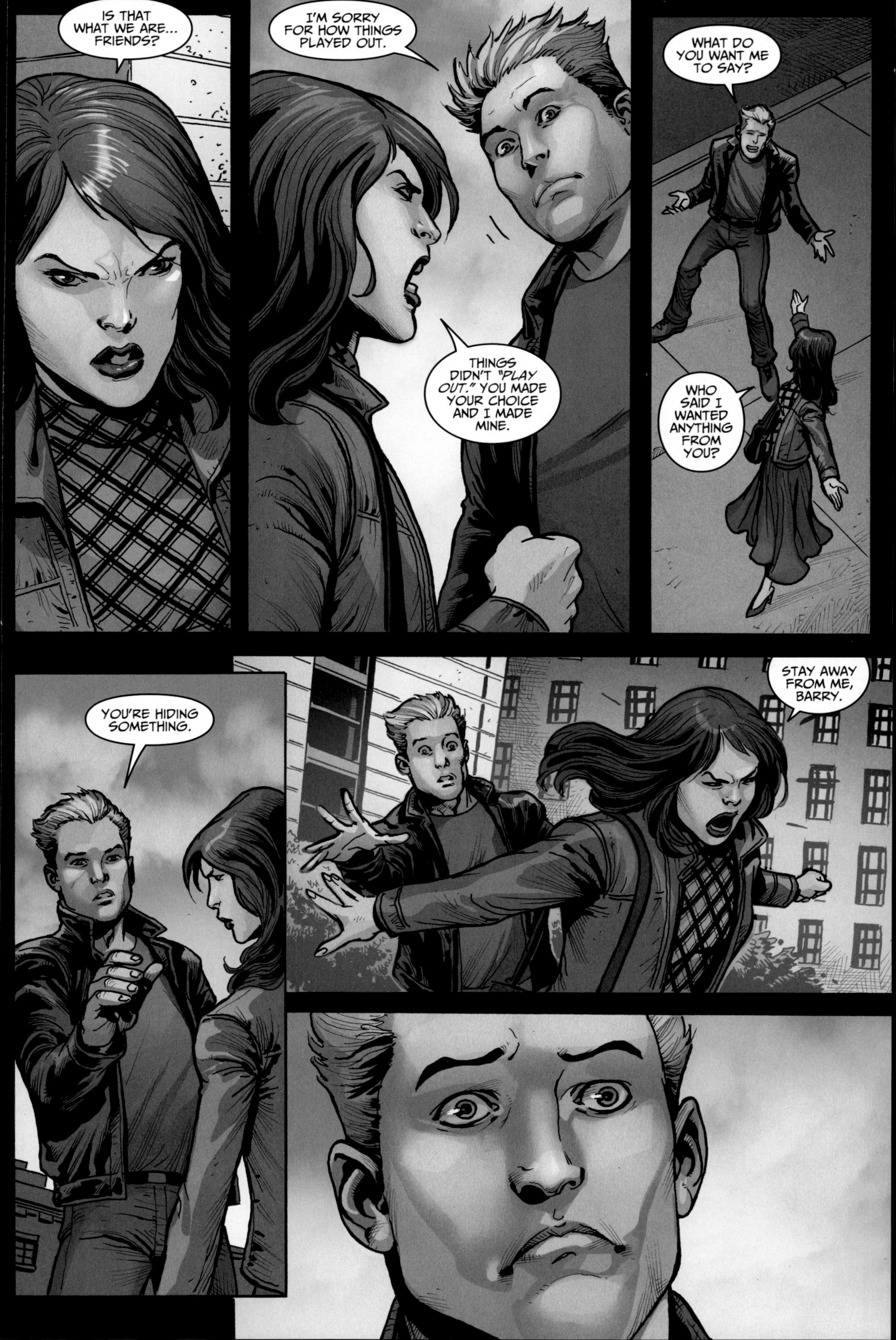
IS THAT WHAT WE ARE... FRIENDS?
I'M SORRY FOR HOW THINGS PLAYED OUT.
THINGS DIDN'T "PLAY OUT." YOU MADE YOUR CHOICE AND I MADE MINE.
WHAT DO YOU WANT ME TO SAY?
WHO SAID I WANTED ANYTHING FROM YOU?
YOU'RE HIDING SOMETHING.
STAY AWAY FROM ME, BARRY.

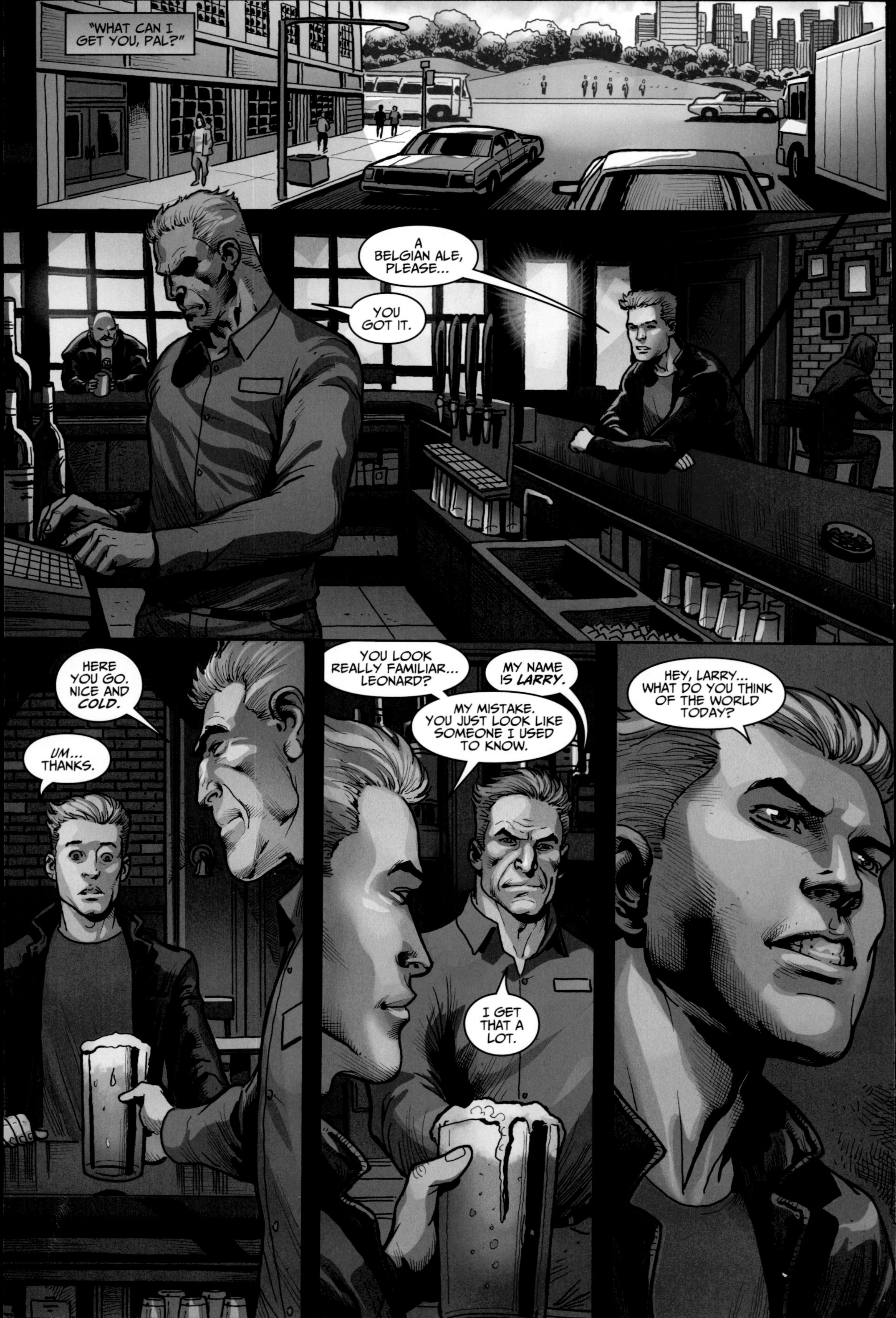
"WHAT CAN I GET YOU, PAL?"
A BELGIAN ALE, PLEASE...
YOU GOT IT.
HERE YOU GO. NICE AND *COLD.*
UM... THANKS.
YOU LOOK REALLY FAMILIAR... LEONARD?
MY NAME IS *LARRY.*
MY MISTAKE. YOU JUST LOOK LIKE SOMEONE I USED TO KNOW.
I GET THAT A LOT.
HEY, LARRY... WHAT DO YOU THINK OF THE WORLD TODAY?

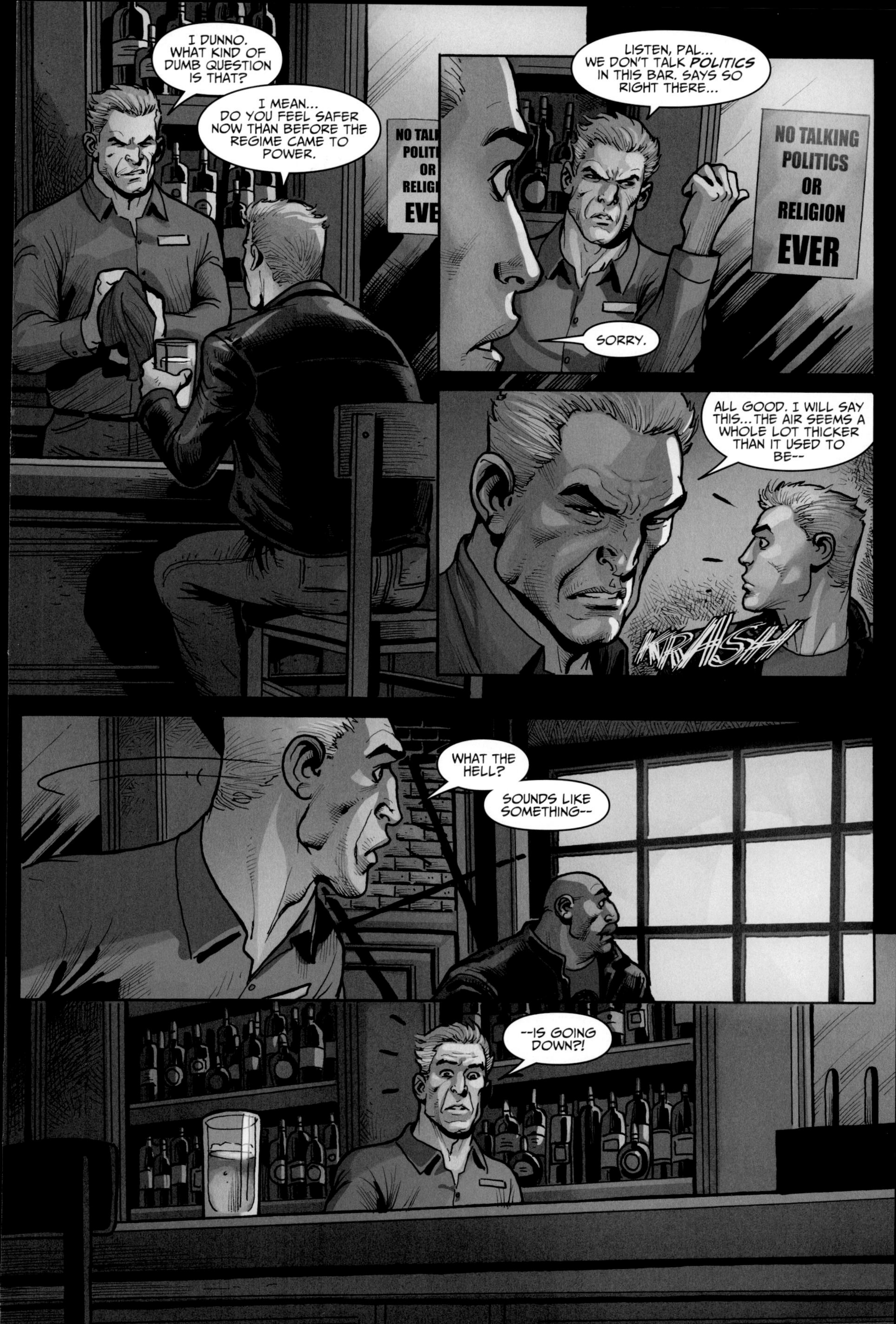
I DUNNO. WHAT KIND OF DUMB QUESTION IS THAT?
I MEAN... DO YOU FEEL SAFER NOW THAN BEFORE THE REGIME CAME TO POWER.
LISTEN, PAL... WE DON'T TALK *POLITICS* IN THIS BAR. SAYS SO RIGHT THERE...
NO TALKING POLITICS OR RELIGION EVER
SORRY.
ALL GOOD. I WILL SAY THIS...THE AIR SEEMS A WHOLE LOT THICKER THAN IT USED TO BE--
KRASH
WHAT THE HELL?
SOUNDS LIKE SOMETHING--
--IS GOING DOWN?!

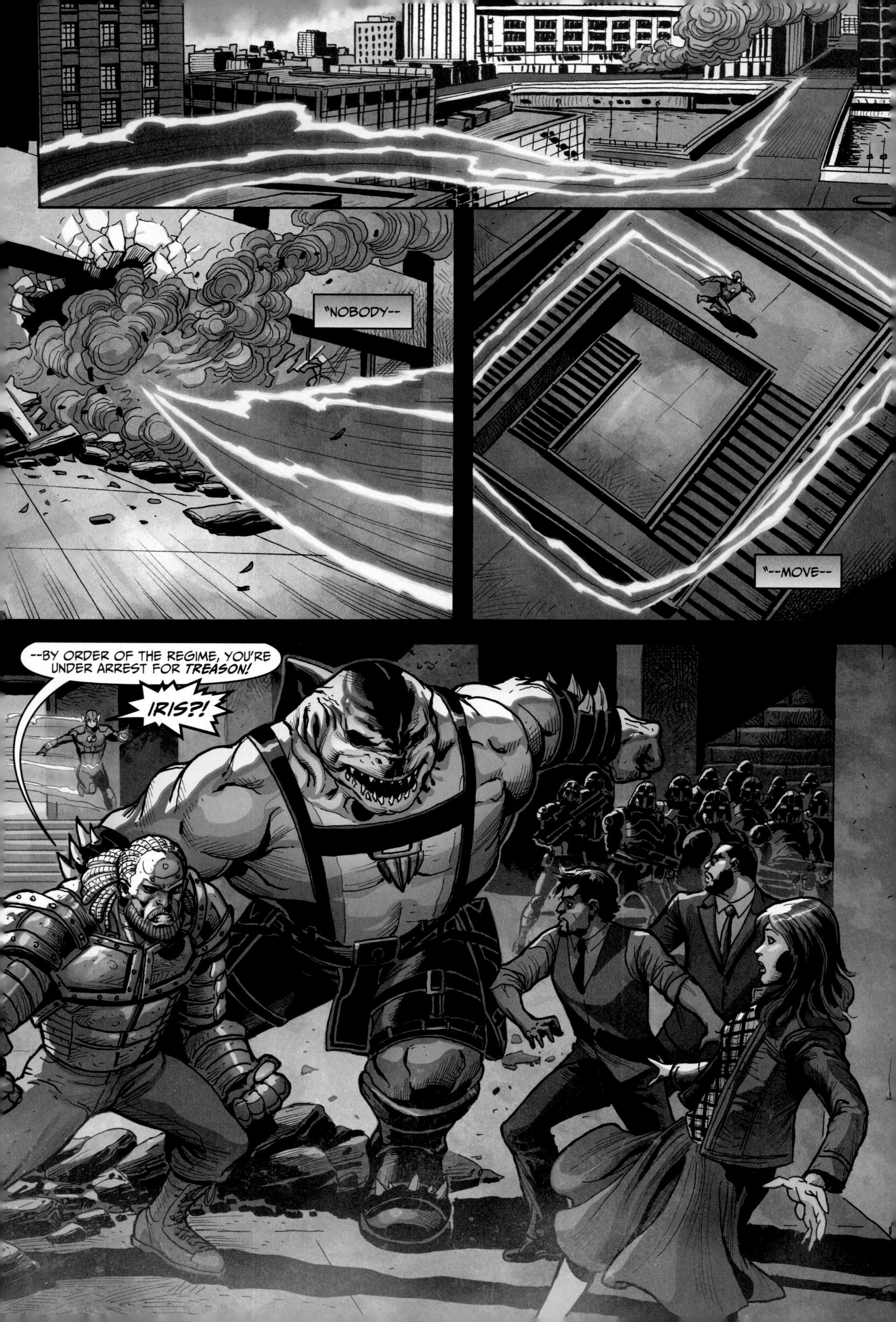
"NOBODY--
"--MOVE--
--BY ORDER OF THE REGIME, YOU'RE UNDER ARREST FOR TREASON!
IRIS?!

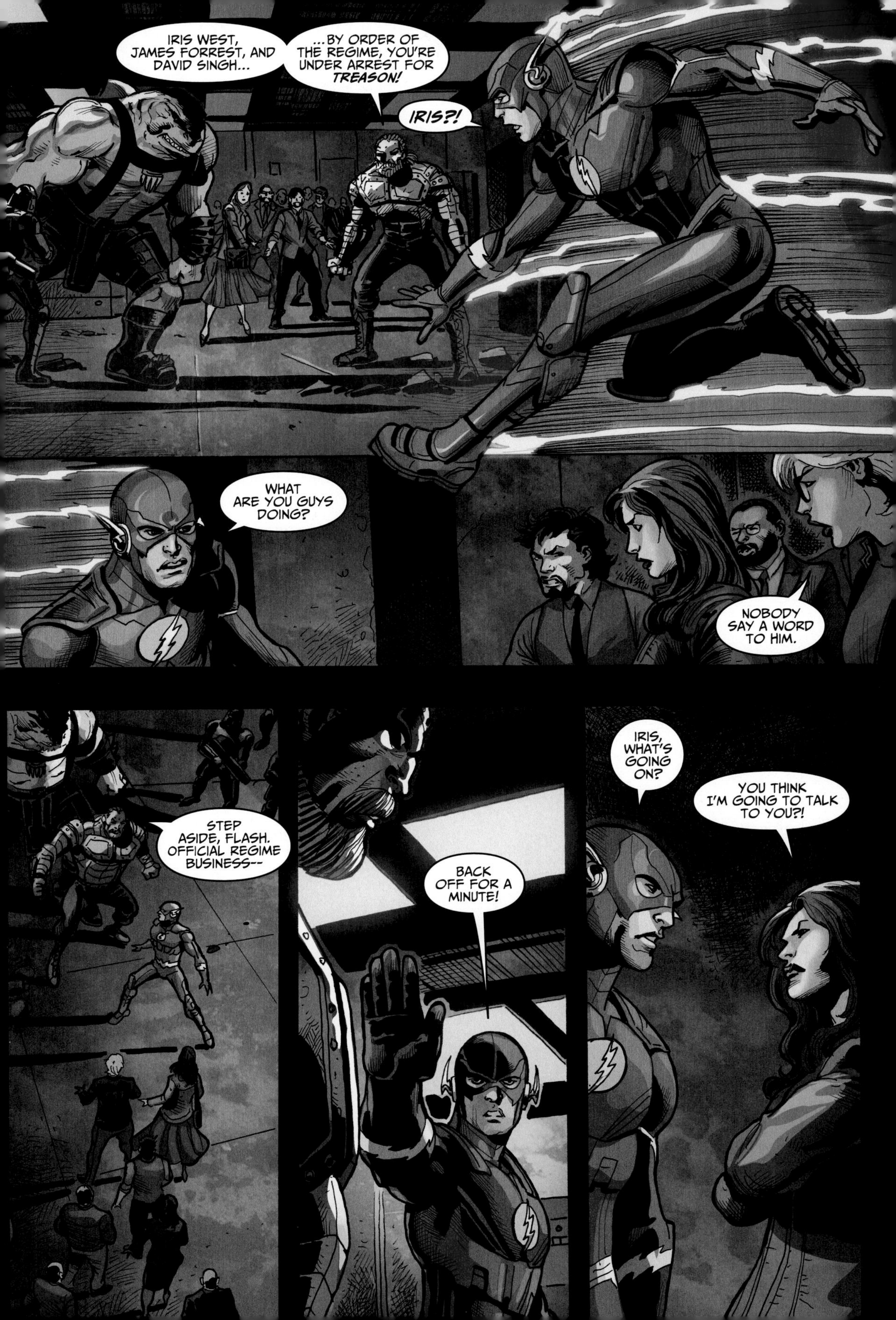
IRIS WEST, JAMES FORREST, AND DAVID SINGH...
...BY ORDER OF THE REGIME, YOU'RE UNDER ARREST FOR *TREASON!*
IRIS?!
WHAT ARE YOU GUYS DOING?
NOBODY SAY A WORD TO HIM.
STEP ASIDE, FLASH. OFFICIAL REGIME BUSINESS--
BACK OFF FOR A MINUTE!
IRIS, WHAT'S GOING ON?
YOU THINK I'M GOING TO TALK TO YOU?!

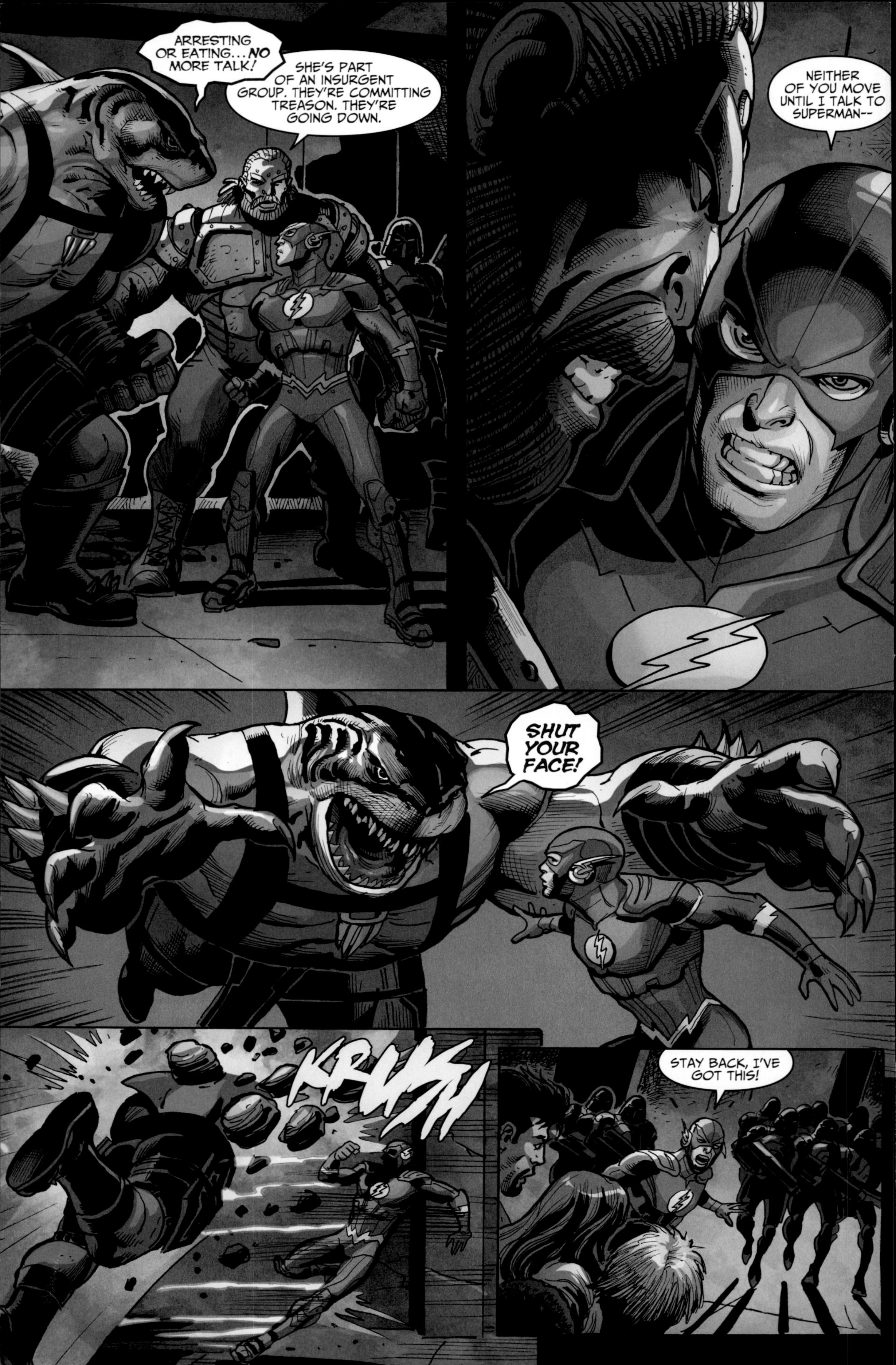
ARRESTING OR EATING... NO MORE TALK!
SHE'S PART OF AN INSURGENT GROUP. THEY'RE COMMITTING TREASON. THEY'RE GOING DOWN.
NEITHER OF YOU MOVE UNTIL I TALK TO SUPERMAN--
SHUT YOUR FACE!
KRUSH
STAY BACK, I'VE GOT THIS!

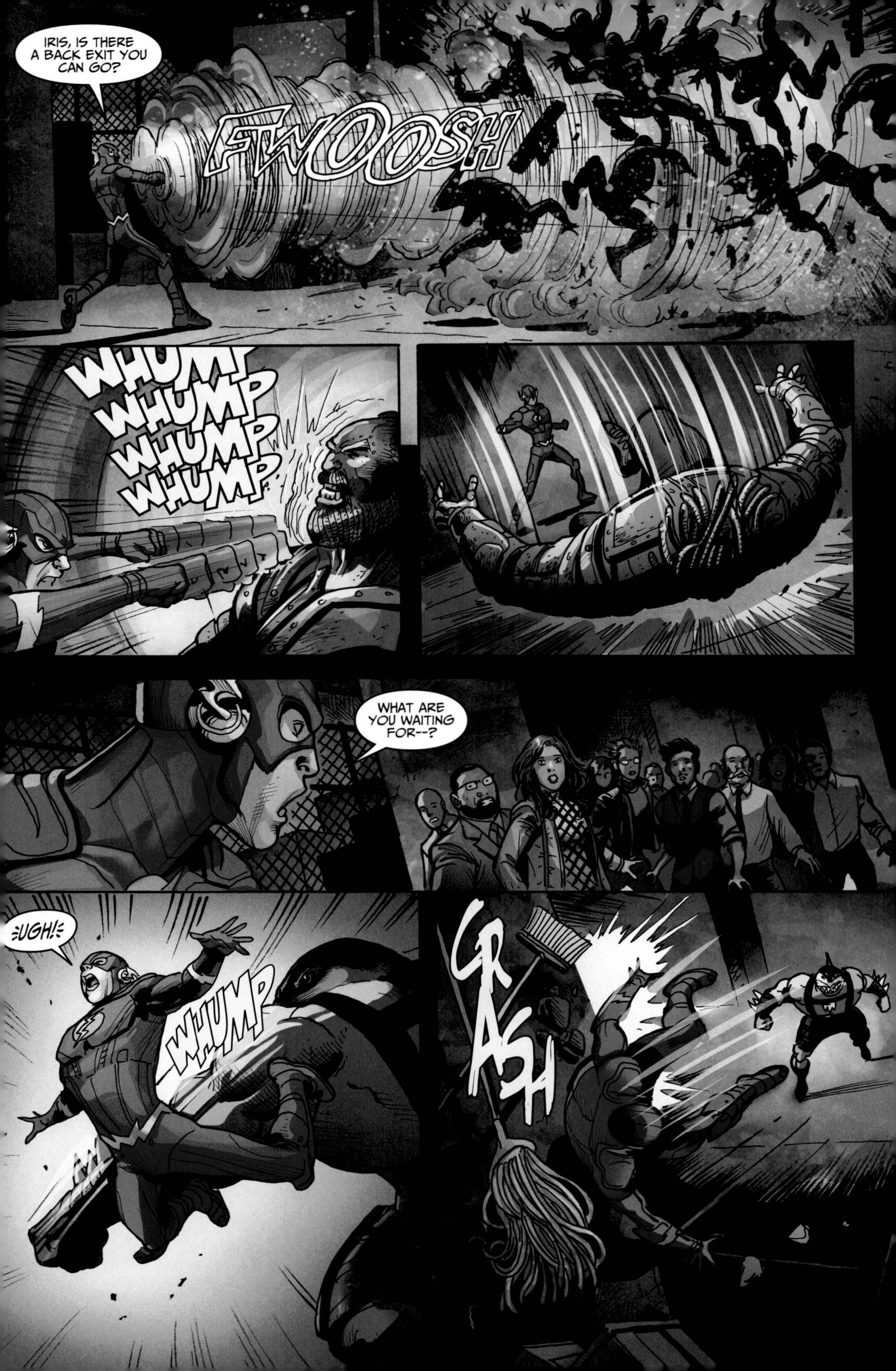
IRIS, IS THERE A BACK EXIT YOU CAN GO?
FWOOSH
WHUMP
WHUMP
WHUMP
WHUMP
WHAT ARE YOU WAITING FOR--?
UGH!
WHUMP
CRASH

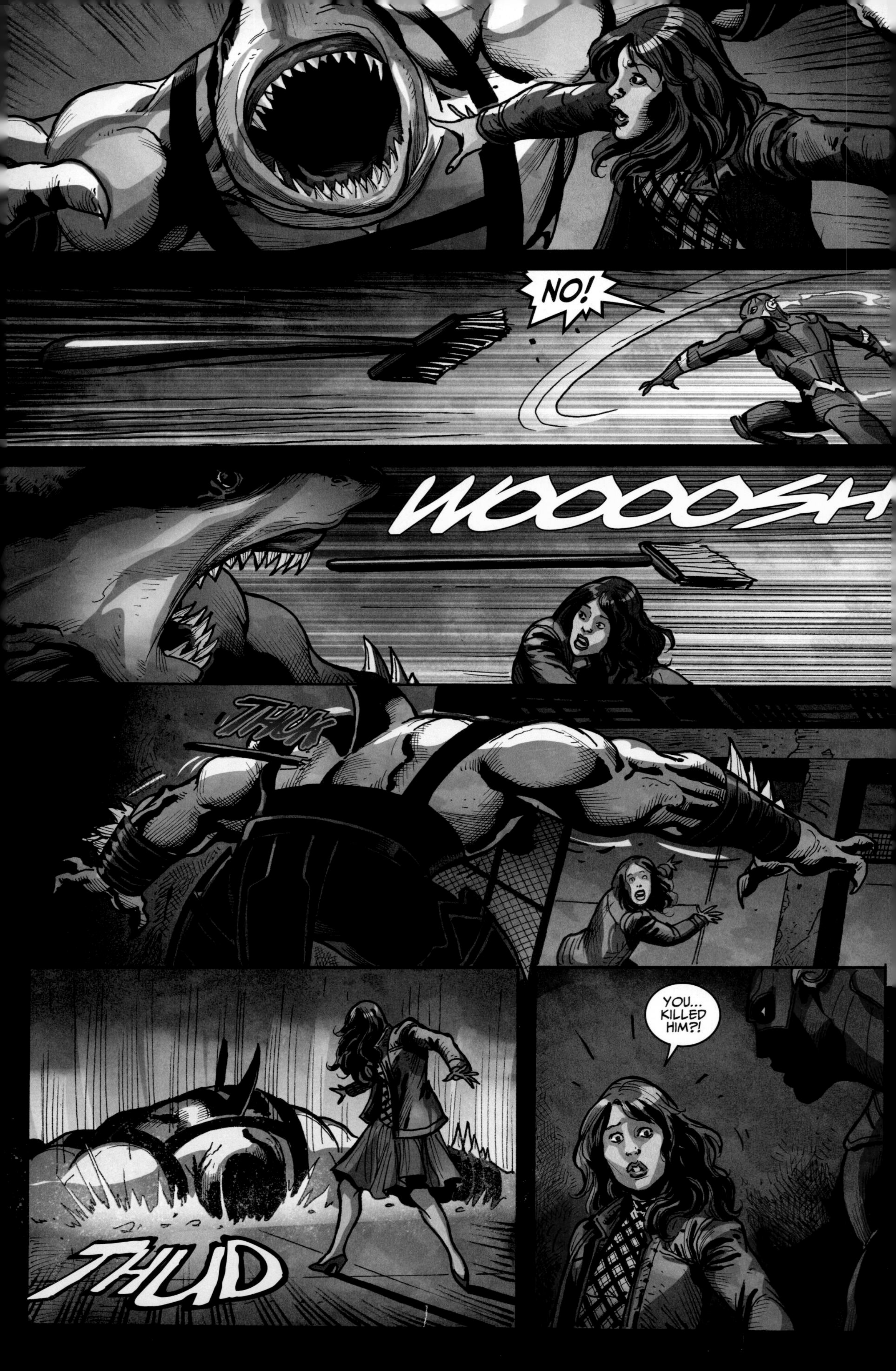
NO!
WOOOOSH
THUK
THUD
YOU... KILLED HIM?!

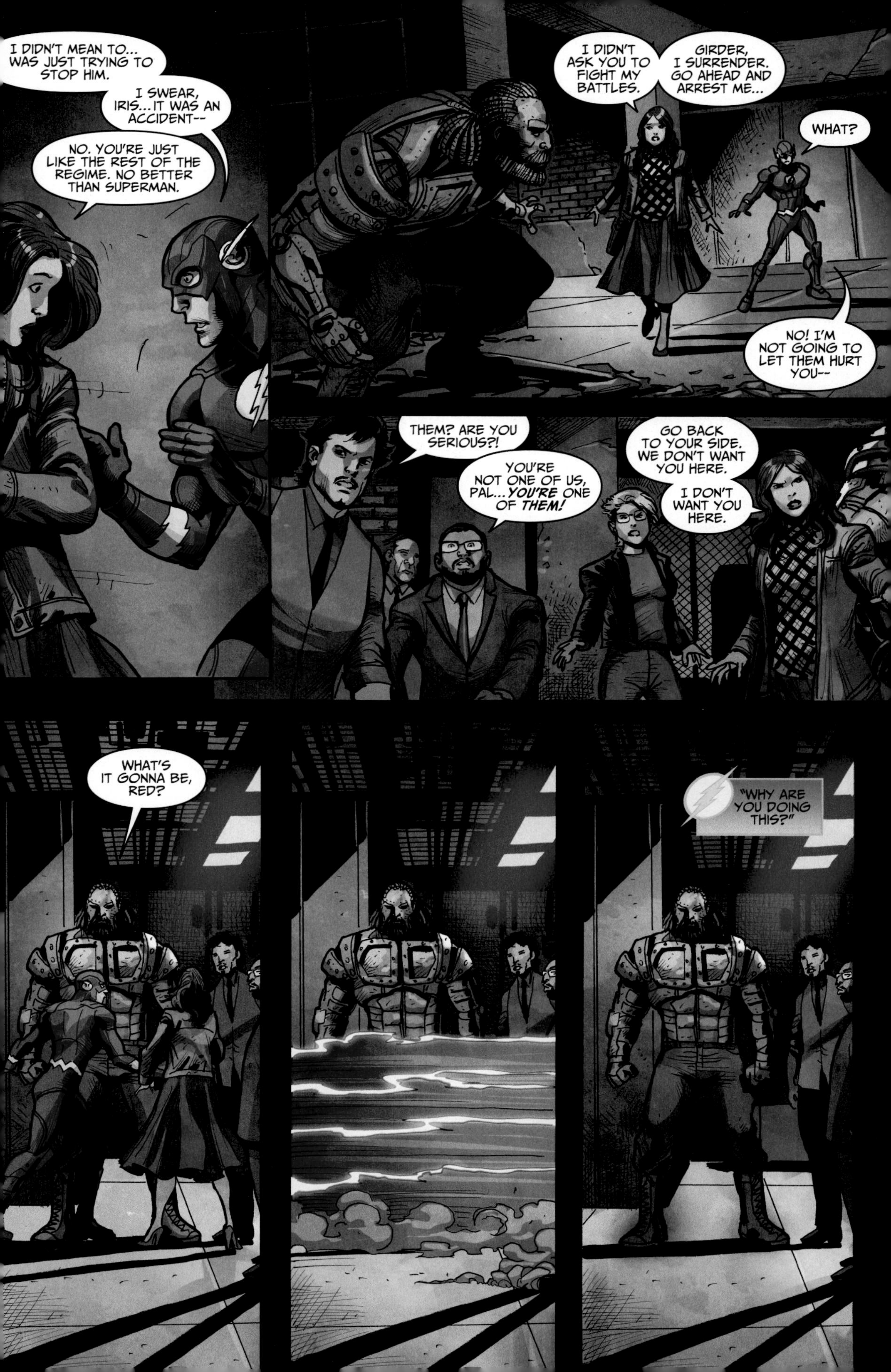
I DIDN'T MEAN TO... WAS JUST TRYING TO STOP HIM.
I SWEAR, IRIS...IT WAS AN ACCIDENT--
NO. YOU'RE JUST LIKE THE REST OF THE REGIME. NO BETTER THAN SUPERMAN.
I DIDN'T ASK YOU TO FIGHT MY BATTLES.
GIRDER, I SURRENDER. GO AHEAD AND ARREST ME...
WHAT?
NO! I'M NOT GOING TO LET THEM HURT YOU--
THEM? ARE YOU SERIOUS?!
YOU'RE NOT ONE OF US, PAL...YOU'RE ONE OF THEM!
GO BACK TO YOUR SIDE. WE DON'T WANT YOU HERE.
I DON'T WANT YOU HERE.
WHAT'S IT GONNA BE, RED?
"WHY ARE YOU DOING THIS?"

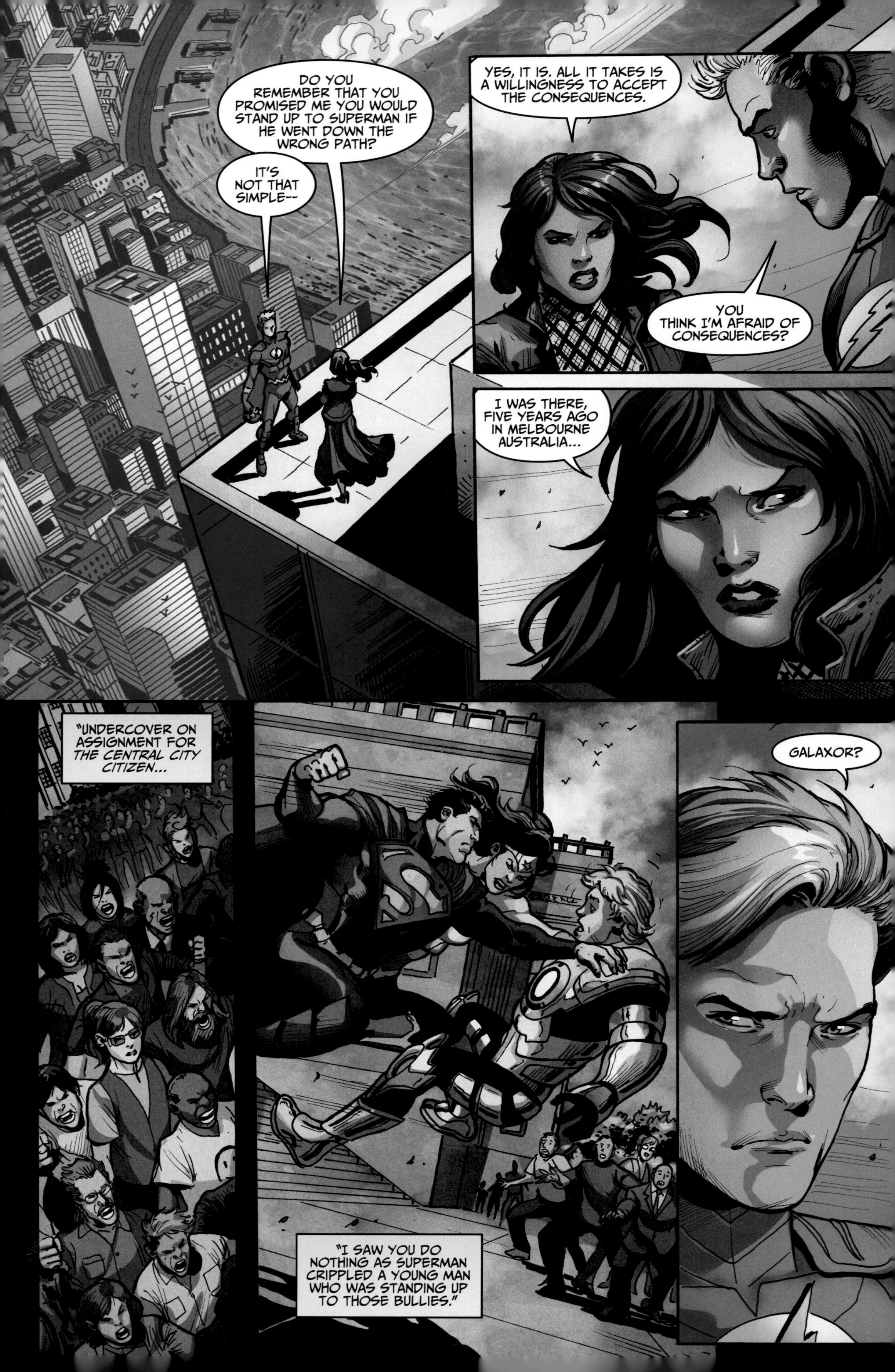
DO YOU REMEMBER THAT YOU PROMISED ME YOU WOULD STAND UP TO SUPERMAN IF HE WENT DOWN THE WRONG PATH?
IT'S NOT THAT SIMPLE--
YES, IT IS. ALL IT TAKES IS A WILLINGNESS TO ACCEPT THE CONSEQUENCES.
YOU THINK I'M AFRAID OF CONSEQUENCES?
I WAS THERE, FIVE YEARS AGO IN MELBOURNE AUSTRALIA...
"UNDERCOVER ON ASSIGNMENT FOR THE CENTRAL CITY CITIZEN...
"I SAW YOU DO NOTHING AS SUPERMAN CRIPPLED A YOUNG MAN WHO WAS STANDING UP TO THOSE BULLIES."
GALAXOR?

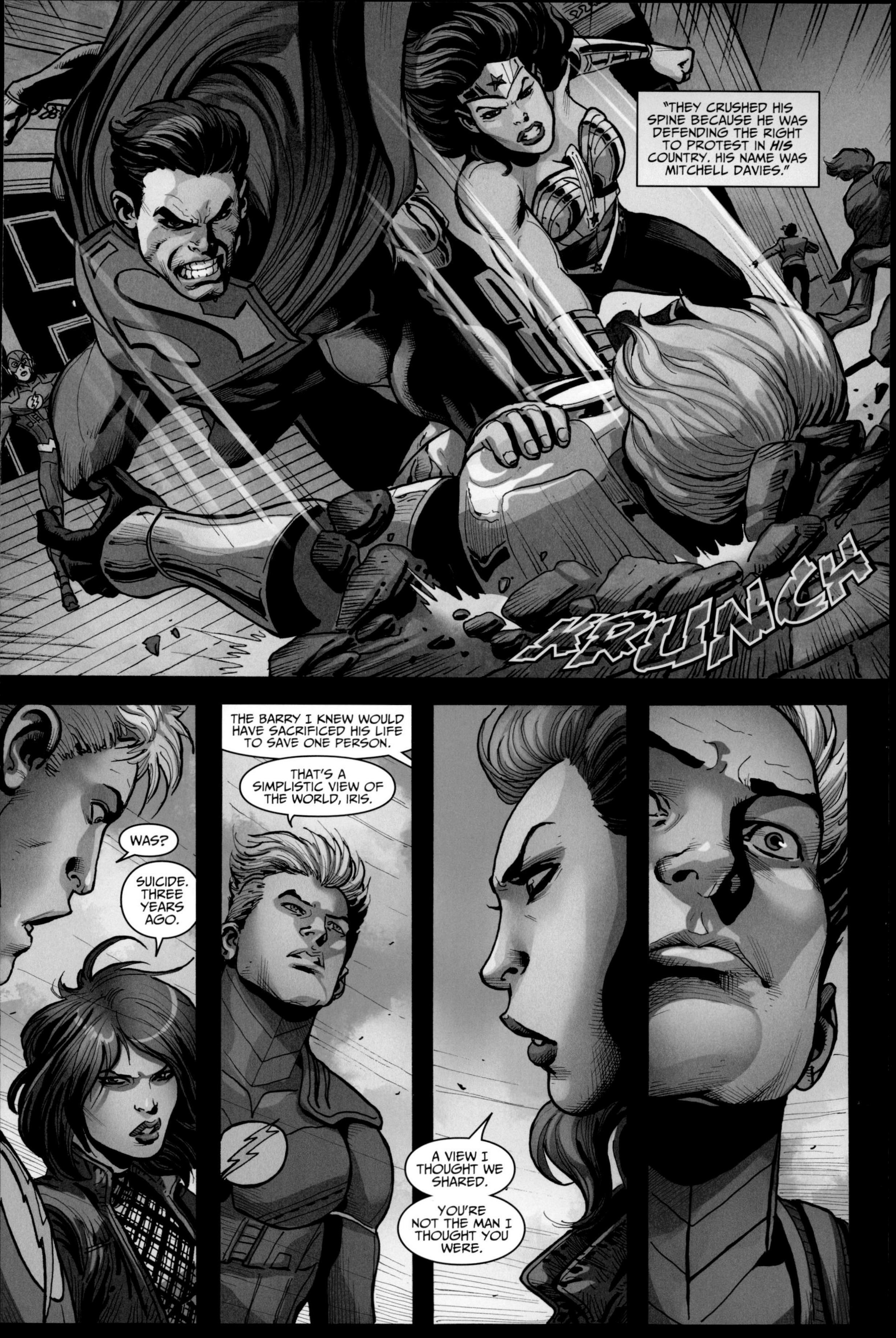
"THEY CRUSHED HIS SPINE BECAUSE HE WAS DEFENDING THE RIGHT TO PROTEST IN *HIS* COUNTRY. HIS NAME WAS MITCHELL DAVIES."
KRUNCH
WAS?
SUICIDE. THREE YEARS AGO.
THE BARRY I KNEW WOULD HAVE SACRIFICED HIS LIFE TO SAVE ONE PERSON.
THAT'S A SIMPLISTIC VIEW OF THE WORLD, IRIS.
A VIEW I THOUGHT WE SHARED.
YOU'RE NOT THE MAN I THOUGHT YOU WERE.

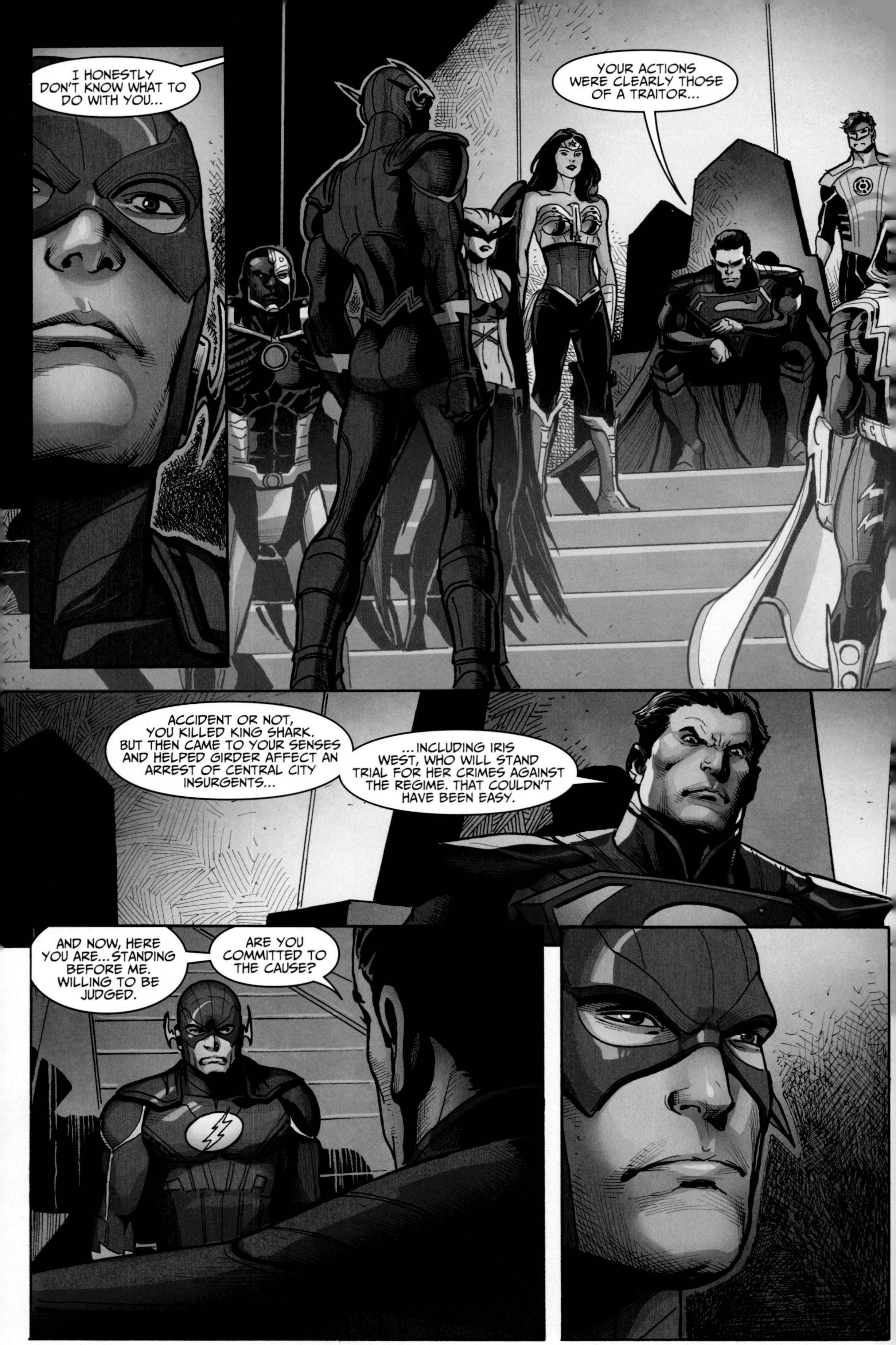
I HONESTLY DON'T KNOW WHAT TO DO WITH YOU...
YOUR ACTIONS WERE CLEARLY THOSE OF A TRAITOR...
ACCIDENT OR NOT, YOU KILLED KING SHARK. BUT THEN CAME TO YOUR SENSES AND HELPED GIRDER AFFECT AN ARREST OF CENTRAL CITY INSURGENTS...
...INCLUDING IRIS WEST, WHO WILL STAND TRIAL FOR HER CRIMES AGAINST THE REGIME. THAT COULDN'T HAVE BEEN EASY.
AND NOW, HERE YOU ARE...STANDING BEFORE ME. WILLING TO BE JUDGED.
ARE YOU COMMITTED TO THE CAUSE?

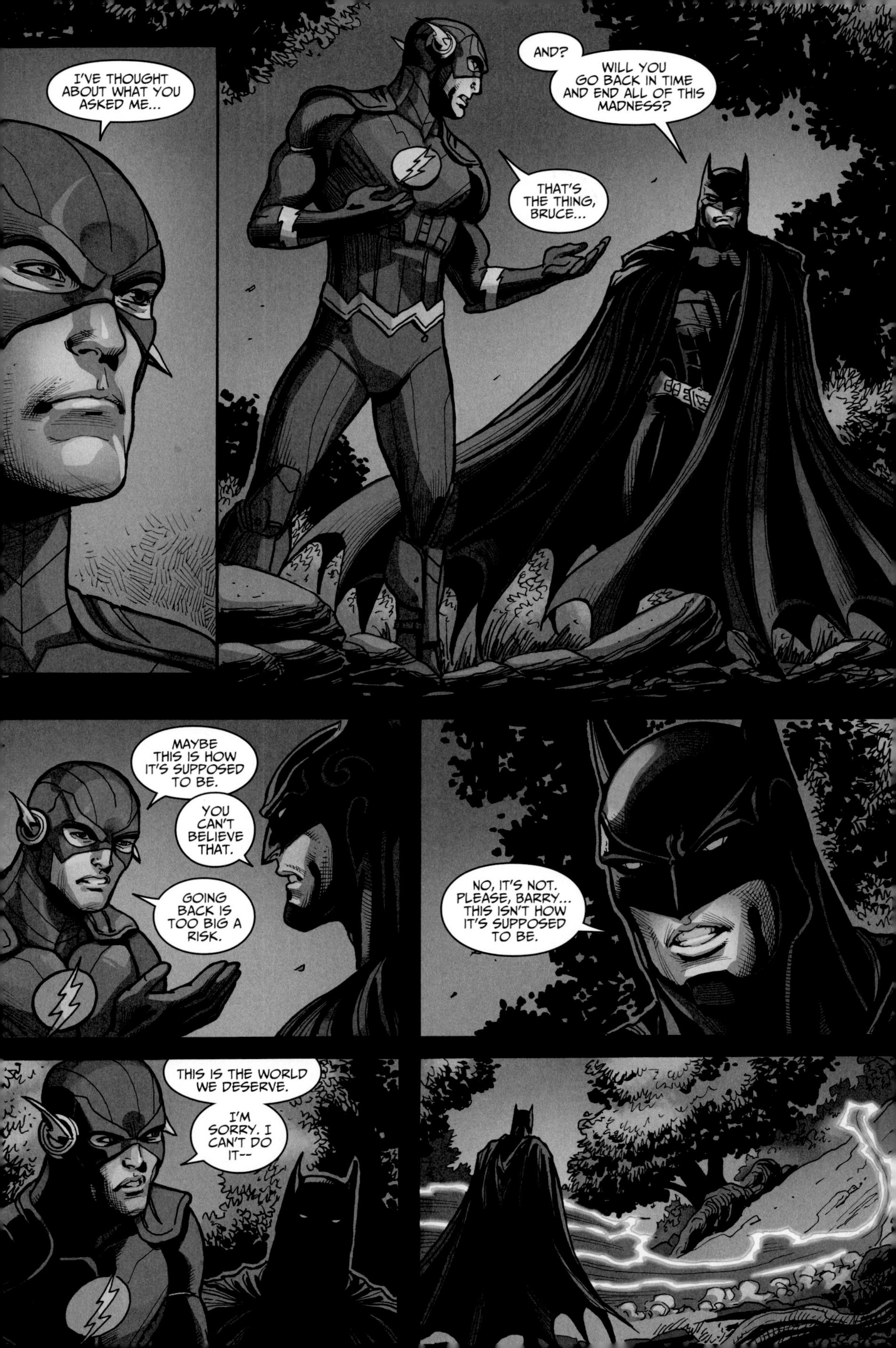
I'VE THOUGHT ABOUT WHAT YOU ASKED ME...
AND?
WILL YOU GO BACK IN TIME AND END ALL OF THIS MADNESS?
THAT'S THE THING, BRUCE...
MAYBE THIS IS HOW IT'S SUPPOSED TO BE.
YOU CAN'T BELIEVE THAT.
GOING BACK IS TOO BIG A RISK.
NO, IT'S NOT. PLEASE, BARRY... THIS ISN'T HOW IT'S SUPPOSED TO BE.
THIS IS THE WORLD WE DESERVE.
I'M SORRY. I CAN'T DO IT--

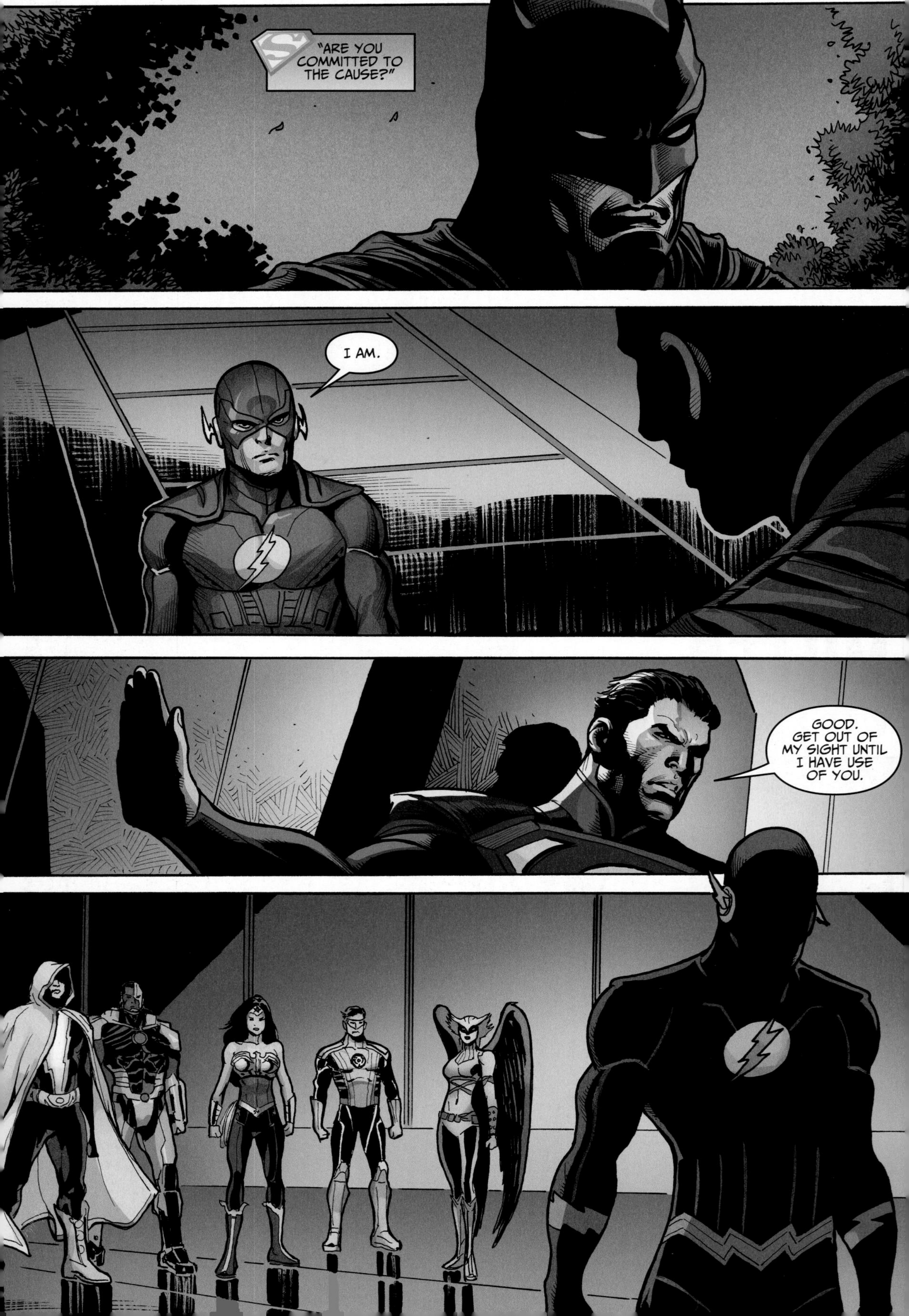
"ARE YOU COMMITTED TO THE CAUSE?"
I AM.
GOOD. GET OUT OF MY SIGHT UNTIL I HAVE USE OF YOU.

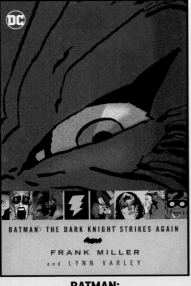
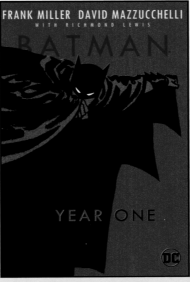

WATCHMEN
ALAN MOORE
with DAVE GIBBONS

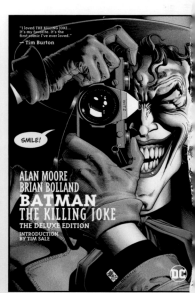

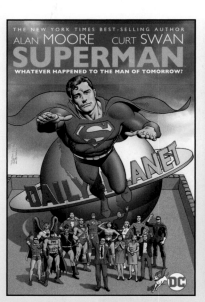

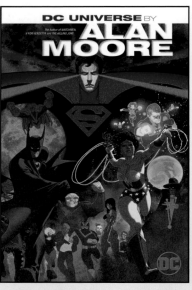

**SUPERMAN: WHATEVER HAPPENED
TO THE MAN OF TOMORROW?**

**THE DC UNIVERSE BY ALAN MOORE
with VARIOUS ARTISTS**

**BATMAN:
THE KILLING JOKE
with BRIAN BOLLAND**